Disability, Human Rights, and Contract Law

An initial glance at the intricate web of the English legal system may perceive human rights and private law as paths leading to different realms. In this vision, contract law, shaped by economic concerns, is confined to a role of enforcing agreements. Yet, given ageing population trends and the increase in the number of people with mental health conditions, such as dementia, entering into grossly asymmetrical contracts, we must re-assess the lens through which we perceive contract law. This book calls for a re-examination of the role of contract law in light of the UN Convention on the Rights of Persons with Disabilities (UNCRPD), insisting on an approach that responds to both economic and social concerns. The book aims to contribute towards bridging the areas of disability equality and contract law, questioning the compatibility of key principles and doctrines in contract law with UNCRPD values, including autonomy and human dignity.

Eliza Varney is Associate Professor in the School of Law, University of Nottingham. She is the author of *Disability and Information Technology* (Cambridge University Press, 2013).

Law in Context

Since 1970, the Law in Context series has been at the forefront of a movement to broaden the study of law. The series is a vehicle for the publication of innovative monographs and texts that treat law and legal phenomena critically in their cultural, social, political, technological, environmental and economic contexts. A contextual approach involves treating legal subjects broadly, using materials from other humanities and social sciences, and from any other discipline that helps to explain the operation in practice of the particular legal field or legal phenomena under investigation. It is intended that this orientation is at once more stimulating and more revealing than the bare exposition of legal rules. The series includes original research monographs, coursebooks and textbooks that foreground contextual approaches and methods. The series includes and welcomes books on the study of law in all its contexts, including domestic legal systems, European and international law, transnational and global legal processes, and comparative law.

Books in the Series

Acosta: *The National versus the Foreigner in South America: 200 Years of Migration and Citizenship Law*

Alaattinoğlu: *Grievance Formation, Rights and Remedies*

Ali: *Modern Challenges to Islamic Law*

Alyagon Darr: *Plausible Crime Stories: The Legal History of Sexual Offences in Mandate Palestine*

Anderson, Schum & Twining: *Analysis of Evidence, 2nd Edition*

Ashworth: *Sentencing and Criminal Justice, 6th Edition*

Barton & Douglas: *Law and Parenthood*

Baxi, McCrudden & Paliwala: *Law's Ethical, Global and Theoretical Contexts: Essays in Honour of William Twining*

Beecher-Monas: *Evaluating Scientific Evidence: An Interdisciplinary Framework for Intellectual Due Process*

Bell: *French Legal Cultures*
Bercusson: *European Labour Law, 2nd Edition*
Birkinshaw: *European Public Law*
Birkinshaw: *Freedom of Information: The Law, the Practice and the Ideal, 4th Edition*
Blick: *Electrified Democracy: The Internet and the United Kingdom Parliament in History*
Broderick & Ferri: *International and European Disability Law and Policy: Text, Cases and Materials*
Brownsword & Goodwin: *Law and the Technologies of the Twenty-First Century: Text and Materials*
Cane & Goudkamp: *Atiyah's Accidents, Compensation and the Law, 9th Edition*
Clarke: *Principles of Property Law*
Clarke & Kohler: *Property Law: Commentary and Materials*
Collins: *The Law of Contract, 4th Edition*
Collins, Ewing & McColgan: *Labour Law, 3rd Edition*
Corrias, *Law and Inhumanity: Dehumanization, Silent Claims and Atrocity Crimes*
Cowan: *Housing Law and Policy*
Cranston: *Making Commercial Law Through Practice 1830–1970*
Cranston: *Legal Foundations of the Welfare State*
Darian-Smith: *Laws and Societies in Global Contexts: Contemporary Approaches*
Dauvergne: *Making People Illegal: What Globalisation Means for Immigration and Law*
David: *Kinship, Law and Politics: An Anatomy of Belonging*
Davies: *Perspectives on Labour Law, 2nd Edition*
Dembour: *Who Believes in Human Rights?: Reflections on the European Convention*
de Sousa Santos: *Toward a New Legal Common Sense: Law, Globalization, and Emancipation*
Diduck: *Law's Families*
Douglas-Scott: *Brexit, Union, and Disunion: The Evolution of British Constitutional Unsettlement*
Dowdle: *Transnational Law: A Framework for Analysis*
Dupret: *Positive Law from the Muslim World: Jurisprudence, History, Practices*
Emon: *Jurisdictional Exceptionalisms: Islamic Law, International Law, and Parental Child Abduction*
Estella: *Legal Foundations of EU Economic Governance*
Fortin: *Children's Rights and the Developing Law, 3rd Edition*
Garnsey: *The Justice of Visual Art: Creative State-Building in Times of Political Transition*
Garton, Probert & Bean: *Moffat's Trusts Law: Text and Materials, 7th Edition*
Ghai & Woodman: *Practising Self-Government: A Comparative Study of Autonomous Regions*
Glover-Thomas: *Reconstructing Mental Health Law and Policy*
Gobert & Punch: *Rethinking Corporate Crime*
Goldman: *Globalisation and the Western Legal Tradition: Recurring Patterns of Law and Authority*
Haack: *Evidence Matters: Science, Proof, and Truth in the Law*
Harlow & Rawlings: *Law and Administration, 4th Edition*
Harris: *An Introduction to Law, 8th Edition*
Harris, Campbell & Halson: *Remedies in Contract and Tort, 2nd Edition*
Harvey: *Seeking Asylum in the UK: Problems and Prospects*

Herring: *Law and the Relational Self*
Hervey & McHale: *European Union Health Law: Themes and Implications*
Hervey & McHale: *Health Law and the European Union*
Holder & Lee: *Environmental Protection, Law and Policy: Text and Materials, 2nd Edition*
Jackson & Summers: *The Internationalisation of Criminal Evidence: Beyond the Common Law and Civil Law Traditions*
Jeutner: *The Reasonable Person: A Legal Biography*
Kennedy: *Inducing Intimacy: Deception, Consent and the Law*
Kostakopoulou: *The Future Governance of Citizenship*
Kreiczer-Levy: *Destabilized Property: Property Law in the Sharing Economy*
Kubal: *Immigration and Refugee Law in Russia: Socio-Legal Perspectives*
Lewis: *Choice and the Legal Order: Rising above Politics*
Likosky: *Law, Infrastructure and Human Rights*
Likosky: *Transnational Legal Processes: Globalisation and Power Disparities*
Lixinski: *Legalized Identities: Cultural Heritage Law and the Shaping of Transitional Justice*
Loughnan: *Self, Others and the State: Relations of Criminal Responsibility*
Lunney: *A History of Australian Tort Law 1901-1945: England's Obedient Servant?*
Maughan & Webb: *Lawyering Skills and the Legal Process, 2nd Edition*
McGaughey: *Principles of Enterprise Law*
McGlynn: *Families and the European Union: Law, Politics and Pluralism*
Mertens: *A Philosophical Introduction to Human Rights*
Miller: *An Introduction to German Law and Legal Culture: Text and Materials*
Moffat: *Trusts Law: Text and Materials*
Monti: *EC Competition Law*
Morgan: *Contract Law Minimalism: A Formalist Restatement of Commercial Contract Law*
Morgan & Yeung: *An Introduction to Law and Regulation: Text and Materials*
Nash: *British Islam and English Law: A Classical Pluralist Perspective*
Ng: *Political Censorship in British Hong Kong: Freedom of Expression and the Law (1842–1997)*
Nicola & Davies: *EU Law Stories: Contextual and Critical Histories of European Jurisprudence*
Norrie: *Crime, Reason and History: A Critical Introduction to Criminal Law, 3rd Edition*
Norrie: *Rethinking Criminal Justice: Punishment, Abolition And Moral Psychology*
O'Dair: *Legal Ethics: Text and Materials*
Oliver: *Common Values and the Public–Private Divide*
Oliver & Drewry: *The Law and Parliament*
Palmer & Roberts: *Dispute Processes: ADR and the Primary Forms of Decision-Making, 1st Edition*
Palmer & Roberts: *Dispute Processes: ADR and the Primary Forms of Decision-Making, 3rd Edition*
Picciotto: *International Business Taxation*
Pieraccini: *Regulating the Sea: A Socio-Legal Analysis of English Marine Protected Areas*
Probert: *The Changing Legal Regulation of Cohabitation, 1600-2010: From Fornicators to Family, 1600-2010*

Qiao: *The Authoritarian Commons: Neighborhood Democratization in Urban China*
Radi: *Rules and Practices of International Investment Law and Arbitration*
Reed: *Internet Law: Text and Materials*
Richardson: *Law, Process and Custody*
Roberts & Palmer: *Dispute Processes: ADR and the Primary Forms of Decision-Making, 2nd Edition*
Rowbottom: *Democracy Distorted: Wealth, Influence and Democratic Politics*
Sauter: *Public Services in EU Law*
Scott & Black: *Cranston's Consumers and the Law*
Seneviratne: *Ombudsmen: Public Services and Administrative Justice*
Seppänen: *Ideological Conflict and the Rule of Law in Contemporary China: Useful Paradoxes*
Siems: *Comparative Law, 3rd Edition*
Stapleton: *Product Liability*
Stewart: *Gender, Law and Justice in a Global Market*
Tamanaha: *Law as a Means to an End: Threat to the Rule of Law*
Taylor: *Fortin's Children's Rights and the Developing Law, 4th Edition*
Tuori: *Properties of Law: Modern Law and After*
Turpin & Tomkins: *British Government and the Constitution: Text and Materials, 7th Edition*
Twining: *General Jurisprudence: Understanding Law from a Global Perspective*
Twining: *Globalisation and Legal Theory*
Twining: *Human Rights, Southern Voices: Francis Deng, Abdullahi An-Na'im, Yash Ghai and Upendra Baxi*
Twining: *Jurist in Context: A Memoir*
Twining: *Karl Llewellyn and the Realist Movement, 2nd Edition*
Twining: *Rethinking Evidence: Exploratory Essays, 2nd Edition*
Twining & Miers: *How to Do Things with Rules, 5th Edition*
Wan: *Film and Constitutional Controversy: Visualizing Hong Kong Identity in the Age of 'One Country, Two Systems'*
Ward: *A Critical Introduction to European Law, 3rd Edition*
Ward: *Law, Text, Terror*
Ward: *Shakespeare and Legal Imagination*
Watt: *The Making Sense of Politics, Media, and Law: Rhetorical Performance as Invention, Creation, Production*
Wells & Quick: *Lacey, Wells and Quick: Reconstructing Criminal Law: Text and Materials, 4th Edition*
Woodhead: *Caring for Cultural Heritage: An Integrated Approach to Legal and Ethical Initiatives in the United Kingdom*
Yeung and Ranchordás: *An Introduction to Law and Regulation: Text and Materials, 2nd Edition*
Young: *Turpin and Tomkins' British Government and the Constitution: Text and Materials, 8th Edition*
Zander: *Cases and Materials on the English Legal System, 10th Edition*
Zander: *The Law-Making Process, 6th Edition*

International Journal of Law in Context: A Global Forum for Interdisciplinary Legal Studies

The *International Journal of Law in Context* is the companion journal to the Law in Context book series and provides a forum for interdisciplinary legal studies and offers intellectual space for ground-breaking critical research. It publishes contextual work about law and its relationship with other disciplines including but not limited to science, literature, humanities, philosophy, sociology, psychology, ethics, history and geography. More information about the journal and how to submit an article can be found at http://journals.cambridge.org/ijc

Disability, Human Rights, and Contract Law

ELIZA VARNEY
University of Nottingham

CAMBRIDGE
UNIVERSITY PRESS

CAMBRIDGE
UNIVERSITY PRESS

Shaftesbury Road, Cambridge CB2 8EA, United Kingdom

One Liberty Plaza, 20th Floor, New York, NY 10006, USA

477 Williamstown Road, Port Melbourne, VIC 3207, Australia

314–321, 3rd Floor, Plot 3, Splendor Forum, Jasola District Centre,
New Delhi – 110025, India

103 Penang Road, #05–06/07, Visioncrest Commercial, Singapore 238467

Cambridge University Press is part of Cambridge University Press & Assessment,
a department of the University of Cambridge.

We share the University's mission to contribute to society through the pursuit of
education, learning and research at the highest international levels of excellence.

www.cambridge.org
Information on this title: www.cambridge.org/9781316516638

DOI: 10.1017/9781009030731

When citing this work, please include a reference to the DOI 10.1017/9781009030731

First published 2025

A catalogue record for this publication is available from the British Library

Library of Congress Cataloging-in-Publication Data
Names: Varney, Eliza, 1978– author.
Title: Disability, human rights, and contract law / Eliza Varney, University of Nottingham.
Description: Cambridge, United Kingdom ; New York, NY : Cambridge
University Press, 2025. | Series: Law in context
Identifiers: LCCN 2025005972 | ISBN 9781316516638 (hardback) |
ISBN 9781009030731 (ebook)
Subjects: LCSH: People with disabilities – Legal status, laws, etc. | People
with disabilities – Employment – Law and legislation. | Convention on the
Rights of Persons with Disabilities and Optional Protocol (2007 March 30) |
Contracts. | Respect for persons – Law and legislation | Interpersonal complementarity.
Classification: LCC K637 .V37 2025 | DDC 342.08/7–dc23/eng/20250212
LC record available at https://lccn.loc.gov/2025005972

ISBN 978-1-316-51663-8 Hardback

To Mike and Alex Varney

Contents

Acknowledgements

This book is dedicated to my husband Mike and our daughter Alex. I am so grateful for their continuous encouragement, support and patience. I have also written this book in the memory of my parents Ioana and Radu. I owe them so much, including my Christian faith and the respect I feel for every person.

I have received a lot of support from colleagues at the University of Nottingham, including Peter Bartlett, Howard Bennett, Peter Cartwright and Richard Hyde. I am also grateful to my colleagues during my time at Keele University, including Kelvin Johnstone and Abi Pearson. I would also like to thank all my students, past and present, for being a great source of inspiration.

I would like to thank everyone who have assisted with this publication, in particular Toby Ginsberg, Gemma Smith, Marianne Nield, Laura Blake (Cambridge University Press), Ramya Selvaraj, and Megha Sharma (Lumina Datamatics), as well as the anonymous reviewers. I am very grateful to *Legal Studies*, *Journal of Business Law* and *King's Law Journal* for allowing me to reuse versions the following articles in this book:

- 'Redefining Contractual Capacity? The UN Convention on the Rights of Persons with Disabilities and the Incapacity Defence in English Contract Law' (2017) 37 *Legal Studies* 493–519.
- 'Agency Contracts and the Scope of the Incapacity Defence in English Contract Law: A Topic too Hot to Handle?' (2020) 5 *Journal of Business Law* 382–401.
- 'The UN Convention on the Rights of Persons with Disabilities and English Contract Law: A Tale of Unfinished Bridges?' (2020) 31(3) *King's Law Journal* 444–66, available online: www.tandfonline.com/doi/full/10.1080/09615768.2020.1815941

I am also very grateful to the Taylor & Francis Group for allowing me to reuse a version of the following chapter in this book:

- 'Beyond Negative Interpretations of Freedom of Contract: The Interplay between Private Law and Human Rights in Light of the UN Convention on the Rights of Persons with Disabilities' in Catalin Gabriel Stanescu and Asress Gikay (eds.) *Discrimination, Vulnerable Consumers and Financial Inclusion* (Routledge, 2020), pp. 35–56.

The empirical research comprised in Chapter 5 (including interviews with representatives from Deaf and Disabled People's Organisations) was funded by the Society of Legal Scholars (SLS) Research Activities Fund (joint bid with Mike Varney). All interviews were given with permission to publish. I am very grateful to the SLS for funding this empirical research, and to Mike Varney for allowing me to use in this book materials from interviews conducted jointly. I also owe my gratitude to the following interviewees who allowed me to use quotes from these interviews in this book (all references to title and affiliation refer to titles and affiliations at the time of the interviews):

- Guido Gybels, policy expert
- Lorna Carter (Chair), Disability Nottinghamshire, Mansfield
- Sophie Fournel (CEO), Centre for Independent Living Kent (CiLK) (now Disability Assist), Ashford
- Emily Morton (Operations Manager), Disability Sheffield
- Dave Thompson (Development Manager), Access Dorset, Bournemouth
- Hannah Tutt (Chairperson), Centre for Independent Living Kent (CiLK) (now Disability Assist), Ashford
- Jonathan Toye (Coordinator), West Norfolk Disability Information Service (WNDIS), King's Lynn.

Any errors and omissions in this book are my own.

Table of Cases

Australia

Canada

Council of Europe

European Union

New Zealand

Singapore

United Kingdom

United Nations

Table of Legislation

Council of Europe

European Union

United Kingdom

United Nations

Abbreviations

ATMs	Automatic teller machines
B2C	Business to consumer
CCRs	Consumer Contracts (Information, Cancellation and Additional Charges) Regulations
CJEU	Court of Justice of the European Union
CMA	Competition and Markets Authority
CPUTRs	Consumer Protection from Unfair Trading Regulations
CRA	Consumer Rights Act
DDA	Disability Discrimination Act
DDPOs	Deaf and Disabled People's Organisations
DED	Disability equality duty
DMCCA	Digital Markets Competition and Consumers Act
ECHR	European Convention on Human Rights
ECtHR	European Court of Human Rights
EqA	Equality Act
EUWA	European Union (Withdrawal) Act
HRA	Human Rights Act
MCA	Mental Capacity Act
OCA	Online choice architecture
OFT	Office of Fair Trading
PSED	Public sector equality duty
REUL	Retained European Union law
REULA	Retained EU Law (Revocation and Reform) Act
SGA	Sale of Goods Act
SGSA	Supply of Goods and Services Act
TFEU	Treaty on the Functioning of the European Union
UCTA	Unfair Contract Terms Act
UN CEDAW	UN Convention on the Elimination of all Forms of Discrimination against Women
UNCRPD	UN Convention on the Rights of Persons with Disabilities
UNCRPD Committee	UN Committee on the Rights of Persons with Disabilities
WAA	European Union (Withdrawal Agreement) Act

1

Introduction

> Never approach a score with eyes of the … past, for they may bring you nothing more in return than Yorick's skull.
>
> Dinu Lipatti, Romanian pianist and composer, 1917–1950

If we could redesign the law of contract starting with a blank canvas, would the end result be the same as our current legal framework? Many of the principles that shaped English contract law, including freedom and sanctity of contract, are rooted in an individualistic conception of autonomy and a perception of contracting parties as economic actors in pursuit of self-interest. Yet, ageing population trends and the likely consequential increase in the number of people with mental health conditions such as dementia,[1] entering into grossly asymmetrical contracts to their detriment,[2] have reinforced the need for an approach that 'humanises' private law[3] and perceives contracting parties as both economic and social actors. It is, therefore, legitimate to re-examine key principles and doctrines of contract law, reflecting on the extent to which these are compatible with the values entrenched in the UN Convention on the Rights of Persons with Disabilities (UNCRPD),[4] in particular the protection of individual and relational autonomy, and human dignity. The Convention was ratified by the United Kingdom (UK) in 2009 and whilst it has not been incorporated into domestic law and, consequently has 'no direct effect in English law',[5] its ratification requires that domestic law conforms 'wherever possible' with the 'norms

[1] Martin Prince and others, *Dementia UK: Second Edition – Overview* (London: Alzheimer's Society, 2014), p. 5.

[2] Ronald Hamdy and others, 'Patients with Dementia Are Easy Victims to Predators' (2017) 3 *Gerontology and Geriatric Medicine* 1–8 at 1.

[3] François Du Bois, 'Private Law in the Age of Rights' in Daniel Visser and Elspeth Reid (eds.), *Private Law and Human Rights in Scotland and South Africa* (Edinburgh: Edinburgh University Press, 2013), pp. 12–36 at p. 35.

[4] UN Convention on the Rights of Persons with Disabilities (UNCRPD), New York, 13 December 2006, in force 3 May 2008, GA Res 61/611, A/61/611, 15 IHRR 255.

[5] *R. (on the application of NM)* v. *Islington LBC* [2012] EWHC 414 (Admin) [98] (Sales J). See Deniz Canruh, 'Use of the UNCRPD in Social Security Cases before UK Courts and Tribunals' (2019) 26 *Journal of Social Security Law* 112–25 at 115.

and values' enshrined in the Convention.[6] The end result of this re-evaluation is not to propose a new framework of principles and doctrines of English contract law. Instead, it considers how the current legal framework can be interpreted in a way that is compatible with the Convention values, which moves away from a focus on people's medical conditions to consider the circumstances of the transactions, and which reinforces the view that even when operating in the private sphere, people never stop being holders of rights.[7]

This book calls for a vision of contract law based not on a single, economic sphere but on two concentric spheres. The inner sphere encompasses an economic realm rooted in values such as freedom and sanctity of contract, reflecting a non-interventionist approach that can accommodate imbalanced transactions, if entered into by parties who exercise their individual autonomy unaffected by vitiating factors.[8] The outer sphere is shaped by public policy concerns and embodies social values such as the protection of relational autonomy and human dignity, recognising our interdependence and reaffirming our equal worth as people.[9] For example, grossly asymmetrical contracts (e.g. purchases at excessively high prices or sales at significant undervalue, to the detriment of a vulnerable party who acted without appropriate and accessible legal advice) would step out of the inner economic sphere into the outer social sphere of contractual relations. Decisions not to enforce such significantly imbalanced transactions could be perceived as circumstances where the state does not give its agreement to enforce such contracts[10] because vitiating factors have caused the transaction to step out of the inner economic sphere into the outer social sphere.

The lens through which we should examine such contracts, and the map that could assist us in this endeavour, is explored in more depth in Chapter 2, which articulates the model of concentric spheres in contract law. This chapter calls for an approach that considers not only economic but also social values, and which assesses vulnerability based on the context of the transactions, rather than the medical conditions of individuals. Once this map has been drawn up in Chapter 2, the structure of Chapters 3–5 rests on the idea of bridges between private law (with a focus on contract law) and human rights (with a focus on disability equality). Rather than exploring the construction of a single bridge, the book examines three such constructions.[11] Chapter 3 centres on the first bridge, which

[6] *AH* v. *West London Mental Health Trust* [2011] UKUT 74 (AAC) [16] (Carnwath LJ).

[7] Rachel Hurst, 'Disabled People's Organisations and Development: Strategies for Change' in Emma Stone (ed.), *Disability and Development: Learning from Action and Research on Disability in the Majority World* (Leeds: Disability Press, 1999), pp. 25–35.

[8] John Adams and Roger Brownsword, *Understanding Contract Law* (5th ed., London: Sweet & Maxwell, 2007), p. 192.

[9] Amita Dhanda, 'Constructing a New Human Rights Lexicon: Convention on the Rights of Persons with Disabilities' (2008) 5 *Sur: International Journal of Human Rights* 43–59 at 49.

[10] Seana Shiffrin, 'Paternalism, Unconscionability Doctrine and Accommodation' (2000) 29 *Philosophy and Public Affairs* 205–50 at 227.

[11] The idea of the three bridges between disability equality and contract law was suggested by the anonymous reviewer to the article: Eliza Varney, 'The UN Convention on the Rights of

can be envisaged between common law doctrines and principles, linking the inner economic sphere of contract law with its outer sphere. This chapter examines vitiating factors affecting the balance between contracting parties, including incapacity, *non est factum*, mistake, misrepresentation, duress, unconscionability, and undue influence. The discussion argues that we should focus not only on the horizontal axis of contractual relations between private parties but also on the vertical axis that governs the relation between individuals and the state. The contractual relations between the parties (A and B) could be envisaged as a lever on a balance scale, with the parties at each end of the scale, and the state in the middle, as a fulcrum. Factors such as the combination of A's vulnerability and B's unacceptable conduct could be perceived as a weight pressing A down into a danger zone of gross asymmetry in the parties' bargaining position, stepping from the inner economic dimension into the outer social sphere of contracting.

After examining the role of private law doctrines and principles in connecting social and economic values in the contractual realm, the discussion moves to explore the second bridge in Chapter 4, which considers the part played by regulation (including the regulation of unfair contract terms) in bringing together these values. The discussion focuses on the regulation of unfair contract terms, unfair commercial practices, implied terms in contracts for the provision of goods, services, and digital content, and on information and cancellation rights in business-to-consumer (B2C) contracts. The analysis explores the extent to which these provisions protect people not only as economic actors but also as social actors, as well as the extent to which this framework safeguards values such as autonomy and human dignity. This chapter also examines the concept of consumer vulnerability in consumer–trader relations. It builds on Cartwright's taxonomy of consumer vulnerability (which includes informational, supply, redress, pressure, and impact vulnerability)[12] to add one further type: influence vulnerability. This refers to the limited opportunities available to consumers, including people with disabilities, to shape the regulatory framework, when compared with the influence exercised by industry players.

The third bridge is explored in Chapter 5 and focuses on the connection between constitutional values and private law. The analysis concentrates on the values of autonomy and human dignity and their interplay with the principle of freedom of contract in English contract law. The discussion also reflects on the link between the UNCRPD, the European Convention on Human Rights (ECHR),[13] the Human Rights Act (HRA) 1998,[14] and English contract

Persons with Disabilities and English Contract Law: A Tale of Unfinished Bridges?' (2020) 31 *King's Law Journal* 444–66. I am very grateful to the anonymous reviewer for this vision of three bridges.

12 Peter Cartwright, 'Understanding and Protecting Vulnerable Financial Consumers' (2015) 38 *Journal of Consumer Policy* 119–38 at 119.

13 Convention for the Protection of Human Rights and Fundamental Freedoms, Rome, 4 November 1950, in force 3 September 1953, ETS No. 005.

14 Human Rights Act (HRA) 1998 (c. 42).

law and suggests that rather than looking for a seamless bridge that links the UNCRPD directly with English contract law, we should look for stepping-stones connecting the UNCRPD, the ECHR, the HRA, and domestic private law. This chapter also discusses the values of participation and inclusion, with a focus on the idea of influence vulnerability explored in Chapter 4, and reflects on the need to enhance the influence of persons with disabilities and Deaf and Disabled People's Organisations (DDPOs) in shaping legislative developments in English law, including consumer contract law.

The idea of bridges between economic and social concerns is brought together in the concluding chapter (Chapter 6). This chapter reinforces the need to recognise the outer sphere of contracting in holding these connections together. The discussion emphasises the role of contract law in protecting economic and social values, individual and relational autonomy, and in enforcing transactions and safeguarding vulnerable parties.[15] A suggested path to succeed in these endeavours is to embrace the idea of complementarity in contract law, which enables us to accept the coexistence of ideas that may appear, initially, to be mutually exclusive.[16] Just as in science we have to accept the idea that an electron can behave both as a particle and as a wave,[17] we can transpose the concept of complementarity in contract law, to enable us to see economic and social values not as antagonistic but as coexisting parts of interconnected spheres.

This research is mostly desk-based. It relies on socio-legal inquiry, focusing on participation barriers encountered by people with disabilities in the contractual sphere, and examining how the legal framework relates to structural problems such as economic and emotional exploitation by, among others, predatory sellers, or family members or carers. Sources include General Comments of UN Committees, reports drafted by government departments, by statutory independent bodies, by registered charities, and by consumer organisations, responses to public consultations, empirical scholarship on the living experiences of persons with disabilities, as well as empirical research conducted with DDPO representatives. The analysis is based on legal inquiry focused on primary and secondary sources examining vitiating factors in contract law and issues concerning the regulation of B2C transactions, including unfair contract terms and unfair commercial practices. The critical analysis of these sources is informed, among other sources, by the literature on disability and economics, feminist critiques of contract law, socio-legal critiques of the vulnerability concept, contract theory, and contract legal history.

[15] Jonathan Herring, *Vulnerable Adults and the Law* (Oxford: Oxford University Press, 2016), p. 258.

[16] Robert Oppenheimer, 'Science and the Common Understanding', The Reith Lectures, BBC Radio 4, 1953; Brian Cox, 'Robert Oppenheimer', Reith Revisited, BBC Radio 4, 27 September 2017.

[17] Oppenheimer, 'Science and the Common Understanding'; Cox, 'Robert Oppenheimer'.

This book aims to contribute towards bridging the areas of disability equality law and contract law. It builds on contract legal research that explores issues of public policy and social values,[18] to focus specifically on disability equality in the contractual sphere, and on disability legal research concerned with equality for consumers with disabilities,[19] by centring the discussion on contract theory. It also seeks to build on studies exploring the link between contract law and human rights,[20] by focusing on questions concerning the compatibility of key principles, doctrines, and statutory provisions in English contract law with UNCRPD values, including autonomy and human dignity. Given the centrality of contractual relations to people's lives,[21] such questions are important for both disability theory and contract theory.

Contract law plays a crucial role in connecting people in mutual relations and contributing to the wider norms that govern how people should treat each other.[22] In the light of ageing population trends and the likely increase in the number of people whose capacity to understand the implications of a transaction has been affected by mental health conditions such as dementia,[23] it is important that the interests of persons with disabilities in the contractual realm are not overlooked. The issue of grossly asymmetrical contracts affecting persons with disabilities is becoming increasingly important, especially if we consider that by 2051, the estimated figure for people living with conditions such as dementia in the UK will approach 2 million.[24] In the contractual sphere, people with this condition are likely to be affected by factors such as difficulty in processing information, communicating and planning, and memory loss, as well as by as insufficient understanding of their condition by other contracting parties (including service providers such as the financial services industry).[25] Further difficulties in the contractual realm are also likely to be encountered by people with cognitive, mobility or sensory disabilities, who may be placed in a vulnerable position of information asymmetry due to environmental barriers such as the absence of information in accessible for-

[18] Stephen Waddams, *Sanctity of Contracts in a Secular Age: Equity, Fairness and Enrichment* (Cambridge: Cambridge University Press, 2019).

[19] Yvette Maker and others, 'From Safety Nets to Support Networks: Beyond "Vulnerability" in Protection for Consumers with Cognitive Disabilities' (2018) 41 *University of New South Wales Law Journal* 818–45.

[20] Roger Brownsword, 'Developing a Modern Understanding of Human Dignity' in Dieter Grimm, Alexandra Kemmerer and Christoph Mollers (eds.), *Human Dignity in Context* (Baden-Baden: Nomos, 2018), pp. 299–324.

[21] Anthony T. Kronman, 'Contract Law and Distributive Justice' (1980) 89 *Yale Law Journal* 472–511 at 472.

[22] Mindy Chen-Wishart, 'Undue Influence: Vindicating Relationships of Influence' (2006) 59 *Current Legal Problems* 231–66 at 239.

[23] Jeremy Dixon, Judy Laing and Christine Valentine, 'A Human Rights Approach to Advocacy for People with Dementia: A Review of Current Provision in England and Wales' (2018) *Dementia* 1–16 at 3.

[24] Prince and others, 'Dementia UK', p. 5.

[25] Eimear O'Brien, 'Are You Treating Your Vulnerable Customers Fairly?' (2017) 6 *Compliance and Risk Journal* 10.

mats. Additional challenges have been posed by the rise in social isolation seen during pandemics such as COVID-19,[26] which increased people's vulnerability to pressure to enter into detrimental transactions. While, in some cases, people may seek to rely on pathways such as complaints to an Ombudsman[27] to challenge such disadvantageous transactions, contract law should also provide an effective path to be pursued. Consequently, it is important to have clarity as to when grossly imbalanced contracts will be unenforceable. Perhaps even more significant is to have a clear understanding as to why such contracts will or will not be enforced, relying on a framework of principles that seeks to protect people not only as economic actors but also as social actors endowed with values such as equality, autonomy, and human dignity. When examining these contracts, it is also important to move away from a focus on people's medical conditions and to consider instead the circumstances of the transactions (including factors such as accessible information) and to perceive people as holders of rights, irrespective of whether they are operating in the public or private spheres.[28]

The book also calls for a regulatory framework, including in relation to unfair commercial practices in B2C transactions, which considers neurodiversity. Neurodiversity recognises 'differences in brain function and behavioural traits' as a 'normal variation in the human population' and includes neurodivergence (e.g. autism, ADHD, dyslexia, dyspraxia, dyscalculia, dysgraphia, Tourette's syndrome), and neurotypicality.[29] As part of the analysis in Chapter 4 of the regulatory framework on unfair commercial practices, the discussion reflects on the challenges posed by harmful 'online choice architecture' (OCA)[30] on consumers in the digital marketplace, including on neurodivergent consumers, calling for an approach that assesses vulnerability based on the context of the transaction, which recognises the variety of ways in which people process information, and which is focused on protecting values such as individual autonomy and human dignity. Harmful OCA (or 'dark patterns')[31] refers to design features employed by traders to present 'information and choices' to consumers,[32] in a way that 'systematically' manipulates them into actions that they would

[26] Debanjan Banerjee and Mayank Rai, 'Social Isolation in COVID-19: The Impact of Loneliness' (2020) 66 *International Journal of Social Psychiatry* 525–27 at 525.

[27] Examples include the Financial Ombudsman Service for issues such as consumer insurance and banking.

[28] Hurst, 'Disabled People's Organisations', p. 25.

[29] Lawrence Fung and others 'Neurodiversity: An Invisible Strength?' (2022) 74(9) *Jom* 3200–2 at 3201.

[30] Information Commissioner's Office (ICO) and the Competition and Markets Authority (CMA), 'Harmful Design in Digital Markets: How Online Choice Architecture Practices Can Undermine Consumer Choice and Control over Personal Information, Joint Position Paper', August 2023.

[31] Ashley Firth, *Practical Web Inclusion and Accessibility: A Comprehensive Guide to Access Needs* (1st ed., New York: Apress, 2019), with reference to Harry Brignull who coined the phrase 'dark patterns'.

[32] ICO and CMA, 'Harmful Design'.

not have taken otherwise.[33] Dark patters include forced urgency (e.g. countdown timers or scarcity claims about low stocks), trick questions (e.g. questions deliberately designed to confuse consumers to agree to a subscription), false hierarchy (e.g. providing consumers with two options, but using an enhanced position, colour or size for the option more favourable to the trader), and forced continuity (e.g. difficult to cancel subscriptions following a free trial).[34] These dark patterns, which work 'on a subconscious level', can influence consumers without their knowledge, can benefit traders (e.g. by increased profits) and result in negative experiences for the consumers,[35] causing, *inter alia*, financial and emotional harm.[36] These deceptive patterns can be particularly problematic for neurodivergent consumers, who may have a lower threshold than neurotypical consumers for when a feature designed by traders to influence consumers becomes a manipulative pattern,[37] and who may experience feelings of panic and anxiety when faced with dark patterns such as 'forced urgency'.[38] Consumer contract law must reflect a contextual understanding of vulnerability, acknowledging human diversity (e.g. the various ways in which people process information), when assessing the scope of unfair commercial practices. In addition, this regulatory framework must be shaped in consultation with key stakeholders, including organisations of neurodivergent people.

Questions regarding the validity of grossly imbalanced transactions involving vulnerable contracting parties should be addressed with reference not only to procedural factors and economic concerns but also to substantive factors and social concerns,[39] including the protection of fundamental values such as human dignity. In this context, a focus on safeguarding human dignity could be understood as the need to ensure that no one is disadvantaged because of their subjective characteristics,[40] and that everyone is treated with respect.[41] Moreover, vulnerability should not be associated with belonging to a particular group, or having a particular medical condition, but should be rooted in the context of the transaction examined (e.g. questioning whether service providers made available appropriate and accessible information to enable the individual to make an informed decision).[42]

The UNCRPD rests on a clear framework of values, based on a rights-based approach for understanding vulnerability in all spheres[43] and, by implication, the contractual realm. As such, the Convention can act as a benchmark against

[33] Adrian Petterson, 'Dark Patterns and Disability: Ethical Failings of Designing for Normal', TEDxUofT, University of Toronto, 29 January 2022.

[34] Which? 'Dark Patterns: How Consumer Choices Are Manipulated Online', 23 March 2023.

[35] Petterson, 'Dark Patterns and Disability'.

[36] Which? 'Dark Patterns'.

[37] Petterson, 'Dark Patterns and Disability'.

[38] Firth, 'Practical Web Inclusion', p. 248.

[39] Stephen Waddams, *Principle and Policy in Contract Law* (Cambridge: Cambridge University Press, 2011), p. 112.

[40] Zoe Apostolopoulou, 'Equal Treatment of People with Disabilities in the EC: What Does 'Equal' Mean?' (2004) Jean Monnet Working Paper 09/04.

[41] Denise Réaume, 'Discrimination and Dignity' (2003) 63 *Louisiana Law Review* 1–51 at 1.

[42] Herring, 'Vulnerable Adults', p. 6.

[43] Articles 3(a) and 4 of the UNCRPD.

which we can assess the effectiveness of English contract law (including consumer contract law) in responding to both economic and social concerns in the contractual sphere. International human rights instruments such as the UNCRPD are clear as to why everyone has the right to exercise their legal capacity on an equal basis with others and to enjoy equal protection of values such as autonomy and human dignity. Nevertheless, there is less clarity as to how these rights are to be exercised in the contractual sphere, on the connection between concepts such as legal capacity and contractual capacity, and on how safeguards from vitiating factors or protection from unfair commercial practices are to operate in practice. Conversely, domestic frameworks such as English contract law provide a certain degree of clarity on how procedural factors, such as freedom from duress, undue influence, or unconscionability, are to operate in practice, but there is less clarity on why intervention is necessary. It is as if the inner sphere of contract law has been isolated from the outer sphere of social values, with incomplete bridges to connect the two. Whilst this book focuses on contract law in a domestic jurisdiction, the lessons to be learnt are not limited to English contract law, due to the universality of the need to protect social values in the private sphere. English contract law and the UNCRPD have much to learn from each other, and this book seeks to explore how to build bridges that would facilitate two-way paths between them. Through these paths, the Convention harnesses the potential of contract law to pursue social objectives (which would be in addition to pursuing these objectives through other areas of law, including public law), and English contract law assesses the extent to which its principles and doctrines are compatible with the values promoted by the UNCRPD, including equal respect for autonomy and human dignity. This vision of concentric economic and social spheres in contract law is articulated more clearly in Chapter 2, which sketches the map to direct the search for connections between these sets of values in the contractual realm.

2

The Map

Contract Law, the UNCRPD and the Concentric Spheres of Economic and Social Values

No pessimist ever discovered the secret of the stars
or sailed to an uncharted land

(Helen Keller, 1880–1968, American writer and social reformer, Optimism: An Essay (1903) pt. 3)

Contract law is pivotal for human connections and needs to have at its core a vision that reflects not only its economic implications but also the social dimension of entering, or being denied the right to enter into contracts. Any approach that looks at the contracting parties (A and B) in the abstract as sole economic actors, without considering more closely the social context of the transaction and the parties' bargaining positions, presents a distorted image. Given the centrality of transactions in people's everyday lives, one of the multifaceted aspects of contract law is to play a role within the wider objectives of shaping a society where everyone has the opportunity to exercise their individual autonomy on an equal basis with others, and where their human dignity is protected. This chapter highlights the interconnection between economic and social values in the contractual realm, rooted in a perception of people as holders of rights rather than merely economic actors, and in a broad interpretation of autonomy and human dignity that looks beyond individualistic values. With a focus on grossly asymmetrical contracts, it also promotes an understanding of vulnerability in the contractual context, based on the circumstances of the transaction, rather than on the medical condition of individuals. These issues are explored in a two parts structure. The chapter begins with a reflection on the merits and drawbacks of the UNCRPD as a potential benchmark for promoting a vision of contract law that responds to both economic and social concerns and recognises the equality of all human beings, emphasising on the view of disability as an aspect of human diversity.[1] The second part of the discussion considers how English contract law could be brought closer to the equality vision promoted by the UNCRPD, proposing an understanding of the contractual realm based on concentric economic and social spheres, shaped by fluid

[1] Article 3(d) of the UNCRPD.

boundaries, and reflecting on the relevance of contract law as part of a broader set of measures to ensure a fairer society.

2.1 The UNCRPD: A Benchmark for Protecting the Rights of Persons with Disabilities in the Contractual Realm?

People with disabilities are confronted with various barriers to participation in the contractual sphere. These include the denial of opportunity to enter into contractual relations due to formal barriers restricting decision-making such as guardianships, or informal barriers imposed, *inter alia*, by family members restricting access to money[2] or to identification documents necessary to open a bank account, resulting in 'de facto' guardianships.[3] They also include attitudinal barriers from service providers who refuse to contract or provide less favourable terms due to a person's disability.[4] Further challenges are posed by environmental barriers such as inaccessible premises, by insufficient understanding of support requirements, including for people with non-visible disabilities (such as anxiety, depression, autism and chronic fatigue syndrome),[5] or by the absence of appropriate and accessible information.[6]

Such barriers create environments that place people in a vulnerable position, resulting in a clear imbalance of power between the parties. The word 'vulnerable' is rooted in the Latin verb '*vulnerare*', meaning 'to wound'.[7] These contexts of power imbalance could harm parties who encounter barriers to participation in the contractual realm. For example, a party (A) may find themselves in a position of vulnerability when the other party (B) (e.g. a bank allowing A to stand as surety for a loan provided to another party) did not ensure that A had access to appropriate and accessible information.[8] This may result in information asymmetry between the contracting parties, placing A in an unequal bargaining position.[9] Other contexts that could place A in a position of vulnerability include the provision by B of a standard form contract on a 'take

[2] Clíona de Bhailís, 'Introduction to Contractual Capacity' in Eilionóir Flynn and others (eds.), *Global Perspectives on Legal Capacity Reform: Our Voices, Our Stories* (London: Routledge, 2019), pp. 47–49 at p. 47.

[3] Joy Rehema and Emer O'Shea, 'I Have the Strength to Speak Up for Myself: Nikona nguvu ya kujiongelelea' in Flynn and others (eds.), *Global Perspectives on Legal Capacity Reform*, pp. 50–60 at p. 57.

[4] Carol Kaufman-Scarborough, 'Social Exclusion: A Perspective on Consumers with Disabilities' in Susan Dunnett, Kathy Hamilton and Maria Piacentini (eds.), *Vulnerable Consumers: Conditions, Contexts and Characteristics* (London: Routledge, 2015), pp. 157–69 at p. 157.

[5] Angelica Guevara, 'Ableness as Property' (2020) *Denver Law Review Forum*, University of Wisconsin Legal Studies Research Paper No. 1593, 1–39 at 18.

[6] Michael Oliver, *The Politics of Disablement* (Basingstoke: Palgrave Macmillan, 1990).

[7] Charles Talbut Onions (ed.), *The Oxford Dictionary of English Etymology* (1st ed., Oxford: Oxford University Press, 1996); Herring, 'Vulnerable Adults', p. 6.

[8] Fiona Burns, 'The Elderly and Undue Influence Inter Vivos' (2003) 23 *Legal Studies* 251–83.

[9] Michael Trebilcock and Steven Elliott, 'The Scope and Limits of Legal Paternalism: Altruism and Coercion in Family Financial Arrangements' in Peter Benson (ed.), *The Theory of Contract Law: New Essays* (Cambridge: Cambridge University Press, 2001), pp. 45–85 at p. 62.

it or leave it' basis, where such contracts include unfair terms,[10] or situations where A is subject to aggressive sales tactics from predatory sellers (e.g. door to door sellers of utility services) or predatory money lenders.[11] Rather than perceiving the contracting parties, A and B, in the abstract, we must look more closely at the parties' bargaining positions, the wider social context of the transaction, and how this context can create vulnerabilities.

A narrow understanding of 'vulnerability', confined to particular groups perceived as 'disadvantaged' within society,[12] and associated with concepts of 'weakness' and 'dependency', can lead to the 'stigmatisation' of individuals belonging to these groups,[13] particularly when contrasted with ideas of 'strength'[14] or 'individual autonomy' (understood narrowly as 'self-sufficiency').[15] Far from being neutral, such 'binary opposition' of terms reflects a 'subordinating structure'[16] that fails to consider values such as equality, the interrelation between people,[17] and the need to protect human dignity. It also fails to consider how economic and social structures can create disadvantage,[18] and the correlation between factors such as the high unemployment rate faced by people with disabilities[19] (especially when this intersects with other grounds such as age, gender and race)[20] and poverty[21] (including digital poverty).[22] Such factors tend to place people in a weak bargaining position when seeking to participate in the contractual sphere, including due to limited access to appropriate information and legal advice. Moreover, a narrow perception of 'vulnerability' confined to people with specific medical conditions,

[10] Friedrich Kessler, 'Contracts of Adhesion: Some Thoughts about Freedom of Contract' (1943) 43 *Columbia Law Review* 629–42 at 632.

[11] Maker, 'From Safety Nets', 834.

[12] Martha Albertson Fineman, 'Vulnerability and Inevitable Inequality' (2017) 4 *Oslo Law Review* 133–49 at 142.

[13] Martha Albertson Fineman, 'Beyond Identities: The Limits of an Antidiscrimination Approach to Equality' (2012) 92 *Boston University Law Review* 1713–70 at 1748.

[14] Shelley Bielefeld, 'Compulsory Income Management and Indigenous Peoples: Exploring Counter Narratives amidst Colonial Constructions of "Vulnerability"' (2014) 36 *Sydney Law Review* 695–726 at 722.

[15] Martha Albertson Fineman, 'The Vulnerable Subject and the Responsive State' (2010) 60 *Emory Law Journal* 251–76 at 259.

[16] Bielefeld, 'Compulsory Income Management', 722.

[17] Martha Albertson Fineman, 'Vulnerability and Social Justice' (2019) 53 *Valparaiso University Law Review* 341–69 at 342.

[18] Nirmala Erevelles, *Disability and Difference in Global Contexts: Enabling a Transformative Body Politic* (New York: Palgrave Macmillan, 2011) at p. 19.

[19] Marta Russell, 'What Disability Civil Rights Cannot Do' in Marta Russell, *Capitalism and Disability: Selected Writings* (edited by Keith Rosenthal) (Chicago: Haymarket Books, 2019), pp. 62–73 at p. 65.

[20] Marta Russell, 'Backlash, the Political Economy, and Structural Exclusion' (2000) 21 *Berkeley Journal of Employment and Labor Law* 335–66 at 337.

[21] Marta Russell and Ravi Malhotra, 'Capitalism and the Disability Rights Movement' in Marta Russell, *Capitalism and Disability: Selected Writings* (edited by Keith Rosenthal) (Chicago: Haymarket Books, 2019), pp. 1–10 at p. 2.

[22] Kerry Dobransky and Eszter Hargittai, 'The Disability Divide in Internet Access and Use' (2006) 9 *Information, Communication and Society* 314–34.

which overlooks other factors that may place parties in a weak bargaining position, could limit the circumstances in which people could be provided with a way out of a grossly imbalanced transaction.[23]

The search for a vision of contract law that reflects a broad understanding of 'vulnerability',[24] focused on the context of the transaction rather than on the medical condition of individuals, which considers the broader social justice impact of legal doctrine and recognises the interconnection between economic and social values in the contractual realm, could rely on the UNCRPD as a potential inspiration. The Convention reaffirms the move away from a medical model of disability centred on people's medical conditions to a predominantly social model.[25] This model perceives disability as a socially constructed phenomenon resulting from 'the interaction between persons with impairments and attitudinal and environmental barriers that hinders their full and effective participation in society on an equal basis with others'.[26] It focuses on adapting society to accommodate the full spectrum of abilities, rather than on adapting individuals to society,[27] and perceives social inclusion and respect for individual autonomy as complementary goals.[28] The Convention seeks to ensure, among other measures, the accessibility of information provided to the public, also calling on private entities that offer services to the public to consider accessibility requirements.[29] Accessibility is also included as one of the general principles advanced by the Convention[30] alongside, *inter alia*, 'full and effective participation and inclusion in society'.[31] Furthermore, general obligations placed by the Convention on States Parties include a call to 'take all appropriate measures to eliminate discrimination on the basis of disability by any person, organization or private enterprise'.[32] These requirements contribute towards the overall objective of the Convention to uphold the full and equal enjoyment of all human rights and fundamental freedoms by persons with disabilities and to promote respect for the inherent dignity of all human beings.[33]

The UNCRPD, which is the first binding international human rights instrument focused specifically on the rights of persons with disabilities,[34]

[23] Fineman, 'Beyond Identities', 1749. [24] Fineman, 'The Vulnerable Subject', 266.

[25] Sarah Fraser Butlin, 'The UN Convention on the Rights of Persons with Disabilities: Does the Equality Act 2010 Measure up to UK International Commitments?' (2011) 40 *Industrial Law Journal* 428–38.

[26] Paragraph (e), Preamble of the UNCRPD.

[27] Anna Lawson, 'The United Nations Convention on the Rights of Persons with Disabilities: New Era or False Dawn?' (2007) 34 *Syracuse Journal of International Law and Commerce* 563–618 at 572.

[28] Articles 3(a) and 3(c) of the UNCRPD. Heiner Bielefeldt, 'New Inspiration for the Human Rights Debate: The Convention on the Rights of Persons with Disabilities' (2007) 52 *Netherlands Quarterly of Human Rights* 397–99 at 398.

[29] Articles 9(1)(b) and (2)(b) of the UNCRPD. [30] Ibid. Article 3(f). [31] Ibid. Article 3(c).

[32] Ibid. Article 4(1)(e). [33] Ibid. Article 1.

[34] Arlene Kanter, 'The Promise and Challenge of the United Nations Convention on the Rights of Persons with Disabilities' (2007) 34 *Syracuse Journal of International Law and Commerce* 287–322 at 288.

reframes the interest of persons with disabilities in terms of human rights[35] and reflects a perception of people as subjects of human rights rather than as objects of care,[36] with full entitlements in society rather than disempowered victims.[37] It emphasises the equal worth of all human beings, aims to ensure 'full and equal enjoyment of all human rights and fundamental freedoms by all persons with disabilities and to promote respect for their inherent dignity',[38] and calls for 'respect for difference' and for the 'acceptance of persons with disabilities as part of human diversity and humanity'.[39] The Convention tackles human rights abuses experienced by persons with disabilities, including the denial of legal capacity on the basis of disability,[40] and adapts the application of established human rights to circumstances particular to persons with disabilities.[41]

The Convention provides a benchmark to recognise the interdependence of people and the interconnection of rights.[42] It reaffirms the indivisibility of all human rights and fundamental freedoms[43] and departs from the artificial distinction between civil and political rights based on negative formulations of non-interference, and economic, social and cultural rights based on positive formulations that call for state action.[44] The Convention brings together these economic and social values to create 'hybrid rights'.[45] The correlation between economic and social values embodied in the UNCRPD should influence our interpretation of key ideas such as autonomy and human dignity, supporting a broad interpretation of these concepts. The Convention promotes individual autonomy, recognising under Articles 12(1) and (2) the equal right of persons with disabilities to possess and exercise legal capacity,[46] which is central to the exercise of human agency as a person.[47] The provisions on equal recognition before the law under Article 12[48] act as a 'sword' to advance personhood (including entering into legally binding agreements) and as a 'shield' against

[35] Rosemary Kayess and Phillip French, 'Out of Darkness into Light? Introducing the Convention on the Rights of Persons with Disabilities' (2008) 8 *Human Rights Law Review* 1–34.

[36] Lawson, 'The United Nations Convention', 584.

[37] Deirdre Smith, 'Who Says You're Disabled? The Role of Medical Evidence in the ADA Definition of Disability' (2007) 82 *Tulane Law Review* 1–76 at 71.

[38] Article 1 of the UNCRPD. [39] Ibid. Article 3(d).

[40] Tara Melish, 'The UN Disability Convention: Historic Process, Strong Prospects and Why the U.S. Should Ratify' (2007) 14 *Human Rights Brief* 37–47 at 43.

[41] Kayess and French, 'Out of Darkness', 3.

[42] Oliver Lewis, 'Advancing Legal Capacity Jurisprudence' (2011) 6 *European Human Rights Law Review* 700–14 at 704.

[43] Paragraph (c), Preamble of the UNCRPD.

[44] Don MacKay, 'The United Nations Convention on the Rights of Persons with Disabilities' (2007) 34 *Syracuse Journal of International Law and Commerce* 323–32 at 330.

[45] Ibid. [46] Articles 12(1) and (2) of the UNCRPD.

[47] Michael Bach, *The Right to Legal Capacity under the UN Convention on the Rights of Persons with Disabilities: Key Concepts and Directions for Law Reform* (Toronto: IRIS, 2009), pp. 2–3.

[48] Article 12 of the UNCRPD.

unwanted interference from others.[49] These provisions also stand as the basis for the enjoyment of other Convention rights, including the right to independent living and inclusion in the community.[50]

Article 12 of the UNCRPD could play a significant contribution in tackling the historical disadvantage and the barriers to participation in society faced by persons with disabilities in general, and persons with cognitive disabilities in particular.[51] Such disadvantages include legal barriers when disability is equated with incapacity, leading to a denial of legal capacity and the institution of guardianship systems and substituted decision-making.[52] These reflect a perception of people as objects of care for whom decisions must be made, rather than as subjects of human rights who may require support in making their own decisions.[53] The denial of legal capacity has been equated with the 'civil death' of the persons concerned.[54] Persons whose decisions have no legal force are left without the opportunity to make their own choices and depend instead on the actions of others.[55] They are denied their individuality and are deprived of their personal autonomy and human dignity,[56] becoming 'non-persons' under the law.[57] Article 12 of the UNCRPD has been has been commended as 'the beating heart of the Convention',[58] with the potential to 'effect revolutionary changes'.[59] It plays a key contribution to the paradigm shift in the perception of persons with disabilities from objects of care to subjects of rights, from substituted decision-making and denial of legal capacity to supported decision-making and the recognition of the right of persons with disabilities to enjoy legal capacity on an equal basis with others, and from exclusion to inclusion.[60] It refers explicitly, in Article 12(5), to the equal right of persons with disabilities to control their own financial affairs and to have access to financial credit.[61]

The concept of universal legal capacity, which recognises the ability of all people to hold and exercise rights and duties,[62] is central to the exercise of

49 Gerard Quinn, 'Personhood and Legal Capacity: Perspectives on the Paradigm Shift of Article 12 UNCRPD', HPOD Conference, Harvard, 2010, p. 10.

50 Article 19 of the UNCRPD.

51 Stanley Herr, Lawrence Gostin and Harold Hongju Koh (eds.), *The Human Rights of Persons with Intellectual Disabilities: Different but Equal* (Oxford: Oxford University Press, 2003).

52 Bach, 'The Right to Legal Capacity', p. 1.

53 Robert Dinerstein, 'Implementing Legal Capacity under Article 12 of the UNCRPD: The Difficult Road from Guardianship to Supported Decision-Making' (2012) 19 *Human Rights Brief* 8–74 at 9.

54 Lawson, 'The United Nations Convention', 569.

55 Dinerstein, 'Implementing Legal Capacity', 9.

56 Lewis, 'Advancing Legal Capacity Jurisprudence', 709.

57 Anna Nilsson, 'Who Gets to Decide? Right to Legal Capacity for Persons with Intellectual and Psychosocial Disabilities', Council of Europe, CommDH/Issue Paper (2012) 2, Strasbourg, 20 February at 4–6.

58 Ibid. 59 Lawson, 'The United Nations Convention', 595.

60 Articles 1 and 12(1)–(3) of the UNCRPD. 61 Ibid. Article 12(5).

62 UN Committee on the Rights of Persons with Disabilities, 'General Comment No. 1: Article 12 (Equal Recognition before the Law)', 19 May 2014, UN Doc CRPD/C/GC/1, [13].

human dignity,[63] enabling people to shape their own lives.[64] Closely linked to universal legal capacity is the concept of universal human dignity. The citizenship value of human dignity contributes towards ensuring substantive equality, which proactively tackles 'systemic' forms of discrimination entrenched in society.[65] These concepts should be interpreted in light of each other, recognising their overlap in promoting respect for everyone. The key for ensuring a clear understanding of these concepts is through social dialogue,[66] including consultations with DDPOs. Persons with disabilities are often confronted by other people's misconceptions about disability, resulting in a 'misrecognition' of their identity.[67] The UNCRPD provides a framework for change from misrecognition to recognition, promoting respect for human diversity.[68] The citizenship value of human dignity plays a key role in achieving this objective, as it is inherent in every person and its recognition aims to ensure that 'everyone is treated as having value or worth'.[69] One understanding of human dignity envisages the empowerment of people to exercise their individual autonomy, including in the contractual sphere.[70] Nevertheless, the Convention adopts a broad interpretation of the concepts of autonomy and human dignity, unconfined to individual autonomy[71] and to an understanding of human dignity as solely the empowerment of parties to exercise individual autonomy.[72]

The UNCRPD recognises a relational understanding of autonomy, linked with a broad view of personhood which connects autonomy with interdependence between people.[73] The Convention aims to facilitate participation and inclusion,[74] recognising in Article 12(3) also the potential need for support in decision-making[75] and, in Article 12(4) the potential need for safeguards such as protection from undue influence,[76] interpreted in light of the general principles advanced by the UNCRPD, including the protection of autonomy and human dignity.[77] This reference to safeguards can be linked to an understanding of human dignity focused not only on emboldening people to exercise individual autonomy (human dignity as 'empowerment') but also to restraining this exercise for pursuing wider social values (human dignity as

63 Bach, 'The Right to Legal Capacity', pp. 2–3. 64 Quinn, 'Personhood and Legal Capacity'.

65 Sandra Fredman, 'Equality: A New Generation?' (2001) 30 *Industrial Law Journal* 145–68 at 154.

66 Réaume, 'Discrimination and Dignity', 51.

67 Halvor Hanisch, 'Recognising Disability' in Jerome Bickenbach, Franziska Felder and Barbara Schmitz (eds.), *Disability and the Good Human Life* (Cambridge: Cambridge University Press, 2014), pp. 113–38 at p. 124.

68 Ibid. 69 Fredman, 'Equality: A New Generation?', 155.

70 Roger Brownsword, 'Freedom of Contract, Human Rights and Human Dignity' in Dan Friedmann and Daphne Barak-Erez (eds.), *Human Rights in Private Law* (Oxford: Hart Publishing, 2001), pp. 181–200 at pp. 183–84.

71 Dhanda, 'Constructing a New Human Rights Lexicon', 50.

72 Brownsword, 'Freedom of Contract', p. 183.

73 Dhanda, 'Constructing a New Human Rights Lexicon', 50. 74 Article 3(c) of the UNCRPD.

75 Ibid. Article 12(3). 76 Ibid. Article 12(4). 77 Ibid. Article 3(a).

'constraint').[78] Furthermore, in the event of a conflict of principles such as a call for non-interference with freedom of contract and a call for the protection of human dignity, the latter ranks higher.[79]

The framework advanced by the UNCRPD is not free from challenges. Unlike the UN Convention on the Elimination of all Forms of Discrimination against Women (UN CEDAW),[80] which refers explicitly to the equal right to conclude contracts,[81] there is no explicit reference to equality in the contractual sphere in the UNCRPD. Instead, there is an unexplored, implicit reference to such equality as part of the provisions on equal recognition before the law.[82] Moreover, while the UN CEDAW calls for both the equal right to exercise legal capacity in concluding contracts, and equal opportunities to exercise legal capacity,[83] cost-related implications may have been at the root of not including explicitly an equivalent provision in the UNCRPD.

The UNCRPD framework lacks clarity regarding the extent to which the right to exercise legal capacity can be restricted (if at all) and the link between legal capacity, mental capacity and contractual capacity.[84] While the adoption of Article 12 represents a victory for persons with disabilities, the practical implications of implementing this provision suggest that 'the hard part begins!'[85] This difficulty is augmented when considering the implications of universal legal capacity in the area of contract law, given the silence of the Convention regarding its application in the contractual sphere. However, despite this silence, the UNCRPD has the potential to be a benchmark in guiding a re-examination of legal concepts such as contractual capacity in light of the values pursued by the Convention, including the protection of autonomy and human dignity.

The implementation of Article 12 of the UNCRPD could be accompanied by the abandonment of the incapacity defence in contract law, relying on other doctrines such as unconscionability, undue influence or duress, to fill in any potential gaps left in the protection of vulnerable contracting parties. However, as we will see in Chapter 3 as part of the discussion on vitiating factors in English contract law, these doctrines are not free from challenges. As things stand, abandoning the incapacity defence would leave a vacuum that could not be filled by other doctrines. Consequently, rather than calling for the abandonment of the incapacity defence in contract law, this discussion calls instead for reconceptualising this doctrine in light of UNCRPD values, including autonomy and human dignity. In the context of English contract law, this

[78] Brownsword, 'Modern Understanding of Human Dignity', p. 302.

[79] *Nyusti and Takács* v. *Hungary*, CRPD/C/9/D/1/2010, 11 March 2010.

[80] UN Convention on the Elimination of All Forms of Discrimination against Women (UN CEDAW), New York, 18 December 1979, in force 3 September 1981, GA Res 34/180, A/34/46, 1249 UNTS 13.

[81] Article 15(2) of the UN CEDAW. [82] Article 12 of the UNCRPD.

[83] Article 15(2) of the UN CEDAW.

[84] Peter Bartlett, 'The United Nations Convention on the Rights of Persons with Disabilities and Mental Health Law' (2012) 75 *Modern Law Review* 752–78.

[85] Dinerstein, 'Implementing Legal Capacity', 8.

analysis is part of a wider call for an expanded interpretation of vitiating factors doctrines, including unconscionability, undue influence and duress, in pursuit of social values.

In a framework which recognises universal legal capacity (the ability possessed by everyone to hold and exercise rights and duties) and distinguishes this from mental capacity (the decision-making skills of an individual, which vary from person to person and may be influenced by external factors),[86] the exercise of universal legal capacity could be facilitated by an effective legal framework where parties can rely, when appropriate, on defences such as contractual incapacity. However, the effectiveness of the incapacity defence in contract law depends on a range of factors. Bach notes that as the incapacity defence in contract law may be invoked by anyone, this defence is compatible with Article 12 of the UNCRPD, but incompatibility would arise if incapacity and disability were conceptually equated.[87] Concerns about incompatibility with the Convention could arise, even in a disability neutral concept of incapacity, if differential treatment on the basis of mental capacity had a disproportionate impact on people with disabilities,[88] leading to an allegation of indirect discrimination on the basis of disability.[89] This could amount to a breach of Article 12(2) (which reaffirms the right to equal enjoyment of legal capacity), read in conjunction with Article 5 of the UNCRPD (which prohibits 'all discrimination on the basis of disability'), including any discriminatory measure that has the 'purpose or effect' of interfering with the right to equal recognition before the law.[90] However, there is an argument (although not without challenges), that the incapacity defence in contract law could be objectively justified within this framework. Whilst the Convention provides 'no schema of defence against charges of indirect discrimination',[91] Martin and others note that the differential treatment which leads to a disproportionate impact on persons with disabilities may be permitted if based on reasonable and objective justifications and pursues a legitimate aim under the Convention.[92] A measure that has disproportionate impact on people with disabilities must meet a three

[86] UNCRPD Committee, 'General Comment No. 1', [13].

[87] Bach, 'The Right to Legal Capacity', p. 5.

[88] Eilionóir Flynn, 'Mental (in)Capacity or Legal Capacity: A Human Rights Analysis of the Proposed Fusion of Mental Health and Mental Capacity Law in Northern Ireland' (2013) 64 *Northern Ireland Legal Quarterly* 485–505 at 497.

[89] Articles 2, 5 and 12 of the UNCRPD.

[90] Ibid. See Wayne Martin and others, 'Achieving CRPD Compliance. Is the Mental Capacity Act of England and Wales Compatible with the UN Convention on the Rights of Persons with Disabilities? If Not, What Next? An Essex Autonomy Project Position Paper', Report submitted to the UK Ministry of Justice, 22 September 2014 at 16.

[91] Martin, 'Achieving CRPD Compliance', 7.

[92] Ibid. Martin and others support this conclusion with reference to the UN Committee on Economic, Social and Cultural Rights, 'General Comment No. 20: Non-discrimination in economic, social and cultural rights (Article 2(2) of the International Covenant on Economic, Social and Cultural Rights)', 2 July 2009, E/C.12/GC/20, [13]; UN Human Rights Committee, 'CCPR General Comment No. 18: Non-discrimination', 10 November 1989, HRI/GsEN/1/Rev.9 (Vol. I), [13].

part test to demonstrate that it serves ‘a legitimate aim’ under the Convention, relies on an ‘objective basis’, which constitutes ‘a reasonable means’ for achieving the relevant aim.[93]

The incapacity defence in contract law, if reconceptualised in light of UNCRPD values, could seek to meet the three parts of this test. Firstly, such defence could pursue ‘a legitimate aim’, as the Convention seeks not only to empower people with disabilities (e.g. respect for individual autonomy) but also to protect individuals in situations of risk or exploitation.[94] A broad reading of Article 11 (to include serious risk not confined to humanitarian emergencies) and Article 16 (to include passive exploitation), read in conjunction with Article 3(a) of the UNCRPD (respect for human dignity) could support a framework which protects A who has entered into a grossly imbalanced transaction, without the mental capacity to understand its nature, without support such as independent legal advice and in the presence of passive unacceptable conduct from B. Care must, however, be exercised in the way in which these articles are interpreted, in order to ensure that this interpretation is reflective of UNCRPD values.[95] Secondly, a reconceptualised incapacity defence could rest on an objective basis. To be compatible with the Convention ethos, this defence must move beyond A’s medical condition (and whether this was known by or apparent to B), to include an assessment of environmental factors such as the circumstances of the transaction. Finally, the basis of this defence could be a reasonable means for achieving a relevant aim. The Convention provides little guidance on how to balance protection of individual autonomy with potential interventions to safeguard human dignity.[96] As highlighted by Martin and others, ‘the core’ of the autonomy concept lies in the notion of ‘self-determination’, and if A cannot understand the implications of a particular transaction (e.g. due to the absence of appropriate and accessible information), it is difficult to argue that A exercised autonomy to enter into that transaction.[97] A reconceptualised incapacity defence in contract law could provide a safety net in such circumstances.

The starting point must always be a presumption of contractual capacity, and parties should have access to support in exercising capacity[98] (e.g. accessible information,[99] assistance with understanding the implications of a

[93] Martin, ‘Achieving CRPD Compliance’, 7.

[94] Articles 3(a), 11 and 16 of the UNCRPD. See Martin, ‘Achieving CRPD Compliance’, p. 30.

[95] In relation to Article 16 of the CRPD and a call for a consistent interpretation of this article ‘with the remainder of the CRPD’, see Peter Bartlett and Marianne Schulze, ‘Urgently Awaiting Implementation: The Right to Be Free from Exploitation, Violence and Abuse in Article 16 of the Convention on the Rights of Persons with Disabilities (CRPD)’ (2017) 53 *International Journal of Law and Psychiatry* 2–14 at 3.

[96] John Dawson, ‘A Realistic Approach to Assessing Mental Health Laws’ Compliance with the UNCRPD’ (2015) 40 *International Journal of Law and Psychiatry* 70–9 at 71.

[97] Martin, ‘Achieving CRPD Compliance’, p. 9.

[98] Article 12(3) of the UNCRPD.

[99] Piers Gooding, Anna Arstein-Kerslake and Eilionóir Flynn ‘Assistive Technology as Support for the Exercise of Legal Capacity’ (2015) 29 *International Review of Law, Computers and Technology* 245–65 at 251.

decision),[100] including informal and formal support arrangements.[101] Support may be 'particularly important' when signing a contract, to enable informed decision-making.[102] The support for exercising legal capacity must respect A's 'rights, will and preferences', be free of conflicts of interest or undue influence and be 'proportional and tailored' to A's circumstances.[103] These safeguards seek to balance the objectives of empowerment and protection but fail to clarify how to address 'troubling situations' where a person's decision places him at a 'serious risk' that he does not understand.[104] Such concerns should not be confined to risks involving personal safety but should also include situations where A's decision to enter into a grossly imbalanced transaction places him at a serious financial risk that he does not understand, as well as personal disadvantage.

A further hurdle when seeking to defend the incapacity defence in contract law is encountered when evaluating such a defence in light of the interpretation of Article 12 of the UNCRPD presented by the UN Committee on the Rights of Persons with Disabilities (UNCRPD Committee).[105] The arguments are likely to meet some difficulty, given the absolute stance adopted by the Committee when insisting that mental capacity assessments based on functional tests (which may question whether A had the ability to use and weigh information and understand the implications of his decision), which may result on denial of legal capacity, are incompatible with Article 12.[106] The Committee focuses on the provision of support in exercising legal capacity, which should not 'hinge on mental capacity assessments'.[107] Furthermore, the Committee stresses that everyone has legal standing (to hold rights) and legal agency (to exercise rights) and these strands cannot be separated.[108]

The UNCRPD Committee is correct in stressing that legal capacity comprises legal standing and legal agency, and in its insistence for supported decision-making.[109] Yet, whilst the Committee focuses on the provision of support when this may be needed to exercise legal capacity and on the necessary safeguards within this framework of support, it fails to consider the position where decisions are taken outside this framework of support by a party who lacks the mental capacity to understand the nature and consequences of his decision and the need for support, resulting in a grossly imbalanced transaction to his detriment. The need to respond to such concerns would justify, in exceptional circumstances, a departure from the Committee's 'hard-line'

[100] Lucy Series, 'Relationships, Autonomy and Legal Capacity: Mental Capacity and Support Paradigms' (2015) 40 *International Journal of Law and Psychiatry* 80–91 at 85.

[101] UNCRPD Committee, 'General Comment No. 1', [17].

[102] Anna Arstein-Kerslake, 'An Empowering Dependency: Exploring Support for the Exercise of Legal Capacity' (2016) 18 *Scandinavian Journal of Disability Research* 77–92 at 81.

[103] Article 12(4) of the UNCRPD.

[104] Series, 'Relationships, Autonomy and Legal Capacity', 87.

[105] UNCRPD Committee, 'General Comment No. 1'. [106] Ibid. [15]. [107] Ibid. [29(i)].

[108] Ibid. [14]. [109] Ibid. See Martin, 'Achieving CRPD Compliance', p. 24.

interpretation of Article 12,[110] which goes much further than the Convention's requirement for ensuring that persons with disabilities enjoy legal capacity 'on an equal basis with others'.[111] A reconceptualised incapacity defence in contract law available to all and reflective of UNCRPD values, could play a role in such circumstances.[112]

Further challenges that extend beyond the text of the Convention itself, but relate to the work of the UNCRPD Committee, include the fact that in its General Comment 1 on Article 12,[113] the Committee refers only three times to the equal right to exercise legal capacity by entering into contracts. These references are made twice regarding Article 15 of the UN CEDAW, and once with reference to Article 12(3) of the UNCRPD when discussing the support to exercise legal capacity.[114] As stressed in General Comment 1, such support should include universal design and accessibility, requiring public and private actors (including banks and other financial institutions) to provide information in accessible formats, which would enable persons with disabilities to perform legal acts required to conclude contracts.[115] Yet, these issues could have been explored in more depth, with further guidance on how they should operate in practice.

There is also unexplored reference to freedom of contract in the jurisprudence of the UNCRPD Committee, particularly in *Nyusti and Takács* v. *Hungary*.[116] This case concerns parties in asymmetrical positions of bargaining power: party A symbolising customers with visual disabilities, unable to access automatic teller machines (ATMs) which had no Braille markings or audio instructions, with B denoting a bank who insisted that any requirement to make their ATMs accessible would infringe on their freedom of contract, that A entered into the contract of their own free will and with full knowledge that the automatic teller machine services would be inaccessible, and that A's human dignity was not infringed by the fact that they could not use these services unaided.[117] While A perceived their contract as being located within a wider, social sphere, B's perception of the contract was confined to the economic sphere, rooted in a non-interventionist approach. Both the Court of Appeal and the Supreme Court of Hungary agreed with B.[118] Having exhausted all domestic remedies, A complained to the UNCRPD Committee. Hungary adopted the view that accessibility obligations are not applicable to private parties such as banks, and do not extend to contractual relations between private parties.[119] The Committee disagreed, stressing that States Parties to the Convention are under an obligation to take 'all appropriate measures to elim-

[110] Sascha Callaghan and Christopher Ryan, 'An Evolving Revolution: Evaluating Australia's Compliance with the Convention on the Rights of Persons with Disabilities in Mental Health Law' (2016) 39 *University of New South Wales Law Journal* 596–624 at 604.

[111] Article 12(2) of the UNCRPD. See Dawson, 'A Realistic Approach', 73.

[112] Chapter 3 discusses in more detail a re-conceptualised incapacity defence in contract law in light of UNCRPD values, in the context on English contract law.

[113] UNCRPD Committee, 'General Comment No. 1'. [114] Ibid. [6], [17], [35]. [115] Ibid. [17].

[116] *Nyusti and Takács* v. *Hungary*, CRPD/C/9/D/1/2010, 11 March 2010. [117] Ibid. [2.12].

[118] Ibid. [2.13] and [2.16]. [119] Ibid. [9.3].

inate discrimination on the basis of disability by any person, organisation or private enterprise'.[120] Furthermore, States Parties must take appropriate measures to ensure equal access to, *inter alia*, services, identify and eliminate accessibility barriers and develop and implement minimum accessibility standards.[121] In addition, States Parties must ensure that all private entities offering services to the public 'take into account all aspects of accessibility'[122] and Hungary was in breach of these obligations.[123]

This decision recognised that Convention rights permeate not only the public domain but also the private realm, and that contractual relations transcend the economic sphere into a wider, social sphere. Implied in this decision is a recognition that when balancing social values (such as human dignity) and economic values (such as freedom of contract), human dignity is ranked as a higher value that justifies interference with freedom of contract, and that freedom of contract does not operate in a vacuum but within a wider framework of social values. However, this may only be read between the lines of the UNCRPD Committee' decision and is not stated explicitly. Despite the merits of this decision, it represents a missed opportunity to engage with issues of freedom of contract and to defy an understanding of this principle unconcerned with the parties' bargaining power (such as the unequal bargaining power of persons with disabilities contracting with the bank on a 'take it or leave it' basis). It also constitutes a missed opportunity to challenge a narrow interpretation of freedom of contract as non-intervention by the state in contractual relations, and to promote a positive, wide understanding of this concept where intervention is permitted if required in pursuit of social values (based on a vision of contract law as having a multidimensional role permeating economic and social spheres).

The UNCRPD rests on a well-defined framework of values, promoting full and equal enjoyment of all human rights and fundamental freedoms by persons with disabilities, which include the equal right to exercise legal capacity.[124] The Convention is less clear how the exercise of legal capacity and the potential application of safeguards (such as protection from undue influence)[125] are to operate in practice.[126] Coupled with this, is the absence of an explicit reference in the Convention to equality in the contractual sphere, albeit this is implied in the provisions on equal recognition before the law.[127] In addition, while the jurisprudence of the UNCRPD Committee recognised the need to interfere with freedom of contract in pursuit of equality and the protection of human dignity, it made no attempt to challenge explicitly a narrow understanding of freedom of contract. It is as if there was no courage to step into the contractual sphere, or to highlight the link between social and economic values in

120 Ibid. [9.4] with reference to Article 4(1)(e) of the UNCRPD.
121 Ibid. with reference to Article 9(2)(a) of the UNCRPD.
122 Ibid. [9.4] with reference to Article 9(2)(b) of the UNCRPD. 123 Ibid. [10].
124 Articles 1 and 12(2) of the UNCRPD. 125 Ibid. Article 12(4).
126 Bartlett, 'The United Nations Convention', 752. 127 Article 12 of the UNCRPD.

this sphere. This is akin to an unfinished bridge. Nevertheless, despite these drawbacks, the merits of the UNCRPD cannot be overlooked in providing a lens for examining whether the contractual legal framework considers not only economic factors (such as the security of transactions) but also social factors (including the protection of values such as autonomy and human dignity). This requires an understanding of vulnerability in the contractual sphere that goes beyond the medical conditions of individuals, to also assess environmental factors, such as the circumstances of the transaction.

2.2 Concentric Economic and Social Spheres in the Contractual Realm: A Map for a Fairer Vision of Contract Law?

When operating in the private sphere and entering into contracts, people should always be perceived as citizens, with all the economic, political and social principles that this entails.[128] The concept of citizenship should be understood in a wider sense, based on values such as equality, autonomy and human dignity, rather than in a narrow sense confined to nationality. Such citizenship values should permeate all areas of law,[129] including contract law. Similar to the image of contract law in Lorenzetti's fourteenth-century painting '*Il Buon Governo*' (tr. the good government),[130] as interpreted by Teubner, this area of law can embrace a multidimensional role (including economic and social spheres), reflecting the interrelatedness between public law and private law and the interdependence of human beings bound together through contracts (a bond depicted as a rope running through people's hands).[131] This imagery is particularly poignant if we consider the etymology of the word 'contract', based on the Latin verb '*contrahere*', meaning 'to bring together'.[132] In this strongly integrated society, the role of contract law is to facilitate private transactions and connect people in mutual relations, going beyond a solely horizontal axis that symbolises the relationship between private parties, to also include the vertical axis that epitomises the relation between citizens and the state.[133] This conception, which contrasts with conventional approaches that reflect a unidimensional role for contract law (as facilitator of market transactions within the economic sphere and perceives individuals as economic actors in pursuit of self-interest),[134] is close to the inter-relational approach adopted

[128] See Thomas Humphrey Marshall, *Citizenship and Social Class, and Other Essays* (Cambridge: Cambridge University Press, 1950), pp. 10–11.

[129] Giovanna Procacci, 'Poor Citizens: Social Citizenship versus Individualisation of Welfare' in Colin Crouch, Klaus Eder and Damian Tambini (eds.), *Citizenship, Markets and the State* (Oxford: Oxford University Press, 2001), pp. 49–68 at p. 63.

[130] Ambrogio Lorenzetti, *Il Buon Governo*, 1338 painting, Palazzo Pubblico di Siena.

[131] Gunther Teubner, 'Contracting Worlds: The Many Autonomies of Private Law' (2000) 9 *Social and Legal Studies* 399–417 at 400–02.

[132] Onions, 'Oxford Dictionary of English Etymology'.

[133] Teubner, 'Contracting Worlds', 400–02. [134] Ibid.

by the UNCRPD, which provides a new lens for re-examining existing legal concepts.[135]

Given that when operating in the contractual realm, people never stop being citizens to become merely economic actors, we should not limit our perception of this domain as being confined solely to an economic sphere separated from social concerns. Instead, we should envisage the contractual realm as being based on two concentric spheres. The inner economic sphere is guided by principles such as freedom of contract and sanctity of contract. Contracting parties have the freedom to choose who they contract with (party freedom), and under which terms (term freedom),[136] and to have their transactions enforced.[137] This sphere reflects values associated with *laissez-faire* ideology,[138] where the primary role of the state is to provide a framework within which parties can deal with confidence,[139] and to enforce agreements entered into freely by the contracting parties.[140] This inner, economic and non-interventionist sphere of contract law, accommodates a conception of autonomy based on individualist values,[141] and an understanding of human dignity as 'empowerment',[142] focusing on the voluntary nature of contractual relations.[143] Provided that the parties exercise these choices unaffected by vitiating factors, they are bound by their bargains,[144] even when the outcome is an imbalanced transaction.[145] The classic example in English contract law of the sale of a house in exchange for a peppercorn is designed to illustrate that the law is generally unconcerned with the equivalence of exchange (or adequacy of consideration).[146]

Circumstances could, however, arise, causing the transaction to step out of the inner, economic and non-interventionist sphere, into the outer, social sphere of contract law, shaped by public policy concerns and fairness-based considerations. This approach reflects a call for 'a more fluid interrelation between the idea of enforceability of contracts and limitations on enforceability', where contracts are enforceable, unless giving effect to a transaction is 'highly unreasonable'.[147] This framework is also compatible with a perspective where principles

135 Series, 'Relationships, Autonomy and Legal Capacity', 80.

136 Roger Brownsword, *Contract Law: Themes for the Twenty-First Century* (Oxford: Oxford University Press, 2006), pp. 50 and 57.

137 *Printing and Numerical Registering Co.* v. *Sampson* (1874–75) LR 19 Eq 462, [465].

138 Adam Smith, *An Inquiry into the Nature and Causes of the Wealth of Nations* (2nd ed., London: Strahan and Cadell eds. 1778), Volume II, p. 35.

139 Dori Kimel, 'Neutrality, Autonomy, and Freedom of Contract' (2001) 21 *Oxford Journal of Legal Studies* 473–94 at 474.

140 Brownsword, 'Themes for the Twenty-First Century', pp. 38 and 51.

141 Patrick Atiyah, *An Introduction to the Law of Contract* (5th ed., Oxford: Clarendon 1995), p. 9.

142 Brownsword, 'Modern Understanding of Human Dignity', p. 302.

143 Kimel, 'Neutrality', 482.

144 Adams and Brownsword, 'Understanding Contract Law', p. 192.

145 Herring, 'Vulnerable Adults', p. 226.

146 Alfred Simpson, *A History of the Common Law of Contract: The Rise of the Action of Assumpsit* (Oxford: Oxford University Press, 1996).

147 Waddams, 'Sanctity of Contracts', p. 221.

such as freedom of contract should be limited only when there are 'good reasons' for doing so.[148] In a structure 'guided by individual rights-led morality', such limitations (e.g. on party freedom) could be justified only 'if more important rights are at stake'[149] (e.g. equal access to goods and services, free from discrimination on grounds of, *inter alia*, disability).[150] Considerations for restricting freedom and sanctity of contract could be classified broadly into measures pursuing wider public policy objectives, and provisions to address a gross imbalance of power between the parties (A and B), resulting in an unfair transaction.[151] In many circumstances, these two justifications overlap (e.g. where a grossly asymmetrical contract raises concerns both regarding the unfairness of the transaction between A and B and wider public policy concerns).[152]

Public policy considerations play an important role in shaping the social sphere in contract law and in drawing the boundaries between enforcement and non-enforcement of transactions[153] on the basis of, *inter alia*, the harm likely to be caused by permitting a transaction to go ahead.[154] This recognises the fact that concepts such as freedom and sanctity of contract are not absolute and can be subject to exceptions, including with reference to 'open-ended' principles such as public policy, which may cover a call for 'the avoidance of unjust, disproportionate, extravagant or unconscionable' transactions that are contrary to the public interest.[155] Reliance on broad concepts such as 'public policy' or 'the public interest' must be approached with caution, as their openness to a wide range of interpretations have led the notion of 'public policy' to be compared with 'a very unruly horse', as 'once you get astride it you never know where it will carry you'.[156] On a similar note, the concept of the 'public interest' has been likened to 'an empty vessel to be filled at different time with different content'.[157] Such concepts must be rooted in citizenship values, including equality of citizenship and the protection of autonomy and human dignity,[158] reflecting an approach that accommodates human rights not only in public law but also in private law.[159]

This vision also recognises that human rights constitute 'a special case' where the separation between public law (focused on the relation between individuals

148 Brownsword, 'Themes for the Twenty-First Century', p. 65. 149 Ibid.

150 See, for example, sections 142–48 (contract) of the Equality Act (EqA) 2010 (c. 15).

151 David Ibbetson, *A Historical Introduction to the Law of Obligations* (Oxford: Oxford University Press, 1999), p. 249.

152 Waddams, 'Sanctity of Contracts', p. 6 with reference to *Horwood* v. *Millar's Timber & Trading Co Ltd* [1917] 1 KB 305.

153 Ibid. p. 221.

154 Hugh Collins, 'The Vanishing Freedom to Choose a Contractual Partner' (2012) 76 *Law and Contemporary Problems* 71–88 at 73.

155 Waddams, 'Sanctity of Contracts', pp. 202–04 and 206–07.

156 *Richardson* v. *Mellish* (1824) 130 ER 294, [252] (Burrough J). See Ibbetson, 'A Historical Introduction', pp. 249–50.

157 Mike Feintuck, *'The Public Interest' in Regulation* (Oxford: Oxford University Press, 2004), p. 3.

158 Ibid. 159 Collins, 'The Vanishing Freedom', 88.

and the state) and private law (concerned with the relation between individuals), 'should not be taken as an absolute barrier to cross-fertilisation', given that both are 'part of an integral legal system' which originates from fundamental rights.[160] Collins makes a convincing analogy between these fundamental individual rights (which are the root of all areas of law, including contract law) and 'the magma at the core of the Earth' (which, once erupted, has led to the formation of several geological features), and calls for an understanding of contract law that is 'true to the origins of private law in the magma of individual rights', where doctrines are interpreted in a way that reflects their foundation in fundamental rights.[161] The framework of concentric spheres of contract law presented in this book is compatible with this vision, and Collins' 'magma theory'[162] can be called upon to support the arguments for the existence of an outer sphere of contract law reflective of values such as autonomy and human dignity, and providing fertile ground for the cross-fertilisation between public and private law principles.

In addition to public policy considerations, the social sphere of contract law is also shaped by social values such as fairness-based concerns, questioning the validity of a grossly imbalanced transaction where a party's decision to enter into the contract was affected by vitiating factors such as incapacity,[163] mistake,[164] misrepresentation,[165] duress,[166] undue influence[167] or unconscionability.[168] Such assessments should be made with a focus on the circumstances of the transaction, guided not only by economic considerations but also by social concerns such as a focus on human dignity. Questions regarding the validity of such transactions should not be understood as instances where the state 'interferes' with freedom and sanctity of contract, but rather, as situations where the state may not give its agreement to enforce such transactions,[169] because vitiating factors have caused the transaction to step out of the inner, economic and non-interventionist sphere into the outer sphere guided by public policy and fairness-based considerations. The framework within which transactions take place is defined by the state, which has the power to enforce or refuse to give effect to contracts entered into by the parties.[170] In the vision of concentric spheres presented in this book, the state can take a non-interventionist stance in the inner economic sphere, while transactions that step outside this sphere warrant state intervention. The triggers causing a transaction to step into the social realm is discussed at the end of this section. At this stage, however, we

[160] Hugh Collins, 'Private Law, Fundamental Rights, and the Rule of Law' (2018) 121 *West Virginia Law Review* 1–25 at 12.
[161] Ibid. 13–15. [162] Ibid.
[163] *Imperial Loan Co Ltd* v. *Stone* [1892] 1 QB 599 (hereafter Imperial Loan v. Stone).
[164] *Thoroughgood's Case* (1582) 76 ER 408.
[165] *Salt* v. *Stratstone Specialist Ltd (t/a Stratstone Cadillac Newcastle)* [2015] EWCA Civ 745.
[166] *Friedeberg Seeley* v. *Klass* [1957] 2 WLUK 63; Times, February 19, 1957.
[167] *Royal Bank of Scotland Plc* v. *Etridge (No.2)* [2001] UKHL 44 (hereafter RBS v. Etridge).
[168] *Fry* v. *Lane* (1888) 40 Ch D 312; *Cresswell* v. *Potter* [1978] 1 WLR 255.
[169] Shiffrin, 'Paternalism', 227. [170] Kimel, 'Neutrality', 478.

must set the basis for the argument as to why the state cannot stay neutral in the event of such transactions.

A system where the state adopts a position of neutrality, confining its role merely to the enforcement of transactions, allows stronger parties to 'capitalise on the vulnerabilities' of weaker parties, with the potential to result in grossly imbalanced transactions.[171] Consequently, 'a system in which everybody is invited to do his own thing, at whatever cost to his neighbour, must work ultimately to the benefit of the rich and powerful'.[172] Therefore, in the context of grossly imbalanced transactions to the detriment of a vulnerable contracting party, rather than staying neutral, the state's failure to assist the weaker party is equivalent to having 'an active role in creating the conditions for its fall'.[173] It is, therefore, important to look at 'cases where neutrality may not be fair', focusing, *inter alia*, on the extent of the power imbalance between the parties and the circumstances of the transaction.[174] The model of concentric spheres of contract law presented in this section can assist with this endeavour.

Calls for state intervention within the contractual realm are also likely to encounter resistance, based on arguments that private law should be confined to issues of transactional (or corrective) justice, whilst leaving distributive justice considerations to the realm of public law.[175] While transactional justice aims to address issues that have arisen in the contractual relations between the parties (e.g. breach of contract), distributive justice is concerned with inequalities resulting from the distribution of resources in society.[176] Nevertheless, there is 'no neat division of labour between public and private law', that would confine transactional justice exclusively to the realm of private law, and distributive justice as solely a matter of concern for public law,[177] especially if we consider that the development of rules in contract law (in particular regarding regulated contracts,[178] but also in the interpretation of contract doctrines in light of fairness-based considerations)[179] require choices to be made regarding 'the distribution of power, risk and resources' between contracting parties.[180] If we accept the vision of contract law based on concentric economic and social spheres, then the actions expected from the state in the social realm of the contractual framework, even if intended in pursuit of transactional justice, are likely to have some distributive justice consequences,[181] given the focus of

[171] Ibid. 480.

[172] Grant Gilmore, *The Death of Contract* (Columbus: Ohio State University Press, 1974), p. 104.

[173] Kimel, 'Neutrality', 480. [174] Ibid. 478.

[175] Peter Benson, 'The Unity of Contract Law' in Benson (ed.) 'The Theory of Contract Law', pp. 118–205 at p. 123.

[176] Atiyah, 'An Introduction', p. 14. [177] du Bois, 'Private Law in the Age of Rights', p. 25.

[178] Hugh Collins, 'Regulating Contract Law' in Christine Parker et al. (ed.), *Regulating Law* (Oxford: Oxford University Press, 2004) pp. 13–32.

[179] Ibbetson, 'A Historical Introduction', pp. 242 and 261.

[180] Andrea Fejős, 'Social Justice in EU Financial Consumer Law' (2019) 24 *Tilburg Law Review* 68–88 at 72.

[181] Kronman, 'Contract Law and Distributive Justice', 472.

these actions for pursuing fairness-based objectives and public policy considerations, including the protection of autonomy and human dignity.

While the inner economic sphere embraces an understanding of autonomy based on individualist values, the outer, social sphere of contract law espouses a relational understanding of autonomy that recognises the interrelation between people.[182] It also seeks to reflect an interpretation of human dignity as 'constraint' for pursuing wider social values,[183] seeking to ensure that every human being is treated with respect.[184] Consequently, the concept of autonomy can be called upon in the inner economic sphere to justify the enforcement of transactions entered into voluntarily by contracting parties,[185] reflective of a definition of individual autonomy as the freedom to make choices in accordance with one's 'view of the good life'.[186] The value of individual autonomy is closely related to an understanding of human rights as the empowerment of an individual to make choices and participate in society without fear from discrimination on the basis of factors such as disability.[187] Yet, the exercise of human dignity as 'empowerment' is reliant on having a contextual framework within which parties can exercise choices[188] and where both parties (A and B) have access to 'real choices'.[189] The state has a role to 'shape the arena within which freedom of contract can be exercised',[190] based on a 'realistic conception of the human subject' which considers 'the implications of human...vulnerability'.[191] The state needs to intervene in the relation between the parties in the case of grossly asymmetrical transactions[192] that step out of the inner economic sphere into the outer social sphere of the contractual realm. In this latter sphere, the focus on autonomy is no longer on its individualistic dimension, but is directed towards its relational aspect, concentrating, *inter alia*, on the potential 'adverse long term effect on the autonomy' of the party detrimentally affected by a grossly imbalanced transaction.[193]

Moreover, the social sphere reveals the 'protective function' of contract law,[194] accommodating a definition of human dignity that justified 'constraining' the actions of contracting parties in pursuit of wider social values.[195] Circumstances where such constraints may be justified include standard form contracts[196] involving an individual consumer (A) and a service provider (B). B, who is in a strong bargaining position, has drafted the standard form to their

[182] Dhanda, 'Constructing a New Human Rights Lexicon', 47.
[183] Brownsword, 'Modern Understanding of Human Dignity', p. 302.
[184] Réaume, 'Discrimination and Dignity', 1. [185] Kimel, 'Neutrality', 482.
[186] Fredman, 'Equality: A New Generation?', 155.
[187] Brownsword, 'Modern Understanding of Human Dignity', p. 302.
[188] Kimel, 'Neutrality', 482. [189] Collins, 'The Vanishing Freedom', 88.
[190] Kimel, 'Neutrality', 482. [191] Fineman, 'The Vulnerable Subject', 273.
[192] Kimel, 'Neutrality', 494. [193] Ibid.
[194] Brownsword, 'Themes for the Twenty-First Century', p. 39.
[195] Brownsword, 'Modern Understanding of Human Dignity', p. 302.
[196] Andrew Burgess, 'Consumer Adhesion Contracts and Unfair Terms: A Critique of Current Theory and a Suggestion' (1986) 15 *Anglo-American Law Review* 255–80.

advantage,[197] offering the agreement on a 'take it or leave it' basis.[198] In contrast, A is in a weak bargaining position due to factors such as limited information and resources, as well as restricted choice regarding available alternatives.[199] In such circumstances, A's agreement to enter into the transaction takes the form of mere 'adherence'[200] (resulting in a description of such agreements as 'contracts of adhesion'),[201] undermining A's 'basic right to negotiate' and his 'honour and dignity'.[202] Given that most contracts required by people to participate in society and live independent lives (including transactions for utility services) involve standard form agreements, these transactions have not just economic implications, but also a social dimension.[203] It is, therefore, important not to overlook the fact that individuals entering into these transactions are not solely economic actors, but are also citizens.[204] Protecting the rights of these parties should be rooted in concerns for fairness and for safeguarding values such as autonomy and human dignity, embracing an understanding of consumer rights as human rights.[205]

While Chapter 4 explores in more detail the issue of regulatory protection of consumer interests and the compatibility of this framework with UNCRPD values (in particular autonomy and human dignity), this book is also concerned with circumstances where vitiating factors (discussed in Chapter 3) could affect the balance of power between contracting parties, placing a party in a position of vulnerability and resulting in a grossly imbalanced transaction to their detriment. The remainder of this section sets the basis for the call that vulnerability should be interpreted in a manner compatible with UNCRPD values and reflects on potential triggers that could justify state intervention. The discussion so far sought to emphasise that state intervention may be necessary to address issues of significant imbalance and a perception of contract law based on concentric spheres can accommodate a role for the state in the contractual realm not just as the enforcer of transactions (in the economic sphere) but also as the protector of vulnerable parties[206] (in the social sphere).

197 Nicholas Wilson, 'Freedom of Contract and Adhesion Contracts' (1965) 14 *International and Comparative Law Quarterly* 172–93 at 185.

198 Sinai Deutch, 'Are Consumer Rights Human Rights?' (1994) 32 *Osgoode Hall Law Journal* 537–78 at 553.

199 Kessler, 'Contracts of Adhesion', 632.

200 Philip Shuchman, 'Consumer Credit by Adhesion Contracts' (1962) 35 *Temple Law Quarterly* 125–40 at 128–9.

201 Kessler, 'Contracts of Adhesion', 632.

202 Deutch, 'Are Consumer Rights Human Rights?', 553.

203 Yvette Maker and others, 'Ensuring Equality for Persons with Cognitive Disabilities in Consumer Contracting: An International Human Rights Law Perspective' (2018) 19 *Melbourne Journal of International Law* 178–99 at 182–83.

204 Cosmo Graham, *Regulating Public Utilities: A Legal and Constitutional Approach* (Oxford: Hart Publishing, 2000), p. 88.

205 Deutch, 'Are Consumer Rights Human Rights?', 537 and 553.

206 Brownsword, 'Themes for the Twenty-First Century', p. 41.

A vision of contract law based on concentric economic and social spheres, and which recognises the relevance of both a horizontal axis (between A and B as private parties) and a vertical axis (between private persons and the state) in the contractual realm is better equipped to respond to challenges encountered by persons with disabilities in this framework, including participation barriers. Such challenges require a multi-layered response reliant on both public and private law measures.[207] Responses include provisions to combat discrimination and promote equality in accessing goods and services,[208] and measures to regulate, *inter alia*, unfair contract terms.[209] They also include an effective framework of private law principles that would enable parties to seek to invalidate transactions entered into as a result of vitiating factors,[210] and which can be invoked by anyone, so that disability and incapacity are never conceptually equated.[211] This framework should not evaluate vulnerability on the basis of having a particular medical condition, but should, instead, base its assessment on an examination of the context of the transaction.[212] In assessing these circumstances in order to question, for example, whether A should be released from an agreement with B, one issue to consider is whether the transaction finds itself within the inner, non-interventionist economic sphere, or whether it is located within the wider social sphere of the contractual realm, which warrants intervention in pursuit of public policy and fairness considerations. To assist with this evaluation, we must look at the triggers that may cause a transaction to step out of the inner economic sphere into the outer social sphere, such as a situation where A's decision-making was affected by vitiating factors, resulting in a grossly imbalanced contract to A's detriment.

If we envisage the relation between A and B as a lever on a balance scale, with the parties at each end of the scale, the state can be visualised in the middle, as a fulcrum. The etymology of the word 'fulcrum' rests on the Latin verb '*fulcire*', which means 'to prop up'.[213] This is illustrative of the role of the state in contractual relations, as it enables the enforcement of transactions freely entered into by contracting parties,[214] while refusing to enforce,[215] *inter alia*, grossly asymmetrical contracts affected by vitiating factors,[216] that harm social values such as human dignity.[217] This is also illustrative of what Brownsword refers to as the 'movement of the law away from its classical bearings towards a greater willingness to adjust for the vulnerability of those contractors who

207 Hugh Collins, *Regulating Contracts* (Oxford: Oxford University Press, 1999), p. 361.
208 See, for example, sections 142–48 of the EqA 2010.
209 See, for example, sections 61–71 of the Consumer Rights Act (CRA) 2015 (c. 15).
210 Peter MacDonald Eggers, *Vitiation of Contractual Consent* (London: Routledge, 2016).
211 Bach, 'The Right to Legal Capacity', 5. 212 Herring, 'Vulnerable Adults', p. 6.
213 Onions, 'Oxford Dictionary of English Etymology'.
214 Printing and Numerical Registering Co v. Sampson (1874–75) LR 19 Eq 462.
215 Shiffrin, 'Paternalism', 227.
216 See, for example, *Credit Lyonnais Bank Nederland NV* v. *Burch* [1997] 1 All ER 144.
217 Hugh Collins, 'The Impact of Human Rights Law on Contract Law in Europe' Cambridge Legal Studies Research Paper 13/2011 at 5.

bargain from a weak position',[218] and such vulnerability should be assessed with reference to the context of the transaction. Consequently, the role of the state would be to 'support private ordering'[219] (by enforcing transactions, as these have no legal force without the power of the state),[220] and to 'shape' such ordering[221] (by setting the rules on how the parties should treat each other and the circumstances where the state may refuse to enforce a transaction that triggered public policy or fairness-based concerns).[222] Some level of restraint is necessary in the contractual realm[223] to prevent 'certain kinds of harm' affecting contracting parties, assessed with reference to 'community ideas of justice and reasonableness'.[224] While the state as enforcer of transactions can be associated with concerns for protecting individual autonomy and human dignity as 'empowerment', the state as protector from harms can be linked with a focus on relational autonomy and human dignity as 'constraint',[225] within the outer, social sphere of contract law.

The refusal to enforce grossly imbalanced transactions affected by vitiating factors and harmful to individual autonomy and human dignity should not be perceived as 'interference' with freedom of contract, rooted in a negative interpretation of this concept as freedom from state control and focused solely on procedural factors regarding the manner in which the contract was entered into.[226] Instead, issues such as vitiating factors could be envisaged as a weight pressing A down into a danger zone of gross asymmetry of power, bringing the transaction within the outer, social sphere of the contractual realm and, unless B could point to a counterweight that would redress this imbalance, lifting A back into the inner economic sphere, the state could refuse to enforce such a transaction. Such counterweight could be provided by the presence of accessible and appropriate independent advice,[227] if this addresses not only economic, but also social considerations.

This model demonstrates concern not only for the procedural fairness of the transaction (focused on the process that led to the conclusion of the agreement between the parties) but also for the substantive fairness of the contract (focused on the outcome of the agreement).[228] The vision of concentric spheres presented in this book does not suggest that substantive unfairness alone should be used as a justification for setting aside a contract as, among other concerns, this would rest on a too uncertain framework.[229] Instead, this

[218] Brownsword, 'Themes for the Twenty-First Century', pp. 72–73.
[219] Collins, 'Regulating Contracts', pp. 56–57. [220] Waddams, 'Sanctity of Contracts', p. 233.
[221] Collins, 'Regulating Contracts', pp. 57–58.
[222] Chen-Wishart, 'Undue Influence: Vindicating Relationships of Influence', 231.
[223] Waddams, 'Sanctity of Contracts', p. 233. [224] Atiyah, 'An Introduction', pp. 35–36.
[225] Brownsword, 'Modern Understanding of Human Dignity', p. 302.
[226] Collins, 'The Impact of Human Rights Law', 5.
[227] Trebilcock and Elliott, 'Scope and Limits of Legal Paternalism', p. 79.
[228] Atiyah, 'An Introduction', pp. 282–84.
[229] David Tiplady, 'The Judicial Control of Contractual Unfairness' (1983) 46 *Modern Law Review* 601–18 at 618.

model supports the view that substantive unfairness, in the form of a significantly imbalanced transaction, could be referred to as a trigger for assessing the procedural fairness of the transaction.[230] Significant imbalance in the outcome of the transaction would be found, for example, if there was 'gross discrepancy' between the price paid (or received) by a party and the value of the subject matter of the transaction, as measured by the market, and the discrepancy cannot be explained by factors such as 'donative intent or assumption of risk' on the part of the party who suffered loss.[231] As Atiyah notes, in a transaction where 'one outcome favours one party vastly more than the other', the 'natural reaction' is to 'believe that something must have gone wrong in the bargaining process'.[232] Factors for considering the procedural fairness of the transaction would include an assessment whether the party who stood to gain from the bargain (B), had knowledge of the factors that placed the disadvantaged individual (A) in a vulnerable position (e.g. gross asymmetry of information between the parties), placing A in a weak position relative to B.[233] Moreover, factors to assess the procedural fairness of the bargain would also consider whether B took any steps to redress this imbalance. As an illustration of what Brownsword terms 'enlightened self-interest',[234] this may include ensuring that A had access to information accessible and appropriate to his circumstances.[235] For this framework to be effective, the triggers that bring the transaction into the outer social sphere must not be interpreted too narrowly. For instance, an assessment of B's behaviour should include passive unacceptable conduct, such as going ahead with a transaction grossly disadvantageous to A, despite having constructive knowledge of A's vulnerable circumstances. Moreover, the counterweight that would lift A out of the danger zone must not be interpreted too broadly. It should not be sufficient to merely show that A was informed about the economic implications of the transactions but instead, there should be an insistence to show that the information was accessible and appropriate to A's circumstance, and that it considered not only economic factors but also substantive factors such as potential harms to A's human dignity.

A wide construal of these triggers and a narrow interpretation of the counterweights mentioned earlier would have the likely consequence of broadening the scope of current doctrines concerned with vitiating factors in contract law (including incapacity, *non est factum*, mistake, misrepresentation, duress, undue influence, and unconscionability). This book supports a wide interpretation of these doctrines in pursuit of both economic and social values, with the result of narrowing any existing gaps between these doctrines that form the piecemeal approach of responding to vitiating factors in the contractual realm. For any remaining gaps, we can rely on the safety net provided by Waddams'

[230] Atiyah, 'An Introduction', pp. 285 and 290.
[231] Benson, 'The Unity of Contract Law', pp. 185–86. [232] Atiyah, 'An Introduction', p. 334.
[233] Ibid. 285. [234] Brownsword, 'Themes for the Twenty-First Century', p. 29.
[235] Maker, 'From Safety Nets', 839.

convincing arguments for the existence of a general power to modify 'highly unreasonable contracts', inherited by the modern courts from the administration of equity under the Court of Chancery, and which can be 'extended, where appropriate, to new circumstances'.[236] This book focuses on a step preceding the need to resort to such residual power, namely an expanded understanding of current doctrines and principles in English contract law, calling for their interpretation in light of UNCRPD values, with a particular focus on autonomy and human dignity.

2.3 Conclusion

The likely increase in the number of grossly imbalanced contracts, due to ageing population trends (increasing the number of people who may be affected by mental health conditions such as dementia),[237] and the rise in social isolation seen during pandemics such as COVID-19[238] (increasing people's vulnerability to pressure to enter into grossly asymmetrical transactions), have reinforced the need to examine whether our current contractual legal framework can respond effectively to such challenges. The UNCRPD provides a lens to assist in this assessment. It enables us to evaluate whether the current framework addresses issues of 'vulnerability' in the contractual sphere by looking at the context of the transaction, rather than at the medical condition of individuals. It also enables us to assess whether the contractual realm is shaped by both economic and social values, and whether concepts such as autonomy and human dignity are interpreted broadly to recognise not only the need for empowerment to pursue individual interests but also the need for protecting parties who find themselves in a vulnerable context such as a gross imbalance of bargaining power caused by information asymmetry.

An understanding of contract law where people are perceived solely as economic actors in pursuit of self-interest, focused only on economic values and reliant on a narrow interpretation of autonomy (based on individual concerns and neglecting its relational dimension)[239] and of human dignity (concerned only with empowerment and overlooking any safeguards in pursuit of social values),[240] presents an incomplete view. Such distorted vision would be unprepared to deal effectively with the challenges posed by any likely increase in the number of grossly asymmetrical transactions. This chapter set the basis for a vision of contract law based in two concentric spheres: an inner sphere shaped by economic considerations and an outer sphere rooted in social values, where most contracts are placed in the inner, non-interventionist realm, but

236 Waddams, 'Sanctity of Contracts', pp. 4, 8–9, 12 and 220; Sections 24 and 25 of the Supreme Court of Judicature Act 1873 (c. 53).

237 Prince and others, 'Dementia UK'.

238 Banerjee and Rai, 'Social Isolation', 525.

239 Dhanda, 'Constructing a New Human Rights Lexicon', 47.

240 Brownsword, 'Freedom of Contract', p. 183.

circumstances could cause a transaction to step into the outer social dimension, warranting intervention. For this framework to be effective, it is important that the economic sphere of contract law is not isolated from its wider social sphere, and that there are sufficient bridges connecting the two spheres. The remaining chapters examine the extent to which these two spheres are connected in English contract law, and the degree to which the process of building bridges between economic and social values in the contractual realm calls for new constructions, or for the reinforcement of existing structures.[241]

[241] Waddams, 'Sanctity of Contracts'.

3

The First Bridge

Common Law Principles and Doctrines

> Science may have found a cure for most evils;
> but it has found no remedy for the worst of them all
> —the apathy of human beings
>
> (Helen Keller, American writer and social reformer, 1880–1968, My Religion (1927))

If English contract law had its own version of a 'periodic table', vitiating factors would form one group of elements. These include factors that enable an innocent party (A) to escape the consequences of a grossly imbalanced transaction with another party (B). In this subject-specific equivalent of the 'periodic table', one way (among other possibilities) in which the 'elements' of contract law could be arranged, would be to group elements on the basis of their relevance to formation (including offer, acceptance, consideration, intention and certainty), vitiating factors (including incapacity, *non est factum*, mistake, misrepresentation, duress, undue influence and unconscionability), terms (including express and implied) and remedies (including discharge for breach of contract, damages and specific performance). This is, of course, an oversimplified and imperfect structure, and 'elements' that would not sit neatly within this construction include doctrines such as privity and frustration. Yet, the reason for this suggestion is to introduce the idea of 'conduits of fairness' within the structure of contract law. This refers to elements within this framework where there is more scope for finding fertile ground to pursue a vision of this area of law which is closer to the values promoted by the UNCRPD, including the protection of autonomy and human dignity. One such potential fertile ground could be found in the 'group of elements' concerned with contract terms (including implied terms), which is explored in the next chapter, centred on regulation. This chapter focuses on the 'group of elements' comprising vitiating factors, examining their potential to expand the way in which the current contractual legal framework embraces fairness. The doctrines of incapacity, *non est factum*, mistake, misrepresentation, duress, undue influence and unconscionability have already been the subject of extensive academic debate.[1] Building on the vision of concentric spheres in contract law introduced in the previous chapter, this discussion proposes an examination of these doctrines through the lens of the inner and outer spheres of contractual relations, questioning the extent to which the inner sphere focused on economic values and rooted in the principles of freedom and sanctity of contract is connected to the wider sphere of social values, as well as the degree of clarity to which English contract law justifies intervention in transactions affected by vitiating factors. The discussion challenges a narrow interpretation of vitiating factors (centred on preserving the sanctity of contracts, holding parties to their transaction and restricting intervention solely to procedural grounds), calling for a broad interpretation of these factors (focused on both procedural and substantive fairness) which is closer to UNCRPD values.

3.1 The Vision of Balance Scales within Concentric Spheres

Imagine the contractual relation between A and B as a lever on a balance scale, with the parties at each end of the scale, and the state in the middle, as a fulcrum. Rather than visualising these parties in perfect balance, a more accurate representation would be to envisage the scales unbalanced. This may be due to differences in the parties' circumstances, including their access to financial resources and information, which affect their bargaining position.[2] Such imbalances are common in contractual relations, where a perfect equilibrium between the parties' bargaining strength may be regarded as merely a myth. As long as A exercises his choices unaffected by vitiating factors, the parties are left to look after their own interests, without questioning the sanctity of the contract, even if this has not resulted in an equivalent exchange.[3] The parties are, therefore, left to operate in the inner, economic sphere of contracting, without interference with their freedom of contract.

There are, however, factors which would cause such gross imbalance in A and B's contractual relations, taking their position from the inner, non-interventionist economic sphere, into the outer, interventionist sphere. Incapacity,[4] *non est factum*, mistake,[5] misrepresentation, duress, undue influence

[1] See, for example, MacDonald Eggers, 'Vitiation of Contractual Consent'; Gareth Spark, *Vitiation of Contracts: International Contractual Principles and English Law* (Cambridge: Cambridge University Press, 2013).

[2] Trebilcock and Elliott, 'Scope and Limits of Legal Paternalism', p. 62.

[3] John Adams and Roger Brownsword, 'The Ideologies of Contract' (1987) 7 *Legal Studies* 205–23 at 207.

[4] This discussion is focused on the doctrine of mental incapacity.

[5] Given the importance for this discussion of reflecting on A's vulnerability and B's unacceptable conduct, the references to mistake focus on unilateral mistake (where A is mistaken about a fundamental aspect of the contract and B may have knowledge of A's mistake, or may have induced A's mistake), rather than on common mistake (where both parties are mistaken about a fundamental aspect of the transaction).

and unconscionability could be understood as providing examples of such factors. Across these doctrines, intervention may be seen as rooted in the presence of a weight pressing A down into a danger zone of gross imbalance (warranting intervention), and the absence of any counterweight (lifting A back up into the non-interventionist zone, had B acted to redress this imbalance). The first element of this test (the presence of weight pressing A down into a danger zone) is based on a combination of two factors: A's weak bargaining position (due, *inter alia*, to gross information asymmetry between the parties) and B's unacceptable conduct (such as going ahead with the contract despite having actual or constructive knowledge of A's weakness). The second element of this test (the absence of any counterweight to lift A out of the danger zone) is based on B's failure to take measures to 'emancipate' A,[6] such as redressing the gross information asymmetry by facilitating A's access to appropriate independent legal advice.[7]

Understood this way, the focus is not solely on A's weakness[8] or B's unacceptable conduct,[9] but also on the relationship between the parties and the role of the state in regulating these relations.[10] This vision is not confined to individual autonomy, but is concerned also with relational autonomy,[11] and is not limited to a unilateral vision of contract law restricted to the economic sphere, but focuses on the wider, social sphere, as an integral part of the contracting world.[12] The following discussion seeks to defend this model, examining the elements of this structure.

3.2 The Lever, the Weight and the Counterweight

In the image of the balance scales highlighted earlier, the parties (A and B) are envisaged at each end of the scale, and the relationship between them is perceived as a lever, resting on a fulcrum which symbolises the state. While the next section is centred on the latter element of this vision, this section focuses on the 'lever' (the relationship between the parties), the 'weight' (referring to the vitiating factors that could cause a transaction to step out of the inner economic, non-interventionist sphere of contract, into the outer, social sphere which warrants intervention) and the counterweight (which could, if present, cause the transaction to step back into the non-interventionist sphere).

6 Rick Bigwood, 'Undue Influence: "Impaired Consent" or "Wicked Exploitation"?' (1996) 16 *Oxford Journal of Legal Studies* 503–15 at 513.

7 Trebilcock and Elliott, 'Scope and Limits of Legal Paternalism', p. 62.

8 Peter Birks and Chin Nyuk Yin, 'On the Nature of Undue Influence' in Jack Beatson and Daniel Friedman (eds.), *Good Faith and Fault in Contract Law* (Oxford: Clarendon Press, 1997), pp. 57–97.

9 Bigwood, 'Undue Influence', 503.

10 Chen-Wishart, 'Undue Influence: Vindicating Relationships of Influence', 231.

11 Herring, 'Vulnerable Adults', p. 243.

12 Teubner, 'Contracting Worlds', 400–02.

3.2.1 Challenging a Narrow Interpretation of the 'Weight' and a Broad Interpretation of Any 'Counterweight' Affecting the Balance between the Parties

Under the current framework concerning vitiating factors in contract law, the connection between the inner economic sphere and the outer social sphere of the contractual realm appears to be insufficiently articulated, with the focus rooted in economic values, procedural justifications for intervention, and a perception of contracting parties as autonomous (detached) individuals[13] in pursuit of self-interest. If there are any concerns for social values, substantive fairness and relational autonomy, these are disguised as part of the intervention to ensure procedural fairness.[14]

As a 'group of elements' concerned with vitiating factors, the doctrines of mental incapacity, *non est factum*, mistake, misrepresentation, duress, undue influence and unconscionability present a certain degree of complexity to any attempts to classify them into sub-groups. One option would be to divide these doctrines based on their effect of rendering the contract void (as if it never existed *ab initio* i.e. from the beginning), or voidable (where the innocent party may affirm or rescind the transaction), with *non est factum* and mistake belonging to the first category,[15] and the remaining doctrines falling within the latter category.[16] Another would group the first three doctrines as being concerned with A's absence of consent, with the remaining doctrines focused on A's impaired consent due to B's actions.[17] There is, however, 'no unified theory' of vitiating factors in English contract law, which remains reliant on a piecemeal approach of 'having separate specific rules for separate specific defects' in contract formation.[18] This chapter does not perceive this reliance on different doctrines with critical eyes, as this could present a vulnerable contracting party with an arsenal of weapons to choose from, as appropriate, when seeking to challenge a grossly imbalanced transaction. However, to address challenges posed by any gaps between these doctrines, the discussion calls for enlarging the scope of these doctrines, where necessary.

Rather than seeking to sub-categorise the vitiating factors doctrines, the present discussion focuses on a commonality between these doctrines, when invoked as a potential way to escape a grossly asymmetrical transaction. These doctrines can be understood as concerned with a degree of contractual

13 Chen-Wishart, 'Undue Influence: Vindicating Relationships of Influence', 241.

14 Patrick Atiyah, 'Contract and Fair Exchange' (1985) 35 *University of Toronto Law Journal* 1–24.

15 Cf. mistake in equity, *Solle* v. *Butcher* [1950] 1 KB 671.

16 Andrew Burrows, *A Restatement of the English Law of Contract* (Oxford: Oxford University Press, 2016), p. 46.

17 Spark, 'Vitiation of Contracts', pp. 1–3.

18 John Cartwright, *Contract Law: An Introduction to the English Law of Contract for the Civil Lawyer* (3rd ed., Oxford: Hart Publishing, 2016), p. 158.

imbalance resulting from a combination of A's vulnerability and B's unacceptable conduct, in the absence of any action from B that could have redressed this imbalance. This chapter calls for a broad interpretation of A's vulnerability (to include vulnerability based on the context of the transaction) and of B's unacceptable conduct (to include the passive unacceptable conduct of going ahead with the transaction, despite having constructive knowledge of A's vulnerability resulting from the transactional context). Conversely, any assessment of whether there has been any action from B that could have redressed the imbalance between the contracting parties, such as ensuring that A had access to independent legal advice, should be interpreted narrowly to refer to accessible and appropriate advice.

A's vulnerability is associated with a range of factors, depending on the doctrine applied. For mental incapacity, the common law approach for assessing A's vulnerability looks at whether, at the time of entering into the contract, 'he was so insane' that 'he did not know what he was doing',[19] while for unconscionability, this may result, among other factors that could create bargaining weakness,[20] from a special susceptibility to exploitation by B due, *inter alia*, to 'infirmity of body or mind' or 'lack of assistance or explanation where assistance or explanation is necessary'.[21] In cases of unilateral mistake, A's vulnerability is due to being mistaken about a fundamental aspect of the transaction, such as the terms of the contract,[22] or the identity of B, the other contracting party.[23] In cases of misrepresentation, A (the representee)'s vulnerability derives from the fact that the 'informational basis' for his judgement[24] whether or not to enter into the contract with B (the representor) either at all, or under those particular terms, has been 'impaired' by a false statement of fact made by B.[25] In situations where A has mistakenly signed a written document that is fundamentally different from the document which he intended to sign, and was not careless in doing so, A may seek to rely on the doctrine of *non est factum* ('this is not my deed') to render the transaction void.[26] In this context, A's vulnerability may derive from either a weakness that impacts on his ability to understand the

[19] *Imperial Loan* v. *Stone* [1892] 1 QB 599, [601].
[20] Mindy Chen-Wishart, 'Duress, Undue Influence and Unconscionable Dealing' in Hugh Beale and others (eds.), *Chitty on Contracts*, 2 vols. (34th ed., London: Sweet & Maxwell, 2021), vol. I, 10–164.
[21] *Blomley* v. *Ryan* (1956) 99 CLR 362, [405] (Fullagar J).
[22] *Hartog* v. *Colin & Shields* [1939] 3 All ER 566.
[23] *Shogun Finance Ltd v. Hudson* [2003] UKHL 62.
[24] Cartwright, 'Contract Law', pp. 189–90.
[25] On the difference between statements of fact and statements of opinion, see *Bisset* v. *Wilkinson* [1927] AC 177; *Esso Petroleum Co Ltd* v. *Mardon* [1976] QB 801; *Smith* v. *Land & House Property Corp* (1884) 28 Ch D 7. On the difference between statements of fact and statements of intention, see *Edgington* v. *Fitzmaurice* (1885) 29 Ch D 459. On the continuing effect of a statement made during contractual negotiations, see *Cramaso* v. *Ogilvie-Grant* [2014] UKSC 9.
[26] *Saunders (Executrix of the Estate of Rose Maud Gallie)* v. *Anglia Building Society (formerly Northampton Town and County Building Society); sub nom. Gallie* v. *Lee* [1971] AC 1004 (hereafter *Saunders* v. *Anglia Building Society*).

document due to facts such as 'defective education, illness or innate incapacity',[27] or from having been tricked into signing the document.[28]

For both undue influence and duress, A's vulnerability may be due to impaired consent resulting from B's influence[29] (in cases of undue influence), or from B's pressure (regarding duress).[30] While in the case of duress and in some cases of undue influence, A is aware of his own actions but has 'no real choice' in the matter, in other cases of undue influence where A has been subjected to more subtle forms of influence, he may be unaware that he is acting under B's control.[31] The issue of A's vulnerability in undue influence cases could involve a party (A) who is in a relationship of 'trust and confidence', or of 'physical and emotional dependence' with another party (B),[32] where B has gained 'an ascendant position' over A, obtained through measures such as encouraging A to put his trust in him, or through more 'subtle coercive techniques'.[33] For duress, B's pressure places A in a vulnerable position of fear for himself or those he cares about, his goods, or his economic interests,[34] resulting in no realistic option but to enter into the contract.[35]

For a level of contractual imbalance that would trigger the application of vitiating factors doctrines, A's vulnerability must have been affected by B's unacceptable conduct. As above, this is associated with a range of factors, depending on the doctrine applied. Where A seeks to set aside a disadvantageous transaction with B on the basis of mental incapacity, he must prove not only his own mental incapacity but also B's unacceptable conduct of entering into that transaction, despite having knowledge of A's condition.[36] For *non est factum*, B's unacceptable conduct could include entering into a written contract signed by A, with the knowledge that A's weakness impacted on A's ability to understand the document, causing A to make the mistake of agreeing to a document which was fundamentally different from the document that A intended to sign.[37] Alternatively, it could take the form of unacceptably inducing A's mistake, such as deliberately misrepresenting to A the contents of the document due to be signed by A.[38] For unilateral mistake, B's unacceptable conduct may be due, for example, to going ahead with the transaction with A,

27 Ibid. [1016] (Lord Reid).
28 Ibid. [1016] and [1025]. See Ewan McKendrick, 'Contract: In General' in Andrew Burrows (ed.), *Principles of the English Law of Obligations* (Oxford: Oxford University Press, 2015), 1.150.
29 *RBS* v. *Etridge* [2001] UKHL 44 [9].
30 *Barton (Alexander)* v. *Armstrong (Alexander Ewan)* [1976] AC 104 [118] (Lord Cross) (hereafter *Barton* v. *Armstrong*).
31 Cartwright, 'Contract Law', p. 190.
32 Chen-Wishart, 'Duress, Undue Influence', 10–072. See *Bank of Credit and Commerce International SA* v. *Aboody* [1990] 1 QB 923.
33 Hugh Collins, *The Law of Contract* (4th ed., London: Lexis Nexis, 2003), p. 144.
34 Jan Smits, *Contract Law: A Comparative Introduction* (2nd ed., Cheltenham: Edward Elgar Publishing, 2017), p. 168.
35 Spark, 'Vitiation of Contracts', p. 212.
36 *Imperial Loan* v. *Stone* [1892] 1 QB 599, [602].
37 *Saunders v. Anglia Building Society* [1971] AC 1004.
38 *Foster* v. *Mackinnon* (1868–69) LR 4 CP 704. See Spark, 'Vitiation of Contracts', pp. 78 and 88.

despite having knowledge[39] of A's fundamental mistake concerning B's identity, or the terms of the contract.[40]

In the case of misrepresentation, B's unacceptable conduct is in the form of a false statement of fact addressed to A, which induces A to enter into the contract.[41] Actionable statements of fact must be distinguished from mere statements of opinion,[42] statements of intention,[43] or from 'sales talk',[44] which would not generally give rise to an action for misrepresentation. B can make the false statement of fact through words[45] or conduct,[46] and can include half-truths,[47] or failure to inform A about a relevant change in circumstances affecting the accuracy of a previous statement made as part of negotiating a transaction.[48] B's state of mind is relevant for classifying the misrepresentation as fraudulent or non-fraudulent. This has implications, *inter alia*, for determining whether the court has discretion to award damages instead of rescission under section 2(2) of the Misrepresentation Act 1967 (for non-fraudulent misrepresentations).[49] A misrepresentation is fraudulent where B made the false statement with knowledge about its untruth, or with disregard as to its accuracy (i.e. a false statement made 'knowingly, or without belief in its truth, or recklessly, careless whether it be true or false').[50]

For unconscionability, B's unacceptable conduct is due to exploitation of weakness, by knowingly taking advantage of A and entering into a transaction disadvantageous for A.[51] For undue influence, to prove B's unacceptable conduct, A may seek to rely on either direct evidence (e.g. witness statements) of B's 'overt acts of improper pressure or coercion such as unlawful threats'[52] or indirect evidence that B abused an 'ascendant position' gained over A,[53] by indirect evidence based on a relationship of trust and confidence between A and B, and

39 *OT Africa Line Ltd* v. *Vickers Plc* [1996] 1 Lloyd's Rep 700, [703] (Mance J) suggests that knowledge includes both actual and constructive knowledge. Cf. *Chwee Kin Keong* v. *Digilandmall.com Pte Ltd* [2005] SGCA 2, [53] and *Longley* v. *PPB Entertainment Ltd* [2022] EWHC 977 (QB), [94] (Ellenbogen J) (obiter), which require actual knowledge. See Beale, Hugh, 'Mistakes as to the Terms or as to Identity' in Hugh Beale and others (eds.), *Chitty on Contracts*, 2 vols. (35th ed., London: Sweet & Maxwell, 2023), vol. I, 5-023.

40 *Hartog* v. *Colin & Shields* [1939] 3 All ER 566. Cf. *Tamplin* v. *James* (1880) 15 Ch D 215.

41 Cartwright, 'Contract Law', pp. 189–90.

42 *Bisset* v. *Wilkinson* [1927] AC 177. See Howard Bennett, 'Statements of Fact and Statements of Belief in Insurance Contract Law and General Contract Law' (1998) 61(6) *Modern Law Review* 886–98.

43 *Jaffray* v. *Society of Lloyd's; sub nom. Society of Lloyd's* v. *Jaffray* [2002] EWCA Civ 1101.

44 *Dimmock* v. *Hallett* (1866–67) LR 2 Ch App 21.

45 *Property Alliance Group Ltd* v. *Royal Bank of Scotland Plc* [2018] EWCA Civ 355.

46 *Horsfall* v. *Thomas* (1862) 1 H & C 90.

47 *Oakes* v. *Turquand* (1867) LR 2 HL 325.

48 *With* v. *O'Flanagan* [1936] Ch 575. See Burrows, 'Restatement' pp. 189–90.

49 Section 2(2) of the Misrepresentation Act 1967 (c. 7). *William Sindall Plc v. Cambridgeshire CC* [1994] 1 WLR 1016.

50 *Derry* v. *Peek* (1889) 14 App Cas 337, [374] (Lord Herschell).

51 *Boustany* v. *Piggott* (1995) 69 P & CR 298. See Spark, 'Vitiation of Contracts', p. 286.

52 *RBS* v. *Etridge* [2001] UKHL 44, [8] (Lord Nicholls).

53 Collins, 'The Law of Contract', p. 144. See *National Westminster Bank Plc* v. *Morgan* [1985] AC 686.

a transaction calling for an explanation (e.g. a grossly imbalanced transaction in B's favour, that cannot be explained on normal grounds), where on a balance of probabilities, B is likely to have exercised undue influence to induce A to enter into the transaction.[54] As confirmed in *Royal Bank of Scotland Plc* v. *Etridge (No.2)* (*Etridge*), these refer to two methods of proving undue influence, rather than two different classes of undue influence.[55] For the purpose of simplicity in terminology in this discussion, the two methods of proving undue influence (through direct proof or evidential presumption), are referred to by relying on the pre-*Etridge* terminology of 'actual undue influence' and 'presumed undue influence'.[56] Actual undue influence includes situations where undue influence is directly proved,[57] and where B's unacceptable conduct takes various forms, including 'coercion, domination or pressure',[58] which can include 'bullying, confrontation and harassment',[59] 'emotional pressure'[60] such as emotional blackmail, as well as threat to abandon[61] or the exercise of excessive control over A's affairs.[62] In the absence of direct proof, the presence of undue influence could be proved indirectly from a relationship of influence and a transaction that 'calls for explanation',[63] such as a grossly imbalanced transaction to A's detriment[64] (e.g. sale at a significant undervalue or purchase at a significant overvalue).[65]

For duress, the reference to B's unacceptable conduct depends on the type of duress, taking the form of illegitimate pressure that ranges from actual or threatened harm to A's person (physical harm[66] or imprisonment,[67] or harm to other persons such as A's family members[68] or employees),[69] to A's goods (including their unlawful seizure[70]), or to A's economic interests[71] (including threats to commit a crime, a tort,[72] and in some circumstances referred to in more detail later on in this section, it may include threatened breach of contract,[73] or threats to commit a lawful act[74]). These illegitimate threats could be

54 *RBS* v. *Etridge* [2001] UKHL 44, [6–8], [93].
55 Ibid. [92]-[93]. See Chen-Wishart, 'Duress, Undue Influence', 10-080.
56 *Allcard v. Skinner* (1887) 36 Ch D 145. 57 *RBS* v. *Etridge* [2001] UKHL 44, [93].
58 Chen-Wishart, 'Duress, Undue Influence', 10-072.
59 Ibid. 10-090; *Drew* v. *Daniel*; sub nom. *Daniel* v. *Drew* [2005] EWCA Civ 507.
60 Ibid. 10-075. 61 Ibid. 10-091; *Langton* v. *Langton* [1995] 2 FLR 890.
62 Ibid. 10-093; *Bank of Montreal* v. *Stuart* [1911] A.C. 120 PC (Can).
63 *RBS* v. *Etridge* [2001] UKHL 44, [93].
64 McKendrick, 'Contract: In General', 1.205 and 1.206; *Hammond* v. *Osborn* [2002] EWCA Civ 885.
65 Collins, 'The Law of Contract', p. 144. 66 *Barton* v. *Armstrong* [1976] AC 104.
67 *Duke de Cadaval* v. *Collins* (1836) 111 ER 1006. 68 *Singh* v. *Redford* [2018] EWHC 2390 (Ch).
69 *Royal Boskalis Westminster NV* v. *Mountain* [1999] QB 674.
70 *Maskell* v. *Horner* [1915] 3 KB 106 CA; Cf. *Skeate* v. *Beale* (1840) 11 A & E 983.
71 *Atlas Express Ltd* v. *Kafco (Importers and Distributors) Ltd* [1989] QB 833; *B&S Contracts and Design* v. *Victor Green Publications* [1984] ICR 419.
72 *Universe Tankships Inc of Monrovia* v. *International Transport Workers Federation; The Universe Sentinel* [1983] 1 AC 366.
73 *Occidental Worldwide Investment Corp* v. *Skibs A/S Avanti; The Siboen and The Sibotre* [1976] 1 Lloyd's Rep 293 QBD (Comm).
74 *Times Travel (UK)* v. *Pakistan International Airline Corp* [2021] UKSC 40 (SC) (hereafter *Times Travel* v. *PIAC*). See Andrew Burrows, *A Restatement of the English Law of Unjust Enrichment* (Oxford: Oxford University Press, 2012), p. 71–73.

express[75] or implied,[76] but they must be distinguished, *inter alia*, from mere commercial pressure. Moreover, B's illegitimate pressure must have caused A to enter into the contract with B, either by being actively present in A's mind when making the decision to transact with B (in the case of duress to the person),[77] or by meeting a 'but for' test (in the case of economic duress), where B's 'illegitimate pressure must have been such as actually caused the making of the agreement, in the sense that it would not otherwise have been made either at all or, at least, in the terms in which it was made'.[78] In the case of economic duress, this may also need to be supplemented by showing that B's acts have left A with no reasonable alternative but to submit to B's pressure.[79]

In cases of undue influence or unconscionability, B could seek to provide a counterbalance to claims regarding his unacceptable conduct by showing that A exercised his free will when entering into the contract[80] (which, in the case of both doctrines, could come into play if B ensured that A received independent legal advice).[81] In cases of duress, the fact that A received independent advice would 'not preclude a finding of duress',[82] although this may be relevant in determining whether B's illegitimate pressure caused A to enter into the contract, and whether A appreciated the availability of any reasonable alternatives to submission to B's pressure.[83] In the case of duress to the person, the causation requirement is not reliant on a 'but for' test, as is the case for economic duress,[84] but is framed broadly to refer to a situation where B's threat was actively present in A's mind when deciding to transact with B,[85] while B could seek to rely on the very narrow counterbalance of showing that his actions had no impact at all on A's decision to enter into the contract.[86]

The above framework shows concern for procedural mechanisms confined to economic values, centred on procedural fairness focused on the manner in which the contract was formed, and overlooking issues of substantive

75 *Vantage Navigation Corp* v. *Suhail and Saud Bahwan Building Materials; The Alev* [1989] 1 Lloyd's Rep 138 QBD (Comm).

76 *Woolwich Equitable Building Society* v. *Inland Revenue Commissioners* [1993] AC 70. See Andrew Burrows, *A Casebook on Contract* (6th ed., Oxford: Hart Publishing, 2018), p. 787.

77 *Barton* v. *Armstrong* [1976] AC 104. Andrew Burrows, *The Law of Restitution* (3rd ed., Oxford: Oxford University Press, 2011), p. 263.

78 *Huyton SA* v. *Peter Cremer GmbH & Co* [1999] 1 Lloyd's Rep 620 (hereafter *Huyton* v. *Peter Cremer*), [250] (Mance J, as he then was).

79 *Hennessy* v. *Craigmyle & Co* [1986] ICR 461. See Mindy Chen-Wishart, 'The Nature of Vitiating Factors in Contract Law' in Gregory Klass, George Letsas and Prince Saprai, *Philosophical Foundations of Contract Law* (Oxford: Oxford University Press, 2014), pp. 294–318 at p. 301.

80 *Inche Noriah* v. *Shaik Allie bin Omar* [1929] AC 127.

81 *RBS* v. *Etridge* [2001] UKHL 44, [153]. See Chen-Wishart, 'Duress, Undue Influence', 10–128.

82 Burrows, 'Casebook on Contract', p. 819.

83 *Hennessy* v. *Craigmyle & Co* [1986] ICR 461. See Chen-Wishart, 'Duress, Undue Influence', 10–037.

84 *Huyton* v. *Peter Cremer* [1999] 1 Lloyd's Rep 620.

85 *Barton* v. *Armstrong* [1976] AC 104, [119].

86 Ibid. See Burrows, 'The Law of Restitution', p. 263.

fairness focused on the contract terms.[87] The emphasis on procedural (rather than substantive) factors is rooted in the need to ensure certainty in the contractual sphere.[88] Yet, despite an apparent advantage of certainty, a focus on procedural factors brings its own challenges. For example, when assessing B's unacceptable conduct in cases of unconscionability, a focus on B's 'deliberate' exploitation of A's weakness (rather than on the circumstances of the transaction) appears to allow B to 'take advantage of [A]'s vulnerable state, short of actively manipulating' A.[89]

Similar concerns regarding A's vulnerability can be raised regarding the doctrine of *non est factum*, where A's weakness is associated with factors such as 'defective education, illness or innate incapacity'.[90] This reflects a 'narrow, perhaps clichéd notion of vulnerability', focused on issues such as A's medical condition, which overlooks wider factors such as the circumstances of the transaction, and the fact that all people could feel vulnerable when faced with lengthy, complex documents presented to them for signature.[91] The doctrine of *non est factum* operates within very narrow confines to ensure certainty, avoid potential conflicts with the objective test of agreement, and protect the security of transactions.[92] Its application is conditioned on A showing both that the document mistakenly signed was fundamentally different from what A intended to sign, and that he was not careless in his actions of signing the document.[93] The issue of fundamental mistake concerns 'the nature or effect' of the document,[94] requiring a 'radical' difference between what A intended to sign and what he actually signed.[95] Questions can, therefore, be raised as to what can amount to radical difference to justify the application of the *non est factum* doctrine. That A must also show he was not careless in signing the document[96] holds A to the standard of the reasonable person in A's 'position and circumstances'.[97] Consequently, A is expected to take 'reasonable precautions to inform himself of the contents' of the document before signing.[98] To show that he was not careless in signing the document, A must refer to either a 'weakness' that affected his ability to understand the document without explanation, or the fact that he was tricked into signing the document, as B (or another party) 'fraudulently or negligently' induced A's mistake.[99]

87 Anthony Hudson, 'Mental Incapacity Revisited' (1986) *The Conveyancer and Property Lawyer* 178–86 at 178.

88 Adams and Brownsword, 'Understanding Contract Law', p. 189.

89 Herring, 'Vulnerable Adults', p. 251.

90 *Saunders* v. *Anglia Building Society* [1971] AC 1004, [1016] (Lord Reid). See Spark, 'Vitiation of Contracts', p. 88.

91 Herring, 'Vulnerable Adults', p. 237.

92 McKendrick, 'Contract: In General', 1.152.

93 *Saunders* v. *Anglia Building Society* [1971] AC 1004, [1023]. See Spark, 'Vitiation of Contracts', pp. 79–80.

94 Atiyah, 'An Introduction', p. 185.

95 *Saunders* v. *Anglia Building Society* [1971] AC 1004, [1016-7].

96 Ibid.

97 Spark, 'Vitiation of Contracts', pp. 82–83.

98 Atiyah, 'An Introduction', p. 185. See *United Dominions Trust* v. *Western* [1976] QB 513.

99 Spark, 'Vitiation of Contracts', pp. 76 and 79.

Some ambiguity concerning the boundaries of the *non est factum* doctrine relates to the question of whether A must show absence of carelessness only when this doctrine is relied on against an innocent third party (C), or whether this applies to all circumstances where A seeks to rely on this doctrine.[100] Spark favours a wider application of this requirement (to promote 'care in contractual decisions'), but notes that B's unacceptable conduct 'should negate this requirement' (justified as a policy decision to 'prevent the procurement of contracts by unacceptable means').[101] In the vision of balance scales promoted in this chapter, both elements should be present (i.e. both the need to show A's absence of carelessness and B's unacceptable conduct) and should be interpreted broadly. As A and B are seen at each end of the balance scale, connected by a lever, if A's justification that he was not careless in signing the document is with reference to a vulnerability, this should be interpreted broadly to include vulnerability based on the circumstances of the transaction. In this approach that emphasises contextual vulnerability, the corresponding reference to B's conduct should include, as unacceptable conduct, not only B's actual knowledge of A's weakness which lead to A's mistake in signing a fundamentally different document, but also any constructive knowledge where B ought to have known about these circumstances. On a similar note, if A's justification that he was not careless in signing the document is with reference to the alternative justification that he was tricked into signing the document, this can connect, via the lever on the balance scale, to B's unacceptable conduct of inducing A's absence of consent by fraudulent or negligent means.

Challenges are also associated with the doctrine of unilateral mistake, given the difficulty of distinguishing between A's fundamental mistakes that could render a contract void (e.g. mistake as to the terms of the contract[102] or to the identity of the other contracting party, B)[103] and non-fundamental mistakes (e.g. as to the quality of the subject matter,[104] or B's attributes such as his creditworthiness).[105] Courts tend to focus on protecting the security of transactions,[106] holding A to his bargain with B, even in situations where B had knowledge of A's mistake, if that mistake was not 'fundamental'.[107] While this approach protects B's interests, it overlooks fairness-based considerations that may justify releasing a vulnerable party from a transaction entered into on the basis of a mistake.[108] A's interests would be protected more effectively if the contract could be set aside in situations where B had knowledge of both A's vulnerability and A's mistake (whether or not fundamental), and B did not take reasonable steps to draw the mistake to A's attention. Under this approach focused on contextual vulnerability, B's knowledge would include both actual and constructive knowledge.

[100] Ibid. pp. 76 and 84. [101] Ibid. p. 85.
[102] *Chwee Kin Keong* v. *Digilandmall.com Pte Ltd* [2005] SGCA 2.
[103] *Ingram* v. *Little* [1961] 1 QB 31. [104] *Smith* v. *Hughes* (1870–71) LR 6 QB 597.
[105] *Phillips* v. *Brooks* [1919] 2 KB 243. See McKendrick, 'Contract: In General', 1.141.
[106] Adams and Brownsword, 'Understanding Contract Law', pp. 48–49.
[107] *Smith* v. *Hughes* (1870–71) LR 6 QB 597. [108] Herring, 'Vulnerable Adults', p. 234.

The difficult distinction between mistakes as to identity (fundamental)[109] and attributes (not fundamental)[110] presents an additional set of challenges, particularly given that mistake as to identity cases tend to involve two innocent parties. One innocent in this context is the original seller (A), who has been tricked by a rogue (B), to part with his property in exchange for a cheque (which A subsequently discovers to be forged), after B presents himself to be someone else (a creditworthy party). Usually, B then sells the goods to an innocent buyer (C). Once A discovers the fraud, he seeks to recover the goods from C. A's success depends on whether his contract with B is void for unilateral mistake as to identity (if B's identity was fundamental to the transaction), which would justify A in claiming title over the goods, as B does not acquire ownership over the goods and cannot pass on title to C, in accordance with the principle *nemo dat quod non habet* ('no one can give what they do not have'). If, on the other hand, A's mistake was not to B's identity and was merely mistaken about B's attributes (a non-fundamental mistake that cannot render the contract void, but may render it voidable for misrepresentation), B had acquired ownership over the goods, which he could have passed on to C (as long as the transaction between B and C took place before A gave notice to rescind a voidable contract between A and B).[111]

The problematic distinction between identity and attributes was characterised by Lord Denning as 'a distinction without a difference'.[112] As Morgan indicates, B's 'identity' is, in most transactions, a means to an end rather than an end in itself.[113] While in some contracts, B's identity may be 'intrinsically important' (e.g. due to B's reputation in a particular field relevant to the transaction),[114] in most contracts, what matters to A is not B's identity 'per se', but 'the creditworthiness attached to that identity'.[115] Spark makes the legitimate point that, rather than relying on the distinction between 'identity' and 'attributes' as 'the guiding principle' in mistake as to identity cases the focus in assessing the transaction between A and B should be instead on whether A would consider a contract with B to be 'different from a contract on the same terms with the person' that A believes B to be.[116]

It is difficult to justify the presumptions applicable within the current framework, that A's mistake was only to B's attributes (not a fundamental mistake) if the contract was face to face,[117] but that A's mistake was to B's identity (a fundamental mistake), if the contract was written and B's alias was based on another

[109] *Cundy* v. *Lindsay* (1878) 3 App Cas 459.

[110] *King's Norton Metal Co* v. *Edridge, Merrett & Co Ltd* (1897) 14 TLR 98.

[111] Jonathan Morgan, *Great Debates in Contract Law* (3rd ed., Palgrave, 2020), p. 160; *Car & Universal Finance Co Ltd* v. *Caldwell* [1965] 1 QB 525.

[112] *Lewis* v. *Averay* [1972] 1 QB 198, [206] (Lord Denning).

[113] Morgan, 'Great Debates', pp. 161–62.

[114] Ibid. p. 162.

[115] Stephen Smith, *Contract Theory* (Oxford: Oxford University Press, 2004), pp. 82–83.

[116] Spark, 'Vitiation of Contracts', p. 131.

[117] *Phillips* v. *Brooks* [1919] 2 KB 243.

(real) person or organisation.[118] Moreover, the current distinction between identity and attributes in the contract between A and B is crucial in determining whether the innocent party C has to return the goods to the original owner A. This is problematic, as C had no knowledge of the transaction between A and B before entering into the contract with B and C was in a weaker position than A to discover B's dishonesty.[119] In the vision of concentric spheres presented in this book, A (as the innocent original seller) finds himself in the 'danger zone' envisaged within the social sphere, but so does C (the innocent party who bought the goods from B in good faith and without notice of A's rights). Given that A is 'more at fault' than C in 'not preventing the fraud' committed by B,[120] a fairer framework would be one where (as suggested by the Law Commission,[121] Lords Nicholls and Millett dissenting in *Shogun Finance Ltd* v. *Hudson*,[122] and by academic commentators),[123] the transaction between A and B was voidable (even if entered into due to a unilateral mistake), rather than void. In addition to the fairer outcome that would be ensure by this step, such reform would also represent a move away from the problematic distinctions reflected within the current framework between B's attributes and identity, and between written and face to face transactions.[124]

Another doctrine which is not free from procedural challenges is the doctrine of misrepresentation. In situations where A was induced to enter into a contract by B's false statement of fact, A may be able to rescind (i.e. set aside) the transaction[125] subject to any potential bars[126] such as unjust enrichment where the parties cannot be satisfactorily restored to their pre-contractual position,[127] intervening third party rights,[128] affirmation,[129] or lapse of time.[130] One source of ambiguity when assessing whether the misrepresentation is actionable concerns the extent to which A is expected to have relied on B's false statement of fact when reaching the decision to enter into the contract with B. This aspect of the misrepresentation doctrine rests on a 'surprisingly opaque' framework,[131] with questions raised both regarding the subjective

[118] *Shogun Finance Ltd* v. *Hudson* [2003] UKHL 62. See McKendrick, 'Contract: In General', 1.142.

[119] Smith, 'Contract Theory', pp. 82–83. [120] Ibid.

[121] Law Commission, 'Twelfth Report on the Transfer of Title to Chattels', Cmnd 2958 (1966).

[122] *Shogun Finance Ltd* v. *Hudson* [2003] UKHL 62, [35] and [82].

[123] See, for example, Catharine MacMillan, 'Rogues, Swindlers and Cheats: The Development of Mistake of Identity in English Contract Law' (2005) 64 *Cambridge Law Journal* 711–44.

[124] Burrows, 'Restatement' p. 183.

[125] For the issue of rescission as an all-or-nothing remedy, see *Glanville* v. *Glanville* [2002] EWHC 1587 (Ch), [50] (Mr Justice Park).

[126] Hugh Beale, 'Misrepresentation' in Beale and others (eds.), *Chitty on Contracts*, 9-132, 9-141, 9-145 and 9-147.

[127] *Spence* v. *Crawford* [1939] 3 All ER 271, [77] (Lord Wright).

[128] *Re Crown Holdings (London) Ltd (In Liquidation)* [2015] EWHC 1876 (Ch).

[129] *Ormes* v. *Beadel* (1860) 2 De GF & J 333.

[130] *Clough* v. *London & North Western Railway Co* (1871–72) LR 7 Ex 26.

[131] Burrows, 'Restatement' p. 191.

impact of B's statement on A's decision to enter into the contract (the issue of inducement),[132] and the objective assessment of the impact of B's statement on the 'reasonable person' in A's position (the issue of materiality),[133] considering, for example, whether the reasonable person would have taken steps to verify the truth of B's statement.[134] Challenges are associated with both of these issues. Questions have been raised about the applicable test to determine whether A has been induced to enter into the contract with B,[135] with indications[136] that the prevalent approach is that fraudulent misrepresentations are subject to a more generous test for A (where B's misleading statement of fact must have been 'actively present' in A's mind),[137] while non-fraudulent misrepresentations reflect a stricter test for A (where B's false statement of fact must have been 'an effective cause' in A's decision to enter into the contract with B).[138] Questions have also been raised regarding the issue of materiality, whether this is 'a discrete requirement' of the doctrine of misrepresentation,[139] or whether it is merely relied on to assess the issue of inducement.[140]

A further source of dissatisfaction with the current framework concerns the award of damages for misrepresentation, with a particular focus on the 'badly worded' provisions[141] in section 2(1) of the Misrepresentation Act,[142] leading to the 'distinctly odd' decision[143] of the Court of Appeal in *Royscot Trust Ltd* v. *Rogerson* (*Royscot*).[144] While, in theory, A could seek to recover damages at common law for the tort of deceit,[145] or for the tort of negligence,[146] in practice A tends to claim damages for misrepresentation under statute, relying on section 2(1) of the Misrepresentation Act.[147] In *Royscot*,[148]

[132] *Pan Atlantic Insurance Co Ltd* v. *Pine Top Insurance Co Ltd* [1995] 1 AC 501.

[133] Spark, 'Vitiation of Contracts', pp. 185 and 188–89.

[134] *Redgrave* v. *Hurd* (1881) 20 Ch D 1. Cf. *Smith* v. *Eric S Bush* [1990] 1 AC 831. See Burrows, 'Restatement' p. 192.

[135] *JEB Fasteners Ltd* v. *Marks Bloom & Co* [1983] 1 All ER 583. See Burrows, 'Restatement' p. 192.

[136] *BV Nederlandse Industrie Van Eiprodukten* v. *Rembrandt Enterprises Inc* [2019] EWCA Civ 596; See Burrows, 'Restatement' p. 191.

[137] *Edgington* v. *Fitzmaurice* (1885) 29 Ch D 459; [483] (Bowen LJ). See also [481] (Cotton LJ); [485] (Fry LJ).

[138] *Assicurazioni Generali SpA* v. *Arab Insurance Group (BSC)* [2002] EWCA Civ 1642, [59], [62] (Clarke LJ); *Raiffeisen Zentralbank Osterreich AG* v. *Royal Bank of Scotland Plc* [2010] EWHC 1392 (Comm), [174] and [180] (Mr Justice Christopher Clarke).

[139] *Mathias* v. *Yetts* (1882) 46 LT 497. See Ewan McKendrick, *Contract Law* (14th ed., London: Red Globe Press, 2021), p. 264.

[140] Spark, 'Vitiation of Contracts', pp. 185 and 188–90.

[141] Stephen Smith, *Atiyah's Introduction to the Law of Contract* (6th ed., Oxford: Clarendon Press, 2005), p. 263.

[142] Section 2(1) of the Misrepresentation Act 1967.

[143] McKendrick, 'Contract Law', pp. 269–71.

[144] *Royscot Trust Ltd v. Rogerson; sub nom. Royscot Trust* v. *Maidenhead Honda Centre* [1991] 2 QB 297.

[145] *Derry v. Peek* (1889) 14 App Cas 337. See Burrows, 'Restatement' pp. 30 and 193.

[146] *Hedley Byrne & Co Ltd* v. *Heller & Partners Ltd* [1964] AC 465; Burrows, 'Restatement' pp. 30 and 193.

[147] Section 2(1) of the Misrepresentation Act 1967.

[148] *Royscot Trust Ltd* v. *Rogerson* [1991] 2 QB 297.

the Court of Appeal indicated that A's action for a non-fraudulent misrepresentation under section 2(1) would lead to the same measure of damages as if the misrepresentation was fraudulent,[149] if B (on whom the burden of proof is reversed) is unable to show that he believed in the truth of his statement, with reasonable grounds to do so.[150] This approach relies on the wording of section 2(1), which notes that if A entered into a contract as a result of B's misrepresentation and suffered loss as a consequence, and if B would have been liable in damages 'had the misrepresentation been made fraudulently', B would be liable 'notwithstanding that the misrepresentation' is not fraudulent, unless B proves that he believed, with reasonable grounds, that the statement was true.[151] This interpretation of section 2(1), as reflected in *Royscot*, allows A to take advantage of the remoteness rule applied to fraudulent misrepresentation (allowing A to recover all loss that resulted directly from B's false statement),[152] which is more generous to A when compared to the remoteness rule applicable to negligent misrepresentations at common law (allowing A to recover only for loss that was 'reasonably foreseeable').[153] The higher degree of B's culpability in the case of fraud, when compared to negligence, can justify allowing A to rely on a more generous remoteness test.[154] Yet, under section 2(1), as A could seek to recover damages for non-fraudulent misrepresentation as if the misrepresentation was fraudulent, A may be able to rely, in the case of non-fraudulent misrepresentation, on the more generous remoteness test for fraudulent misrepresentations.[155] Smith comments that 'it is unlikely' that the drafters of the Misrepresentation Act 'actually intended such a result', and that 'their clumsy wording' and the refusal of the Court of Appeal in *Royscot* 'to go around the Act's literal words' resulted in 'what can only be described as an embarrassment for English law'.[156] A preferable approach would be for damages under section 2(1) of the Misrepresentation Act to be based not on the tort of deceit, but on the tort of negligence, adopting the appropriate remoteness test for negligence, based on 'reasonable foreseeability'.[157]

Further difficulties are posed by the 'ill conceived' provisions[158] presented in section 2(4) of the Misrepresentation Act. This provision removes the possibility for consumers to claim damages for misrepresentation under section

[149] Ibid.; *Doyle* v. *Olby (Ironmongers) Ltd* [1969] 2 QB 158.
[150] Section 2(1) of the Misrepresentation Act 1967; *Howard Marine & Dredging Co Ltd* v. *A Ogden & Sons (Excavations) Ltd* [1978] QB 574.
[151] Ibid. See Smith, 'Atiyah's Introduction to the Law of Contract', p. 263.
[152] *Smith New Court Securities Ltd v. Citibank NA; sub nom. Smith New Court Securities Ltd* v. *Scrimgeour Vickers (Asset Management) Ltd* [1997] AC 254. See Burrows, 'Restatement' p. 193.
[153] Burrows, 'Restatement' p. 193.
[154] Smith, 'Atiyah's Introduction to the Law of Contract', p. 263. [155] Ibid.
[156] Ibid.; *Smith New Court Securities Ltd* v. *Citibank NA* [1997] AC 254, [283] (Lord Steyn, *obiter*); *Gran Gelato Ltd* v. *Richcliff (Group) Ltd* [1992] Ch 560, [573] (Sir Donald Nicholls).
[157] Burrows, 'Restatement' p. 193. [158] Ibid. 194.

2(1),[159] if they have a right of redress under consumer law.[160] The right of redress under these provisions for consumers affected by unfair commercial practices (including misleading statements that led A, as a consumer, to enter into the contract) include the right to unwind (i.e. bring to an end) the contract, to discounts regarding payments under the contract, and to damages for consequential financial loss, distress, physical inconvenience or discomfort.[161] While the approach reflected in section 2(4) of the Misrepresentation Act was based on an attempt to 'avoid duplication'[162] in the recovery of damages for misrepresentation on the basis of statutory provisions, this has, in fact, resulted in complexity. Moreover, the necessity for adding this provision has been questioned by the fact that the issue of avoidance of double recovery has already been addressed in consumer law.[163]

Concerns can also be raised regarding the doctrine of undue influence, given questions over the circumstances in which B's conduct can be deemed to as 'undue', and the extent to which this may include B's passive unacceptable conduct of going ahead with the transaction despite having knowledge (actual or constructive) of A's vulnerability.[164] Challenges are also present when assessing the scope of actual undue influence, where although it may not be necessary to show that the transaction 'call[ed] for explanation',[165] A may need to show that B 'preferred his own interests',[166] leading to questions whether A could set the transaction aside if B genuinely thought that he was acting in A's best interest.[167] Cases of imbalanced transactions could fall under the category of presumed undue influence, even where B thought that he was acting in A's best interest, if A and B were in a relationship of trust and confidence.[168] Yet, for cases of 'coercion, domination or pressure'[169] where A and B

[159] Section 2(1) of the Misrepresentation Act 1967. In theory, consumers could still seek to recover damages for negligent misrepresentation under the common law for the tort of negligence. See *Hedley Byrne & Co Ltd* v. *Heller & Partners Ltd* [1964] AC 465. See Burrows, 'Restatement' p. 194.

[160] Initially, this referred to part 4A of the Consumer Protection from Unfair Trading Regulations (CPUTRs) 2008, SI 2008 No. 1277, as amended by the Consumer Protection (Amendment) Regulations 2014, SI 2014 No. 870. The CPUTRs are revoked by the Digital Markets, Competition and Consumers Act (DMCCA) 2024 (c. 13) which received royal assent on the 24th of May 2024, and which migrates an amended version of the CPUTRs provisions within part 4 of the DMCCA (consumer rights and disputes). See section 251(1) (consequential amendments) of the DMCCA 2024. Many of the DMCCA provisions are expected to come into force in the autumn of 2024. See sections 252 and 339 of the DMCCA 2024.

[161] Section 233 of the DMCCA 2024.

[162] Burrows, 'Restatement' p. 194.

[163] Initially, this referred to Regulation 27L of the CPUTRs 2008 (as amended). See section 235 of the DMCCA 2024. See Burrows, 'Restatement' p. 194.

[164] Chen-Wishart, 'Duress, Undue Influence', 10-079.

[165] *RBS* v. *Etridge* [2001] UKHL 44, [30].

[166] Ibid. 9. See Chen-Wishart, 'Duress, Undue Influence', 10-090.

[167] Chen-Wishart, 'Duress, Undue Influence', 10-098. See *Dunbar Bank Plc* v. *Nadeem* [1998] 3 All ER 876.

[168] *Cheese* v. *Thomas* [1994] 1 WLR 129. See Chen-Wishart, 'Duress, Undue Influence', 10-098.

[169] Chen-Wishart, 'Duress, Undue Influence', 10-072.

are not in a relationship of trust and confidence, which fall outside presumed undue influence, and where B genuinely believed that he was acting in A's interest, A would benefit from a greater degree of protection if the focus on B's knowledge included constructive knowledge where B ought to have known that the transaction was not in A's interest, based on the circumstances of the transaction. An approach focused on contextual vulnerability would ensure a broader interpretation of B's unacceptable conduct to include passive unacceptable conduct.

Further challenges are present in tripartite situations involving a surety, a debtor and a bank, where the bank is fixed with constructive notice of undue influence whenever the surety and the debtor are in a non-commercial relation.[170] Burns questions the scope of this approach, asking whether this would cover the relation between an elderly person with dementia and his employed carer.[171] Further difficulties are posed by the problematic assumptions that if A was informed by an independent legal adviser, A exercised his free will by going ahead with the transaction.[172] Auchmuty notes that once a bank has shifted the responsibility for providing A with advice on the solicitors, 'they could afford to be as careless as they liked', based on the assumption that if A received legal advice, that advice was adequate.[173] When assessing whether A has been lifted out of the danger zone by the presence of independent legal advice, these considerations should look at A as both an economic and social actor, taking into account, *inter alia*, associated social values such as the protection of human dignity.[174]

A's reliance on the doctrine of duress presents an additional set of challenges, due to the 'unstable nature'[175] of this doctrine. For example, one of the most challenging issues when seeking to define the boundaries of duress concerns the debate whether an act, or the threat to commit an act which is lawful, should amount to illegitimate pressure for the purpose of finding duress.[176] The question concerning 'the existence in English law of the concept of lawful act duress' was settled by the Supreme Court in *Times Travel* v. *Pakistan International Airline Corp* (*Times Travel*).[177] However, as noted by Lord Hodge, 'the boundaries of the doctrine of lawful act duress are not fixed',

170 *Barclays Bank Plc* v. *O'Brien* [1994] 1 AC 180.

171 Burns, 'The Elderly and Undue Influence', 277–78.

172 Peter Millett, 'Equity's Place in the Law of Commerce', (1998) 114 *Law Quarterly Review* 214–22 at 220.

173 Rosemary Auchmuty, 'Men Behaving Badly: An Analysis of English Undue Influence Cases' (2002) 11 *Social and Legal Studies* 257–82 at 263.

174 For a more detailed discussion on human dignity, see Chapter 2.

175 Mindy Chen-Wishart, 'Practical Benefit and the Emperor's New Clothes' in Beatson and Friedman (eds.), 'Good Faith and Fault in Contract Law', pp. 123–50 at 143.

176 Collins, 'The Law of Contract', p. 141. See *CTN Cash and Carry Ltd* v. *Gallaher Ltd* [1994] 4 All ER 714 CA (Civ Div).

177 *Times Travel* v. *PIAC* [2021] UKSC 40 (SC), [1]. See Nelson Enonchong, *Duress, Undue Influence and Unconscionable Dealing* (4th ed., London: Sweet & Maxwell, 2023), 3-016.

although any attempt to expand this doctrine must be approached 'with caution', particularly in a commercial context.[178] Given the absence of a 'doctrine of inequality of bargaining power' and of 'a general principle of good faith in contracting', in English contract law,[179] B's actions, if lawful, can only amount to 'illegitimate pressure', if B behaved in 'a highly reprehensible way'.[180] As recognised by Lord Hodge in *Times Travel*, 'the scope for lawful act economic duress is extremely limited in the sphere of commercial transactions',[181] being so far recognised in two circumstances: threats of criminal prosecution,[182] or manoeuvring cases.[183] B's threat to prosecute A or A's relatives, or to publish information concerning A or his family members, could amount to illegitimate pressure within the framework of duress.[184] Alternatively, B may have used 'reprehensible means' to 'manoeuvre' A into a position of vulnerability to 'exploit that vulnerability', where A has no alternative but to submit to B's request.[185]

An alternative assessment to whether a lawful act can amount to illegitimate pressure for the purpose of finding duress was presented in *Times Travel* by Lord Burrows, in the minority.[186] Lord Burrows sought to condition lawful act duress to situations where B's threat was accompanied by 'bad faith'[187] (e.g. if B requested from A something that B was not entitled to request and B had actual knowledge of this), whilst no illegitimate pressure would be found if B made the demand believing that he was entitled to make the request, and the parties operated within a commercial context.[188] This approach was dismissed by the majority in *Times Travel* for, *inter alia*, risking the creation of 'undesirable uncertainty in commercial transactions'.[189]

Certainty and predictability are indeed very important factors in defining the boundaries of legal doctrines, but so are fairness and flexibility,[190] particularly when A is not only placed in a vulnerable position due to B's actions, but also when, in addition to this, their starting point in their negotiations with B was also from a position of vulnerability. In that respect, an approach closer to a vision of contract law that responds to both economic and social values is that suggested in his *obiter* remarks by Leggatt LJ (as he then was), in *Al*

178 *Times Travel* v. *PIAC* [2021] UKSC 40 (SC), [3] (Lord Hodge). 179 Ibid. [27], [28].
180 Ibid. [4], [57]. 181 Ibid. [57].
182 Ibid. [4]. See *Williams* v. *Bayley* (1866) LR 1 HL 200 HL; *Kaufman* v. *Gerson* [1904] 1 KB 591; *Mutual Finance Ltd* v. *John Wetton & Sons Ltd* [1937] 2 KB 389 KBD.
183 *Times Travel* v. *PIAC* [2021] UKSC 40 (SC), [4]. See *Progress Bulk Carriers Ltd* v. *Tube City IMS LLC; The Cenk Kaptanoglu* [2012] EWHC 273 (Comm) (hereafter *The Cenk Kaptanoglu*); *Borrelli* v. *Ting* [2010] UKPC 21.
184 See *Mutual Finance Ltd* v. *John Wetton & Sons Ltd* [1937] 2 KB 389 KBD. See Chen-Wishart, 'Duress, Undue Influence', 10-058.
185 See *Times Travel* v. *PIAC* [2021] UKSC 40, [17], [58]; *The Cenk Kaptanoglu* [2012] EWHC 273 (Comm). See Chen-Wishart, 'Duress, Undue Influence', 10-063 and 10-063A.
186 *Times Travel* v. *PIAC* [2021] UKSC 40. 187 Ibid. [138] (Lord Burrows, minority).
188 Ibid. See Chen-Wishart, 'Duress, Undue Influence', 10-057 and 10-068.
189 *Times Travel* v. *PIAC* [2021] UKSC 40, [55] (Lord Hodge, majority).
190 Adams and Brownsword, 'Understanding Contract Law', pp. 188–92.

Nehayan v. Kent,[191] a case which precedes the approach to lawful act duress settled in *Times Travel*. In his comments on the boundaries of lawful act duress, Leggatt LJ suggested an assessment of B's conduct based on 'basic minimum standards of acceptable behaviour'.[192] Predicting potential criticisms that this standard would be seen as too uncertain, Leggatt LJ insisted that 'it is only in cases where the demand made and means used to reinforce it are completely indefensible that the courts will intervene'.[193] According to Leggatt LJ's vision, B's conduct involving 'a demand coupled with a threat to commit a lawful act' would amount to an illegitimate threat only in circumstances where B's demand was made without 'reasonable grounds', and B's threat 'would not be considered by reasonable and honest people to be a proper means of reinforcing the demand'.[194] Within the vision of concentric spheres of contract law presented in this book, the 'basic minimum standards of acceptable behaviour' referred to by Leggatt LJ in his judgement would need to be shaped by both economic and social values.

The second set of challenges regarding the boundaries of the doctrine of duress concerns the causation test and the extent to which this differs, depending on the type of duress.[195] This test seeks to determine whether B's illegitimate pressure has caused A to enter into the contract with B,[196] either by being actively present in A's mind when making the decision to transact with B (in the case of duress to the person),[197] or by meeting a 'but for' test (in the case of economic duress).[198] The test is less clearly articulated in the case of duress to goods,[199] with suggestions that the 'but for' test applicable to economic duress applies in this context as well,[200] especially if duress to goods is perceived as being subsumed within the concept of economic duress.[201] However, other suggestions insist on a scale approach where the test for goods is stricter than the more generous approach adopted regarding duress to the person, but not as strict as the test applied to economic duress, resulting in an 'intermediary causative standard' for duress to goods.[202] There is an attraction to this latter approach, which recognises the different degrees of 'illegitimacy' adopted by B, as he employs 'unacceptable means' of pressuring A to enter into a disadvantageous transaction.[203] Moreover, due to the severity of B's illegitimate pressure in the case of duress to the person, not only is the causation requirement framed broadly to refer to a situation where B's threat was actively present in

[191] *Al Nehayan* v. *Kent* [2018] EWHC 333 (Comm). [192] Ibid. [187] (Leggatt LJ, as he then was).
[193] Ibid. [194] Ibid. [188]. [195] Burrows, 'Casebook on Contract', p. 787.
[196] Smith, 'Contract Theory', p. 320. See *Dimskal Shipping Co SA* v. *International Transport Workers Federation; The Evia Luck (No.2)* [1992] 2 AC 152 (hereafter The Evia Luck).
[197] *Barton* v. *Armstrong* [1976] AC 104, [119]-[120].
[198] *Huyton* v. *Peter Cremer* [1999] 1 Lloyd's Rep 620. See discussion above.
[199] Spark, 'Vitiation of Contracts', p. 26.
[200] *Astley* v. *Reynolds* (1731) 2 Str. 915. See Chen-Wishart, 'Duress, Undue Influence', 10-032.
[201] *The Alev* [1989] 1 Lloyd's Rep 138 QBD (Comm). See Burrows, 'Casebook on Contract', p. 793.
[202] Spark, 'Vitiation of Contracts', pp. 25 and 230. [203] Ibid. p. 25.

A's mind when deciding to transact with B,[204] but there is also an indication that once this is proven by A, the burden reverts onto B to show that B's actions had no impact at all on A's decision to enter into the contract.[205] As discussed in more detail in Section 3.3, given that the causation test is more generous to A in the case of duress to the person, A would benefit from an expansion of the category of duress to the person to move beyond physical pressure and to include emotional pressure. This would be particularly beneficial to A, as the reversed burden of proof applied to duress to the person does not apply to other forms of duress such as duress to goods, or economic duress,[206] for fear that a more generous doctrine would undermine the security of transactions[207] and disadvantage B.

A third challenge concerning the boundaries of duress focuses on the question of whether the doctrine of economic duress is subject to an extra requirement (in addition to illegitimate pressure and causation), to show that A had no reasonable or practical alternative but to submit to B's pressure.[208] While one perspective sees this latter assessment as merely part of the causation requirement for economic duress, rather than as a separate test,[209] an alternative approach is to perceive this as a separate, independent element of economic duress.[210] The reasonable or practical alternative ask the question whether 'any reasonable person in the same predicament' as A 'would have acted in the same way',[211] barring relief where A had a reasonable or practical alternative course of action that he could have chosen, instead of submitting to B's requests.[212] Such alternatives include securing substitute performance from a different contracting party, together with an action for damages for any loss.[213] Consequently, A will be denied relief if a 'reasonable person' would have pursued a reasonable or practical alternative even if A himself did not appreciate the availability of this alternative course of action or did not feel that his circumstances enabled him to pursue this, and the only reason why he submitted is because of B's illegitimate pressure.[214] The reasonable or practical alternative test fails to look more closely at A and the particular circumstances of his transaction with B, perceiving the parties in the abstract, expecting A to be 'a person of reasonable courage' who is not 'weak or foolish to give in'

204 *Barton* v. *Armstrong* [1976] AC 104, [119].

205 Ibid. See Burrows, 'Casebook on Contract', p. 788.

206 Chen-Wishart, 'Duress, Undue Influence', 10-032 and 10-034.

207 *Al Nehayan* v. *Kent* [2018] EWHC 333 (Comm).

208 Burrows, 'Casebook on Contract', p. 787.

209 *Kolmar Group AG* v. *Traxpo Enterprises Pvt Ltd* [2010] EWHC 113 (Comm) (hereafter *Kolmar* v. *Traxpo*). See Chen-Wishart, 'Duress, Undue Influence', 10-021 and 10-046.

210 *The Universe Sentinel* [1983] 1 AC 366. See Chen-Wishart, 'Duress, Undue Influence', 10-041 and 10-046.

211 Chen-Wishart, 'Duress, Undue Influence', 10-041. See *Huyton* v. *Peter Cremer* [1999] 1 Lloyd's Rep 620.

212 *Hennessy* v. *Craigmyle & Co* [1986] ICR 461. See Martin Hogg, *Promises and Contract Law: Comparative Perspectives* (Cambridge: Cambridge University Press, 2011), p. 261.

213 Morgan, 'Great Debates', p. 214.

214 Chen-Wishart, 'Duress, Undue Influence', 10-044.

to B's demands.[215] This approach overlooks human diversity, as A appears to be expected to stand up to B's threats, rather than submit and subsequently rely on duress to challenge the transaction with B.[216] Yet, as Dawson points out, while 'the constant man' has 'stalked the fields of common law duress' for a considerable period of time, it is important not to overlook the need for a greater level of legal protection required by 'the weak, the timid, the anxious and submissive'.[217] An insistence on the reasonable or practical alternative test as a separate requirement for economic duress would provide a more favourable approach to B and the security of transactions, making it harder for A to challenge the contract on the basis of economic duress.

A fourth challenge regarding the scope of the duress doctrine is centred in the current classification of this doctrine into duress to the person, goods and economic duress.[218] As Lucy notes, these categories are 'fairly limited', covering actual or threatened pressure to A's person, property or prosperity.[219] Due to these limited categories, if, for example, B's threat is causing A anxiety that he will face financial ruin, A would likely need to rely on economic duress (concerning threats to his 'economic wellbeing'), rather than on duress to the person (which appears to be limited to threats to his 'physical wellbeing').[220] Parties seeking to rely on duress to the person benefit from a wider interpretation of the causation requirement where B's illegitimate pressure must have caused A to enter into the contract with B by being actively present in A's mind when making the decision to transact with B).[221] However, they are also faced with a narrow interpretation of the types of illegitimate pressures that fall under this category which appear to be focused on physical pressure.[222] Conversely, economic duress appears to cover a wider range of factors amounting to illegitimate pressure (including threats to commit a crime or a tort, and could include, in certain circumstances, threatened breach of contract[223] or threats to perform a lawful act),[224] but the causation requirement is narrow (reliant on a 'but for' test),[225] and this may need to be supplemented by the additional requirement for A to show that he had no reasonable or practical alternative to entering into the contract with B.[226]

The narrow classification of the doctrine of duress (confined to the categories of duress to the person, to goods and economic duress), and the narrow tests adopted under each category, are rooted in concerns for protecting the

[215] Burrows, 'The Law of Restitution', p. 272. [216] See Morgan, 'Great Debates', pp. 213–14.
[217] John Dawson, 'Economic Duress: An Essay in Perspective' (1947) 45 *Michigan Law Review* 253–90 at 265. See Morgan, 'Great Debates', pp. 214–15.
[218] Chen-Wishart, 'The Nature of Vitiating Factors', p. 308.
[219] William Lucy, *Philosophy of Private Law* (Oxford: Oxford University Press, 2007), p. 135.
[220] McKendrick, 'Contract Law', p. 337. See *Holyoake* v. *Candy* [2017] EWHC 3397 (Ch) at 397.
[221] *Barton* v. *Armstrong* [1976] AC 104, [119]-[120].
[222] *Holyoake* v. *Candy* [2017] EWHC 3397 (Ch) at 397.
[223] *Adam Opel GmbH* v. *Mitras Automotive (UK) Ltd* [2007] EWHC 3481 (QB).
[224] *Times Travel* v. *PIAC* [2021] UKSC 40.
[225] *Huyton* v. *Peter Cremer* [1999] 1 Lloyd's Rep 620. [226] *The Universe Sentinel* [1983] 1 AC 366.

security of transaction.[227] A focus on safeguarding the sanctity of contract and on ensuring that the doctrine of duress does not provide A with an easy escape route from a bad bargain, consequently safeguarding B's interests in the transaction, is legitimate. Yet, it is also legitimate to question whether A's interests are protected adequately, and whether the framework places sufficient weight on considerations of fairness, whilst ensuring that the doctrine operates within 'reasonably tangible parameters' that would avoid the 'danger that the doctrine will burst its banks'.[228] The current approach to duress to the person has so far been concerned with acts that harm, or threaten harm to A's body, mirroring the torts of trespass to the person (assault, battery and false imprisonment).[229] This approach, focused on physical harm, can be traced back to medieval times, where the writ of debt (a medieval method of contractual action developed in the twelfth century) could be challenged by relying on the defence of duress with reference to actual or threatened imprisonment, or 'menace to life or limb'.[230] Current interpretations of duress to the person need to reflect a modern understanding of forms of pressure (including the impact of B's threats on A's mind, rather than just his body), raising the need to either develop an additional category of duress ('emotional duress'), or to adopt an extended interpretation of the current category of duress to the person, to include not only threats to A's body through physical force or imprisonment, but also threats to A's mind through emotional pressure.

Further challenges which are discussed in more detail in Section 3.3 are associated with the doctrine of mental incapacity, regarding the assessment of both A's vulnerability (reliant on a medicalised approach centred on A's medical condition, rather than on the circumstances of the transaction) and B's unacceptable conduct (where questions are raised whether the knowledge requirement is limited to actual knowledge, or whether it also includes constructive knowledge of A's condition, and if the latter approach is accepted, whether this is limited to situations where A's mental incapacity was apparent).[231] This chapter calls for a broad understanding of the knowledge requirement to include constructive knowledge interpreted broadly to refer not only to situations where A's mental incapacity would have been 'apparent' to B but also to instances where B ought to have been put 'on notice' of the possibility of A's mental incapacity, based on the circumstances of the transaction. This approach would broaden the circumstances where A could rely on the doctrine of mental incapacity to point towards the 'weight' (based on a combination of A's vulnerability and B's unacceptable conduct) that pushed A into the 'danger

227 Morgan, 'Great Debates', p. 210.

228 Andrew Phang, 'Economic Duress: Uncertainty Confirmed' (1992) 5 *Journal of Contract Law* 147–56 at 154.

229 Burrows, 'The Law of Restitution', p. 71.

230 Simpson, 'History of the Common Law of Contract', p. 52.

231 Simon Whittaker, 'Personal Incapacity' in Beale and others (eds.), 'Chitty on Contracts', 11-088.

zone' that led to the conclusion of a grossly imbalanced contract to his detriment. In circumstances where B is put 'on notice' of the possibility of A's mental incapacity, based on the circumstances of the transaction, B could rely on a 'counterweight' to lift the transaction out of the 'danger zone' by showing that he took steps to ensure that A understood the transaction (e.g. ensuring that A received independent advice). However, as stressed earlier, such counterweights need to be interpreted narrowly to refer to advice that is accessible and appropriate to A's circumstances, and that considers both economic factors and social concerns such as the protection of human dignity.[232]

While procedural factors may appear, at first, easier to determine when compared to substantive considerations, in reality, it is difficult to establish where to draw the line to justify intervention on the basis of vitiating factors.[233] This can only be assessed effectively with reference to substantive factors such as the outcome of the transaction,[234] especially if they resulted in a grossly imbalanced contract.[235] Yet, under the current framework, courts are reluctant to recognise openly that they give weight to substantive factors when determining whether parties should be released from their contractual obligations on the basis of vitiating factors.[236] The concept of substantive fairness is vulnerable to criticism for being uncertain, difficult to define and lacking a clear scope.[237] Tiplady highlights the risk that if this concept becomes an end in itself in contract law, 'judges will begin to make choices which they are ill equipped to make', with unpredictable consequences.[238] In Tiplady's words, there is a danger that 'though they know the word to start the sorcerer's broom, they will be unable to control it'.[239] Lord Denning's attempt in *Lloyds Bank Ltd* v. *Bundy*[240] to establish a fairness threshold for assessing the validity of contracts when there is imbalance in the parties' bargaining position,[241] received little support in subsequent cases and was disapproved by Lord Scarman in *National Westminster Bank Plc* v. *Morgan*.[242] Substantive fairness may, in reality, play an important role in assessing the validity of contracts, but this has, so far, been 'disguised'.[243] Atiyah expresses concern that 'the extreme reluctance of courts to acknowledge openly' that substantive fairness is considered when evaluating the validity of a contract, 'often obscures what is actually going on'.[244]

[232] For a discussion of the importance of re-examining contract law principles and doctrines in light of social values such as human dignity, see Chapter 2.
[233] Morgan, 'Great Debates', p. 214.
[234] *Cheese* v. *Thomas* [1994] 1 WLR 129. See Spark, 'Vitiation of Contracts', p. 288.
[235] Morgan, 'Great Debates', p. 214.
[236] *Credit Lyonnais Bank Nederland NV* v. *Burch* [1997] 1 All ER 144. See Morgan, 'Great Debates', pp. 213–14.
[237] Stephen Smith, 'In Defence of Substantive Fairness' (1996) 112 *Law Quarterly Review* 138–58.
[238] Tiplady, 'Judicial Control of Contractual Unfairness', 618. [239] Ibid.
[240] *Lloyds Bank Ltd* v. *Bundy* [1975] QB 326. [241] Ibid. [336]-[337].
[242] *National Westminster Bank Plc* v. *Morgan* [1985] AC 686, [707].
[243] Spencer Thal, 'The Inequality of Bargaining Power Doctrine: The Problem of Defining Contractual Unfairness' (1988) 8 *Oxford Journal of Legal Studies* 17–33 at 19–21.
[244] Atiyah, 'Contract and Fair Exchange', 9.

On a similar note, Chen-Wishart comments that 'judicial articulations do not accurately reflect judicial actions',[245] implying a 'mass deception' by the courts when they insist that they are unconcerned with substantive fairness.[246] Yet, courts remain reluctant to evaluate openly the fairness of contract terms and, as Morgan suggests, 'perhaps honesty, in this instance, would be dangerous if it led to a general judicial power to regulate' contract terms.[247]

A framework focused on the certainty of rules, rather than on the fairness of outcomes and which is not concerned with whether the parties started from a balanced position, tends to favour the stronger contracting party.[248] A preferable approach is one where both parties are protected and where substantive fairness plays a role, without sacrificing certainty and without going as far as advancing a general principle of fairness in English contract law.[249] Certainty would indeed be endangered by a framework which would allow A to be released from his contractual obligations solely on the basis of substantive fairness. The vision of the balance scales presented in this book does not suggest this. Instead, it proposes a model where concerns for the substantive fairness of the transaction are seen as a trigger for raising procedural protections. While this is not a novel suggestion,[250] the proposed vision differs from previous discussions by insisting on a wide interpretation of B's constructive knowledge (to include the circumstances of the transaction) which, when combined with A's vulnerability, acts as a weight pushing A down into a danger zone that warrants intervention, and that such intervention should be rooted in social considerations (including the protection of human dignity).

Under the current framework, this weight is too narrowly constructed, as it is unclear whether, when applying doctrines such as undue influence and unconscionability, it includes B's passive unacceptable conduct to continue the contract with A despite having constructive knowledge (interpreted widely to include the circumstances of the transaction) of A's weakness. The proposed vision also looks at the presence of independent advice as a counterweight that lifts A out of the danger zone (when considering the application of doctrines such as duress and undue influence), but only if this is consistent with social values. Under the current framework, this counterweight is too broadly constructed, as it does not give sufficient weight to the parties' circumstances, before concluding that A entered into the transactions with full knowledge of what he agreed to. Any independent advice should be appropriate to A,[251] and must address any accessibility barriers that

[245] Mindy Chen-Wishart, 'The *O'Brien* Principle and Substantive Unfairness' (1997) 56 *The Cambridge Law Journal* 60–70 at 64.

[246] Morgan, 'Great Debates', p. 213. [247] Ibid. p. 214.

[248] Herring, 'Vulnerable Adults', pp. 228–29. [249] *Lloyds Bank Ltd* v. *Bundy* [1975] QB 326.

[250] See, for example, Chen-Wishart, 'Undue Influence: Vindicating Relationships of Influence', 265.

[251] Trebilcock and Elliott, 'Scope and Limits of Legal Paternalism', p. 79.

may be faced by A, focusing on environmental factors such as A's access to appropriate information and on social values such as the equal protection of human dignity.[252]

The role of social values in protecting contracting parties affected by gross asymmetry in their bargaining positions has not been articulated to a desired degree of clarity in English contract law. This is coupled with the reluctance of the courts to recognise overtly that substantive fairness has a role in English contract law. Instead, we are faced with a covert pursuit of substantive fairness, under the guise of procedural fairness.[253] This is similar to being aware of the desired destination but lacking the courage to forge a clear path to get there. It is akin to an unfinished bridge.

3.2.2 Challenging a One-Sided Approach that Overlooks the 'Lever' Connecting the Two Parties

A contractual framework focused mainly on procedure may attempt to provide clarity on *how* interference with freedom of contract could be justified in narrow circumstances, but is likely to be less clear as to *why* intervention may be necessary. The following discussion seeks to illustrate this point with reference to the doctrines of duress and undue influence, where there has been considerable academic debate regarding the purpose of intervention.[254] In the case of undue influence, while Birks and Chin advance an approach focused on A's impaired consent (due to 'excessive dependence' on B),[255] and Bigwood support a focus on B's unacceptable conduct (based on 'transactional neglect' of A's interests),[256] Chen Wishart challenges one-sided approaches, stressing the need to look at the relationship between both parties and their social context within which the parties operate.[257] Such an approach would recognise the interdependence between contracting parties, based on a relational understanding of autonomy.[258]

Similar concerns have been expressed regarding the doctrine of duress, where initial justifications for intervention centred on A's impaired consent,[259] with subsequent justifications focused on B's unacceptable conduct,[260]

[252] Lisa Vanhala, *Making Rights a Reality? Disability Rights Activists and Legal Mobilization* (Cambridge: Cambridge University Press, 2011), p. 229.

[253] Chen-Wishart, 'Undue Influence: Vindicating Relationships of Influence', 265.

[254] See, for example, Morgan, 'Great Debates', p. 206.

[255] Birks and Chin, 'On the Nature of Undue Influence', p. 67. See *Pesticcio* v. *Huet*; sub nom. *Niersmans* v. *Pesticcio* [2004] EWCA Civ 372.

[256] Rick Bigwood, 'Contracts by Unfair Advantage: From Exploitation to Transactional Neglect' (2005) 25 *Oxford Journal of Legal Studies* 65–96; See *Tate* v. *Williamson* (1866–67) LR 2 Ch App 55.

[257] Chen-Wishart, 'Undue Influence: Vindicating Relationships of Influence', 265.

[258] Ibid. 242.

[259] *Pao On* v. *Lau Yiu Long* [1980] AC 614, [635]-[636]. See Ibbetson, 'A Historical Introduction', pp. 252–53.

[260] *The Universe Sentinel* [1983] 1 AC 366. See Spark, 'Vitiation of Contracts', pp. 213–14.

providing merely one-sided approaches[261] based on problematic tests.[262] The focus on A's impaired consent considers the effect of B's pressure on A's ability to provide 'true consent' to the agreement, due to A's 'overborne' will,[263] overlooking the fact that the impact of B's pressure is not to deprive A of choice, but to restrict A's options to 'a choice between two evils'.[264] Conversely, an approach centred on B's unacceptable conduct[265] considers the source of the pressure,[266] but is faced with the difficulty of distinguishing between legitimate and illegitimate conduct in the contractual realm, particularly given the risk that 'more subtle and insidious forms of pressure'[267] could fall just outside the scope of illegitimate behaviour currently caught by the doctrine of duress.[268]

An approach focused on the relation between the parties and the social context within which the parties operate moves away from a narrow vision of autonomy confined to individualistic values which currently dominates contract law,[269] and which promotes values such as profit maximisation and the pursuit of self-interest.[270] Such an approach rooted in individualism reflects a perception of a rational contracting party who is 'intelligent' and 'powerful', and who is 'able to stand up for himself' in order to 'drive a hard bargain', an image which is in sharp contrast with the more realistic perception of a non-commercial contractor who may be 'ignorant about many things', is vulnerable to 'emotional and physical pressure', and is 'short of time and energy to read mountains of paperwork'.[271] A focus on individualistic values presents an incomplete, distorted image. It centres only on A and B as economic actors pursuing their own interests and overlooks the lever that connects the two (symbolising the interrelation between contracting parties). It misses out the broader set of values that govern the parties' relationship, including social values such as interdependence and mutuality.[272] It also overlooks the responsibilities associated with these relationships, including the need to perceive contracting parties as 'fellow vulnerable people who need to be looked out for' (rather than as 'a source of profit')[273] and who need to be treated with respect.[274]

An approach centred on individualistic values is also unconcerned with who the parties are,[275] as 'the abstract A and B of contract textbooks' are generally seen as 'disembodied unsituated persons', unaffected by the challenges

261 Chen-Wishart, 'Duress, Undue Influence', 10-010.
262 Waddams, 'Sanctity of Contracts', p. 45.
263 Smith, 'Contract Theory', pp. 316–17. See *Pao On* v. *Lau Yiu Long* [1980] AC 614, [635]-[636].
264 *DPP for Northern Ireland* v. *Lynch* [1975] AC 653, [691] (Lord Simon) (in the context of criminal law). See Patrick Atiyah, *The Rise and Fall of Freedom of Contract* (Oxford: Clarendon Press, 1979), p. 436.
265 The Universe Sentinel [1983] 1 AC 366.
266 Smith, 'Contract Theory', pp. 316–17.
267 Atiyah, 'An Introduction', p. 268.
268 Herring, 'Vulnerable Adults', p. 242.
269 Chen-Wishart, 'Undue Influence: Vindicating Relationships of Influence', p. 203.
270 Herring, 'Vulnerable Adults', p. 257.
271 Ibid. pp. 228, 258 and 261.
272 Ibid. p. 228.
273 Ibid. pp. 258–59.
274 Chen-Wishart, 'The Nature of Vitiating Factors', pp. 302–03.
275 Adams and Brownsword, 'Understanding Contract Law', p. 194.

experienced by real people in everyday life.[276] Moreover, this abstract contracting framework rests on the assumption that the starting point for A and B's bargaining position is one of balance.[277] Consequently, this distorts any subsequent assessments of whether access to independent advice has redressed the balance between the parties' positions, and any attempt to achieve an outcome that 'balances' the interests of these parties. For example, regarding undue influence, the House of Lords in *Etridge* may have attempted to 'balance' the parties' interests (an individual and a bank),[278] but as Auchmuty comments, the 'balance argument rests on a false premise', given the significant asymmetry between the parties' bargaining positions and their access to resources, including information.[279] This framework also overlooks the social context within which the parties operate[280] and any structural inequalities that may affect these parties.[281]

3.3 The Fulcrum

In the vision imagining the contractual relations between the parties (A and B) as a lever on a balance scale, with A and B at each end of the scale, the state is envisaged in the middle as a fulcrum. The state plays the role of a central pivot in contractual relations, enforcing transactions, or refusing to enforce them, as appropriate.[282] Doctrines such as mental incapacity, *non est factum*, mistake, misrepresentation, duress, undue influence and unconscionability could be understood not as instances where the state interferes with the parties' freedom of contract, or undermines the sanctity of contract, but as circumstances where the state refuses to enforce grossly asymmetrical contracts[283] which have stepped out of the inner, non-interventionist sphere, into a wider sphere shaped by social concerns.

3.3.1 Challenging an Imbalanced Approach that Places More Weight on the Security of Transactions, to the Detriment of Vulnerable Parties

Rather than providing a framework that balances concerns for freedom and sanctity of contract (for transactions that could be envisaged within the inner economic sphere of the contractual framework) with the need to safeguard vulnerable contracting parties who entered into grossly asymmetrical contracts (for transactions that stepped into the wider, social sphere), the current

276 Collins, 'The Law of Contract', p. 137. 277 Herring, 'Vulnerable Adults', pp. 228 and 257.
278 *RBS* v. *Etridge* [2001] UKHL 44, [35]-[37]; Burns, 'The Elderly and Undue Influence', 252.
279 Auchmuty, 'Men Behaving Badly', 271.
280 Alison Diduck, '*Royal Bank of Scotland Plc* v. *Etridge* (No 2): Commentary' in Rosemary Hunter, Clare McGlynn and Erika Rackley (eds.), *Feminist Judgments, from Theory to Practice* (Oxford: Hart Publishing, 2010), p. 152.
281 Auchmuty, 'Men Behaving Badly', 266. 282 Shiffrin, 'Paternalism', 227.
283 Chen-Wishart, 'Undue Influence: Vindicating Relationships of Influence', 251–52.

framework places more weight on protecting the security of transactions, resulting in an imbalanced approach to the detriment of the vulnerable party. The following discussion, centred on mental incapacity, seeks to illustrate this point.

English contract law relies on a prima facie presumption that all adults have capacity to contract.[284] Consequently, a contract involving a party (A), who lacked the mental capacity to understand the transaction would be valid unless, *inter alia*, A's property or affairs were subject to the control of the court,[285] or the other party to the transaction (B) had knowledge of the mental incapacity.[286] Even if the contract falls within one of these exceptions, if the subject matter involves a necessary good or service, party A must still pay a reasonable price for these necessaries.[287] Under the Mental Capacity Act (MCA) 2005, a person is considered to lack capacity regarding a certain matter if, 'at the material time', he was 'unable to make a decision for himself in relation to the matter, because of an impairment of, or a disturbance in the functioning of, the mind or brain'.[288] Under the common law test, A must prove that, at the time of entering into the contract, 'he was so insane' that 'he did not know what he was doing'.[289] The level of understanding required for upholding the validity of a transaction depends on the nature of that transaction.[290] The MCA test for determining lack of capacity is 'broadly consistent' with the common law test[291] and may be adopted even in cases not covered by this Act, if this is 'appropriate' and the courts have 'regard to' the existing common law principles.[292]

Parallels can be drawn between the MCA and the common law approaches in seeking to protect the interest of the person who lacked the mental capacity to understand the transaction. However, the discussion on mental incapacity included in this chapter focuses only on a narrow issue: the common law approach to the question of validity of contracts entered into between A (who lacked the mental capacity to understand the transaction) and B (who was unaware of the incapacity and acted in good faith).[293] Although this is a narrow focus, it raises wider policy questions regarding the extent to which this protection is guided by a framework of citizenship values, including the

[284] Whittaker, 'Personal Incapacity', 11-001.

[285] Sections 2 and 3 of the Mental Capacity Act (MCA) 2005 (c. 9). See Peter Bartlett, 'Re-thinking the Mental Capacity Act 2005: Towards the Next Generation of Law' (2023) 86(3) *Modern Law Review* 659–700.

[286] *Imperial Loan* v. *Stone* [1892] 1 QB 599.

[287] Section 7 of the MCA 2005.

[288] Ibid. section 2(1). See also section 3(1).

[289] *Imperial Loan* v. *Stone* [1892] 1 QB 599, [601].

[290] *Manches* v. *Trimborn* (1946) 115 LJ KB 305.

[291] Edwin Peel, *Treitel on the Law of Contract* (15th ed., London: Sweet and Maxwell, 2020), 12-054.

[292] *Local Authority X* v. *MM (an adult)* [2007] EWHC 2003 (Fam), [79]-[80] (Munby J). See Whittaker, 'Personal Incapacity', 11-093.

[293] For a more detailed discussion of the MCA 2005, see Whittaker, 'Personal Incapacity', 11-099 and 11-100 (property and affairs under the control of the court), and 11-096 and 11-097 (liability for necessaries).

protection of autonomy and human dignity. Whilst recognising the relevance of the MCA in defining capacity regarding contracts for necessary goods and services[294] and its potential influence in areas currently covered by the common law,[295] the discussion sees this influence as a two-way street. An effective interpretation of contractual capacity under common law, reflective of UNCRPD values, which considers both economic and social factors, and looks beyond the medical condition of individuals to consider the circumstances of the transaction, could act as a positive influence on the way capacity is constructed under the MCA. Given the impact of the common law in shaping section 7 of the MCA (regarding necessary goods and services), replicating the economic focus reflected in the common law jurisprudence,[296] there is potential that a redefined concept of contractual capacity under the common law could influence positively the assessment of contractual capacity in areas governed by the MCA (including contracts with parties whose property is subject to the control of the court[297] and contracts for necessary goods and services).[298]

The issue of mental incapacity in English contract law has been noted for its 'topsy-turvy' history.[299] Influenced by the approach adopted in Roman Law, Bracton's thirteenth-century account of English law noted that contracts with parties who lacked the mental capacity to understand the transaction were void.[300] This provided complete protection to A who, in the absence of mental capacity to understand the contract, could not have consented to that transaction to voluntarily assume contractual obligations.[301] However, as this approach allowed mere proof of incapacity to invalidate the contract, it was criticised for being subjective, encouraging fraudulent claims, undermining the security of transactions and failing to consider B's interests.[302] A few centuries later, the balance shifted to the other extreme. The desire to limit the opportunities where parties could escape their contractual obligations on grounds of mental incapacity coincided with the development of trading and commerce in England.[303] Writing in the sixteenth century, Chief Justice Coke noted that no adult could avoid a contract by pleading his own incapacity (or 'stultifying' himself).[304] This approach was the basis for the seventeenth-century decision

[294] Sections 2, 3 and 7 of the MCA 2005.

[295] *Local Authority X* v. *MM (an adult)* [2007] EWHC 2003 (Fam).

[296] *Rr Rhodes; sub nom. Rhodes* v. *Rhodes* (1890) LR 44 Ch D 94; *Aster Healthcare Ltd* v. *Shafi* [2014] EWCA Civ 1350.

[297] Section 15 of the MCA 2005.

[298] Ibid. section 7.

[299] Peter Watts, 'Contracts Made by Agents on Behalf of Principals with Latent Mental Incapacity: The Common Law Position' (2015) 74 *Cambridge Law Journal* 140–54 at 145.

[300] Henry of Bracton, *De Legibus Et Consuetudinibus Angliæ (The Laws and Customs of England)*, c. 1210–1268.

[301] Spark, 'Vitiation of Contracts', pp. 57–58.

[302] Watts, 'Contracts Made by Agents', 145.

[303] W. G. H. Cook, 'Mental Deficiency and the English Law of Contract' (1921) 21 *Columbia Law Review* 424–41.

[304] Chief Justice Coke (1552–1634). See Cook, 'Mental Deficiency', 429.

in *Beverley's case*[305] and ensured that A was 'absolutely liable for his alleged contract'.[306] This provided certainty, protected B's expectations and strengthened the security of transactions,[307] but was criticised for going 'too far', 'bringing about injustice'[308] and being 'absurd' and 'mischievous', as it overlooked A's interests.[309]

Nineteenth-century contract law witnessed an attempt to find a middle ground between the interests of both parties. In *Molton* v. *Camroux* (*Molton*), Pollock CB commented that the rule in *Beverley's Case* 'has been relaxed' and that 'unsoundness of mind' could constitute a good defence to set aside a contract if A could show that he lacked the capacity to enter into a contract and this was known by B.[310] However, courts would not set aside a contract if B was unaware of the incapacity and contracted fairly and in good faith, the contract was executed and the parties could not be restored to their original position.[311] On appeal, this decision was affirmed in the Exchequer Chamber by Patteson J.[312] While Pollock CB noted that courts would not set aside a contract where B was unaware of the incapacity and contracted fairly, he did not state explicitly that the unfairness of a contract could justify invalidating it, irrespective of B' knowledge.[313] The focus on the security of transactions was made clear in *Imperial Loan Co Ltd* v. *Stone*[314] (*Imperial Loan*), where fairness was mentioned briefly in only one of the three judgments delivered in the Court of Appeal. Lopes LJ stated that 'to avoid a fair contract on grounds of insanity', A had to prove both his own mental incapacity and B's knowledge of the incapacity.[315] Yet, Lopes LJ did not state explicitly that fairness was a condition for enforcing a contract and that an unfair contract could be set aside irrespective of whether B was aware of the incapacity.[316] Unlike Lopes LJ, Fry LJ and Lord Esher MR made no reference to fairness in their judgments. Both judgments indicated that B's knowledge of A's mental incapacity was an essential element for rendering a contract voidable. Furthermore, Lord Esher noted that without such knowledge, the contract was valid irrespective of whether it was executory or executed.[317] To prove his lack of capacity at the time of entering into a contract, A must show that 'he was so insane…that he did not know what he was doing'.[318] A must prove both his lack of capacity and that B 'knew him to be so insane as not to be capable of understanding what he was about'.[319] This set a high threshold for invalidating a contract for want of capacity.

305 *Beverley's Case* (1603) 4 Co. rep. 123b. 306 Cook, 'Mental Deficiency', 429. 307 Ibid.
308 See *Archer* v. *Cutler* [1980] 1 NZLR 386, [396].
309 Cook, 'Mental Deficiency', 431, quoting Joseph Story, *Commentaries on Equity Jurisprudence* (13th ed., Boston: Little, Brown and Co, 1886), p. 239.
310 *Molton* v. *Camroux* (1848) 2 Exch 487, [501]. 311 Ibid. [503].
312 *Molton* v. *Camroux* (1849) 4 Exch. 17, [17]–[19]. See Henry Goudy, 'Contracts by Lunatics' (1901) 17 *Law Quarterly Review* 147–54 at 152.
313 See *Archer* v. *Cutler* [1980] 1 NZLR 386, [400]; *Hart* v. *O'Connor* [1985] AC 1000, [1020].
314 *Imperial Loan* v. *Stone* [1892] 1 QB 599. 315 Ibid. [602].
316 See *Archer* v. *Cutler* [1980] 1 NZLR 386, [398]–[400]; *Hart* v. *O'Connor* [1985] AC 1000, [1021].
317 *Imperial Loan* v. *Stone* [1892] 1 QB 599, [601]. 318 Ibid. 319 Ibid.

Whilst twentieth-century contract law revisited the question of balance between the interests of A and B, the approach adopted in *Imperial Loan* remained prevalent. In *York Glass Co Ltd* v. *Jubb*[320] (*York Glass*), the Court of Appeal considered the question whether a contract concluded between A and B could be invalidated for being unfair. Although the case did not require this issue to be decided, Sargant LJ indicated that his mind was 'entirely open' to that question.[321] However, he did not go as far as saying that the unfairness of a transaction could justify setting it aside. The Privy Council decision in *Hart* v. *O'Connor*[322] (*Hart*) confirmed the *Imperial Loan* approach and the preference for upholding the security of transactions. Lord Brightman rejected the conclusions reached by the New Zealand Court of Appeal in *Archer* v. *Cutler* (*Archer*), where McMullin J. stated that earlier decisions (including the judgments of Pollock CB in *Molton*, Lopes LJ in *Imperial Loan* and Sargant LJ in *York Glass)* implied that an unfair transaction could be invalidated for want of capacity, irrespective of B's knowledge of the incapacity.[323] Lord Brightman considered the fairness-based approach adopted in *Archer* as being 'illogical' and 'unsupported by authority', and expressed concerns about its divergence from Australian and English contract law.[324] In assessing the validity of a contract between A and B, the 'unfairness' of the transaction did not constitute a ground for rendering the contract voidable, 'unless such unfairness amounts to equitable fraud'.[325] The emphasis on B's knowledge of the incapacity as a condition for rendering the contract voidable seeks to protect B from hardship and reflects a preference for holding parties to their agreements.[326] This approach can be defended for its focus on certainty and clear rules to facilitate transactions and for upholding the security of transactions. Yet, far from providing a 'middle course' that seeks to protect the interests of both parties,[327] this approach can be criticised for being 'harsh' on A.[328] It places insufficient weight on A's interests and fails to assess the hardship caused to A by upholding a transaction that A entered into whilst lacking the mental capacity to understand its nature.[329] The rule adopted in *Imperial Loan* and confirmed in *Hart* may protect B from hardship, but it fails to 'look at the other side of the picture',[330] resulting in an imbalanced approach.

The requirement imposed in *Imperial Loan* on A to prove both his lack of capacity and B's knowledge of it, places a 'heavy burden' on A, particularly given the increased number of contracts where parties do not meet face to face.[331] Furthermore, *Imperial Loan* makes no reference to 'the character or degree of insanity' required to fall within the protection of the incapacity defence.[332]

[320] *York Glass Co Ltd* v. *Jubb* [1925] All ER 285. [321] Ibid.
[322] *Hart* v. *O'Connor* [1985] AC 1000.
[323] *Archer* v. *Cutler* [1980] 1 NZLR 386, [401]. See *Hart* v. *O'Connor* [1985] AC 1000.
[324] *Hart* v. *O'Connor* [1985] AC 1000, [1027]. [325] Ibid.
[326] Peel, 'Treitel on the Law of Contract', 12-053. [327] Watts, 'Contracts Made by Agents', 145.
[328] Smits, 'Contract Law'. [329] Goudy, 'Contracts by Lunatics', 150. [330] Ibid. [331] Ibid.
[332] Ibid.

In addition, unlike *Molton*, the decision in *Imperial Loan* makes no distinction between executory and executed contracts and the validity of a contract is upheld even in cases where *restitutio in integrum* is possible.[333] A may also be seen to be in need of protection.[334] As Lord Millett noted in *Barclays Bank Plc* v. *Schwartz*, mental incapacity may not only deprive A 'of understanding the transaction, but also deprive him of the awareness that he [does] not understand it'.[335] When compared to B, A is 'in an unequal bargaining position' when negotiating a contract[336] and in a weaker position to protect his interests.[337] Furthermore, it is difficult to argue that A gave his free consent to enter into a legally binding agreement.[338] Moreover, the other party's knowledge of the incapacity is not considered crucial when assessing the validity of contracts with minors.[339] At common law, such contracts are generally voidable (with a few exceptions, including contracts for necessary goods and services, for apprenticeships, education and services) and are not binding on the minor, but are binding on the other party.[340] Commenting on the courts' readiness to set aside such contracts, Goudy questions why the minor is preferred to the person lacking mental capacity.[341] Moreover, while *Imperial Loan* and *Hart* consider B's knowledge of the mental incapacity to be essential for setting aside a contract, such knowledge is not required in other jurisdictions, including Scotland.[342] Furthermore, the incapacity defence under the *Imperial Loan* rule appears to be confined to face-to-face contracting and may not protect A when his dealings with B were by remote communications (including letters or electronic forms of communication), although the position remains unclear.[343] In searching for a way out of such 'penumbral uncertainties', Watts questions whether the law should allow B 'to be better off by having dealt by post, email or the internet', where A's incapacity 'would have been apparent in a face-to-face transaction'.[344] However, the need to protect A in such circumstances must be balanced against the need to protect B, especially in situations where A's incapacity would not have been apparent to the reasonable person in B's position.[345] Perhaps a broader interpretation of constructive knowledge to include the circumstances of the transaction may provide a more balanced response and a way forward in such situations where A and B deal remotely.

333 Cook, 'Mental Deficiency', 438.

334 Robert Brucken and others, 'Mental Illness and the Law of Contracts' (1959) 57 *Michigan Law Review* 1020–1118 at 1025.

335 *Barclays Bank Plc* v. *Schwartz*, Times, 2 August 1995 CA (Civ Div).

336 Brucken and others, 'Mental Illness and the Law of Contracts', 1029.

337 Goudy, 'Contracts by Lunatics', 150. 338 Ibid. 339 Goudy, 'Contracts by Lunatics', 153.

340 *Proform Sports Management Ltd* v. *Proactive Sports Management Ltd* [2006] EWHC 2903 (Ch). See Whittaker, 'Personal Incapacity', 11-007.

341 Goudy, 'Contracts by Lunatics', 153.

342 *Loudon & Co* v. *Hunter; sub nom. John Loudon & Co* v. *Elder's Curator Bonis* (1922) 13 Ll L Rep 500. See Smits, 'Contract Law: A Comparative Introduction', p. 98.

343 Watts, 'Contracts Made by Agents', 143. 344 Ibid.

345 Whittaker, 'Personal Incapacity', 11-081.

The twenty-first century decision of the Supreme Court in *Dunhill* v. *Burgin*[346] (*Dunhill*) provides reasons for cautious optimism that a middle ground can be found between the interests of A and B. In this decision, Lady Hale noted that B's knowledge of incapacity required in *Imperial Loan* was not limited to actual knowledge and that A could avoid a contract by showing that B 'ought to have known' about the incapacity.[347] Lady Hale presented the inclusion of both actual and constructive knowledge as the 'generally accepted' approach,[348] and this understanding was not contested by the other four Supreme Court justices (Lords Kerr, Dyson, Wilson and Reed), who agreed with Lady Hale's judgment. The inclusion of constructive knowledge brings the advantage of objectivity,[349] as it allows questioning whether the reasonable person in B's position would have known about the incapacity.[350] It also has the potential to balance the interests of A and B, because it extends the grounds where A could invalidate a contract for want of capacity (not limited to B's actual knowledge of the incapacity to include constructive knowledge) but continues to operate within limited confines (as some degree of knowledge is still required from B). In doing so, *Dunhill* avoids the pitfalls of the approach in *Archer*.

Whilst Lady Hale's comments in *Dunhill* could facilitate a balanced approach in cases involving contracts where A alleges mental incapacity, this matter is far from being settled. Lady Hale's interpretation of the *Imperial Loan* rule has been attacked for potentially resting on an unclear basis.[351] A narrow interpretation of Lady Hale's comments, where B may be fixed with constructive knowledge only when the incapacity is apparent, but where actual knowledge is required where the incapacity is not apparent, is believed to be in line with earlier authorities.[352] However, such an interpretation would be 'limited in its extent' and restricted in its significance.[353] Conversely, a broader interpretation of Lady Hale's formulation, where B is fixed with constructive knowledge when the circumstances surrounding the transaction put him 'on notice of the possibility' of mental incapacity, and he did not take steps to 'avoid being fixed with constructive knowledge', would extend the significance of Lady Hale's statement, but would face challenges for resting on less clear authorities.[354] Yet, such authority could be found in *York Glass*, where Warrington LJ stated that 'if circumstances are proved which are such' that any reasonable person in B's position 'would have inferred from these circumstances' that A lacked the mental capacity to understand the transaction, B 'would be taken to know' about the incapacity, even without actual knowledge.[355] The strength of this authority for supporting a broad interpretation of Lady Hale's formulation in *Dunhill* should not be weakened by the fact that reliance on *York Glass* 'formed part of the alleged distinct and (possibly) equitable wider ground of avoidance

[346] *Dunhill* v. *Burgin* [2014] UKSC 18. [347] Ibid. [25]. [348] Ibid. [349] Ibid.

[350] Spark, 'Vitiation of Contracts', p. 58. [351] Peel, 'Treitel on the Law of Contract', 12-056.

[352] Whittaker, 'Personal Incapacity', 11-088. [353] Ibid. 11-081. [354] Ibid.

[355] *York Glass Co Ltd v. Jubb* [1925] All ER 285, [292]. See Whittaker, 'Personal Incapacity', 11-082.

on the basis of unfairness rejected by the Privy Council' in *Hart*.[356] *Archer* failed because it could have opened up the possibility for substantive fairness alone to justify invalidating a contract with a party who lacked the mental capacity to understand the transaction. Even in its broader interpretation, Lady Hale's formulation in *Dunhill* cannot be equated with such a proposition.

Lady Hale's interpretation of the *Imperial Loan* rule to include both actual and constructive knowledge, and the potential significance of a broad understanding of constructive knowledge to include the circumstances of the transaction, would provide a welcome degree of balance between the interests of A and B. However, enthusiasm must be tempered by an acknowledgement of the context in which Lady Hale presented her remarks.[357] In *Dunhill*, the Supreme Court was asked to decide, *inter alia*, whether the validity of a settlement of claim between a party who lacked the mental capacity to understand its nature and another party who was unaware of the incapacity, was determined by the general rule in *Imperial Loan*, or whether it was subject to the Civil Procedure Rules (CPR) (which required the court's approval to be valid).[358] The Supreme Court held that the validity of such settlement of claim is to be determined in accordance with the CPR, rather than by reference to the *Imperial Loan* rule, and Lady Hale's remarks about the latter were expressed *obiter*.[359] However, despite the context of Lady Hale's remarks, their significance cannot be undermined. In *Josife* v. *Summertrot Holdings Ltd*, Lady Hale's interpretation of the *Imperial Loan* rule was presented by the High Court as an accurate statement of the law for assessing the validity of contracts which fall under this rule.[360]

A reinterpretation of the *Imperial Loan* rule to include a broad interpretation of constructive knowledge could also have implications for the law of agency, and may prove relevant when re-evaluating the potential of this area of law to provide a legal framework for some forms of supported decision-making.[361] While an assessment of these implications is outside the scope of this chapter, we must draw a brief parallel between the two-party circumstances discussed earlier, which may involve two innocents, and the more complex framework of an agency agreement,[362] which could potentially involve three innocent parties. The interplay between economic and social concerns is also manifested in this context,[363] although the balance seems focused on protecting A's interests,

356 Whittaker, 'Personal Incapacity', 11-082 with reference to *Hart* v. *O'Connor* [1985] AC 1000, [1024]-[1026].

357 Ibid. 11-079.

358 Civil Procedure Rules 1998/3132, Rule 21.10(1). See Whittaker, 'Personal Incapacity', 11-084.

359 Whittaker, 'Personal Incapacity', 11-084.

360 *Josife* v. *Summertrot Holdings Ltd* [2014] EWHC 996 (Ch), [19]. See Whittaker, 'Personal Incapacity', 11-078, footnote 359.

361 See Art 12(3) of the UNCRPD.

362 This discussion refers only to the common law framework and makes no reference to powers of attorney under the *Powers of Attorney Act* 1971 (c 27) or lasting powers of attorney under the MCA 2005. For a discussion of these issues, see Whittaker, 'Personal Incapacity', 11-103, 11-104.

363 Watts, 'Contracts Made by Agents', 140.

with limited protection conferred to the agent or the third party who transacted with A through an agent.

The question whether the *Imperial Loan* rule applies to agency contracts has led to conflicting answers.[364] The first editions of *Bowstead and Reynolds on Agency* (the first to the twelfth editions from 1896 to 1959) and the latest editions of this publication (from the twentieth edition of 2015 to present),[365] as well as Watts' writing on this subject, suggest a positive answer.[366] If a principal (A) who appears to have mental capacity appoints an agent (B) whilst A lacks the mental capacity to understand the nature of the transaction, that appointment should be valid but could be voidable if A could show both his mental incapacity at the time of the appointment and B's (actual or constructive) knowledge of this condition.[367] Consequently, A could confer on B actual authority to contract on his behalf with another party (C) and the contract between A and C would be valid if A could have entered into that contract in person and C had no knowledge of A's mental incapacity.[368] Furthermore, A's representations to C about B's authority to act on his behalf could confer on B apparent authority, subject to C's knowledge about A's mental incapacity.[369]

The *Imperial Loan* rule should also apply in cases concerning A's supervening mental incapacity.[370] If A appoints B as agent whilst A has full mental capacity, but A subsequently loses his mental capacity, the agency contract between A and B should remain valid and B should continue to have actual authority to act on A's behalf, as long as B has no actual or constructive knowledge of A's mental incapacity, and A and B did not agree expressly that A's mental incapacity would terminate B's actual authority.[371] Furthermore, where A made representations to C about B's authority, which conferred on B apparent authority to act on A's behalf,[372] A's subsequent mental incapacity should not terminate B's apparent authority without C's actual or constructive knowledge of A's mental incapacity.[373] The general rule in *Imperial Loan* should also apply to the relation between A and C, and the contract between these parties should remain valid, even after A's subsequent loss of mental capacity (if A would have been bound had he contracted directly with C), unless C had actual or constructive knowledge of A's mental incapacity.[374]

When assessing the impact of A's mental incapacity on the validity of a contract, that assessment should rely on the same principles, whether we are looking at a direct contract between two parties, or whether the transaction is an agency contract between A and B, or a contract between A and C negotiated

[364] Peter Watts, *Bowstead and Reynolds on Agency* (23rd ed., London: Sweet & Maxwell, 2023), 10-020.
[365] Ibid. 2-009. [366] Watts, 'Contracts Made by Agents'. [367] Ibid. 144. [368] Ibid.
[369] Ibid. p. 140; *Rama Corp Ltd* v. *Proved Tin & General Investments Ltd* [1952] 2 QB 147.
[370] Watts, 'Contracts Made by Agents', 143. [371] Ibid. p. 153.
[372] *Rama Corp Ltd* v. *Proved Tin & General Investments Ltd* [1952] 2 QB 147.
[373] Watts, 'Bowstead and Reynolds on Agency', 2-009.
[374] Watts, 'Contracts Made by Agents', 153.

by B (as agent) on A's behalf.[375] There should be no distinction between the approach adopted in direct contracts and contracts adopted in an agency context, particularly if we consider that the law of agency aims to ensure that A's decision to appoint B as agent, to act on his behalf in a contract with C, should not place A in a different position than A would have been in, had he contracted with C directly.[376] As Pollock noted, 'by agency, the individual's legal personality is multiplied in space'.[377] Adopting the *Imperial Loan* rule in an agency context has the advantage of clarity, as it moves away from any ambiguities that may be associated with an exception from the general rule. However, there is also a risk that adopting this approach comes at a cost, as the application of the *Imperial Loan* rule in an agency context also brings with it the challenges associated with this rule highlighted earlier, including the insufficient protection conferred to A's interest if the courts were to insist on a strict interpretation of the knowledge requirement. It is, therefore, crucial that knowledge is not limited to actual knowledge and includes constructive knowledge which attaches to the other party (B or C) if either A's mental incapacity ought to have been apparent to the other party, or the circumstances were such that the other party ought to have known about A's mental incapacity.

The agency contract, however, presents an additional set of challenges, particularly when we look at the relation between B and C.[378] In this three-party setting, the way in which we assess the validity of the contract between A and B has consequences for the contractual relation (and any liability that may arise under these contracts), involving B and C, and A and C, respectively. If the agency contract between A and B remains valid even after A's subsequent mental incapacity (because B had no actual or constructive knowledge of A's mental incapacity), B continues to have actual authority to bind A, which could lead to a valid contract between A and C. Furthermore, by continuing to have authority to bind A, B is not liable for breach of warranty of authority under the implied collateral contract with C.[379] If the agency contract between A and B becomes voidable following B's actual or constructive knowledge of A's mental incapacity, B may lose the actual authority to act on A's behalf, although he may continue to have apparent authority if A made representations to C about B's authority, which were relied on by C and C had no knowledge of A's mental incapacity.[380] If B acts without authority from A, B may be liable for breach of warranty of authority under a collateral contract between B and C, where B impliedly warranted his authority to act on A's behalf,[381] unless

[375] Ibid. 141. [376] Ibid.

[377] Frederick Pollock, *Principles of Contract* (13th ed., London: Stevens & Sons, 1950), p. 45.

[378] Gerard McMeel, 'Philosophical Foundations of the Law of Agency' (2000) 116 *Law Quarterly Review* 387–411.

[379] *Collen* v. *Wright* (1857) 120 ER 241.

[380] Watts, 'Bowstead and Reynolds on Agency', 10-020; *Rama Corp Ltd* v. *Proved Tin & General Investments Ltd* [1952] 2 QB 147.

[381] *Collen* v. *Wright* (1857) 8 El & Bl 647.

C had knowledge that B acted without authority.[382] However, the trigger for this liability depends on a range of factors. If *Imperial Loan* applies to agency relations, the contract between A and B (the agency contract) becomes voidable upon B's knowledge of A's mental incapacity. In such circumstances, B would likely lose his actual authority, although there is some suggestion that if B is acting under an agency contract (e.g. as a solicitor acting on behalf of a client), that may enable B to retain residual authority to take steps to ensure that A's wishes are 'properly adhered to'.[383] Questions can be raised regarding the scope of such residual authority and the extent to which court assessments of such residual authority would operate, within a framework that takes into consideration values such as the protection of autonomy and dignity. The application of the *Imperial Loan* rule to the complex setting of agency contracts is not free from challenges but, as the following discussion emphasises, it is preferable to an alternative where A's mental incapacity automatically terminates the contractual relations between A and B, irrespective of A's wishes, and renders B vulnerable to liability for breach of warranty of authority without regards to B's (actual or constructive) knowledge of A's mental incapacity.

The thirteenth to the nineteenth editions of *Bowstead and Reynolds on Agency* (from 1968 to 2010) doubted the application of the *Imperial Loan* rule to agency contracts and considered instead that a principal (A)'s mental incapacity rendered the contract with an agent (B) automatically void.[384] This approach is also reflected in Hudson's writing, who considered that *Imperial Loan* did not apply to the relation between A and B (whether mental incapacity affected A at the time of appointing B or subsequently), nor did it apply to the relation between A and C.[385] He commented that the source of A's liability to C may derive from B's apparent authority to act on A's behalf (in cases where A, before being affected by mental incapacity, made representations to C about B's authority),[386] but conceded that C may be 'depriv[ed] of all rights' against A in cases that fall outside the scope of apparent authority.[387] Hudson's support for an exception from the *Imperial Loan* rule for agency contracts was influenced by his concern that this rule fails to protect A effectively, which, as he noted, led to considerable 'hostile criticism' of the decision in *Imperial Loan*.[388] Nevertheless, a broad reading of the knowledge requirement in *Imperial Loan* (to include constructive knowledge based on the circumstances of the transaction) would address such concerns and make *Imperial Loan* a more attractive alternative.

[382] *Jones* v. *Hope* (1880) 3 TLR 247.

[383] Watts, 'Bowstead and Reynolds on Agency', 10-020, with reference to *Blankley* v. *Central Manchester and Manchester Children's University Hospitals NHS Trust* [2015] EWCA Civ 18, [36].

[384] Ibid. 2-009.

[385] Anthony Hudson, 'Agency and Insanity' (1959) 37 *Canadian Bar Review* 497–503.

[386] Ibid. 498. See *Drew* v. *Nunn* (1878–79) LR 4 QBD 661 CA.

[387] Hudson, 'Agency and Insanity', 498–99.

[388] Ibid. 503.

Those who doubt the application of the *Imperial Loan* rule to agency contracts tend to refer, as authority, to the early twentieth-century decision of the Privy Council in *Daily Telegraph Newspaper Co Ltd* v. *McLaughlin* (*McLaughlin*),[389] which affirmed a decision of the High Court of Australia.[390] The courts noted that a principal who lacked the mental capacity to understand the nature of the transaction could not execute a power of attorney and that the deeds of transfer executed under that power of attorney were also a nullity.[391] However, this decision was based on the *non est factum* doctrine, which applies when a party, without being negligent, mistakenly signs a document that is fundamentally different from what he thought he was signing.[392] The party who mistakenly signed a power of attorney in *McLaughlin* (a document rendered void on the basis of *non est factum*) had been affected by 'profound' and 'self-evident' mental incapacity.[393] As the decision in *McLaughlin* was not based on the mental incapacity defence, this decision should not be used to undermine the application of the *Imperial Loan* rule to agency contracts.[394]

Those reluctant to apply the *Imperial Loan* rule to agency contracts tend to refer, as a further source of support, to the mid twentieth-century decision of the High Court of Australia in *Gibbons v. Wright* (*Gibbons*).[395] This decision appears to confirm that a person who lacks the mental capacity to understand the nature of the transaction cannot appoint an agent.[396] If *Gibbons* is to be understood as 'an accurate statement of the law' which confirms an exception from the *Imperial Loan* rule in an agency context, this exception is 'odd'.[397] More likely, however, is that the court in *Gibbons* appears to have 'misread' its previous decision in *McLaughlin*,[398] which found that A could not execute a power of attorney on the basis of the *non est factum* doctrine. Furthermore, as Watts notes, cases referred to in *Gibbons* to support the non-application of the *Imperial Loan* rule to agency contracts[399] do not support that approach on closer inspection.[400] For example, *Elliott* v. *Ince* is concerned with a gift rather than a contract,[401] *Stead* v. *Thornton* and *Tarbuck* v. *Bispham* involve situations

389 *Daily Telegraph Newspaper Co Ltd v. McLaughlin* [1904] AC 776 PC (Aus).

390 *Daily Telegraph Newspaper Co Ltd* v. *McLaughlin* (1904) 1 CLR 423. See Hudson, 'Agency and Insanity', 498.

391 *Daily Telegraph Newspaper Co Ltd* v. *McLaughlin* [1904] AC 776 PC (Aus), [779]-[780] (Lord Macnaghten).

392 Francis Reynolds, 'Agency' in Beale and others (eds.), 'Chitty on Contracts', 21-041. See *Thoroughgood's Case* (1582) 76 ER 408.

393 Watts, 'Bowstead and Reynolds on Agency', 2-009.

394 Watts, 'Contracts Made by Agents', 142.

395 *Gibbons* v. *Wright* (1954) 91 CLR 423 HC (Aus).

396 Ibid. [486] (Dixon CJ, Kitto and Taylor JJ). See Hudson, 'Agency and Insanity', 498.

397 MacDonald Eggers, 'Vitiation of Contractual Consent', p. 132.

398 *Daily Telegraph Newspaper Co Ltd* v. *McLaughlin* (1904) 1 CLR 423; *Daily Telegraph Newspaper Co Ltd* v. *McLaughlin* [1904] AC 776 PC (Aus). See Watts, 'Contracts Made by Agents', 148.

399 *Gibbons* v. *Wright* (1954) 91 CLR 423 HC (Aus) at 486.

400 Watts, 'Bowstead and Reynolds on Agency', 2-009.

401 *Elliott* v. *Ince* (1857) 7 De GM & G 475. See Watts, 'Contracts Made by Agents', 151.

where B had knowledge of A's mental incapacity,[402] as did the case of *Drew* v. *Nunn* (*Drew*) which was decided on the basis of apparent authority,[403] while in *Yonge* v. *Toynbee* (*Yonge*), the automatic termination of B's authority by A's mental incapacity was assumed without further analysis.[404]

If agency contracts were to be rendered automatically void by A's mental incapacity, as appeared to be suggested in *Yonge*, B would be left with insufficient protection.[405] B would automatically lose his actual authority to act on A's behalf, irrespective of his knowledge of A's mental incapacity. Under this approach, in the choice between two innocents (A and B), A appears to receive absolute protection to B's detriment (although, as discussed below, this approach fails to consider A's wishes, as it renders the contract void rather than voidable). Once B loses the authority to act on A's behalf, he becomes vulnerable to liability for breach of warranty of authority under the implied collateral contract with C,[406] unless C is aware that B acted outside authority.[407] Once again, B's knowledge of the loss of authority is irrelevant,[408] and once again, at a choice between two innocents (this time the choice being between B and C), B loses out.[409] This would be a double blow for B, and the difficulty would stem from a framework where the *Imperial Loan* rule did not apply to the agency contract between A and B and where B's knowledge of A's mental incapacity was irrelevant.

Conversely, in a framework that does apply the *Imperial Loan* rule to agency contracts, the contract between A and B is rendered voidable (rather than void) only if B had knowledge of A's mental incapacity. Therefore, B would lose his actual authority to act on A's behalf if he knew or ought to have known about A's mental incapacity, and there is an argument that even in such circumstances, B may retain residual authority to take steps that would protect A's interests.[410] Then, when examining B's potential liability under his collateral contract with C, B's liability for breach of warranty of authority would depend on whether B had originally lost his actual authority under the contract with A, based on his knowledge of A's mental incapacity and on the scope of any residual authority to act on A's behalf.[411] Consequently, B's knowledge (which should include both actual and constructive knowledge) of A's mental incapacity becomes indirectly relevant for assessing B's potential liability under the collateral contract between B and C.

[402] *Stead v. Thornton* (1832) 3 B & Ad 357; *Tarbuck v. Bispham* (1836) 2 M & W 2. See Watts, 'Contracts Made by Agents', 151.
[403] *Drew* v. *Nunn* (1878–79) LR 4 QBD 661. [404] Watts, 'Contracts Made by Agents', 152.
[405] Gerald Fridman, 'Lawyers as Agents' (1987) 36 *University of New Brunswick Law Journal* 9-40 at 21-2.
[406] *Collen* v. *Wright* (1857) 8 El & Bl 647. [407] *Jones* v. *Hope* (1880) 3 TLR 247.
[408] *Yonge* v. *Toynbee* [1910] 1 KB 215 CA, [227].
[409] Watts, 'Bowstead and Reynolds on Agency', 2-009.
[410] Ibid. 10-020, with reference to *Blankley* v. *Central Manchester and Manchester Children's University Hospitals NHS Trust* [2015] EWCA Civ 18, [36].
[411] Ibid.

Such an approach would reverse *Yonge*,[412] but would not necessarily undermine *Collen* v. *Wright* (*Collen*),[413] because *Collen* 'left uncertain' the time at which liability for breach of warranty of authority attached to B.[414] *Yonge* took the view that liability attached to B as soon as authority ceased and that B's authority ceased automatically with A's loss of mental capacity.[415] However, if the *Imperial Loan* rule applied in an agency context, liability could attach to B only once he had knowledge of A's mental incapacity (and would depend, *inter alia*, on the scope of any residual authority that B may have).[416] The application of the *Imperial Loan* rule to the agency context would resurrect, to some extent, the approach adopted in *Smout* v. *Ilbery* (*Smout*) (a mid-nineteenth-century case of the Court of Exchequer), according to which liability could attach to B when he had actual or constructive knowledge that authority had been revoked.[417] This case, which some believed to be compatible with *Collen*,[418] was given a final blow in *Yonge*, when the latter confirmed that *Smout* had been overruled by *Collen*.[419] The departure from *Smout* may be seen as regrettable, as the incorporation of both actual and constructive knowledge (when B ought to have known about A's mental incapacity by exercising 'due diligence')[420] in assessing B's liability, had the potential to ensure an objective and balanced approach which considered the circumstances of the transaction and the interests of both parties. Nevertheless, the application of the *Imperial Loan* rule in the context of agency contracts, if based on a broad reading of knowledge to include both actual and constructive knowledge, brings back some of the positive elements previously associated with *Smout*, but does so indirectly, focused not on the contractual relation between B and C, but on the contract between A and B. In *Yonge*, the potential for B to be found liable for breach of warranty of authority was 'carried too far'.[421] Holding B 'personally responsible' where his actual authority to act on A's behalf is lost without his fault or knowledge, is 'unreasonable' and 'inconsistent' with the general principle confirmed in *Imperial Loan*.[422] In assessing the parties' obligations and liabilities under a contract where A lost the mental capacity to understand the nature of the transaction, the other party (B or C)'s knowledge of A's mental incapacity

[412] P Higgins, 'The Effect of Insanity on Agency Transactions' (1961) 1 *University of Tasmania Law Review* 569–79 argues that *Yonge* could be explained as being isolated to its facts.

[413] *Collen* v. *Wright* (1857) 8 El & Bl 647.

[414] 'Notes on Recent Cases' (1909–1910) 35 *Law Magazine and Review; A Quarterly Review of Jurisprudence*, 5th Ser 339 at 341.

[415] Ibid.

[416] Watts, 'Bowstead and Reynolds on Agency', 10-020.

[417] *Smout* v. *Ilbery* (1842) 10 M & W 1, [11] (Alderson B).

[418] *Salton* v. *New Beeston Cycle Co* [1900] 1 Ch. 43 Ch D. See 'Liability of Solicitor Acting after Revocation of Authority' (1910) 30 *Canadian Law Times* 734–38 at 736.

[419] *Yonge* v. *Toynbee* [1910] 1 KB 215, [226]-[228] (Buckley LJ), cf [235] (Vaughan Williams LJ).

[420] *Smout* v. *Ilbery* (1842) 10 M & W 1, [11] (Alderson B).

[421] 'Implied Warranty of Authority' (1911) 31 *Canadian Law Times* 363–67 at 367.

[422] Fridman, 'Lawyers as Agents', 22.

should be relevant[423] and it should make no difference that A is contracting via an agent.[424]

Further challenges are posed by the inconsistency between *Yonge* and *Drew* in determining the parties' liabilities.[425] Both cases seem to agree that A's mental incapacity revokes B's actual authority to act on A's behalf, rendering the agency contract void.[426] However, *Drew* seems to suggest that B may retain power to bind A to a contract with C if there is apparent authority,[427] while *Yonge* appears to confirm that B is deprived of such power.[428] As Higgins notes, *Drew* and *Yonge* should be 'confined to their special facts', which would 'leave the door open' for the development of 'a reasonable rule to cover all cases' involving A's loss of mental capacity.[429] Both *Drew* and *Yonge* are decisions where the courts were concerned with protecting C's interests. In *Yonge*, Buckley LJ agreed with Willes J's approach in *Collen*, that in a choice between B and C's interests, the party more deserving of protection was C, as B represented to C that he had authority to act on A's behalf.[430] In *Drew*, when faced with a choice between protecting A or C's interests, Bramwell LJ indicated a preference for C, commenting with reference to A that 'insanity' was 'a misfortune' rather than 'a privilege' and justified the choice to protect C by stressing that A's condition 'must not be allowed to injure innocent persons'.[431]

The focus on protecting C's interests indicates a concern for protecting the security of transactions. Nevertheless, the protection of C's interests must be balanced against the need to also protect A and B's interests. In a framework where A's mental incapacity renders the contract with B automatically void and B loses the actual authority to act on A's behalf irrespective of B's knowledge of A's condition, neither A, nor B are effectively protected. The failure to consider B's knowledge (whether actual or constructive) of A's mental incapacity leaves B vulnerable to breach of warranty of authority under the implied collateral contract with C.[432] Furthermore, if A's mental incapacity renders the agency contract with B automatically void, this fails to provide sufficient protection to A's interests, as it overlooks his preferences and choices. Bramwell LJ's dictum in *Drew*, that 'if a man becomes so far insane as to have no mind, perhaps he ought to be deemed dead for the purpose of contracting',[433] appears

[423] Guenter Treitel, *An Outline of the Law of Contract* (6th ed., Oxford: Oxford University Press, 2004), p. 309.
[424] Fridman, 'Lawyers as Agents', 22.
[425] Higgins, 'The Effect of Insanity on Agency Transactions', 569.
[426] Robert Dick, 'Administration of Estates and the Mentally and Physically Infirm' (1975) 2 *Estates and Trusts Quarterly* 256–302 at 266.
[427] *Drew* v. *Nunn* (1878–79) LR 4 QBD 661, [667] (Brett LJ).
[428] Higgins, 'The Effect of Insanity on Agency Transactions', 575 and 578.
[429] Ibid. 579.
[430] *Yonge* v. *Toynbee* [1910] 1 KB 215, [225]-[6] (Buckley LJ).
[431] *Drew* v. *Nunn* (1878–79) LR 4 QBD 661, [668] (Bramwell LJ).
[432] *Collen* v. *Wright* (1857) 8 El & Bl 647.
[433] *Drew* v. *Nunn* (1878–79) LR 4 QBD 661, [668]-[9] (Bramwell LJ).

to equate A's mental incapacity with his 'civil death'[434] and reflects no concern for A's wishes and for the need to respect his autonomy and human dignity.

Conversely, a framework that recognises the application of the *Imperial Loan* rule to the agency context and which relies on a broad interpretation of the knowledge requirement to include both actual and constructive knowledge could achieve a more balanced approach between the interests of A, B and C. B's loss of his actual authority to act on A's behalf would depend on his knowledge of A's mental incapacity. The inclusion of constructive knowledge, in addition to actual knowledge, would protect A (or C respectively), as it would cover the situations where B ought to have known about A's mental incapacity (including based on the circumstances of the transaction). Even where B loses his actual authority to act on A's behalf, based on his (actual or constructive) knowledge of A's mental incapacity, he may still retain residual authority to take steps to ensure that A's interests are effectively protected.[435] Furthermore, a framework where the agency contract between A and B is rendered voidable (rather than void), places more weight on A's preferences and provides greater protection for values such as autonomy and dignity.[436] In addition, a broad interpretation of constructive knowledge moves the focus away from A's medical condition (and whether this was known by, or apparent to B) to include the circumstances of the transaction.

When Brett LJ delivered his judgment in the Court of Appeal decision in *Drew*, at the end of the nineteenth century, he reflected on the question whether a principal's mental incapacity ended the agent's authority and remarked that 'one would expect to find that this question has been long decided on clear principles' but that 'no satisfactory conclusion has been arrived at'.[437] The Court of Appeal found ultimately that 'insanity' of the kind affecting the principal did 'put an end to' the agent's authority, but that this conclusion may not apply to every type of 'insanity'.[438] A case comment published shortly after the decision in *Drew* noted that this decision 'can hardly be said to have settled the general question' regarding the effect of a principal's mental incapacity on the agent's authority.[439] In the twenty-first century, despite the fact that both the Court of Appeal and the Supreme Court have engaged with this question,[440] the issue continues to be clothed with uncertainty.[441] In the Supreme Court decision in *Dunhill*, Lady Hale made the *obiter* comment that the authorities in this area of law are 'in a

434 Lawson, 'The United Nations Convention', 569.

435 Watts, 'Bowstead and Reynolds on Agency', 10-020, with reference to *Blankley* v. *Central Manchester and Manchester Children's University Hospitals NHS Trust* [2015] EWCA Civ 18, [36].

436 MacDonald Eggers, 'Vitiation of Contractual Consent', p. 141.

437 *Drew* v. *Nunn* (1878–79) LR 4 QBD 661, [665] (Brett LJ).

438 Ibid. [669] (Bramwell LJ).

439 'Effect of the Lunacy of a Principal' (1878–9) 23 *Solicitors' Journal and Reporter* 813–30 at 815–16.

440 *Blankley* v. *Central Manchester and Manchester Children's University Hospitals NHS Trust* [2015] EWCA Civ 18; *Dunhill* v. *Burgin* [2014] UKSC 18.

441 Watts, 'Bowstead and Reynolds on Agency', 2-009.

state of some confusion', before voicing relief that 'fortunately, the issue does not arise', making it unnecessary for the court 'to express any opinion, one way or another, as to the present state of the law' (in particular whether the *Imperial Loan* rule applies to the relation between principal and agent).[442] While the High Court in *Blankley* v. *Central Manchester and Manchester Children's University Hospitals NHS Trust* (*Blankley*) indicated preference for the application of the *Imperial Loan* rule in an agency context,[443] the Court of Appeal was less forthright in confirming this, recognising instead the need for a 'fresh examination or reconsideration' of *Yonge* and 'related authorities' and indicating preference for an approach where B's knowledge of A's condition has relevance in determining the contractual relation between A and B.[444] According to Richards LJ, A's supervening mental incapacity should not terminate automatically the contractual relation between A and B (which, in *Blankley*, involved a client and a solicitor), B should continue to have authority to act on A's behalf while B has no knowledge of A's mental incapacity and should continue to have authority 'to take necessary steps' to protect A's position upon becoming aware of A's mental incapacity.[445] However, these remarks were made *obiter* and the Court of Appeal expressed relief that the case did not require the court 'to re-examine the principle' in *Yonge* or 'to grasp the "hot potato" left on one side by the Supreme Court' in *Dunhill*.[446] A choice between confirming the principle in *Yonge* or recognising the application of the *Imperial Loan* rule to agency contracts may appear, in the first instance, as a choice between two unattractive alternatives. However, while both options are open to criticism, the challenges associated with the *Imperial Loan* rule can be addressed by adopting a wide interpretation of the knowledge requirement to include constructive knowledge based on the circumstances of the transaction. This provides a more balanced framework for protecting the interests of the contracting parties, an approach that considers not only economic values (such as the security of transactions) but also social values (such as the protection of human dignity) and, consequently, a way out of this dilemma of conflicting authorities.

3.3.2 Challenging a Narrow Interpretation of Freedom and Sanctity of Contract

Earlier on in this chapter, the discussion has called for an interpretation of vitiating factors that considers not only procedural factors but also substantive considerations of fairness, which reflects an understanding of autonomy

[442] *Dunhill* v. *Burgin* [2014] UKSC 18, [31] (Lady Hale). See Whittaker, 'Personal Incapacity', 11-102.

[443] *Blankley* v. *Central Manchester and Manchester Children's University Hospitals NHS Trust* [2014] EWHC 168 (QB), [30] (Phillips J).

[444] *Blankley* v. *Central Manchester and Manchester Children's University Hospitals NHS Trust* [2015] EWCA Civ 18, [36] (Richards LJ).

[445] Ibid. See Watts, 'Bowstead and Reynolds on Agency', 2-009.

[446] *Blankley* v. *Central Manchester and Manchester Children's University Hospitals NHS Trust* [2015] EWCA Civ 18, [37] (Richards LJ). See Whittaker, 'Personal Incapacity', 11-102.

that includes both its individualistic and its relational aspects, and which is concerned not only with economic factors but also with social considerations, including for the protection of citizenship values such as human dignity. The discussion stressed the need for an approach that considers the relationship between the parties, their staring bargaining positions, the social context of the transaction, broader issues of social inequality that impact on their bargaining position and that any assessment of whether the balance between the parties has been redressed by measures such as the provision of independent advice considers whether such advice was appropriate, accessible and reflective of both the economic and social implications of the transaction. To support such calls, the arguments pointed towards some of the challenges associated with the current framework, which reflects a narrow perception of the contractual sphere, confined to economic values.[447] The current framework also reflects a unidimensional understanding of the role of contract law limited to enforcing agreements on the basis of procedural considerations.[448]

The calls highlighted earlier to address such challenges should not be seen as a step that would risk undermining freedom and sanctity of contract as pillars of the contractual legal framework. Only a 'particularly rigid conception' of freedom of contract understands this principle to mean 'unrestricted freedom to make contracts', irrespective of moral considerations that 'cry out for the imposition of some restrictions'[449] and understands the role of contract law as limited to enforcing the parties' agreements.[450] As Kimel notes, a rigid conception of freedom of contract is 'highly unrealistic', given the many forms in which the law intervenes to protect 'vulnerable contracting parties'.[451] The function of contract law is not limited to enforcing the parties' agreements, but includes the prevention of 'certain kinds of harm', considering values such as fairness,[452] and reflecting an understanding of human dignity not only as 'empowerment' (regarding the provision of a framework within which the parties can exercise choice) but also as 'constraint' (regarding the protection from harms).[453] In the context of mental incapacity, the call presented in this chapter for a broad interpretation of Lady Hale's formulation in *Dunhill*[454] to include constructive knowledge based on the circumstances of the transaction, should not be seen to undermine freedom of contract, as it would be equated with a justifiable intervention in the parties' contractual relations. Jessel MR's discussion of freedom of contract adopted in *Printing and Numerical Registering Co* v. *Sampson* states that adults with 'competent understanding shall have the utmost liberty of contracting' and 'their contracts when entered into

[447] Herring, 'Vulnerable Adults', p. 252. [448] Ibid. p. 225.
[449] Dori Kimel, *From Promise to Contract: Towards a Liberal Theory of Contract* (Oxford: Hart Publishing, 2005), p. 117.
[450] See Atiyah, 'An Introduction', p. 8. [451] Kimel, 'From Promise to Contract', p. 119.
[452] See Atiyah, 'An Introduction', p. 35.
[453] Brownsword, 'Modern Understanding of Human Dignity', p. 302.
[454] *Dunhill* v. *Burgin* [2014] UKSC 18.

freely and voluntarily shall be held sacred and shall be enforced' by courts.[455] Interventions may, therefore, be justified when a contract has been entered into without such understanding due to mental incapacity, and B had actual or constructive knowledge of the incapacity. Given that the enforcement of transactions between contracting parties is reliant on the 'coercive power of the state', operating through its courts,[456] the state may refuse to enforce an agreement entered into as a result of vitiating factors.[457] This illustrates that freedom of contract is not absolute, as it must be balanced against other values, including the protection of vulnerable parties from 'imposition and oppression',[458] which may require the courts to determine whether B's influence over A was 'undue', or whether B's pressure exercised over A was 'illegitimate'.[459]

Questions regarding the validity of a contract between A and B may require courts to make a choice not only between two contracting parties but also between two competing policies. They may involve a choice between fairness considerations that call for releasing a vulnerable contracting party from a transaction concluded due to vitiating factors, balanced against concerns framed as upholding the 'sanctity of contracts' (or the security of transactions), particularly given that the security of transaction principle is not absolute.[460] For example, with reference to the mental incapacity defence in contract law, the broad interpretation of Lady Hale's formulation in *Dunhill* promoted in this chapter may be seen to undermine 'the practical need for commerce to take place without traders and others requiring to consider the mental incapacity of their contracting parties where it is not apparent'.[461] Nevertheless, a framework which considers the circumstances of the transaction and includes reference to grossly imbalanced contracts, may not be that objectionable. In fact, 'legal intervention over one sided bargains' may have considerable social benefits, as it may lead to a reduction in 'extreme claims in negotiations' and an increase in the number of contracts that parties are willing to enter into, resulting in 'a wealthier society'.[462]

An emphasis on social values would skew the balance between the narrow and broad reading of Lady Hale's formulation in *Dunhill* in favour of the latter. While the narrow interpretation reflects individualist values focused on leaving parties to look after their own interests, the broad interpretation of Lady Hale's statement reflects concern for wider community values, including fairness.[463] It also moves the focus away from an individual-centred approach (assessing A's mental incapacity and whether this was known by, or apparent

455 *Printing and Numerical Registering Co* v. *Sampson* (1874–75) LR 19 Eq 462, [465].

456 Waddams, 'Sanctity of Contracts', p. 233.

457 Atiyah, 'An Introduction', p. 265.

458 Waddams, 'Sanctity of Contracts', p. 269.

459 Patrick Atiyah, *Essays on Contract* (Oxford: Clarendon Press, 1986), p. 132.

460 Stephen Waddams, 'Unconscionability in Contracts' (1976) 39 *Modern Law Review* 369–93 at 369–70.

461 Whittaker, 'Personal Incapacity', 11-087.

462 Morgan, 'Great Debates', p. 215.

463 Atiyah, 'Contract and Fair Exchange', 24.

to B), to consider the environment in which the transaction was conducted (e.g. the gross imbalance of consideration, the absence of independent legal advice and whether courts should enforce such a transaction). Parallels can be drawn with discussions in the context of undue influence and unconscionability, which resist approaches centred only on A's absent consent or B's wrongful conduct, consider wider norms that govern how contracting parties should treat each other[464] and assess the circumstances when the state would consider 'an exploitative contract' as 'an unworthy endeavour to support' and enforce.[465]

A broad reading of Lady Hale's statement in *Dunhill* in the context of mental incapacity becomes even more significant if we consider wider social factors. For example, a contract entered into by an elderly person who experiences memory loss (which could potentially be associated with a form of dementia) is likely to be problematic.[466] McKendrick comments that such a situation raises 'an acute conflict of policy', as the need to protect such parties from exploitation must be weighed against the 'wish not to infantilise the elderly'.[467] The number of cases involving contracts with parties who may lack the mental capacity to understand the nature of the transaction is likely to grow, including because of an increase in the number of people who develop mental health conditions such as dementia.[468] Hudson notes that in a legal framework where courts place more weight on upholding the security of transactions over considerations of fairness, the family members of such contracting parties may be tempted to take the management of financial affairs out of their hands, risking 'tension and distress'.[469] A vision of contract law which overlooks fairness-based considerations and wider social concerns is unlikely to provide a satisfactory response to such situations.[470]

Care must, however, be exercised with referring to fairness-based considerations, to avoid the pitfalls encountered by the decision of the New Zealand Court of Appeal in *Archer*,[471] referred to in the previous section. In *Archer*, the New Zealand Court of Appeal recognised the importance of safeguarding A's interests. In a decision that 'clearly diverged' from the approach confirmed in *Imperial Loan*,[472] *Archer* considered that in assessing the validity of a contract entered into by a party who lacked the mental capacity to understand its nature, courts should consider not only if B was aware of the incapacity, but also, irrespective of B's knowledge, whether the agreement was 'unfair'

464 Mindy Chen-Wishart, 'Undue Influence: Beyond Impaired Consent and Wrongdoing towards a Relational Analysis' in Andrew Burrows and Alan Rodger (eds.), *Mapping the Law: Essays in Memory of Peter Birks* (Oxford: Oxford University Press, 2006), pp. 201–22.

465 Shiffrin, 'Paternalism', 227.

466 Ewan McKendrick, *Contract Law: Text, Cases, and Materials* (10th ed., Oxford University Press, 2022).

467 Ibid.

468 Prince and others, 'Dementia UK'.

469 Hudson, 'Mental Incapacity Revisited', 181.

470 Ibid.

471 *Archer* v. *Cutler* [1980] 1 NZLR 386.

472 *Imperial Loan* v. *Stone* [1892] 1 QB 599, [601]. See Hudson, 'Mental Incapacity Revisited', 178.

to A.[473] Factors which could indicate unfairness and which must be assessed objectively include the absence of independent legal advice for A, disparity in the parties' mental capacities, leading to an unequal bargaining position and a sale for a price significantly below the market value.[474] Despite the absence of such classification in *Archer*, the first two factors could be associated with procedural fairness, whilst the latter could be equated with a concern for substantive fairness.[475] McMullin J's 'indicia of unfairness' adopted in *Archer* mirrored the test of an unfair bargain considered in *York Glass*.[476] Yet, unlike *York Glass*, the judgment in *Archer* was explicit in stating that a contract entered into by a person who lacked the mental capacity to understand its nature could be invalidated on grounds of its unfairness. In *Archer*, fairness prevailed over concerns for the security of transactions. Nevertheless, this victory for fairness was short lived, as the subsequent decision in *Hart*[477] saw a return to the traditional approach established in *Imperial Loan*. In *Hart*, Lord Brightman looked critically at the unfairness factors considered in *Archer*, arguing that McMullin J. dealt 'indifferently' with procedural and substantive fairness.[478] Yet, when rejecting the fairness approach adopted in *Archer*, Lord Brightman focused explicitly on substantive unfairness (or 'contractual imbalance').[479]

The rejection of substantive fairness in *Hart* is unsurprising, given the ambiguity that could be associated with this open-ended concept.[480] *Archer*'s main failing consists in its failure to articulate clearly how its fairness-based regime would work in practice, the relation between procedural and substantive fairness as part of this framework and the confines within which this regime would operate. By merely providing indicators of unfairness that included both procedural and substantive factors, without distinguishing between the two or articulating the limits of this proposed regime, *Archer* opened up the possibility that substantive unfairness alone may constitute a ground for invalidating a contract entered into with a party who lacked the mental capacity to understand the transaction.

The broad interpretation of Lady Hale's formulation in *Dunhill*, which would allow a contract to be invalidated for want of capacity when B ought to have known about the incapacity from the circumstances of the transaction involves significant practical challenges.[481] Such a reading of Lady Hale's interpretation of the *Imperial Loan* rule could require the courts 'to work out the circumstances' in which B 'should have known' of A's mental incapacity[482] and this may prove particularly challenging in cases where the parties are not dealing face to face.[483] Parallels have been drawn with the 'considerable

[473] *Archer* v. *Cutler* [1980] 1 NZLR 386, [401]. [474] Ibid. [402].
[475] Hudson, 'Mental Incapacity Revisited', 178. [476] *York Glass Co Ltd v. Jubb* [1925] All ER 285.
[477] *Hart* v. *O'Connor* [1985] AC 1000. [478] Ibid. [1018]. [479] Ibid. [1027].
[480] Tiplady, 'Judicial Control of Contractual Unfairness', 618.
[481] Whittaker, 'Personal Incapacity', 11-079. [482] Ibid.
[483] Watts, 'Contracts Made by Agents', 215.

litigation' regarding constructive notice in undue influence cases, following the House of Lords decision in *Barclays Bank* v *O'Brien*.[484] On a similar note, a constructive knowledge test in incapacity cases 'could lead to certain types of factual circumstance' which would put B on notice about the possibility of A's mental incapacity, and which may be avoided 'by investigation or third party advice'.[485] The use of constructive knowledge in Canada, as part of the test for invalidating contracts on grounds of incapacity, illustrates that such challenges are not insurmountable.[486] A three-part test requires courts to consider whether A lacked mental capacity at the time of the contract, whether due to this condition 'he was not capable of understanding the terms of the transaction and of forming a rational judgment of its effect upon his interests' and whether B had actual or constructive knowledge of such incapacity.[487] In assessing the latter part of the test, the courts may consider whether the circumstances surrounding the transaction 'ought to have put' B on inquiry regarding A's mental incapacity.[488]

A broad reading of Lady Hale's formulation in *Dunhill* would permit A to invalidate a contract on grounds of incapacity if A could show (i) B's actual knowledge of the incapacity or (ii) B's constructive knowledge of the incapacity, if this were apparent or (iii) B's constructive knowledge of the incapacity, based on the circumstances of the transaction. The first two grounds involve fairness in its procedural form, as B either knew of the incapacity but decided to go ahead with the contract regardless of the lack of consent or ignored what any reasonable person would have recognised as incapacity, to secure the transaction despite the lack of consent. Such reliance on procedural unfairness is also present in *Imperial Loan*, although not explicitly articulated. The last of these grounds could involve fairness in both its procedural and substantive form, but unlike *Archer* (which could have opened up the possibility for substantive unfairness alone to justify invalidating a contract), unfairness based on the circumstances of the transaction could require either procedural unfairness alone, or substantive unfairness combined with procedural unfairness. If the trigger for assessing the unfairness of a transaction is based on substantive factors (e.g. grossly imbalanced contract terms to A's detriment),[489] this would need to be supported by procedural factors (e.g. the absence of independent legal advice). Consequently, B would be fixed with constructive knowledge of the incapacity based on the circumstances of the transaction, not by reliance on substantive unfairness alone, but by reference to either procedural unfairness alone, or substantive unfairness in conjunction with procedural unfairness.

Such an approach could be accommodated within the current parameters of English contract law. It would not rely on a general principle of fairness,

[484] *Barclays Bank Plc* v. *O'Brien* [1994] 1 AC 180. See Whittaker, 'Personal Incapacity', 11-079.
[485] Whittaker, 'Personal Incapacity', 11-079. [486] Ibid.
[487] *Bank of Nova Scotia* v. *Kelly* [1973] CarswellPEI 31 [9].
[488] *Hardman* v. *Falk* [1955] BCJ No 199, [16]. [489] Atiyah, 'Contract and Fair Exchange', 6.

but rather be part of a piecemeal approach to ensure fairness, which is already a feature of English contract law. As noted by Bingham LJ in *Interfoto Picture Library Ltd* v. *Stiletto Visual Programmes Ltd*, English law has 'developed piecemeal solutions in response to demonstrated problems of unfairness'.[490] Furthermore, such an approach would not undermine the importance of certainty in English contract law. B would be fixed with constructive knowledge of incapacity based on the circumstances of the transaction, only within a clearly defined framework which would establish when the substantive unfairness trigger would come into play (e.g. grossly imbalanced transactions to A's disadvantage) and only when there is also proof of procedural unfairness (e.g. passive exploitation by B).[491]

3.3.3 Challenging a Narrow Interpretation of the 'Piecemeal' Approach to Vitiating Factors

In his excellent book, *Sanctity of Contract in a Secular Age*, Waddams makes a convincing argument for the existence of a general power in English contract law, inherited by the modern courts from the administration of equity under the Court of Chancery,[492] which could enable courts to modify 'highly unreasonable contracts'.[493] The reference to this general power could address some of the challenges posed by the current fragmented approach for responding to vitiating factors in the contractual framework, which may lead to parties being left without a remedy if they fall outside the protection provided by this piecemeal approach.[494] Resting on the reassurance of the safety net provided by the general power of the courts highlighted by Waddams,[495] this chapter has sought to make the argument for a step which precedes the need to resort to this residual power. The discussion has called for an expanded interpretation of current doctrines in contract law concerned with vitiating factors, and of principles such as freedom and sanctity of contract, to reflect not only economic considerations but also social concerns (including the protection of values such as relational autonomy and human dignity). The arguments insisted on a broad interpretation of the triggers that call for intervention based on vitiating factors, envisaged as 'weights' pressing A down into a 'danger zone'. They also called for a narrow interpretation of factors that could be presented by B in an attempt to argue that any imbalance between the parties has been redressed, such as the presence of independent advice (seen as a 'counterweight' that could lift A out of the 'danger zone'), as such advice should be accessible, appropriate to A's circumstances, and reflective of both economic and social concerns. This section aims

[490] *Interfoto Picture Library Ltd* v. *Stiletto Visual Programmes Ltd* [1989] QB 433, [439].

[491] Rick Bigwood, *Exploitative Contracts* (Oxford: Oxford University Press, 2003), p. 269.

[492] Waddams, 'Sanctity of Contracts', p. 7; Sections 24 and 25 of the Supreme Court of Judicature Act 1873.

[493] Ibid. pp. 12 and 220. [494] Ibid. p. 4. [495] Ibid. pp. 8–9.

to add one further argument in support of this discussion, by seeking to highlight that without such expanded interpretation of the doctrines concerned with vitiating factors, gaps could be left between these doctrines, which could limit the options available to vulnerable contracting parties who enter into grossly asymmetrical transactions to their detriment (particularly in situations where courts are reluctant to use the residual power highlighted by Waddams).[496] When someone has to cross a narrow bridge, they can draw some comfort from the existence of a safety net that could catch a fall. In the context of a bridge between economic and social values in the contractual realm, to assist with cases such as those involving grossly asymmetrical transactions at the detriment of a vulnerable contracting party, Waddams presents us with a safety net.[497] Perhaps further reassurance could be provided by the knowledge that efforts have been made to expand that bridge, with reinforced structures aimed to reduce the gaps between the planks.

Before discussing some of the gaps between vitiating factors doctrines and the need to expand these doctrines to provide increased protection to vulnerable contracting parties, we must stress that vitiating factors are merely one potential 'conduit of fairness' within the structure of contract law, and that measures adopted within this framework may need to be supplemented by further actions focused on other areas of contract law. Further 'conduits of fairness' within the contract law structure could include measures focused on regulating contract terms, including the common law measures regulating the incorporation of contract terms. The following paragraphs reinforce this point with references to common law rules of incorporation of contract law terms by signature, calling for a more generous approach for A, which would require B to provide 'reasonable notice' of terms, such as onerous or unusual terms.

A narrow interpretation of vitiating factors doctrines, including misrepresentation or *non est factum*, is particularly problematic for a vulnerable party A, who may seek to rely on one of these doctrines to escape the consequences of the 'signature rule' confirmed in *L'Estrange* v. *F Graucob* (*L'Estrange*).[498] According to this rule, once A has signed a document containing contractual terms, A is bound by these terms, irrespective of whether he has (or has not) read or understood the document.[499] Unlike the requirement for the incorporation of contract terms by notice,[500] the incorporation of terms by signature is not subject to a requirement of 'reasonable notice' of terms.[501] The 'signature rule' is rooted in the need to ensure certainty and to protect the security of transactions in the contractual sphere,[502] and this rule may be applicable even when B has knowledge (actual or constructive) that A has signed without having read or understood the document.[503] Nevertheless, such concerns for

[496] Ibid. p. 4. [497] Ibid. pp. 7, 12 and 220. [498] *L'Estrange* v. *F Graucob Ltd* [1934] 2 KB 394.
[499] Ibid. [403]. [500] *Parker* v. *South Eastern Railway Co* (1876–77) LR 2 CPD 416 CA.
[501] Morgan, 'Great Debates', p. 75. [502] Herring, 'Vulnerable Adults', p. 236.
[503] Atiyah, 'An Introduction', p. 183.

certainty and sanctity of contract must be balanced against fairness-based considerations aimed to ensure that A is not bound to 'a bargain to which he has not brought a consenting mind'.[504] While some protection may be provided by statutory control mechanism such as the regulation of exemption clauses in business contracts under the Unfair Contract Terms Act (UCTA) 1977,[505] or the regulation of unfair contract terms in consumer contracts under the Consumer Rights Act (CRA) 2015,[506] and by vitiating factors such as misrepresentation and *non est factum*,[507] this protection is not free from challenges. Drawbacks may include the exclusion of terms such as the subject matter or the price of the contract from assessing the fairness of terms under the CRA 2015[508] (if sufficiently 'transparent'[509] and 'prominent', assessed with reference to a 'reasonably well-informed, observant and circumspect' consumer),[510] or the strict application of vitiating factors doctrines such as *non est factum*.[511] Moreover, the *non est factum* doctrine relies on a narrow understanding of vulnerability focused on factors such as 'defective education, illness or innate incapacity',[512] where disability is assessed in medicalised terms, and which places insufficient weight on the wider social context of the transaction, and on the 'innate vulnerability that any of us can face' when presented with lengthy, complex documents for signature.[513]

Far from the fictional image of the 'time-rich and knowledgeable consumer', people often sign complex standard form documents containing small print, without reading or understanding these, with the actual (or constructive) knowledge of service providers that the document has not been fully read or understood by the consumer.[514] The interest of vulnerable contracting parties would be protected more effectively by a wider interpretation of the concept of vulnerability in the application of the *non est factum* doctrine,[515] and by extending the requirement of 'reasonable notice' (which in the case of incorporation by notice of onerous or unusual terms, requires more from B to bring these terms to A's attention)[516] to the incorporation of terms by signature.[517] Lessons could be learnt from the Canadian legal system, from the approach adopted by the Ontario Court of Appeal in *Tilden Rent-A-Car Co.* v. *Clendenning* (*Clendenning*).[518] In *Clendenning*, Dubin JA noted that in the

504 McKendrick, 'Contract Law', p. 174.
505 Sections 2(1) and 2(2), 11 and Schedule 2 of the Unfair Contract Terms Act 1977 (c. 50).
506 Sections 61–71 and Schedule 2 of the CRA 2015.
507 *Curtis* v. *Chemical Cleaning & Dyeing Co* [1951] 1 KB 805; *Saunders* v. *Anglia Building Society* [1971] AC 1004.
508 Section 64(1) of the CRA 2015.
509 Ibid. sections 64(2) and (3).
510 Ibid. sections 64(2), (4) and (5).
511 *Saunders* v. *Anglia Building Society* [1971] AC 1004.
512 Ibid. [1016] (Lord Reid). See Herring, 'Vulnerable Adults', p. 237.
513 Herring, 'Vulnerable Adults', p. 237.
514 Ibid.
515 Ibid.
516 *Interfoto Picture Library Ltd* v. *Stiletto Visual Programmes Ltd* [1989] QB 433. See Morgan, 'Great Debates', p. 76.
517 Morgan, 'Great Debates', p. 76.
518 *Tilden Rent-A-Car Co.* v. *Clendenning* [1978] CarswellOnt 125.

case of standard form contracts where B has actual or constructive knowledge that A's signature does not reflect A's 'true intention', as A signed 'unaware of stringent and onerous provisions' comprised in the standard form contract, B can only rely on such terms, if he has taken 'reasonable measures' to draw these terms to A's attention.[519] It remains to be seen whether the English courts will follow the Canadian approach presented in *Clendenning*.[520] While some decisions reinforce their loyalty for the 'signature rule' confirmed in *L'Estrange*,[521] and while the courts insist that, 'as a general rule', A 'should find time to read the document before signing',[522] Bryan J's *obiter* remarks in the High Court decision in *Cargill International Trading Pte Ltd* v. *Uttam Galva Steels Ltd* provide some hope for the 'exceptional cases' involving parties who had 'no real opportunity to read and consider' the document prior to signature.[523]

An approach which would prevent B from enforcing a contract signed by A, where B had actual or constructive knowledge that A did not assent to the onerous or unusual terms comprised in the written document, would not undermine the objective test of agreement.[524] This is because B should be unable to rely on 'outward appearance' when he has actual or constructive knowledge of the true position,[525] preventing B from relying on the 'appearance of consent' where he knows or ought to know that A signed without being aware of the unusual terms comprised in the document.[526] In the vision of balance scales presented in this chapter, A would find himself in the 'danger zone' (warranting intervention) if he signed a document agreeing to a grossly imbalanced transaction containing onerous or unusual terms, where B had actual or constructive knowledge that A was unaware of these terms. In this framework, a counterbalance could be provided by B (seeking to ensure the enforcement of the transaction) if B could show that he took reasonable steps to draw these terms to A's attention and this was done in an appropriate and accessible manner. This would reduce the circumstances where A would need to rely on the exceptions to the 'signature rule' provided by vitiating factors doctrines such as *non est factum* or misrepresentation, and would be a welcomed addition (for the protection of A's interests) to steps for reforming these doctrines. The remainder of this section focuses on some of the gaps between vitiating factors doctrines, calling for an expanded interpretation of these doctrines to provide an increased level of protection to vulnerable contracting parties.

Challenges faced by gaps between the vitiating factors doctrines, triggered by a narrow reading of these doctrines, can also be illustrated, for example,

519 Ibid. (Dubin JA). 520 See Herring, 'Vulnerable Adults', p. 237.

521 *L'Estrange* v. *F Graucob Ltd* [1934] 2 KB 394; *Peekay Intermark Ltd* v. *Australia & New Zealand Banking Group Ltd* [2006] EWCA Civ 386.

522 McKendrick, 'Contract Law', p. 173. See *Higgins & Co Lawyers Ltd* v. *Evans* [2019] EWHC 2809 (QB).

523 *Cargill International Trading Pte Ltd* v. *Uttam Galva Steels Ltd* [2019] EWHC 476 (Comm), [89] (Bryan J). See McKendrick, 'Contract Law', p. 173. See *Amiri Flight Authority* v. *BAE Systems Plc* [2003] EWCA Civ 1447, [15]–[16].

524 Morgan, 'Great Debates', pp. 75–76. 525 Ibid. 526 Atiyah, 'An Introduction', p. 183.

with reference to the relation between mental incapacity, undue influence, and unconscionability. When questions are raised regarding the capacity of a party (A) to contract with another (B), the doctrines of undue influence and unconscionability could act both as a prequel and as a sequel to such concerns. The doctrines could be seen as a prequel to this structure, because in assessments where A's *prima facie* presumption of contractual capacity cannot be rebutted on the basis of incapacity (either under the MCA or the common law test), these equitable doctrines could offer a way out of the contract, rendering it voidable. These doctrines could also be seen as a sequel to questions regarding A's contractual capacity, because even if A's *prima facie* presumption of contractual capacity can be rebutted on the basis of incapacity (under the MCA or the common law test), a contract where A's property is not under the court's control,[527] or where B had no knowledge of A's mental incapacity,[528] remains valid, unless it could be rendered voidable on the basis of, *inter alia*, undue influence or unconscionability. Consequently, these doctrines could assist a contracting party (A) whose capacity to understand the implications of a transaction has been affected by a mental health condition such as dementia, in circumstances where A does not meet the MCA or the common law test for incapacity, but where A is, nevertheless in a vulnerable position of cognitive asymmetry, due to the absence of accessible or appropriate information.[529] Even where A's condition falls within the incapacity test, these doctrines could offer a safety net in protecting A's interests, especially if the knowledge requirement under the common law test in *Imperial Loan* (which enables A to set the contract aside if he can prove both his incapacity and B's knowledge of his condition)[530] is interpreted narrowly not to include constructive knowledge based on the circumstances of the transaction.[531]

The doctrines of undue influence and unconscionability could be available as grounds of relief to any contracting party, irrespective of mental capacity, and cases such as *Imperial Loan* and *Hart* stress that if A cannot set aside a contract by showing that B was aware of A's mental incapacity, the contract may be set aside on other grounds, including these two doctrines.[532] Judging the validity of these contracts by the same standards, without regard to the mental capacity of the contracting parties, may provide 'an attractive simplicity'.[533] However, as Hudson comments, this places A at a 'serious disadvantage' when compared with B.[534] The fact that A must show, as required in *Imperial Loan*, that 'he did not know what he was doing',[535] may 'prevent him from giving vital evidence' for any allegations of undue influence or unconscionability involving

[527] Sections 2, 3, 15–19 and part 2 of the MCA 2005 (subject to amendments under the Mental Capacity (Amendment) Act 2019 (c. 18). See Whittaker, 'Personal Incapacity', 11-092.

[528] *Imperial Loan* v. *Stone* [1892] 1 QB 599.

[529] Smith, 'Contract Theory', 343.

[530] *Imperial Loan* v. *Stone* [1892] 1 QB 599, [601].

[531] See Whittaker, 'Personal Incapacity', 11-076.

[532] *Hart* v. *O'Connor* [1985] AC 1000, [1018].

[533] Hudson, 'Mental Incapacity Revisited', 184.

[534] Ibid.

[535] *Imperial Loan* v. *Stone* [1892] 1 QB 599, [601].

B.[536] As noted by Hudson, 'in providing his extreme mental impairment', A 'would simultaneously disable himself from giving credible evidence' regarding B's actions 'at the time of the transaction'.[537] Furthermore, the failure to show B's knowledge of the mental incapacity, which would prevent A from relying on the incapacity defence, may also prevent A from relying on undue influence or unconscionability. If A seeks to rely on undue influence in the case of a relationship of influence and a transaction not readily explained by the parties' relationship,[538] but where B acted in good faith, Bigwood comments that A must also show that B had actual knowledge of A's mental incapacity.[539] Similarly, if unconscionability is pleaded by A when B acted in good faith, Devenney and Chandler note that passive unacceptable conduct can be attributed to B only if B had knowledge of A's incapacity.[540] Consequently, despite the availability of potential grounds of relief such as undue influence or unconscionability, if A is unable to show that B was aware of the incapacity, A is left unprotected.[541] Yet, A should be entitled to a greater degree of protection than that conferred by a narrow reading of the *Imperial Loan* test.

Further challenges posed by the gaps between vitiating factors doctrines, which could be brought by a narrow reading of these doctrines, can also be illustrated with reference to the relation between duress and undue influence, in particular actual undue influence. There is an argument that following the development of economic duress in the 1970s,[542] cases of actual undue influence involving pressure[543] should be treated as cases of duress.[544] However, this approach must be accompanied by a certain degree of caution. If A can refer to B's failure to protect from a relationship of trust and confidence and a 'transaction which calls for explanation', he may seek to pursue the route of presumed undue influence, as the burden of proof reverts onto B to rebut the presumption of undue influence.[545] Should this route not be available, A may seek to pursue actual undue influence,[546] as A may not need to show the existence of a relationship of influence with B,[547] or that the transaction calls

536 Hudson, 'Mental Incapacity Revisited', 184. 537 Ibid. 538 *RBS* v. *Etridge* [2001] UKHL 44.

539 Bigwood, 'Exploitative Contracts', p. 466.

540 James Devenney and Adrian Chandler, 'Unconscionability and the Taxonomy of Undue Influence' (2007) *Journal of Business Law* (August) 541–68. See *Fry* v. *Lane* (1888) 40 Ch D 312.

541 Smits, 'Contract Law: A Comparative Introduction', p. 99.

542 See, for example, *North Ocean Shipping Co* v. *Hyundai Construction Co*; The Atlantic Baron [1979] QB 705.

543 See, for example, *Williams* v. *Bayley* (1866) LR 1 HL 200 HL. See Chen-Wishart, 'Duress, Undue Influence', 10-072.

544 *RBS* v. *Etridge* [2001] UKHL 44, [8] (Lord Nicholls); *Times Travel* v. *PIAC* [2021] UKSC 40, [90] (Lord Burrows).

545 *RBS* v. *Etridge* [2001] UKHL 44, [14].

546 Birks and Chin, 'On the Nature of Undue Influence', p. 66. Note, however, that *RBS* v. *Etridge* [2001] UKHL 44, [92]-[93] (Lord Clyde), confirmed that the reference to actual and presumed undue influence concerns two methods of proving undue influence, rather than two different classes of undue influence.

547 *RBS* v. *Etridge* [2001] UKHL 44, [103]. See Chen-Wishart, 'Duress, Undue Influence', 10-089.

for explanation,[548] although A may need to prove that B preferred his own interest.[549] Yet, the position appears to be unclear if B genuinely considered the transaction to be in A's best interest.[550]

One way to address this challenge, which would confer a greater degree of protection on A as a vulnerable contracting party, would be for the courts to consider not only B's actual knowledge but also his constructive knowledge that the transaction was not in A's best interest,[551] looking not only at whether B knew this but also at whether he ought to have known this based on the circumstances of the transaction. Pursuing the route of actual undue influence rather than that of duress (particularly if actual undue influence is interpreted more widely, as suggested earlier) may present certain advantages to A. The trigger for actual undue influence may be lower than that for duress[552] to include more subtle forms of pressure such as emotional pressure.[553] A may wish to rely on actual undue influence to justify being relieved from a contract with B, when B exercised influence on A (such as through 'emotional ties', 'financial dependence', or 'physical dependence'), to pressure A into a disadvantageous transaction.[554] Conversely, A may seek to rely on the doctrine of duress, where B's unacceptable conduct took the form of an act, or the threat of an act of physical violence (in the case of duress to the person),[555] or the wrongful threat to prosecute A or A's relative.[556]

If a narrow interpretation of actual undue influence is adopted regarding the circumstances referred to above, so that no relief is granted when the transaction does not call for explanation as such, and B exercised pressure over A, but genuinely believed the transaction to be in A's best interests (even though he ought to have known that this was not the case), we could probably look to duress for a solution. Nonetheless, it would be better for A if the solution were to fall within the heading of duress to the person, rather than that of economic duress.[557] Such an approach would be preferable not only with regards to the particular issues discussed earlier, but

[548] *CIBC Mortgages Plc* v. *Pitt* [1994] 1 AC 200, [209]. See Chen-Wishart, 'The Nature of Vitiating Factors', p. 303.

[549] *RBS* v. *Etridge* [2001] UKHL 44, [9]. See Chen-Wishart, 'Duress, Undue Influence', 10-098.

[550] Chen-Wishart, 'Duress, Undue Influence', 10-097 and 10-098.

[551] Hugh Beale, 'Undue Influence and Unconscionability' in Andrew Dyson, James Goudkamp and Frederick Wilmot-Smith (eds.), *Defences in Contract* (Oxford: Hart Publishing, 2019), pp. 87–110 at p. 92.

[552] Treitel, 'An Outline of the Law of Contract', p. 177.

[553] Cartwright, 'Contract Law', pp. 160 and 194.

[554] Beale, 'Undue Influence and Unconscionability', pp. 91–92.

[555] *Barton* v. *Armstrong* [1976] AC 104.

[556] Beale, 'Undue Influence and Unconscionability', p. 91. Cases concerning threats to prosecute A or A's relative, which were treated under the heading of undue influence prior to the development of economic duress but would be more likely now to be treated as duress cases, include *Turnbull & Co* v. *Duval* [1902] AC 429 PC (Jam). See Burrows, 'Casebook on Contract', p. 809.

[557] Beale, 'Undue Influence and Unconscionability', p. 92.

also more broadly, regarding the availability of duress as a potential way out of a transaction affected by vitiating factors. In the case of duress to the person, B's illegitimate pressure must have caused A to enter into the transaction, but the causation requirement is set quite low, referring to a situation where B's threat was actively present in A's mind when deciding to transact with B, while B must show that his pressure had absolutely no impact on A.[558] In contrast, economic duress relies on a stricter causation requirement, as in addition to referring to B's illegitimate pressure, A must also show that he would not have entered into the agreement 'but for' B's pressure.[559] Moreover, A may also have to meet the additional requirement of proving that he had no reasonable or practical alternative but to comply with B's request.[560]

Yet, duress to the person appears to be focused on the action or threat of imprisonment, on the action or threat of physical harm,[561] with insufficient weight given to emotional harm. A preferable approach would be an expanded interpretation of the doctrine of duress to the person to include 'emotional duress' as well. This would broaden the weight that presses A down into the 'danger zone', coupled with an already narrow counterweight where B is to show that his pressure had absolutely no impact at all on A's decision to enter into the contract.[562] A's emotional strain due to B's pressure appears to be apparent in cases such as *Williams* v. *Bayley* (where A was frightened that B will prosecute A's son for forgery),[563] *Kaufman* v. *Gerson* (where A was worried that B will dishonour A's husband and children),[564] and *Mutual Finance Ltd* v. *John Wetton & Sons Ltd* (where A was scared that B will prosecute A's brother, which could then cause upset that had the potential to have a very serious impact on A's ill father).[565] These were considered as undue influence cases at the time, but now they would be treated, more likely, under the heading of duress.[566] However, rather than considering these as cases of economic duress, they should fall under a more generous heading of duress to the person, expanded to include emotional duress. This would be a positive move away from what appears to be the confinement of duress to the person to physical forms of pressure, which was based on an understanding of harm and threats to harm, developed in medieval times.

558 *Barton* v. *Armstrong* [1976] AC 104, [119].

559 *Kolmar* v. *Traxpo* [2010] EWHC 113 (Comm).

560 *The Evia Luck* [1992] 2 AC 152.

561 McKendrick, 'Contract Law', p. 337. See *Holyoake* v. *Candy* [2017] EWHC 3397 (Ch), [397], referring to duress to the person as 'threat of *physical* violence' which is 'directed against the claimant or a close relation or associate of the claimant' (emphasis added).

562 *Barton* v. *Armstrong* [1976] AC 104.

563 *Williams* v. *Bayley* (1866) LR 1 HL 200 HL. See Waddams, 'Sanctity of Contracts', p. 383.

564 *Kaufman* v. *Gerson* [1904] 1 KB 591. See Burrows, 'The Law of Restitution', p. 280.

565 *Mutual Finance Ltd* v. *John Wetton & Sons Ltd* [1937] 2 KB 389 KBD. See Birks and Chin, 'On the Nature of Undue Influence', pp. 64–65.

566 Chen-Wishart, 'Duress, Undue Influence', 10-001 and 10-089.

3.4 Conclusion

This book proposes a model for bridging the economic and social realms of contract law. Starting with a vision of two concentric spheres, the discussion perceives the economic realm as an inner sphere rooted in a non-interventionist approach and on values such as freedom and sanctity of contract, which can accommodate imbalanced transactions, if these are entered into by parties exercising their free will, unhindered by vitiating factors. Grossly imbalanced transactions (such as sales at significant undervalue or purchases at excessively high prices, combined with A's vulnerability and the absence of independent advice) would, however, step outside this inner sphere into the social realm which takes the form of the outer sphere of contractual relations. Rather than focusing solely on the horizontal axis of contractual relations between private parties, this sphere engages the vertical axis that governs the relation between individuals and the state. In such circumstances, we must move beyond a non-interventionist understanding of freedom of contract and consider factors such as the substantive fairness of the transaction and the need for intervention based not just on economic concerns (e.g. A's significant financial loss) but also social considerations (e.g. safeguarding A's human dignity). In this vision, the contractual relation between the parties (A and B) is perceived as a lever on a balance scale, with the parties at each end of the scale, and the state in the middle, as a fulcrum. A's weak bargaining position (e.g. due to gross information asymmetry between the parties) and B's unacceptable conduct (e.g. going ahead with the contract despite having actual or constructive knowledge of A's weakness) could be perceived as a weight pressing A down into a danger zone of gross imbalance, warranting intervention. Assessments of whether A is in this danger zone should include social considerations, such as environmental barriers elicited by inaccessible information, and adopt a wide interpretation of constructive knowledge when looking at B's unacceptable conduct. The contract should be allowed to stand if B can prove that A has been lifted out of this danger zone by a counterweight, assessed by looking at the actions taken by B to redress this imbalance. A could be lifted out of this danger zone only by responding to both economic concerns affecting A (e.g. did A receive independent legal advice about protecting his interests) and to social considerations (e.g. was the advice accessible and did it consider A's position as a social actor and the need to protect his human dignity). While this should be supplemented by other measures within contract law (e.g. the regulation of unfair contract terms) and outside contract law (e.g. measures to address structural inequalities, such as accessibility barriers faced by people with disabilities in society), this vision reinforces the fact that contract law has a role to play in the endeavour of bridging social and economic concerns. This discussion has concentrated on the first bridge between these values, within contract law principles and doctrines, with a focus on vitiating factors, which could be envisaged as conduits of fairness within the structure of contract law. Staying within the contractual legal framework, the next chapter is centred on a second bridge between economic and social considerations, examining the role of regulation in connecting these values in the contractual realm.

4

The Second Bridge

Regulation

> Right, as the world goes, is only in question between equals in power,
> while the strong do what they can
> and the weak suffer what they must.
>
> (Thucydides, Ancient Greek Historian, c. 460–404 BC
> History of the Peloponnesian War)

The contractual realm is not a level-playing field, and regulation has a role in addressing some of the imbalances of power between consumers and traders with potential to lead to asymmetrical transactions to the disadvantage of individuals. When directed in pursuit of citizenship values, regulatory measures could act as conduits of fairness within the contractual realm, providing fertile ground to follow a vision of contract law closer to UNCRPD values, including the protection of autonomy and human dignity. This chapter focuses on the second bridge between economic and social values in contract law, examining the role played by regulation in bringing together these values. The discussion questions the effectiveness of regulatory responses to B2C relations in English consumer contract law, in protecting people not just as economic actors, but also as citizens. Regulation, which is the 'sustained and focused control exercised by a public agency' over activities 'valued by a community',[1] can play an important role in connecting economic and social values in the contractual spheres. Regulation is necessary at various stages of the contractual journey, including the pre-contractual framework (e.g. to combat disability discrimination[2] and promote accessible products),[3] the entry into contract (e.g. to combat unfair commercial practices),[4] and the contents of the contract (e.g. to control the fairness of express terms).[5] The discussion focuses on four key areas

[1] Philip Selznick, 'Focusing Organisational Research on Regulation' in Roger Noll (ed.), *Regulatory Policy and Social Sciences* (Barkley: University of California Press, 1985), pp. 363–67, at p. 363.

[2] Sections 13–27 (prohibited conduct) and 142–48 (contract) of the EqA 2010.

[3] Ibid. sections 28–31 (services).

[4] Sections 226–28 of the DMCCA 2024.

[5] Part II (Unfair terms) of the CRA 2015.

of regulation in B2C transactions,[6] namely the regulation of unfair contract terms, measures implying terms in contracts for goods, digital content and services, the regulation of unfair commercial practices, and measures concerning information and cancellation rights. This analysis uses the lens of the inner economic and outer social spheres of contract law (introduced in Chapter 2 and developed in Chapter 3) to assess the extent to which regulatory responses consider social concerns alongside economic factors, to protect individuals as both citizens and consumers. The discussion also challenges unrealistic visions of well-informed and rational consumers, calling for a broad definition of vulnerability[7] based on the context of transactions, and for a regulatory approach that promotes the principle of universal design advanced by the UNCRPD, which requires the provision of products to be usable by all, 'to the greatest extent possible', without the need for specialised design or adaptation.[8]

4.1 Protecting Citizenship Values in the Contractual Realm

The perception of individuals as citizens (defined broadly to refer not to nationality, but to the values linked to this concept, such as equality, autonomy and human dignity) tends to be associated with the public realm, focused on the relation between individuals and the state. Yet, when stepping into the private realm (focused on the relationship between private parties, including consumers and traders), people do not stop being citizens. Consequently, consumer protection measures must address not only the economic interests of individuals but also their social interests, recognising the importance of contracts in everyday life, and the role of regulatory responses in reflecting the wider social norms of how parties should treat each other.

The role of the state in the contractual realm has been the subject of extensive academic discussion.[9] This book, which proposes a vision of contract law based on concentric economic and social spheres, reflects an understanding of the state as having a role in both spheres. The state has a role as protector of vulnerable parties within the social sphere (function one), and as facilitator and enforcer of transactions within the economic sphere (function two). In the event of a conflict between these functions, the state's responsibilities within the social sphere should prevail over its obligations within the economic sphere.

For 'function one' within the social sphere of contract law, vulnerability is understood to be based on the circumstances surrounding the transaction, rather than on the medical condition of individuals. In the context of B2C

[6] The issue of enforcement of consumer rights is outside the scope of this analysis. For a discussion of the enforcement, see Simon Whittaker, 'Consumer Contracts' in Beale and others (eds.), *Chitty on Contracts*, vol. II, ch. 41.

[7] See also Herring, 'Vulnerable Adults'. [8] Article 2 of the UNCRPD.

[9] See, for example, Teubner, 'Contracting Worlds'.

transactions, consumers are in a vulnerable position compared to traders due to power asymmetries regarding access to resources such as information, time, money, or legal advice. In protecting vulnerable parties, the state responds to power imbalances experienced by individuals in consumer-trader relations. Regulatory interventions could include measures to ensure that traders provide consumers with sufficient and appropriate information and time to make informed decisions, that traders do not engage in unfair commercial practices, do not include unfair contract terms, or that goods are of satisfactory quality and services are provided with reasonable care and skill. Such measures could lift consumers from the 'danger zone' created by imbalances of power in B2C relations, to enable them to transact with confidence. These measures must be rooted in the social sphere of contract law, reflecting a concern to protect individuals as both consumers and citizens. When exercising 'function one' as protector of vulnerable parties, regulatory responses focus on fairness and public policy considerations.[10] The boundaries between these two concerns may overlap, including in cases of grossly asymmetrical transactions based on unfair terms.[11] Public policy considerations include the likely harm caused by transactions that are 'unjust, disproportionate, extravagant, or unconscionable', making them 'contrary to the public interest'.[12] 'Public interest' considerations trigger concerns for the protection of citizenship values,[13] including autonomy, and human dignity. These values are also relevant when considering fairness-based justifications for regulating B2C relations, including provisions challenging grossly asymmetrical transactions based on unfair terms.[14]

The core values guiding the state's exercise of 'function two' within the economic sphere of contract law are the protection of freedom and sanctity of contract. Within this sphere, the state seeks to facilitate transactions within an environment that 'inspires confidence, rather than fear'.[15] The state also seeks to 'enforce promises' and to 'protect the reasonable expectations generated by promises'[16] with contract law, providing a 'safety net' in the event of breach of contract by one of the parties.[17] Yet, when the state exercises 'function two' as the facilitator and enforcer of transactions, it does not do so in a vacuum, but pursues these objectives within a wider structure based on fairness and public policy considerations associated with the social sphere and the pursuit of 'function one'.[18] As Scanlon notes, contract law is 'clearly a social institution' which is 'backed up by the coercive power of the state'.[19] Atiyah acknowledges the

[10] See also Ibbetson, 'A Historical Introduction', p. 249.
[11] Waddams, 'Sanctity of Contracts', p. 8. [12] Ibid. p. 206.
[13] Feintuck, 'The Public Interest in Regulation'. [14] Kimel, 'Neutrality', 478.
[15] Brownsword, 'Themes for the Twenty-First Century', p. 38.
[16] Atiyah, 'An Introduction', p. 35.
[17] Brownsword, 'Themes for the Twenty-First Century', p. 38.
[18] Collins, 'Regulating Contracts', p. 56.
[19] Thomas M. Scanlon, 'Promises and Contracts' in Benson (ed.), *The Theory of Contract Law*, pp. 86–117, at p. 86.

protective function of contract law to safeguard vulnerable parties, noting that assessments such as the reasonableness of a party's reliance on another's promise must be done with reference to the wider community's 'ideas of justice and reasonableness'.[20] On a similar note, Eisenberg comments that the legitimacy of contract law 'as an institution' depends on 'the basic structure of society being fair'.[21] Contract law tends to be associated with transactional justice (e.g. compensating a party for losses resulting from another party's breach of contract), rather than distributive justice (e.g. redistribution of resources considering structural inequalities within society).[22] Eisenberg resists the recognition of a redistributive role for contract law but concedes that the 'moral acceptability' of contract law depends on 'reflecting relevant social norms' about 'unfair advantage taking'.[23] Conversely, Kronman posits that contract law does have a distributive justice effect, and that the 'moral acceptability' of contractual rules depends on a framework that promotes the fair distribution of resources and risk between parties.[24]

In the vision of contract law promoted by this book, social norms are relevant for shaping the contractual framework, providing the values that guide the state's exercise of 'function one' within the social sphere of contract law, and the structure within which the state exercises 'function two' in the economic sphere. However, in this vision, distributive justice is a relevant aspect of the social sphere, particularly regarding factors such as risk allocation (e.g. when considering the fairness of exemption clauses in standard form contracts, where a stronger party seeks to allocate the risk of defective performance onto a party in a weaker bargaining position).

One example of an economic value that must be interpreted within the framework of social values is the idea of freedom of contract, both regarding party freedom (to choose your contracting party) and term freedom (to choose the terms of the agreement).[25] Freedom of contract is at the core of the non-interventionist sphere of contract law, embodies 'the proud spirit of individualism and *laissez-faire*',[26] and refers to both freedom to enter into contracts, and freedom from government interference with contracts.[27] Regarding this latter meaning, the state is expected to enforce agreements irrespective of whether the substance of the bargain is fair, as parties are believed to be in the best position to determine whether an agreement is in their best interest.[28] However, when looking at freedom of contract in the sense of freedom from state interference, we must acknowledge that this is subject to the first meaning

20 Atiyah, 'An Introduction', p. 36.

21 Melvin Eisenberg, 'The Theory of Contracts' in Benson (ed.), *The Theory of Contract Law*, pp. 206–64, at p. 256.

22 Atiyah, 'An Introduction', p. 7.

23 Eisenberg, 'The Theory of Contracts', p. 256.

24 Kronman, 'Contract Law and Distributive Justice', 472.

25 Brownsword, 'Themes for the Twenty-First Century', p. 53.

26 Kessler, 'Contracts of Adhesion', 630.

27 Wilson, 'Freedom of Contract', 172.

28 Herring, 'Vulnerable Adults', p. 226.

of freedom of contract (i.e. freedom to enter into contracts).[29] If A (a party in an unequal bargaining position compared with B) enters into a standard form contract presented on a 'take it or leave it' basis, to A's detriment, it is difficult to argue that A exercised freedom of contract in the sense of freedom to enter into contracts, and to defend freedom of contract as freedom from state interference.[30] We must move away from a narrow interpretation of freedom of contract understood as non-interference with contractual relations between parties, and rely instead on a broad interpretation of this concept that considers the context of transactions and the wider 'values underpinning the relations between the parties'.[31] Consequently, the starting point must be the social sphere of contract law, the values shaping this context, and the state's exercise of 'function one' in pursuit of these values. Such an approach is also compatible with Kessler's observation that the meaning of freedom of contract 'must change with the social importance of the type of contract and the degree of monopoly enjoyed by the author of a standard form contract'.[32]

One aspect of freedom of contract is the concept of party freedom, which refers to freedom to choose your contracting party and implies the freedom to refuse to deal with a prospective party.[33] This aspect of the economic sphere of contract law can only be exercised within the framework of values advanced by the social sphere of contract law and its connection with the equality framework under the Equality Act (EqA) 2010. The EqA prohibits traders who provide services to the public from discriminating, *inter alia*, against persons with disabilities in the provision of goods, facilities, or services.[34] Under the EqA, the definition of disability refers to a 'physical or mental impairment' which has 'a substantial and long-term adverse effect' on a person's 'ability to carry out normal day-to-day activities', and the impairment is treated as having a long-term effect if it has lasted, or is likely to last for at least 12 months, or for the rest of a person's life.[35] Discriminatory treatments by service providers include, among others, direct discrimination (e.g. treating consumers with disabilities less favourably than consumer without disabilities)[36] or discrimination arising from disability (e.g. treating customers unfavourably 'because of something arising in consequence' of the disability, where traders had actual or constructive knowledge of the disability, and cannot justify the treatment as 'a proportionate means' to achieve 'a legitimate aim').[37] The concept of discriminatory treatment also includes indirect discrimination (e.g. practices applied in the same way to all customers, which put persons with disabilities at a particular disadvantage compared to persons without disabilities, and are not a 'proportionate means to achieve a legitimate aim'),[38] or failure to comply with the duty to make adjustments (e.g. failure to take reasonable steps to

[29] Wilson, 'Freedom of Contract', 172. [30] Ibid. 174. [31] Herring, 'Vulnerable Adults', p. 227.
[32] Kessler, 'Contracts of Adhesion', 642.
[33] Brownsword, 'Themes for the Twenty-First Century', p. 57.
[34] Sections 28–31 of the EqA 2010. [35] Ibid. sections 6(1)(a) and (b), (6) and Schedule 1.
[36] Ibid. section 13. [37] Ibid. section 15. [38] Ibid. section 19.

avoid 'substantial' disadvantages caused to persons with disabilities, compared to persons without disabilities, by changing practices, the built environment, or providing auxiliary aids).[39] The EqA also prohibits traders from harassing persons with disabilities (e.g. 'unwanted conduct' regarding a customer's disability, with the 'purpose or effect' of violating their dignity, or 'creating an intimidating, hostile, degrading, humiliating, or offensive environment') and from victimising persons with disabilities (e.g. treating customers with disabilities in a detrimental manner because they brought proceedings under the EqA).[40]

Regrettably, the disability definition adopted by the EqA focuses on medical conditions[41] and their impact on individuals, rather than on social barriers to participation such as inaccessible environments or information.[42] Further provisions that narrow the reach of the EqA include the expectations on traders to make reasonable adjustments where their practices put persons with disabilities at a 'substantial disadvantage' (rather than merely at a 'disadvantage'), with similar references to 'substantial disadvantages' being made regarding the absence of auxiliary aids.[43] This reflects a focus on the economic costs of inclusion, rather than on the wider social costs of exclusion.[44]

Additional challenges are associated with EqA provisions concerning the advancement of equality, such as the 'public sector equality duty' (PSED).[45] While before the EqA, the 'disability equality duty' (DED) (introduced in 2005 as an amendment to the Disability Discrimination Act 1995) required public authorities to 'have due regard' to 'the need to promote positive attitudes' towards persons with disabilities, and 'encourage participation' of persons with disabilities in public life,[46] the PSED is more limited. The EqA presents a more confined duty requiring public authorities to 'have due regard' to, *inter alia*, the need to 'advance equality of opportunity' and 'foster good relations' between persons with and without disabilities.[47] The Government's response to the House of Lord Select Committee report on the impact of the EqA on persons with disabilities concluded that it has 'achieved more by initiating conversations' between persons with disabilities and other relevant stakeholders (including in public and private sectors) than the 'blunt instrument of regulation' and 'regulation alone' will not change 'hearts and minds'.[48] Nevertheless,

39 Ibid. sections 20 and 21 and Schedule 2. 40 Ibid. sections 26 and 27. 41 Ibid. section 6(1).

42 Anna Lawson, 'Disability and Employment in the Equality Act 2010: Opportunities Seized, Lost and Generated' (2011) 40(4) *Industrial Law Journal* 359–83.

43 Sections 20(3) and (5) of the EqA 2010.

44 Interview with Guido Gybels, RNID, 17 August 2009 in Eliza Varney, *Disability and Information Technology* (Cambridge: Cambridge University Press, 2013).

45 Sections 149 et. seq. of the EqA 2010.

46 Section 49A of the Disability Discrimination Act 1995 (c. 50), as amended by section 3 of the Disability Discrimination Act 2005 (c 13).

47 Sections 149 of the EqA 2010.

48 Government Response to the Select Committee Report on the Equality Act 2010's Impact on Disabled People, 7 July 2016, preamble, [2], [3].

regulation remains an important element of the overall framework for pursuing equality in society, including in the contractual realm, especially if rooted in the social sphere of contract law and shaped by the involvement in policy-making of persons with disabilities and DDPOs.

In addition to party freedom, the concept of freedom of contract also includes the notion of term freedom, referring to the liberty of contracting parties to choose the terms of their bargain, without state interference.[49] Just as we have seen in the case of party freedom, the exercise of term freedom within the economic sphere of contract law must be conducted within a framework of values set under the social sphere of the contractual realm. For example, if a contract comprises terms that discriminate against individuals on grounds of disability, these terms are unenforceable.[50] Limitations on term freedom may also be permitted when there are 'good reasons' for doing so, including where 'more important rights are at stake', such as in the case of terms that undermine the public interest.[51] We must resist a narrow understanding of term freedom which would view a grossly asymmetrical transaction as merely a manifestation of the freedom of contracting parties to make unwise decisions, without looking at the context of the transaction that led a party to enter into such an imbalanced contract. Section 4.2 examines regulatory measures designed to ensure that contract terms are fair, that consumers have sufficient time and information to enter into contracts away from business premises, that they are not subjected to unfair commercial practices, and that goods sold in the course of a business are of satisfactory quality. The analysis questions whether these provisions are shaped with reference to both social and economic justifications. Then, Section 4.3 reflects on the issue of vulnerability in B2C transactions, calling for an approach based on a contextual understanding of consumer vulnerability.

4.2 Challenging an Approach Focused on Economic Values, with Insufficient Emphasis on the Social Values of Consumer Protection

Before assessing in more detail the effectiveness of selected regulatory provisions in English law for protecting citizenship interests in B2C transactions, we must note the implications for domestic consumer contract law caused by the UK's decision to exit from the European Union (EU). Many provisions discussed in this chapter are based on Directives that the UK had to implement during its membership of the EU.[52] Particular reference is made to Directive

[49] Brownsword, 'Themes for the Twenty-First Century', p. 50. [50] Section 142 of the EqA 2010.

[51] Brownsword, 'Themes for the Twenty-First Century', p. 50.

[52] Article 288 of the Treaty on the Functioning of the European Union (TFEU) (Consolidated Version) [2010] OJ 2010 No. C83, 30 March 2010, pp. 1–388. The United Kingdom was a member of the European Union for 47 years, between 1973 and 2020. See European Communities Act 1972 (c. 68) (repealed) and European Union (Withdrawal Agreement) Act 2020 (c. 1).

93/13/EEC[53] (implemented first by SI 1994 No. 3159,[54] then by SI 1999 No. 2083,[55] and then by the CRA 2015),[56] Directive 1999/44/EC[57] (implemented first by amendments to the Sale of Goods Act (SGA) 1979[58] and reimplemented by the CRA), Directive 2011/83/EU[59] (implemented by Consumer Contracts (Information, Cancellation and Additional Charges) Regulations (CCRs) SI 2013 No. 3134[60] and by specific provisions of the CRA),[61] and Directive 2005/29/EC[62] (implemented by the Consumer Protection from Unfair Trading Regulations (CPUTRs) SI 2008 No. 1277, as amended by SI 2014 No. 870,[63] which are revoked and replaced by the Digital Markets, Competition and Consumers Act (DMCCA) 2024).[64]

Following the result of a referendum held on the 23rd of June 2016, the UK left the EU on the 31st of January 2020[65] (a process known as Brexit). To ensure legal certainty and continuity, the European Union (Withdrawal) Act (EUWA) 2018 made provisions to incorporate into domestic law the EU law applicable in the UK up to the end of the Brexit transition period, set for the 31st of December 2020.[66] This new body of domestic law became known as 'retained EU law' (REUL) and included EU-derived domestic legislation

[53] Council Directive 93/13/EEC of 5 April 1993 on unfair terms in consumer contracts (Unfair Terms Directive), OJ 1993 No. L95, 21 April 1993, pp. 29–34. This directive was amended by Directive 2011/83/EU of the European Parliament and of the Council of 25 October 2011 on consumer rights, OJ 2011 No. L304, 22 November 2011, pp. 64–88 and by Directive (EU) 2019/2161 of the European Parliament and of the Council of 27 November 2019 as regards the better enforcement and modernisation of Union consumer protection rules, OJ 2019 No. L328, 18 December 2019, pp. 7–28.

[54] The Unfair Terms in Consumer Contracts Regulations 1994 (SI 1994 No. 3159) (revoked by Regulation 2 of SI 1999 No. 2083).

[55] The Unfair Terms in Consumer Contracts Regulations 1999 (SI 1999 No. 2083) (revoked by Schedule 4(34) of the CRA 2015).

[56] Part 2 (Unfair terms) of the CRA 2015.

[57] Directive 1999/44/EC of the European Parliament and of the Council of 25 May 1999 on certain aspects of the sale of consumer goods and associated guarantees, OJ 1999 No. L171, 7 July 1999, pp. 12–16, amended by Directive 2011/83/EU and repealed by Directive 2019/2161.

[58] Sale of Goods Act (SGA) 1979 (c. 54).

[59] Directive 2011/83/EU, amended by Directive 2019/2161.

[60] SI 2013 No. 3134 (CCRs).

[61] Sections 28–29, 11(4) and (5), 12, 36(3) and (4), 37, and 50(3) and (4) of the CRA 2015.

[62] Directive 2005/29/EC of the European Parliament and of the Council of 11 May 2005 concerning unfair business-to-consumer commercial practices in the internal market (Unfair Commercial Practices Directive) OJ 2005 No. L149, 11 June 2005, pp. 22–39, amended by Directive 2019/2161.

[63] SI 2008 No. 1277 (CPUTRs), as amended by SI 2014 No. 870.

[64] The CPUTRs are revoked by the DMCCA 2024, which received royal assent on the 24th of May 2024, and which migrates an amended version of the CPUTRs provisions within part 4 of the DMCCA (consumer rights and disputes). See section 251(1) (consequential amendments) of the DMCCA 2024. Many of the DMCCA provisions are expected to come into force in the autumn of 2024. See sections 252 and 339 of the DMCCA 2024.

[65] European Union (Notification of Withdrawal) Act 2017 (c. 9); European Union (Withdrawal) Act (EUWA) 2018 (c. 16); European Union (Withdrawal Agreement) Act (WAA) 2020 (c. 1).

[66] Section 1A of the EUWA 2018, as inserted by section 1 of the WAA 2020.

(e.g. primary or secondary domestic legislation incorporating EU directives), direct EU legislation (e.g. EU regulations, which were directly applicable during the UK's membership of the EU, becoming part of domestic law without the need for implementing measures)[67] and, among others, directly effective EU rights.[68] Moreover, retained general principles of EU law (e.g. equality and non-discrimination), and retained case law of the Court of Justice of the European Union (CJEU) were to assist with interpretating the REUL.[69] Under this approach, CJEU decisions adopted before the end of the transition period, and the general principles of EU law, remained binding on UK laws for interpretating REUL, although the Supreme Court and the Court of Appeal could depart from these sources.[70] Conversely, CJEU cases decided after the end of the transition period, and EU law coming into force after that period (e.g. regulations or directives which had to be implemented after the end of the transition period) had no binding force in UK law.[71] This includes Directive 2019/2161 on the better enforcement and modernisation of EU consumer protection rules, which had to be implemented by the 28th of November 2021.[72] Regarding the status of CJEU decisions adopted after the end of transition period, the EUWA 2018 provided that the domestic courts should consider such decisions where appropriate.[73]

The Retained EU Law (Revocation and Reform) Act (REULA) 2023 revoked by the end of the 31st of December 2023 legislation expressly identified in Schedule 1 of the Act (about 600 pieces of REUL, largely obsolete), with the remaining REUL (known after the end of 2023 as 'assimilated EU law') still in force (unless amended, repealed or replaced by the UK Government), but stripped off associated EU law features such as the supremacy of EU law over national law.[74] The REULA also repealed, with effect from the 31st of December 2023, directly effective retained EU rights,[75] without, however, providing a list of the specific rights revoked.[76] The REULA also abolished the principle of supremacy of EU law over national law[77] (a principle developed by the CJEU to prioritise EU law in the event of conflict with domestic provisions),[78] moving away from the stance initially adopted under EUWA, which preserved this principle for national provisions adopted before the end of the transition period, confirming the abolition of this principle for all domestic legislation, irrespective of when

[67] Sections 2 and 3 of the EUWA 2018. See Article 288 of the TFEU.
[68] Section 4 of the EUWA 2018. [69] Ibid. section 6. [70] Ibid. sections 6(3) and (4).
[71] Ibid. section 6(1)(a). [72] Article 7(1) of Directive 2019/2161.
[73] Sections 6(1)(a) and (2) of the EUWA 2018.
[74] Sections 1, 3 and 5, and Schedule 1 of the Retained EU Law (Revocation and Reform) Act (REULA) 2023 (c. 28).
[75] Ibid. section 2, which repealed section 4 of the EUWA 2018.
[76] David Gauke, Christopher Charlton, and Jonathan Pratt, 'Retained EU Law Act Receives Royal Assent', Macfarlanes, 13 July 2023.
[77] Section 3 of the REULA 2023.
[78] See, for example, Case 6/64, *Costa* v. *ENEL* [1964] ECR 585.

it was adopted.[79] Moreover, REULA also abolished in UK law the general principles of EU law, which had previously been preserved into domestic law by the EUWA to assist with the interpretation of REUL.[80] These general principles had been developed by the CJEU as an aid in interpreting EU law, and include the principles of legal certainty,[81] equality[82] and the protection of fundamental rights.[83] Nevertheless, there is 'scope for dispute as to whether some of these principles otherwise form part of English domestic law'.[84]

Regarding the interpretation of REUL by UK courts, EUWA initially made provisions for the domestic courts to be bound by CJEU decisions adopted before the end of the transition period, unless the Court of Appeal or the Supreme Court considered it right to depart from the CJEU jurisprudence.[85] By contrast, REULA abolishes the principle of supremacy of EU law in the UK[86] and seeks to provide UK courts with increased freedom to depart from retained EU case law.[87] Under the REULA, when assessing whether to depart from retained EU case law, courts such as the Court of Appeal or the Supreme Court must consider that 'decisions of a foreign court are not (unless otherwise provided) binding'.[88] They must also consider relevant changes of circumstances affecting retained EU case law, and 'the extent to which' this case law 'restricts the proper development of domestic law'.[89] The REULA also provides mechanisms for lower courts to refer points of law to the higher courts for rulings on whether the lower courts should follow retained EU case law.[90] These measures could be seen as providing domestic courts with an encouragement to depart from EU-derived case law, raising questions about the status of this body of case law, and providing incentives 'to litigate about issues that had previously been considered settled'.[91] The REULA also confers UK ministers and devolved authorities the power to restate, revoke, replace, and update secondary assimilated EU law.[92] These provisions have been seen as a source of concern, as they give ministers wide ranging powers with limited guidance and limited Parliamentary scrutiny.[93]

[79] Section 3 of the REULA 2023, which amended section 5 of the EUWA 2018.

[80] Ibid. section 4 and section 6 of the EUWA 2018.

[81] See, for example, Case 84/78, *Tomadini* v. *Amministrazione delle finanze dello Stato* [1979] ECR 1801.

[82] See, for example, Case 117/76, *Ruckdeschel & Co* v. *Hauptzollamt Hamburg-St. Annen* [1977] ECR 1753.

[83] See Explanatory Notes to the REULA 2023, [28].

[84] Gauke, Charlton and Pratt, 'Retained EU Law'.

[85] Section 6 of the EUWA 2018.

[86] Section 3 of the REULA 2023.

[87] Ibid. section 6 (at the time of writing, this provision was not yet in force).

[88] Section 6(5)(a) of the EUWA 2018 as amended by section 6 of the REULA 2023 (amendment pending).

[89] Sections 6(5)(b) and (c) of the EUWA 2018 as amended by section 6 of the REULA 2023 (amendment pending).

[90] Section 6A of the EUWA 2018 as inserted by section 6 of the REULA 2023 (not yet in force).

[91] Gauke, Charlton and Pratt, 'Retained EU Law'.

[92] Sections 11–14 of the REULA 2023.

[93] Gauke, Charlton and Pratt, 'Retained EU Law'.

4.2.1 Regulating Unfair Contract Terms

The key provisions in English contract law regulating unfair terms in consumer transactions are found in part 2 of the CRA 2015, which implements Directive 93/13/EEC.[94] Initially, due to shortage of parliamentary time,[95] this Directive was implemented by regulations (firstly by SI 1994 No. 3159,[96] and then by SI 1999 No. 2083)[97] rather than by amending UCTA 1977, resulting in two complex and overlapping regimes for regulating unfair terms.[98] While the application of SI 1999 No. 2083 was restricted to terms that had not been individually negotiated,[99] UCTA applied to both individually negotiated and non-negotiated terms.[100] Conversely, while SI 1999 No. 2083 applied to a wide range of provisions, UCTA focused generally on exemption clauses, despite the reference in the title of this Act to unfair contract 'terms'.[101]

The CRA brings together under one instrument the provisions regulating unfair terms in consumer contracts, revoking SI 1999 No. 2083,[102] and removing the consumer-related provisions from UCTA,[103] which continues to apply, *inter alia*, to contracts between business transactors.[104] The CRA applies to consumer contracts,[105] which are contracts between a consumer (i.e. 'an individual acting for purposes that are wholly or mainly outside' their 'trade, business, craft or profession')[106] and a trader (i.e. 'a person acting for purposes relating to' their 'trade, business, craft or profession').[107] This is a broad definition although it does not include, among others, contracts of employment.[108] In addition to its application to consumer contracts, the CRA extends the scope of protection previously provided under SI 1994 No. 3159 and SI 1999 No. 2083, as it also applies to consumer notices.[109] These refer to communications such as announcements (whether or not in writing), which concern rights or obligations in B2C relations, or the traders' attempt to exempt their liability to consumers.[110]

[94] Directive 93/13/EEC, as amended by Directive 2011/83/EU and by Directive 2019/2161.

[95] Hugh Beale, 'Legislative Control of Fairness: The Directive on Unfair Terms in Consumer Contracts', in Beatson and Friedman (eds.), 'Good Faith and Fault in Contract Law', pp. 231–61, at p. 237.

[96] The Unfair Terms in Consumer Contracts Regulations 1994 (SI 1994 No. 3159) (revoked by Regulation 2 of SI 1999 No. 2083).

[97] The Unfair Terms in Consumer Contracts Regulations 1999 (SI 1999 No. 2083) (revoked by Schedule 4(34) of the CRA 2015).

[98] The Law Commission and the Scottish Law Commission, 'Unfair Terms in Contracts', Law Com No. 292, Cm 6464, February 2005, 1.4 and 2.4(2).

[99] Regulation 5(1) of SI 1999 No. 2083.

[100] Sections 2, 3, 6 and 13 of the UCTA 1977. See Whittaker, 'Consumer Contracts', 40-227.

[101] See Beale, 'Legislative Control of Fairness', p. 233. [102] Schedule 4(34) of the CRA 2015.

[103] Ibid. Schedules 4(2)–(27)

[104] See sections 2(4), 3(3) and 6(5) of the UCTA 1977. See Whittaker, 'Consumer Contracts', 40-226 and 40-235.

[105] Section 61(1) of the CRA 2015. [106] Ibid. sections 2(3) and 76(2).

[107] Ibid. sections 2(1) and 76(2). [108] Ibid. section 61(2). [109] Ibid. sections 61(4) and (7).

[110] Ibid. sections 61(7) and (8). See Explanatory Notes to the CRA 2015, [289].

Consumer contract terms and notices covered by the CRA must be fair, must not seek to exempt liability for death or personal injury resulting from negligence, and if presented in writing, they must be transparent.[111] A consumer contract term is unfair if 'contrary to the requirement of good faith', the term 'causes a significant imbalance' in the parties' contractual rights and obligations to the consumer's detriment, and this assessment must be made considering the nature of the contractual subject matter, 'all the circumstances existing' when the parties agreed the term, all other terms in that contract, and other contracts on which the relevant contract term depends.[112] Similar provisions are included in the CRA for evaluating the fairness of consumer notices.[113] For assessing the transparency of written terms in consumer contracts and consumer notices, the courts must consider whether the term is 'expressed in plain and intelligible language' and is 'legible'.[114]

The inclusion of consumer notices in part 2 of the CRA[115] goes beyond the requirements of Directive 93/13/EEC, which focuses only on contract terms.[116] However, despite this positive development, many challenges remain. Firstly, the CRA does not extend to consumer notices the requirement mandated in section 71, which expects courts to consider the fairness of contract terms, even where the issue of fairness was not raised by either party in the proceedings.[117] As Whittaker notes, this may be due to the fact that this requirement is rooted in the CJEU case law related to Directive 93/13/EEC, applicable only to consumer contract terms.[118] The CJEU has justified the exercise of this duty on courts to consider the fairness of contract terms with reference to 'public interest' rationales for adopting provisions that compensate for imbalances of power between consumers and traders.[119] An approach to consumer contract law rooted in the 'public interest' would reflect the vision presented in this book, where social values (including the citizenship values of equality, autonomy and human dignity)[120] frame the interpretation of economic values. Section 71 of the CRA does not go as far as recognising explicitly the social dimension of consumer protection. Moreover, when exercising the duty to consider the fairness of contract terms, courts are only expected to consider the fairness of terms in consumer contracts if they have 'sufficient legal and factual material' to enable such fairness-based assessment,[121] and if so, they are expected to focus only on the fairness of terms which are the subject of the proceedings, rather than the fairness of the whole contract between the parties.[122]

111 Sections 62, 65 and 68 of the CRA 2015. 112 Ibid. sections 62(4) and (5).
113 Ibid. sections 62(6) and (7). 114 Ibid. sections 68(1) and (2).
115 See, for example, sections 62(2), (6) and (7), 65 and 68(1) and (2) of the CRA 2015.
116 Article 1 of Directive 93/13/EEC. 117 Sections 71(1) and (2) of the CRA 2015.
118 Whittaker, 'Consumer Contracts', 40-258. See Article 1 of Directive 93/13/EEC.
119 Case C-168/05, *Mostaza Claro* v. *Centro Móvil Milenium* [2006] ECR I-10421. See Explanatory Notes to the CRA 2015, [334].
120 Feintuck, 'The Public Interest in Regulation'. 121 Section 71(3) of the CRA 2015.
122 Explanatory Notes to the CRA 2015, [334].

A second challenge concerns the consequences for not complying with the requirements presented under part 2 of the CRA, which differ, depending on whether the challenged term or notice seeks to exempt liability for death or personal injury, or is unfair, or is not transparent. Contract terms or notices that seek to exclude or restrict liability for death or personal injury resulting from negligence are generally void.[123] Unfair contract terms or notices are not binding on consumers[124] (even though the rest of the contract continues to apply 'in every other respect', if practicable),[125] although consumers may continue to rely on any unfair contract terms or notices if they choose to do so.[126] For non-transparent written contract terms or notices,[127] there is no equivalent provision to state that these are not binding on consumers,[128] but if such contract terms or notices could give rise to different interpretations, the meaning most favourable to consumers should prevail.[129] A stronger degree of protection would have been provided by the inclusion of a provision stating that non-transparent contract terms or notices are not binding on consumers.

A third challenge is associated with the fairness test under section 62 of the CRA. According to section 62(4), a term in a consumer contract can be regarded as unfair if 'contrary to the requirement of good faith, it causes a significant imbalance in the parties' rights and obligations under the contract', to the consumer's detriment.[130] Section 62(5) explains that when determining whether a contract term is fair, courts must consider 'the nature' of the contractual subject matter[131] (e.g. if the goods are second hand),[132] and 'all the circumstances existing' when the parties agreed the terms[133] (e.g. consumers' knowledge and experience),[134] 'all other' terms under that contract[135] (e.g. if traders' duties go beyond what is required under the general law)[136] and 'any other contracts' on which the term examined depends.[137] Similar provisions are presented for assessing the fairness of consumer notices under sections 62(6) and (7).[138] The reference to 'significant' imbalances in the parties' rights and obligations under sections 62(4) and (6) places a high threshold for consumers.[139] A preferable approach would have been to refer to 'significant imbalance' and 'incompatibility with good faith' as alternative, rather than cumulative factors for assessing unfairness,[140] as provided in an earlier draft of Directive 93/13/EEC.[141]

[123] Section 65(1), subject to section 66 of the CRA 2015. [124] Ibid. sections 62(1) and (2).
[125] Ibid. section 67. [126] Ibid. section 62(3). [127] Ibid. section 68.
[128] See Whittaker, 'Consumer Contracts', 40-227, comparing sections 68 and 62 of the CRA 2015.
[129] Section 69 of the CRA 2015. [130] Ibid. section 62(4). [131] Ibid. section 62(5)(a).
[132] Andrew Burrows (ed.), *Principles of the English Law of Obligations* (Oxford: Oxford University Press, 2015), 1.122.
[133] Section 62(5)(b) of the CRA 2015.
[134] *Green* v. *Petfre (Gibraltar) Ltd (t/a Betfred)* [2021] EWHC 842 (QB), [181].
[135] Section 62(5)(b) of the CRA 2015.
[136] Burrows, 'Principles of the English Law of Obligations', 1.222.
[137] Section 62(5)(b) of the CRA 2015. [138] Ibid. sections 62(6) and (7).
[139] Burrows, 'Principles of the English Law of Obligations', 1.222.
[140] Beale, 'Legislative Control of Fairness', p. 243.
[141] Article 2 in the Commission Proposal for a Council Directive on Unfair Terms in Consumer Contracts, COM(90) 322 fin. See Beale, 'Legislative Control of Fairness', p. 243.

Before discussing in more detail the limitations of the fairness test, we must stress the merits of the reference to 'good faith' as part of the fairness test,[142] clarified under recital 16 of Directive 93/13/EEC to refer to 'fair and equitable dealings', where the trader considers the consumer's legitimate interests.[143] With reference to the preceding provisions under SI 1994 No. 3159 (replaced first by SI 1999 No. 2083 and then by the CRA), in a statement which 'remain[s] good law',[144] Lord Bingham noted in *Director General of Fair Trading* v. *First National Bank* (*Director General of Fair Trading*) that the good faith requirement (in the context of assessing the fairness of terms in consumer-trader agreements) refers to 'fair and open dealings'.[145] Openness requires terms to be 'expressed fully, clearly, and legibly', with 'no concealed pitfalls and traps' and with 'appropriate prominence' given to any terms that may disadvantage the consumer.[146] Furthermore, the requirement of fair dealings expects traders not to take advantage, 'whether deliberately or unconsciously', of factors such as the customer's need, inexperience, lack of familiarity with the contractual subject matter, or 'weak bargaining position'.[147] By referring to both the openness and fairness of contract terms in the assessment of good faith, Lord Bingham considered not only concerns for procedural fairness (associated with the way in which terms are presented to the consumers), but also substantive fairness (regarding the substance of the bargain).[148] A similar approach is also reflected in Lord Steyn's judgement in this case, where he rejects 'any purely procedural or even predominantly procedural interpretation of the requirement of good faith'.[149]

This decision could have been strengthened by the adoption of an inclusive vision of the 'representative consumer' as being a vulnerable consumer,[150] reflective of the imbalance of power faced by individuals when dealing with traders. Instead, the House of Lords in *Director General of Fair Trading* relied on a perception of the consumer as being 'relatively active', rather than vulnerable,[151] influenced by the CJEU's vision of the 'average consumer' as someone who is 'reasonably well informed, reasonably observant and circumspect'.[152] This is an unrealistic vision of individuals which overlooks the social dimension of contract law, and the need to understand vulnerability as being based on the context of the transaction. When considering the 'representative consumer', we must take into account not only economic values and a perception of individuals as economic actors but also social values, including a recognition

142 Sections 62(4) and (6) of the CRA 2015. 143 Recital 16 of Directive 93/13/EEC.
144 *Longley* v. *PPB Entertainment Ltd* [2022] EWHC 977 (QB), [102.3].
145 *Director General of Fair Trading* v. *First National Bank Plc* [2001] UKHL 52, [17] (Lord Bingham).
146 Ibid. 147 Ibid. 148 Burrows, 'Principles of the English Law of Obligations', 1.222.
149 *Director General of Fair Trading* v. *First National Bank Plc* [2001] UKHL 52, [36] (Lord Steyn). See Brownsword, 'Themes for the Twenty-First Century', p. 186.
150 Brownsword, 'Themes for the Twenty-First Century', p. 186. 151 Ibid.
152 Case C-210/96, *Gut Springenheide and Tusky* v. *Oberkreisdirektor des Kreises Steinfurt* [1998] ECR I-3599, [38].

of our universal vulnerability[153] and the need to protect autonomy and human dignity. Consequently, good faith-based assessments of 'fair and open' dealings should interpret the 'openness' requirement broadly, in light of social values, to include accessibility. Moreover, as Herring notes, when considering the fairness of terms, courts should 'recall that a wide range of consumers' are dealing with traders and 'a term should be regarded as unfair, even if it would have been unfair to a section of consumers (e.g. more vulnerable consumers)'.[154] Such an approach would take into account human diversity and the wide range of abilities and accessibility needs encountered among consumers.

In the CJEU decision in *Aziz* v. *Caixa*, referred to by the Supreme Court in *Parking Eye* v. *Beavis*, the CJEU noted that when making a good faith assessment, courts must consider whether the trader 'dealing fairly and equitably with the consumer, could reasonably assume that the consumer would have agreed to such terms in individual negotiations'.[155] A stronger degree of protection would have been provided to consumers if such an assessment considered whether consumers 'would have agreed to such terms in individual negotiations',[156] had these terms been presented in a manner appropriate to their circumstances, and in an accessible format. Such an approach would consider wider social values, including human dignity, and would place greater weight on the context of the transaction.

Regarding the inclusion of vulnerability-based considerations, when assessing the fairness of contract terms, the reference in section 62(5) of the CRA to 'all the circumstances existing when the term was agreed',[157] could include references to consumer vulnerability. However, this is not stated explicitly in this provision. Regrettably, the protection of vulnerable consumers in the context of unfair terms is hidden between the lines, rather than made unequivocal, and this sends the problematic message that when it comes to assessing the fairness of terms in consumer contracts and notices, vulnerable consumers are merely an afterthought.

A fourth challenge concerns the provisions under section 63 and Schedule 2 of the CRA regarding a list of terms that 'may be' considered to be unfair, which has been presented to assist courts when applying the fairness test under section 62.[158] On a positive note, this is a 'non-exhaustive' list,[159] which means that terms not included in Schedule 2 could still be found to be unfair.[160] Conversely, this is merely an indicative list and the included terms are not automatically considered to be unfair.[161] As noted by Beale, the adoption of a 'grey list' rather than a 'black list' is problematic, as it places on consumers the

153 Herring, 'Vulnerable Adults', p. 232. 154 Ibid. p. 255.

155 Case C-415/11, *Aziz* v. *Caixa d'Estalvis de Catalunya*, Judgment of 14 March 2013, not reported, [69]; *Parking Eye Ltd* v. *Beavis* [2015] UKSC 67, [105].

156 Herring, 'Vulnerable Adults', p. 255. 157 Section 62(5)(b) of the CRA 2015.

158 Ibid. sections 62 and 63 and Schedule 2. See Explanatory Notes to the CRA 2015, [296], [299].

159 Section 63(1) of the CRA 2015. 160 Explanatory Notes to the CRA 2015, [296].

161 Section 63(1). See Explanatory Notes to the CRA 2015, [299].

burden of proving the unfairness of the term challenged.[162] This illustrates an approach that seeks to balance the interests of traders and consumers, rather than prioritise consumer interests, as parties in a vulnerable position due to power imbalances to their detriment.

The list of 'consumer contract terms which may be regarded as unfair' is included in part 1 of Schedule 2, while part 2 modifies this list to exclude certain types of terms such as some terms regarding financial services. Examples comprised in part 1 of Schedule 2 as terms that 'may be regarded as unfair', include terms that have the 'object or effect of inappropriately excluding or limiting' the consumer's legal rights regarding the trader's inadequate performance.[163] Further examples include terms with the 'object or effect' of enabling traders to 'terminate a contract of indeterminate duration without reasonable notice', unless there are 'serious grounds' for doing so, or of 'automatically extending a contract of fixed duration where the consumer does not indicate otherwise', in a context in which 'the deadline for the consumer to express preference not to extend' is 'unreasonably early'.[164] Despite the merits of these provisions in seeking to ensure the fairness of contract terms, Herring is justified in his observation that unfairness is perceived in the abstract and that these provisions fail to respond to 'any specific vulnerability of consumers'.[165] A stronger degree of protection would be provided if fairness-based assessments considered the context of the transaction, assessed in light of economic and social values. For example, Schedule 2(10) includes as an indicative term that may be regarded as unfair, a term with the 'object or effect of irrevocably binding the consumer to terms with which the consumer has had no real opportunity of becoming acquainted' prior to concluding the contract.[166] A fairness-based assessment should include considerations of vulnerabilities due to limited time or inaccessible information.

A fifth challenge concerns the fact that rather than prioritising consumer interests over the interests of traders, the CRA aims to provide a 'balance' between these interests. On the one hand, the Act states that unfair contract terms and notices are not binding on consumers,[167] while on the other hand, it excludes from the application of the fairness test terms concerning the main subject matter of the contract, or the appropriateness of the contract price compared with the value of the goods supplied.[168] This is referred to as the 'core exemption', because it covers essential features of the agreement.[169] Section 64 excludes such terms from the fairness test under section 62 only if these terms are 'transparent' and 'prominent'.[170] For a term to be transparent, it must be

[162] Beale, 'Legislative Control of Fairness', p. 240. [163] Schedule 2(2) of the CRA 2015.
[164] Ibid. Schedules 2(8) and (9). [165] Herring, 'Vulnerable Adults', pp. 253–55.
[166] Schedule 2(1) of the CRA 2015. [167] Ibid. sections 62(1) and (2).
[168] Ibid. sections 64(1)(a) and (b).
[169] Competition and Markets Authority, 'Unfair Contract Terms Explained', CMA37(a), 31 July 2015, 15.
[170] Section 64(2) of the CRA 2015.

'expressed in plain and intelligible language' and, 'in the case of a written term', it must be 'legible'.[171] For a term to be prominent, it must be 'brought to the consumer's attention in such a way that an average consumer would be aware of the term', with the average consumer being defined as someone who is 'reasonably well-informed, observant and circumspect'.[172]

A prevalent value in setting this 'balanced' approach is to provide traders with certainty on the circumstances when contract terms would be assessed for fairness.[173] Such a concern for certainty is also reflected in the Supreme Court decision in *Office of Fair Trading* v. *Abbey National* (with reference to SI 1999 No. 2083 which preceded the CRA), where the court took the view that the 'price' referred to under the core exemptions cannot be split into 'headline price' and 'other prices', and considered charges for unauthorised overdrafts to be part of the price.[174] Before the adoption of the CRA, the Government suggested that 'in many cases it is not possible to distinguish the price payable and future charges', and that rather than relying on a system which would seek to make such a distinction, it is preferable to rely on a framework that only exempts price-related terms if they are transparent and prominent.[175] Provisions such as hidden charges in B2C transactions would still be subject to a fairness test.[176] However, the core exemption should be interpreted narrowly[177] because, as indicated by Lord Steyn in *Director General of Fair Trading*, without a 'restrictive interpretation', the regulatory framework risks being 'frustrated by endless formalistic arguments' whether provisions fall within the fairness test, or whether they fall within the exemption to this test.[178] Consequently, while terms cannot be challenged for the fairness of the 'price/quality ratio', other price-related aspects could fall within the scope of the fairness test,[179] such as the timing of the payment.[180] In a consultation that preceded the CRA, the Office of Fair Trading (OFT) (replaced by the Competition and Markets Authority), referred to their call for a narrow interpretation of the core exemption as merely their second choice for responding to challenges associated with the price/subject matter exception to the fairness test.[181] Their

171 Ibid. section 64(3). See Kathy Conklin, Richard Hyde and Fabio Parente, 'Assessing Plain and Intelligible Language in the Consumer Rights Act: A Role for Reading Scores?' (2019) 39(3) *Legal Studies* 378–97.

172 Sections 64(4) and (5) of the CRA 2015

173 Explanatory Notes to the CRA 2015, [309].

174 *Office of Fair Trading* v. *Abbey National Plc* [2009] UKSC 6 (hereafter *OFT* v. *Abbey National*). See Herring, 'Vulnerable Adults', p. 254.

175 HC Deb 6 March 2014, col 494.

176 Ibid. Burrows, 'Principles of the English Law of Obligations', 1.222.

177 Office of Fair Trading, 'Response to the Law Commission Issues Paper: Unfair Terms in Consumer Contracts', OFT1465, November 2012, 2.13.

178 *Director General of Fair Trading* v. *First National Bank Plc* [2001] UKHL 52, [34] (Lord Steyn).

179 *OFT* v. *Abbey National* [2009] UKSC 6, [41]. See Burrows, 'Principles of the English Law of Obligations', 1.222.

180 Explanatory Notes to the CRA 2015, [310], [311]. See Herring, 'Vulnerable Adults', p. 254.

181 OFT, 'Unfair Terms in Consumer Contracts', 2.13.

first choice was 'the outright removal of the core exemption as a whole'.[182] Such an approach would have achieved 'greater legislative simplicity',[183] ensuring an increased level of protection for consumer interests, bringing more contract terms within the scope of the fairness test. Regrettably, the CRA kept the core exemptions within the regulatory framework on unfair terms.[184]

Some of the justifications for the core exemptions are based on arguments for protecting freedom and sanctity of contracts.[185] Where terms about the contractual subject matter and price are transparent and prominent, consumers exercise their freedom of contract when choosing to enter into contracts with traders under these terms, because 'in a free market economy', contracting parties are 'in theory, able to shape the principal obligations'.[186] Moreover, parties should be held to their freely made agreements and not expect the courts to question the fairness of the exchange or to apply statutory provisions on consumer protection 'as a mechanism for quality/price control'.[187] As discussed earlier in this chapter, protecting freedom and sanctity of contract is one of the state functions exercised within the economic sphere of contract law ('function two'). However, this function should be understood as being secondary to the role of the state in protecting wider social values, including human dignity ('function one'). Consequently, concerns for protecting economic values embodied in the concepts of freedom and sanctity of contract should be interpreted in light of wider social values, considering the context of the transaction. This is particularly relevant where the transaction is based on standard form contracts drafted by traders to their own advantage,[188] where consumers would find it hard to look for alternative contracts because the trader's competitors use similar provisions.[189] Such contracts have been referred to as 'contracts of adhesion' because consumers (as the weaker parties) merely submit (or 'adhere') to the terms presented by traders (as the dominant parties).[190]

Most of the contracts that are important for everyday life are based on standard form contracts, including contracts for financial products or utilities.[191] As Burgess notes, 'adhesion contract' is 'co-terminus with consumer contract'.[192] Standard form contracts often include unfair terms weighted in favour of traders, who are in a stronger bargaining position compared with consumers.[193] Atiyah observes that traders have 'every advantage' over consumers, including 'resources, legal advice, being able to litigate if it came to that, without having to worry unduly about costs', and knowledge that consumers need their services.[194] Terms in these contracts have not just economic implications, but also social consequences (e.g. 'over-indebtedness' caused by long-term financial

[182] Ibid. 2.8. [183] Ibid. [184] Section 64 of the CRA 2015.
[185] *Director General of Fair Trading* v. *First National Bank Plc* [2001] UKHL 52, [12].
[186] OFT, 'Unfair Terms in Consumer Contracts', 2.15.
[187] Burrows, 'Principles of the English Law of Obligations', 1.222.
[188] Atiyah, 'An Introduction', p. 7. [189] Kessler, 'Contracts of Adhesion', 623. [190] Ibid.
[191] Fejős, 'Social Justice', 70. [192] Burgess, 'Consumer Adhesion Contracts', 259.
[193] Kessler, 'Contracts of Adhesion', 623 [194] Atiyah, 'An Introduction', p. 7.

commitments to an unsuitable product or service can have significant consequences for the individuals concerned and their families).[195] In circumstances where the only choice before individuals is between entering into a standard form contract favourable to traders, or not entering into the agreement, it is difficult to argue that these contracts reflect the principles of freedom and sanctity of contract.[196] When contract terms are 'not agreed in any real sense', then 'the theoretical edifice of freedom of contract is questionable'.[197] In the context of the core exemption, we could extend this argument to say that theoretical justifications for this exemption based on freedom and sanctity of contract rest on shaky grounds. A preferable approach would be for all terms in B2C contracts to be subject to the fairness test, based either on procedural fairness alone, or on substantive fairness as a trigger to question the procedural fairness of the transaction.[198] As this approach would not be based on substantive fairness alone, it should avoid the risk of being used 'as a mechanism for quality/price control'.[199]

When assessing the procedural fairness of agreements, closer attention should be paid to the context of transactions and whether consumers have made an informed decision, based on information accessible and appropriate to their circumstances. Atiyah observes that 'there are at least some circumstances' where 'we can know or guess with reasonable accuracy that the terms of the written contract do not actually represent what the parties did intend or agreed to, had they thought about it'.[200] Any assessment of transactional circumstances must be done in light of social values, including assessing the accessibility of information. While this chapter agrees with the OFT's call for abandoning the core exemption to the fairness test, even without such a step, the call for a framework that considers social values to assess the context of transactions, and the accessibility needs of consumers remains relevant. This is particularly pertinent when assessing the transparency and prominence requirements under section 64 of the CRA, which condition the application of the core exemptions regarding the price and the subject matter of the contract.[201] Within the current framework, the transparency requirement refers to terms expressed in 'plain and intelligible language', with additional requirements of legibility in the case of written contract terms.[202] However, there is no explicit reference to the need for these terms to be accessible for consumers, including consumers with disabilities. In the absence of such an explicit reference, it is important that the current provisions on transparency are read broadly in light of social values such as autonomy, and human dignity.

[195] Fejős, 'Social Justice', 69. [196] Shuchman, 'Consumer Credit', 130.
[197] Atiyah, 'An Introduction', p. 7.
[198] The distinction between procedural and substantive fairness is discussed in more detail in Chapter 3.
[199] Burrows, 'Principles of the English Law of Obligations', 1.222.
[200] Atiyah, 'Essays on Contract', p. 363. [201] Section 64(2) of the CRA 2015.
[202] Ibid. section 64(3).

Before the adoption of the CRA, the OFT[203] called for the statutory provisions to reflect the definition of 'plain and intelligible language' reflected in cases such as *Office of Fair Trading* v. *Foxtons*,[204] which question whether the term under scrutiny is 'sufficiently clear to enable the typical consumer to have a proper understanding' of the term 'for sensible and practical purposes'.[205] This would consider not just 'the actual wording used in the contractual documentation but also its effect'.[206] Focusing on both how terms are presented by traders and how they are received by individuals, would ensure a stronger degree of consumer protection. However, rather than concentrating on the effect of terms on 'typical' consumers, the framework should consider how the scrutinised terms are received by vulnerable consumers, reflective of a universal design approach that considers the wide range of abilities that exist in society. This approach would be more reflective of wider social values such as universal human dignity, equality and inclusivity, and would place greater weight on the need for information to be accessible.

Regarding the 'prominence' provision under the CRA, a term would comply with this requirement if 'brought to the consumer's attention in such a way' that a 'reasonably well-informed, observant and circumspect' consumer 'would be aware of the term'.[207] The provision makes no reference to any accessibility requirements that would enable consumers to become well informed. Furthermore, references to the presentation of terms in a manner that ensures that consumers are 'aware' of them[208] do not go further to refer to the effect of such terms on individuals' decisions whether to enter into the contract. As noted by the OFT before the adoption of the CRA (but regrettably, not reflected into the wording of the Act), 'terms should only be excluded' if drafted in a manner in which they can 'reasonably be expected to be factored into consumer decisions to enter the contracts in which they appear'.[209]

Further difficulties are posed by the fact that the 'prominence' requirement relies on the standard of the average consumer, based on the unrealistic threshold of the 'reasonably well informed, observant and circumspect' individual.[210] A stronger degree of protection would be provided by a framework reliant on

[203] OFT, 'Unfair Terms in Consumer Contracts', 2.42.

[204] *Office of Fair Trading* v. *Foxtons Ltd* [2009] EWHC 1681 (Ch).

[205] Ibid. [59] with reference to the first instance decision in *OFT* v. *Abbey National* [2008] EWHC 875 (Comm), referred to as 'Bank Charges 1' (to distinguish this judgement from the appeal decisions), [119] (Andrew Smith J).

[206] Ibid. with reference to *OFT* v. *Abbey National* [2008] EWHC 875 (Comm), [103] (Andrew Smith J). See also *Van Hove* v. *CNP Assurances SA*, C-96/14, 23 April 2015, which stated at [40] that the transparency requirement regarding contract terms 'cannot be reduced merely to their being formally and grammatically intelligible', and at [47], included in this assessment the question whether the average consumer would 'be able to assess the potentially significant economic consequences, for him' of the contract term.

[207] Sections 64(4) and (5) of the CRA 2015.

[208] Ibid. section 64(4).

[209] OFT, 'Unfair Terms in Consumer Contracts', 2.10.

[210] Sections 64(4) and (5) of the CRA 2015. See OFT, 'Unfair Terms in Consumer Contracts', 1.9.

the standard of the vulnerable consumer. Such an approach would lead to a broader interpretation of the 'prominence' requirement to include the accessibility of contract terms. It would also place more weight on traders to consider principles of universal design, including making contract terms available in accessible formats. Examples of accessible formats include Easy Read , which is 'a term that has come into common use in the UK to describe information designed specifically for people with intellectual disabilities as a group with particular literacy needs'.[211] Vulnerable consumers are implicitly protected under the fairness test, under the reference to 'all circumstances' related to the conclusion of the contract and the reference to good faith.[212] For a stronger degree of protection, vulnerable consumers should be acknowledged explicitly under both the fairness test within section 62, and under the core exemption within section 64.

4.2.2 Regulating Standards for the Provision of Goods, Digital Content and Services

Part 1 of the CRA 2015 comprises key provisions on substantive consumer rights regarding contracts for goods (Chapter 2),[213] digital content (Chapter 3)[214] and services (Chapter 4).[215] These measures implement Directive 1999/44/EC (Consumer Sales Directive),[216] as amended by Directive 2011/83/EU (Consumer Rights Directive).[217] Subsequently, Directive 2019/2161 (Omnibus Directive) repealed Directive 1999/44/EC,[218] and amended Directive 2011/83/EU,[219] but as these developments were reliant on transposing the 2019 Directive by the 1st of July 2021, with effect from the 1st of January 2022,[220] they did not become part of retained EU law in the post-Brexit domestic legislation in the UK. Directive 1999/44/EC was initially implemented in the UK by amendments to the SGA 1979,[221] the Supply of Goods and Services Act (SGSA) 1982,[222] and UCTA 1977,[223] following the adoption of the Sale and Supply of Goods to Consumers Regulations 2002 (SI 2002 No. 3045).[224] When the CRA re-implemented Directive 1999/44/EC (as amended by Directive 2011/83/EU) in part 1 on the Act, it removed B2C transactions from the scope of the SGSA

211 Deborah Chinn and Homeyard, Claire, 'Easy Read and Accessible Information for People with Intellectual Disabilities: Is it worth it? A Meta-Narrative Literature Review' (2017) 20(6) *Health Expectations* 1189–200 at 1191.

212 Section 62(4) of the CRA 2015. See OFT, 'Unfair Terms in Consumer Contracts', 5.19.

213 Sections 3–32 of the CRA 2015. 214 Ibid. sections 33–47. 215 Ibid. sections 48–57.

216 Directive 1999/44/EC, amended by Directive 2011/83/EU and repealed by Directive 2019/2161.

217 Directive 2011/83/EU, amended by Directive 2019/2161.

218 Article 23 of Directive 2019/2161. 219 Ibid. Article 4. 220 Ibid. Articles 23 and 24.

221 Part 5A of the SGA 1979 repealed by Schedule 1(27) of the CRA 2015.

222 Part 1B of the Supply of Goods and Services Act (SGSA) 1982 (c. 29) repealed by Schedule 1(50) of the CRA 2015.

223 Section 12(1A) of UCTA 1977 repealed by Schedule 4(11) of the CRA 2015.

224 Sale and Supply of Goods to Consumers Regulations 2002 (SI 2002 No. 3045), revoked by Schedule 1(53) of the CRA 2015. See Whittaker, 'Consumer Contracts', 40-462.

and UCTA,[225] most of the B2C transactions from the scope of the SGA,[226] and revoked SI 2002 No. 3045.[227]

The adoption of part 1 of the CRA aimed to reform the substantive rights of consumers contracting with traders for the supply of goods, digital content, or services.[228] A trader is 'a person acting for purposes relating to' their business,[229] while a consumer is 'an individual' (i.e. a natural person) acting for purposes 'wholly or mainly outside' their business.[230] The CRA sought to consolidate and simplify the legal framework on consumer contract law.[231] For example, Chapter 2 concerning the consumers' statutory rights regarding the supply of goods brings together under the scope of the CRA sales contracts,[232] contracts for the hire of goods,[233] hire purchase agreements,[234] and contracts for the transfer of goods.[235] Such transactions were previously covered under different statutes, including the SGA, the SGSA, and the Supply of Goods (Implied Terms Act) 1973.[236] Following this process, the remedies presented in Directive 1999/44/EC and implemented by SI 2002 No. 3045 have been extended to contracts for the hire of goods and hire purchase agreements.[237] Traders generally cannot exclude or restrict liability for breach of the substantive provisions under the CRA regarding the supply of goods,[238] digital content,[239] or services.[240] These provisions seek to address the inequality of bargaining power between traders and consumers, constraining traders'

[225] Schedules 1(50) and 4(11) of the CRA 2015 (regarding the SGSA 1982 and UCTA 1977). The Explanatory Notes to the CRA 2015 [24] state that for B2C transactions, the provisions of the SGSA and UCTA are replaced by the CRA, and that the SGSA and UCTA are amended so that they cover only business to business and consumer to consumer contracts.

[226] Schedule 1(27) of the CRA 2015. The Explanatory Notes to the CRA 2015 [24] state that for B2C contracts, these are 'mainly' replaced by the CRA, but that 'some provisions of SGA' continue to apply, such as 'rules which are applicable to all contracts of sale of goods' regarding 'matters such as when property in goods passes'. Furthermore, the SGA 1979 continues to apply to business to business and consumer to consumer contracts.

[227] Schedule 1(53) of the CRA 2015. See Whittaker, 'Consumer Contracts', 40-463.

[228] Part 1 of the CRA 2015. [229] Ibid. section 2(2).

[230] Ibid. section 2(3). See James Devenney, 'The Legacy of the Cameron-Clegg Coalition Programme of Reform of the Law on the Supply of Goods, Digital Content and Services to Consumers' (2018) 6 *Journal of Business Law* 485–511 at 494–95.

[231] Geraint Howells and Christian Twigg-Flesner (eds.), 'Consolidation and Simplification of UK Consumer Law', Report for the Department for Business, Innovation and Skills, November 2010, 2.

[232] Sections 3(2)(a) and 5 of the CRA 2015. [233] Ibid. sections 3(2)(b) and 6.

[234] Ibid. sections 3(2)(c) and 7.

[235] Ibid. sections 3(2)(d) and 8. See Simon Whittaker, 'Distinctive Features of the New Consumer Contract Law' (2017) 133 (Jan) *Law Quarterly Review* 47–72, at 47.

[236] Supply of Goods (Implied Terms) Act 1973 (c. 13). See, for example, section 14 of the Supply of Goods (Implied Terms) Act 1973, repealed by Schedule 1(6) of the CRA 2015.

[237] Devenney, 'The Legacy of the Cameron-Clegg Coalition', 492.

[238] Section 31(1) of the CRA 2015, with reference to consumer rights under sections 9–17 and 28–29.

[239] Ibid. section 47(1), with reference to consumer rights under sections 34–37 and 41.

[240] Ibid. sections 57(1), (2) and (3), with reference to consumer rights under sections 49–52. See Whittaker, 'Consumer Contracts', 40-463, 40-471 and 40-590.

ability to avoid or limit their liability by including exemption clauses in their contracts with consumers.[241]

Some of the provisions included in part 1 of the CRA reflect to a great extent the approach adopted in previous statutes. For example, the SGA provides the basis for several provisions included the CRA regarding the supply of goods. Reflecting the approach adopted under section 14(2) of the SGA,[242] section 9 requires contracts for the supply of goods to be 'treated as including a term that the quality of the goods is satisfactory', assessed with reference to the standard of the reasonable person, considering, *inter alia*, the goods' description, price, and 'all other relevant circumstances'.[243] The broad reference to 'all other relevant circumstances', which relies on 'intentionally vague' words,[244] includes 'any public statement' made by traders regarding the 'specific characteristics of the goods', such as public statements 'made in advertising or labelling'.[245] Assessments of the quality of the goods must consider matters such as their 'state and condition', fitness for purpose, appearance and finish, safety, or durability.[246] Further provisions based on the SGA include section 10 (reflecting section 14(3) of the SGA) concerning the fitness of the goods for a particular purpose, where consumers inform traders of this purpose and it is reasonable to rely on the traders' skill or judgement.[247] They also include section 13 (reflecting section 15 of the SGA), concerning goods matching with the sample, where consumers have seen or examined the sample before the contract.[248] Conversely, while section 11 (goods to be as described) is based on section 13 of the SGA,[249] it also includes new provisions, including section 11(4) regarding information provided by traders on the main characteristics of the goods, which is to be treated as an integral part of the contract.[250] New provisions also include section 14 concerning the conformity of the goods with a model seen or examined by the consumer before concluding the contract.[251]

Another statute which provides the basis for part 1 of the CRA is the SGSA, reflected in some of the provisions regarding the supply of services in B2C contracts.[252] Reflecting the approach in section 13 of the SGSA, section 49 requires contracts for the supply of services to be 'treated as including a term' that traders will provide services with 'reasonable care and skill'.[253] Furthermore, similar to section 14 of the SGSA, section 52 requires services where the time for performance was not agreed under the contract, to be performed within a

241 Brownsword, 'Themes for the Twenty-First Century', p. 74.

242 Section 14(2) SGA 1979.

243 Sections 9(1) and (2) of the CRA 2015.

244 Peter Cartwright, *Consumer Protection and the Criminal Law* (Cambridge: Cambridge University Press, 2001).

245 Sections 9(5) and (6) of the CRA 2015.

246 Ibid. section 9(3).

247 Ibid. sections 10(1), (3) and (4).

248 Sections 13(1) and (2)(a) of the CRA 2015. See Whittaker, 'Consumer Contracts', 40-503.

249 See sections 11(1), (2) and 3 of the CRA 2015. See Whittaker, 'Consumer Contracts', 40-501.

250 Sections 11(4) and (5) of the CRA 2015. See also sections 12(2) and (3).

251 Ibid. section 14.

252 Ibid. section 48. See Whittaker, 'Consumer Contracts', 40-470.

253 Section 49(1) of the CRA 2015.

'reasonable time'.[254] Moreover, in a provision which reflects section 15 of the SGSA, but which updates its language,[255] section 51 requires the payment of a 'reasonable price' for services where the price was not agreed under the contract.[256] The CRA also comprises new provisions with no equivalence in the SGSA, particularly section 50 on the provision of information about traders or services.[257] Oral or written information provided by traders regarding traders or their services, is generally to be 'treated as included' into the contract if consumers took this information into account when deciding to enter into the contract, or when making decisions about the service.[258] This provision adopts a broad choice of words, referring to 'anything' said or written to consumers by traders or on their behalf, regarding traders or their service, without restricting this to factual information.[259] However, as Whittaker notes, while this could include statements of opinion or intention, it does not include conduct.[260]

Perhaps the most significant introduction of new provisions within the CRA is the inclusion of an original set of consumer protection measures regarding digital content.[261] These provisions, which are not based on EU legislation or on previously enacted domestic legislation, were adopted to 'modernise' consumer contract law and adapt it to the digital age.[262] Before the CRA, the question whether consumers purchasing computer software could rely on the protection provided by the SGA depended on whether the software was provided on a physical format such as a disk (bringing the transaction within the scope of the SGA), or in a digital format such as a downloaded programme (falling outside the scope of the SGA).[263] The CRA now covers agreements where traders supply 'digital content' to consumers for a price.[264] Similar to the approach adopted for goods contracts, these provisions follow a strict liability standard regarding matters such as satisfactory quality, fitness for a particular purpose and description.[265]

[254] Ibid. section 52. See James Devenney, 'The Consumer Rights Act 2015 and Related Reforms: An Epic Disappointment?' in Roger Halson and David Campbell (eds.), *Research Handbook on Remedies in Private Law* (Cheltenham: Edward Elgar Publishing, 2019), pp. 257–93, at p. 281.

[255] Explanatory Notes to the CRA 2015, [254]. [256] Section 51 of the CRA 2015.

[257] Ibid. section 50. [258] Ibid. sections 50(1)(a), (b) and (2).

[259] Ibid. section 50(1). See Whittaker, 'Consumer Contracts', 40-577.

[260] Whittaker, 'Consumer Contracts', 40-577.

[261] Chapter 3 in part 1 of the CRA 2015. See Whittaker, 'Consumer Contracts', 40-470.

[262] Devenney, 'The Legacy of the Cameron-Clegg Coalition', 489.

[263] *St Albans City and District Council* v. *International Computers Ltd* [1996] 4 All ER 481 [265]-[6]. See Devenney, 'The Consumer Rights Act 2015', p. 262.

[264] Section 33(1) of the CRA 2015. Digital content supplies in return for the provision of personal data is not caught by the CRA 2015. This is in contrast with Article 3(1) of Directive (EU) 2019/770 of the European Parliament and of the Council of 20 May 2019 on certain aspects concerning contracts for the supply of digital content and digital services, OJ 2019 No. L136, 22 May 2019, pp. 1–27.

[265] Sections 34–36 of the CRA 2015. See also section 37 regarding other pre-contract information. See Chris Willett, 'Re-theorising Consumer Law' (2018) 77(1) *Cambridge Law Journal*, 179–210, at 192–93.

The CRA sought to simplify the 'unnecessarily complex' regulatory framework on consumer protection.[266] The Act moves away from the language of implied terms, referring instead to terms treated as included into contracts for the supply of goods, digital content, or services.[267] This revised terminology aims to ensure that consumers find the legislative framework easier to understand,[268] although, as Devenney notes, 'it is difficult to envisage' that this change in terminology 'will have any more than a marginal gain in this respect'.[269] While the CRA spells out the remedies available to consumers for breach of terms treated as included in B2C transactions, without the need to understand the distinction between different types of terms (in contrast to the SGA which referred to implied terms as conditions and warranties),[270] this detailed reference to remedies adds a new layer of complexity.[271]

The issue of complexity can be identified as a first challenge associated with the regulatory framework under part 1 of the CRA. The remedies provided to consumers for lack of conformity of the goods to the contract[272] include the short-term right to reject,[273] the right to repair or replacement,[274] price reduction[275] and the final right to reject.[276] Despite original intentions to simplify this area of law, this framework is 'complicated and unnecessarily wordy',[277] 'cumbersome', and reliant on a 'rather elaborate framework of remedies'.[278] While all these remedies are available for goods following a breach of sections 9–11, 13, 14 or 16, the remedies for breach of sections 12 or 15[279] are different. For breach of section 15, consumers could seek all the above remedies, except the short-term right to reject,[280] while for breach of section 12, consumers could seek to recover 'the amount of any cost incurred' due to the breach, 'up to the amount paid', or the 'value of other considerations given for the goods'.[281] Consumers can also pursue other remedies under general contract law, including damages for breach of contract, as long as they do not seek to recover twice for the same loss.[282] Yet, as Whittaker, notes, if consumers can supplement the remedies provided under the CRA by claiming damages under general contract law, 'it is difficult to see' what is the 'practical role' of the more restrictive remedies under the CRA.[283]

[266] Explanatory Notes to the CRA 2015, [17].
[267] See, for example, section 9(1) (goods), section 34(1) (digital content) and 49(1) of the CRA 2015 (services).
[268] Whittaker, 'Consumer Contracts', 40-480.
[269] Devenney, 'The Consumer Rights Act 2015', p. 267.
[270] See, for example, section 19(11) of the CRA 2015 and sections 14(6) and 15A of the SGA 1979.
[271] Devenney, 'The Consumer Rights Act 2015', p. 267. [272] Section 19(3) of the CRA 2015.
[273] Ibid. sections 20 and 22. [274] Ibid. section 23. [275] Ibid. section 24.
[276] Ibid. sections 20 and 24. [277] Whittaker, 'Distinctive Features', 50.
[278] Devenney, 'The Consumer Rights Act 2015', p. 273. [279] Sections 19(3)–(5) of the CRA 2015.
[280] Ibid. sections 15 and 19(4). [281] Ibid. sections 12 and 19(5).
[282] Ibid. sections 19(10)(a) and (11). See Whittaker, 'Distinctive Features', 58.
[283] Whittaker, 'Consumer Contracts', 40-502.

The short-term right to reject is available for goods[284] for breach of sections 9–11, 13, 14 and 16, but not for, *inter alia*, breach of section 15.[285] Moreover, the right to repair or replacement[286] is available for goods for breach of sections 9–11 and 13–16, unless this is impossible or disproportionate.[287] These are based on the first-level remedies under Directive 1999/44/EC, which provide consumers with a right to corrective performance.[288] The right to repair or replacement is also available for digital content following a similar approach to the application of these remedies in goods contracts.[289] The right to price reduction or the final right of rejection[290] are available regarding goods for breach of sections 9–11 and 13–16. These are based on the second-level remedies presented under Directive 1999/44/EC,[291] which are available only after the consumer has sought to rely on the first-level remedy of repair or replacement and this was unsuccessful or impossible.[292] The right to price reduction is also available for digital content,[293] following to some extent the approach adopted for goods contracts.[294] However, unlike goods contracts, the right to price reduction is not accompanied by the alternative of a final right of rejection.[295] The availability of a final right of rejection for faulty digital content could have presented traders with 'greater incentive[s]' to ensure that their products are free from defects.[296] As noted by the OFT in response to a consultation that preceded the CRA, while recognising the difficulties associated with the 'return' of faulty digital content downloaded by consumers, potential 'industry solutions' should be explored to address these challenges.[297] Consequently, the OFT called for 'further research into technical solutions to allow consumers to reject faulty digital content and receive a full refund', ensuring at the same time that traders 'can have confidence' that consumers will not abuse this remedy.[298] Under the CRA, consumers may, however, seek a full refund in relation to faulty digital content by relying on the provisions on price reduction,[299] and this may respond to some of challenges associated with the absence of a final right of rejection, without having to address the technical challenges of 'returning' digital content.

[284] Sections 20 and 22 of the CRA 2015 [285] Ibid. sections 15 and 19(4). [286] Ibid. section 23.
[287] Ibid. section 23(3).
[288] Article 3(3) of Directive 1999/44/EC. See Whittaker, 'Consumer Contracts', 40-461.
[289] Section 43 of the CRA 2015 regarding breaches of sections 34–36.
[290] Ibid. sections 20 and 24. [291] Articles 3(5) and (6) of Directive 1999/44/EC.
[292] Section 24(5) of the CRA 2015. [293] Ibid. section 44 regarding breaches of sections 34–36.
[294] Section 24 of the CRA 2015. See Devenney, 'The Consumer Rights Act 2015', p. 280.
[295] Whittaker, 'Consumer Contracts', 40-563.
[296] Office of Fair Trading, 'Response to the Draft Consumer Rights Bill Proposals' OFT1502, September 2013, 1.6.
[297] Ibid. 3.6.
[298] Ibid. See also discussion in Devenney, 'The Consumer Rights Act 2015', pp. 279–80. See also Article 14 of Directive 2019/770, which refers to the remedy of bringing digital content 'into conformity'.
[299] Section 44(2) of the CRA 2015. See Whittaker, 'Consumer Contracts', 40-563.

Further remedies include, for contracts for the supply of services, the rights to repeat performance and to price reduction.[300] The right to repeat performance, when available, is a first-level remedy which must be attempted before consumers can access the second-level remedy of price reduction.[301] This remedy requires traders to bring services in conformity with the contract,[302] such as providing services with 'reasonable care and skill' in compliance with section 49.[303] The right to price reduction to an 'appropriate amount' is a second-level remedy available if repeat performance has been unsuccessful or impossible.[304] Nevertheless, as observed by the OFT in response to a consultation which preceded the CRA, in the event of the provision of a poor service, the remedy of price reduction 'will, in many cases, not cover the costs the consumer will incur to put right or redo the poor service'.[305] Consumers can also seek to rely on remedies for breach of contract under general contract law in the event of services that do not conform with the contract, including damages, although consumers cannot recover twice for the same loss.[306]

The CRA also sought to address the issue of fragmentation of consumer contract law[307] but in doing so, it has created 'different fault lines'.[308] The issue of fragmentation can, therefore, be identified as a second challenge associated with this regulatory framework. For example, while section 29 includes provisions regarding the passing of risk,[309] the rules comprised in the SGA regarding the passing of property in goods continue to apply to B2C transitions.[310] The CRA missed out an opportunity to consolidate the rules on the passing of property regarding B2C contracts, which could have provided more clarity, including the case of traders' insolvency.[311] This led to calls from the Law Commission for an amendment to section 4 of the CRA[312] 'to include new rules' on when consumers acquire the ownership of goods.[313]

A third challenge is posed by the predominant perception of individuals under the CRA as economic actors, rather than also as social actors. The CRA reflects a vision of 'confident consumers' as 'key ingredients' to economic

300 Sections 54(3), 55 and 56 of the CRA 2015.

301 Ibid. section 55. See Whittaker, 'Consumer Contracts', 40-584.

302 Sections 54 and 55 of the CRA 2015. 303 Ibid. section 49(1).

304 Ibid. section 56. See Whittaker, 'Consumer Contracts', 40-584.

305 OFT, 'Response to the Draft Consumer Rights Bill Proposals', 4.3.

306 Sections 54(6) and (7) of the CRA 2015. See Devenney, 'The Consumer Rights Act 2015', p. 281.

307 Explanatory Notes to the CRA 2015, [2].

308 Devenney, 'The Consumer Rights Act 2015', p. 260. 309 Section 29 of the CRA 2015.

310 Explanatory Notes to the CRA 2015, [24]. See Devenney, 'The Consumer Rights Act 2015', p. 260.

311 Devenney, 'The Legacy of the Cameron-Clegg Coalition', 488.

312 Section 4 of the CRA 2015.

313 Law Commission, 'Consumer Prepayments on Retailer Insolvency', Law Com No. 368, July 2016, recommendation 5a, p. 114. See Devenney, 'The Consumer Rights Act 2015', p. 258.

development and the 'efficient functioning of the market'.[314] This is in line with the vision pursued by Directive 1999/44/EC, which was rooted in economic, rather than social foundations.[315] Even when Directive 2011/83/EU (which amended Directive 1999/44/EC) made an explicit reference to the need to respect fundamental rights in the context of consumer protection, this was confined to the non-binding preamble of the Directive.[316] In addition to responding to economic concerns, the regulatory framework on consumer protection must also reflect concerns for 'social justice', including when protecting consumers as parties in a weaker bargaining position.[317] As Cartwright notes, 'social regulation' is 'increasingly important' in the context of consumer protection, as measures designed to protect consumer interests should pursue both economic and social goals, and should reflect a perception of individuals as both consumers and citizens.[318] Such an approach could help us 'look beyond the narrow economic function of the consumer' and 'consider the individual's wider role in society'.[319] The concentric sphere model presented in this book can accommodate the dual objective of addressing both economic and social concerns within the contractual realm, as it reflects an understanding of consumers as both economic and social actors, but sees economic objectives as subordinate to social values such as the protection of equality of citizenship, autonomy and human dignity.

The vision of consumer contract law reflected in part 1 of the CRA is 'fuelled by a market-driven approach focused on 'consumers as economic actors',[320] and shaped by an 'ethical vision of the ideal market order',[321] reliant on 'choice in exchange' and freedom of contract.[322] This vision places significant weight on a 'substantial degree of self-reliance' on the part of consumers.[323] This approach can be contrasted with 'an ethical position' that allows intervention when needed to achieve 'a fair balance' in the interest of contracting parties.[324] This interventionist approach is necessary due to imbalances of power between parties in B2C transactions. As Willett notes, consumers have a more 'limited capacity to absorb economic losses caused by defective goods and services', and the impact of breaches of contract can extend beyond economic interest into the social aspects of consumers' lives, including with regards to 'loss of time, distress, inconvenience in personal lives, frustration of obtaining no redress',

314 Devenney, 'The Consumer Rights Act 2015', p. 257.

315 Recital 1 and Article 1 of Directive 1999/44/EC. See Brownsword, 'Themes for the Twenty-First Century', p. 182.

316 Recital 6 of Directive 2011/83/EU, with reference to the need to observe the principles recognised in the Charter of Fundamental Rights of the European Union. See Iris Benöhr, *EU Consumer Law and Human Rights* (Oxford: Oxford University Press, 2013), p. 66.

317 David Campbell, *Contractual Relations: A Contribution to the Critique of the Classical Law of Contract* (Oxford: Oxford University Press, 2022), p. 4.

318 Cartwright, 'Consumer Protection', p. 3.

319 Ibid.

320 Devenney, 'The Consumer Rights Act 2015', pp. 257 and 263.

321 Willett, 'Re-theorising Consumer Law', 179.

322 Campbell, 'Contractual Relations', p. 201.

323 Willett, 'Re-theorising Consumer Law', 185.

324 Ibid. 184.

'lost leisure time', and 'emotional costs'.[325] Consumer protection measures must be rooted in a 'needs-based' ethic that prioritises consumers' interests as the weaker parties, over traders' interests as the stronger parties.[326] To use the language of concentric spheres presented in this book, consumer protection measures must be rooted in the social sphere of the contracting framework.

Unfortunately, the CRA stops short from reflecting such a vision. For example, while the provisions on agreements for the supply of goods and digital content rely on a strict liability approach[327] which promotes a needs-based vision of consumer law, as it holds traders accountable 'even if they have exercised reasonable care',[328] the measures concerning the supply of services are reliant on a negligence-based approach where traders can escape liability if they have exercised reasonable care in the provision of the service.[329] Despite calls before the adoption of the CRA to extend the strict liability approach to services directed at consumer goods and digital content, such as repair or storage, which can provide a measurable outcome based on the state of the goods or digital content after the service (as opposed to pure services such as education, where the outcome is more difficult to measure),[330] these calls were not reflected in the final text of the CRA.[331] Instead, the Government was more responsive to industry voices which called for reliance on the fault-based approach for all services.[332] Although this approach was less favourable to consumers, the industry voices were louder and ultimately won the argument.[333] The need for a regulatory framework which is more responsive to the voices of consumers, including persons with disabilities and DDPOs, is discussed in more detail in the last section of this chapter and in Chapter 5, with a focus on the values of participation and inclusion.

4.2.3 Regulating Unfair Commercial Practices

For over two decades, the key instrument regulating unfair commercial practices in English contract law have been the CPUTRs (as amended),[334] which implemented in the UK Directive 2005/29/EC on unfair commercial practices.[335] The DMCCA, which received royal assent on the 24th of May 2024,

[325] Ibid. 187. On the issue of mental distress in the context of damages for breach of contract, see for example *Watts* v. *Morrow* [1991] 1 WLR 1421, [1445] (Bingham LJ), *Jarvis* v. *Swans Tours Ltd.* [1973] 2 QB 233; *Farley* v. *Skinner* [2001] UKHL 49.

[326] Willett, 'Re-theorising Consumer Law', 185 and 191.

[327] Sections 9 and 34 of the CRA 2015.

[328] Willett, 'Re-theorising Consumer Law', 184 and 187.

[329] Section 49(1) of the CRA 2015. See Willett, 'Re-theorising Consumer Law', 187.

[330] Ibid. 199. Department for Business, Innovation and Skills, 'Enhancing Consumer Confidence by Clarifying Consumer Law: Consultation on the Supply of Goods, Services and Digital Content', July 2012, 115–20.

[331] Willett, 'Re-theorising Consumer Law', 185 and 199.

[332] Ibid.

[333] Ibid.

[334] SI 2008 No. 1277 (CPUTRs), as amended by SI 2014 No. 870, revoked and replaced by the DMCCA 2024.

[335] Directive 2005/29/EC, amended by Directive 2019/2161.

revokes the CPUTRs and migrates an amended version of the CPUTRs measures within part 4 of the DMCCA (consumer rights and disputes).[336] Many of the provisions of the DMCCA are expected to come into force in the autumn of 2024.[337]

Chapter 1 (protection from unfair trading) in part 4 of the DMCCA presents a revised definition of unfair commercial practices, whose use and promotion is prohibited by section 225 (1) and (2).[338] Section 225(4) presents three sets of circumstances where a commercial practice is unfair, while section 225(3) precedes this with an explanation of what is meant by a 'commercial practice' (which include traders' acts or omissions regarding the promotion or supply of their products to consumers), and what is meant by references to 'consumer' (an individual acting for purposes wholly or mainly outside their business) and 'trader' (a person acting for purposes related to their business and can include persons acting on their behalf, such as agents).[339]

The first set of circumstances in which a 'commercial practice' can amount to an 'unfair commercial practice' is presented under section 225(4)(a). This involves a two-step approach. Firstly, the practice must fall within one of four categories of practices involving (i) a misleading action,[340] (ii) a misleading omission,[341] (iii) an aggressive practice[342] or (iv) a contravention of the requirements of professional diligence[343] (we could call this step one). Secondly, the practice must meet what has become known as the 'transactional decision test' (we could call this step two), referring to a situation where the practice identified in step one 'is likely to cause the average consumer to take a transactional decision that the consumer would not have taken otherwise'.[344]

For a misleading action to fall within 'step one', it must involve one of four circumstances.[345] These include, in relation to products (i.e. goods, services or digital content),[346] traders, or 'any other matter relevant to a transactional decision', the provision of false or misleading information, or an overall presentation 'likely to deceive the average consumer' about one of the above matters.[347] Included in this definition is information which although factually correct, 'is presented in a misleading way', and an overall presentation which contains true information but is, nonetheless, deceiving.[348]

A misleading omission falls within 'step one' if, it involves, *inter alia*, a commercial practice where traders omit 'material information' needed by 'an average consumer' to take 'an informed transactional decision'.[349] It can also involve a commercial practice where traders omit information required to be provided to consumers under another enactment, which includes failure to provide such

[336] Section 251(1) of the DMCCA 2024. [337] Ibid. sections 252 and 339.
[338] Ibid. sections 225(1) and (2). [339] Ibid. sections 225(3), (6) and 249.
[340] Ibid. sections 225(4)(a)(i) and 226. [341] Ibid. sections 225(4)(a)(i) and 227.
[342] Ibid. sections 225(4)(a)(i) and 228. [343] Ibid. sections 225(4)(a)(i) and 229.
[344] Ibid. section 225(4)(a). [345] Ibid. sections 225(4)(a)(i) and 226(1). [346] Ibid. section 248(1).
[347] Ibid. section 226(1). [348] Ibid. sections 226(2) and (3).
[349] Ibid. sections 225(4)(a)(i) and 227(1)(a) and (2).

information, or its provision in an 'unclear or untimely' manner, or in a way in which it is unlikely be seen by consumers.[350] When assessing whether a commercial practice amounts to a misleading omission, matters to be considered include 'any limitations resulting from the means of communication used' in that practice, including 'limitations of space or time', and 'any steps' which traders have taken to 'overcome those limitations by providing information by other means'.[351] The inclusion of this provision reflects a need to balance the interests of traders and consumers. It is, however, important to recognise the inherent imbalance of power between these parties, which should inform any assessment of traders' compliance with the prohibition of unfair commercial practices. This is particularly relevant, given that while the CPUTRs referred explicitly to 'all the features and circumstances of the commercial practice'[352] as matters to be considered when assessing if practices amounted to misleading omissions, such reference is not included explicitly in the DMCCA.

For an aggressive practice to fall within 'step one', the commercial practice must involve 'harassment, coercion or undue influence'.[353] While 'harassment' is not explicitly defined, the DMCCA clarifies that 'coercion' includes using 'threat of physical force', and that 'undue influence' refers to 'exploiting a position of power in relation to a consumer' to 'apply pressure in a way which significantly limits the consumer's ability to make an informed decision'.[354] Unlike the CPUTRs, the DMCCA does not include explicitly in the definition of undue influence reference to traders' use of pressure 'even without using or threatening to use physical force', but this should be implied in the definition of undue influence.[355] The Explanatory Notes to the DMCCA specify that traders may enjoy a 'position of power' due to their product expertise, or the consumers' 'particular circumstances', including situations where consumers are 'indebted to the trader' or are otherwise 'in a vulnerable position'.[356] While these references to circumstantial vulnerability in the Explanatory Notes are to be welcomed, a stronger degree of protection could have been provided if these references were included in the DMCCA. When assessing if a commercial practice uses harassment, coercion or undue influence, account must be taken of the nature, timing or location of the practice, and whether the practice involves the use of 'any threatening or abusive language or behaviour', threats to take unlawful actions, exploits consumer vulnerability (including due to age, physical or mental health, credulity or circumstances), or requires consumers to take 'onerous or disproportionate' actions to exercise their rights regarding a product.[357] While the CPUTRs referred expressly to the 'factual context' and the need to consider all the 'features and circumstances' of the commercial practice

[350] Ibid. sections 227(1)(b) and (4). [351] Ibid. section 227(3).
[352] Regulation 6(2)(a) of the CPUTRs 2008.
[353] Sections 225(4)(a)(i) and 228(1) of the DMCCA 2024. [354] Ibid. section 228(3).
[355] Regulation 7(3)(b) of the CPUTRs 2008; Section 228 of the DMCCA 2024.
[356] Explanatory Notes to the DMCCA 2024, [1368].
[357] Sections 228(2) and 247(4) of the DMCCA 2024.

when assessing if a practice is aggressive, the DMCCA does not refer explicitly to the contextual nature of the practice, and it is therefore, important that these factors are interpreted broadly to consider the transactional context.[358]

The final commercial practice identified under 'step one' refers to 'a contravention of the requirements of professional diligence'.[359] This refers to a practice which 'falls short of the standard of skill and care' reasonably expected from traders to be exercised towards consumers, 'commensurate with either honest market practice', or with 'the general principle of good faith', both assessed with reference to 'the trader's field of activity'.[360] The Explanatory Notes to the DMCCA note the objective standard adopted by this provision.[361] They also specify, regarding the considerations of 'honest market practice' and 'good faith', that these involve assessing whether traders have considered 'the legitimate interests or expectations of the average consumer in the particular sector'.[362] They clarify that 'good faith' refers to 'fair and open dealing', and traders should 'not take advantage of consumer's lack of experience or unfamiliarity with a product'.[363]

Within the first set of circumstances in which a 'commercial practice' can amount to an 'unfair commercial practice', presented under section 225(4)(a), 'step two' requires meeting the 'transactional decision test'.[364] This refers to a situation where the practice identified in 'step one' (i.e. a misleading action or omission, an aggressive practice, or a contravention of the requirements of professional diligence) 'is likely to cause the average consumer to take a transactional decision' that they 'would not have taken otherwise'.[365] Previously, under the CPUTRs, while misleading actions or omissions, or aggressive commercial practices were subject to the transactional decision test,[366] contraventions of the requirements of professional diligence were formulated with reference to a material distortion test, which questioned if the practice 'materially distorts' or 'is likely to materially distort the economic behaviour of the average consumer' regarding the product.[367] The CPUTRs also specified that references to the material distortion of economic behaviour referred to a practice that impaired the ability of the average consumer 'to make an informed decision', causing him to 'take a transactional decision he would not have taken otherwise'.[368] As noted by the OFT regarding the CPUTRs, a 'material distortion is comprised of an appreciable impairment test and a transactional decision test'.[369] The DMCCA simplified the language of these assessments, so that all four types of commercial practices identified under 'step one' are subject to the transactional decision test under 'step two'.

[358] Regulation 7(1) of the CPUTRs; Section 228 of the DMCCA 2024.
[359] Ibid. sections 225(4)(a)(i) and 229. [360] Ibid. sections 229(1)(a) and (b).
[361] Explanatory Notes to the DMCCA 2024, [1369]. [362] Ibid. [363] Ibid. [1372].
[364] Section 225(4)(a) of the DMCCA 2024. [365] Ibid. sections 225(4)(a) and 226–29.
[366] Regulations 5(2)(b) and 5(3)(b) (misleading actions), 6(1)(d) (misleading omissions) and 7(1)(b) (aggressive commercial practice) of the CPUTRs 2008.
[367] Ibid. Regulation 3(3)(b) and Regulation 2(1). [368] Ibid. Regulation 2(1).
[369] Office of Fair Trading, 'Guidance on the Consumer Protection from Unfair Trading Regulations 2008', May 2008, 14.16.

The second set of circumstances in which a 'commercial practice' can amount to an 'unfair commercial practice' is presented under section 225(4)(b) of the DMCCA, and refers to a situation in which the trader 'omits material information from an invitation to purchase'.[370] Unlike the first set of circumstances discussed earlier, and unlike the position previously adopted for this commercial practice under the CPUTRs,[371] this assessment is not subject to a 'transactional decision test'. A commercial practice which is 'an invitation to purchase', omits 'material information' if it omits, among others, information regarding the product (e.g. its main characteristics), the trader (e.g. its identity), consumer rights (e.g. cancellation), information required under other enactments, whether traders' practices depart from their published practice (e.g. regarding payment), and the extent of such departure.[372] References to the omission of information include not only the failure to provide material information, but also the provision of such information in an 'unclear or untimely manner', or 'in such a way that the consumer is unlikely to see it'.[373] This has the effect of considering 'how the words used in a commercial practice may be interpreted by the consumer', and how the information was displayed, taking into account matters such as the prominence, positioning, font size and colour of the text.[374]

The third and final set of circumstances in which a 'commercial practice' can amount to an 'unfair commercial practice' is presented under section 225(4)(c), referring to commercial practices listed in Schedule 20 of the DMCCA and considered as unfair 'in all circumstances' (this has become known as 'the blacklist').[375] This assessment is not subject to a 'transactional decision test'.[376] Schedule 20 contains many references to commercial practices that were also part of Schedule 1 of the CPUTRs. It includes reference to the practice described in the CPUTRs as 'bait advertising', which concerns 'making an invitation to purchase products at a specified price', although the trader has 'reasonable grounds' to believe that they would be unable to 'offer these products for supply at that price, in reasonable quantities, for a reasonable period of time' and fails to disclose that fact.[377] Schedule 20 also includes the practice described in the CPUTRs as 'bait and switch',[378] which concerns 'making an invitation to purchase' a product 'at a specified price', but then refusing to show this product, to take orders for it, or deliver it 'within a reasonable time', or 'demonstrating a defective sample of it', where the trader's intention is to promote a different product.[379] In addition, Schedule 20 includes the practice described in the CPUTRs as 'advertorial',[380] which refers to 'using editorial

[370] Section 225(4)(b) of the DMCCA 2024. [371] Regulation 6 of the CPUTRs 2008.
[372] Sections 230(1)–(3) of the DMCCA 2024. [373] Ibid. section 230(9).
[374] Explanatory Notes to the DMCCA 2024, [1381].
[375] Section 225(4)(c) and Schedule 20 of the DMCCA 2014.
[376] Explanatory Notes to the DMCCA 2024, [1347]. [377] Schedule 20(5) of the DMCCA 2024.
[378] Schedule 1(6) of the CPUTRs 2008. [379] Schedule 20(6) of the DMCCA 2024.
[380] Schedule 1(11) of the CPUTRs 2008.

content in the media to promote a product where the trader has paid for the promotion', without making this clear to the consumer.[381] Further provisions within Schedule 20 which mirror measures previously comprised in the CPUTRs include, among others, giving consumers the impression that they 'cannot leave the premises until a contract is formed', and 'explicitly telling a consumer' that the trader's 'job or livelihood' would be at risk unless the consumer buys a product.[382]

Schedule 20 of the DMCCA has also strengthened some of the provisions previously included in the CPUTRs. For example, Schedule 20(7) includes in the list of practices considered as unfair in all circumstances, 'falsely stating that a product will only be available *for a limited time*', in order to 'elicit an immediate decision and deprive consumers of sufficient opportunity or time to make an informed choice'.[383] Under the CPUTRs, this provision relied on narrower language, referring to a false statement that the product will be available only '*for a very limited time*'.[384] Moreover, while the CPUTRs condemned false claims that a product can 'cure illnesses, dysfunction or malformations',[385] Schedule 20(19) goes further, condemning false claims that a product can 'prevent or treat disease or a malformation', or 'restore, correct or modify a physiological function', or 'modify a person's appearance'.[386] The reference to 'disease' in this provision is defined broadly to include 'any injury, ailment or adverse condition, whether of body or mind'.[387]

The DMCCA has also simplified the language of some of the measures previously included in the CPUTRs. For example, the provisions condemning the practice referred to in the CPUTRs as 'inertia selling'[388] are framed in much clearer language under Schedule 20(31), which describes this practice as 'supplying products' to consumers without having been requested, and 'demanding' that consumers pay for, return, or safely store these products.[389] Inertia selling is also covered by section 236, which clarifies that where products are supplied by traders without having been requested, consumers are not obliged to pay for these products and may 'use, deal with or dispose of' these goods 'as if they were an unconditional gift to the consumer'.[390] The mere fact that consumers did not respond, following the unrequested supply of products by traders, does not amount to consent to the traders' request to pay for, return, or safely store the products.[391]

Schedule 20 has also introduced new provisions to strengthen the protection provided to consumers. The key example is Schedule 20(13), which classifies the submission or commissioning of fake consumer reviews as a commercial practice to be treated as unfair in all circumstances.[392] A fake consumer review

[381] Schedule 20(12) of the DMCCA 2024. [382] Ibid. Schedules 20(26) and (32).
[383] Ibid. Schedule 20(7) (emphasis added).
[384] Schedule 1(7) of the CPUTRs 2008 (emphasis added). [385] Ibid. Schedule 1(17).
[386] Schedule 20(19)(1) of the DMCCA 2024. [387] Ibid. Schedule 20(19)(2).
[388] Schedule 1(29) of the CPUTRs 2008. [389] Schedule 20(31) of the DMCCA 2024.
[390] Ibid. sections 236(2) and (3). [391] Ibid. section 236(4). [392] Ibid. Schedule 20(13)(1)(a).

falsely claims to be 'based on a person's genuine experience'.[393] The reference to the 'commissioning' of a review includes 'incentivising' the review writer 'by any means'.[394] This provision also condemns, *inter alia*, the submission or commissioning of a review that 'conceals the fact it has been incentivised'.[395]

There are many reasons why the DMCCA should be commended, some of which have already touched upon in the above discussion. Firstly, many of the key concepts central to the DMCCA rely on broad definitions. The definition of 'commercial practices', described by the Explanatory Notes to the DMCCA as 'far reaching',[396] includes a trader's act or omission concerning the promotion or supply of their product to consumers.[397] Commercial practices can be derived not only from 'repeated behaviour and a course of conduct' but also from 'a single act or omission', depending on the circumstances of the transaction.[398]

The revised definition of 'unfair commercial practices' under the DMCCA is also broad, covering three sets of circumstances where a commercial practice is unfair, including where (i) it is 'likely to cause' an average consumer to take 'a transactional decision' that he 'would not have taken otherwise' (the 'transactional decision test') due to a misleading action or omission, an aggressive commercial practice, or a contravention of a professional diligence requirement, or where (ii) it omits material information from an invitation to purchase, or (iii) is a banned commercial practice under Schedule 20.[399] Commercial practices in the form of a contravention of a professional diligence requirement are now subject to the 'transactional decision test',[400] compared to the previous position under the CPUTRs where these practices were subject to a material distortion test,[401] consisting of an appreciable impairment test (i.e. whether the practice impaired the ability of the average consumer 'to make an informed decision') and the 'transactional decision test'.[402] Moreover, the 'transactional decision test' is not required for the omission of material information from an invitation to purchase[403] (although this was required previously under the CPUTRs),[404] or for commercial practices banned under Schedule 20.[405]

Another broad definition under the DMCCA is that of 'transactional decisions', defined as 'any decision made by a consumer' regarding a product, including its 'purchase or supply', 'retention, disposal or withdrawal', or the exercise of related contractual rights.[406] The Explanatory Notes to the DMCCA observe that the concept of 'transactional decisions' is 'broad', as it covers 'both

[393] Ibid. Schedules 20(13)(5)(a) and (b). [394] Ibid. Schedule 20(13)(5)(g).
[395] Ibid. Schedules 20(13)(1)(b) and (5)(c). [396] Explanatory Notes to the DMCCA 2024, [902].
[397] Section 225(3)(a) of the DMCCA 2024. See also Sections 225(3)(b) and (c).
[398] Explanatory Notes to the DMCCA 2024, [1342].
[399] Sections 225(4) and 226–30 and Schedule 20 of the DMCCA 2024.
[400] Ibid. sections 225(4)(a) and 229.
[401] Regulation 3(3)(b), Regulation 2(1) of the CPUTRs 2008.
[402] Ibid. Regulation 2(1). See OFT, 'Guidance on Consumer Protection', 14.16.
[403] Sections 225(4)(b) and 230 of the DMCCA 2024. [404] Regulation 6 of the CPUTRs 2008.
[405] Section 225(4)(c) and Schedule 20 of the DMCCA 2024. [406] Ibid. section 245.

pre-purchase and post-purchasing decisions', and these include 'decisions on whether or not to do something'.[407] For a consumer decision to fall within the definition of a transactional decision, 'there does not need to be an actual transaction' between a trader and a consumer.[408] This may include pre-contractual decisions (e.g. to visit a shop 'as a result of a commercial offer', or to click on a web link due to information regarding a product), and post-contractual decisions (e.g. not to change service provider).[409] Moreover, when applying the 'transactional decision test' to assess if a commercial practice was 'likely to cause' an average consumer to take a different transactional decision,[410] the Explanatory Notes to the DMCCA clarify that it may be necessary to consider the cumulative effect of 'any or all of the misleading acts and omissions that the trader may have engaged in'.[411]

The DMCCA also presents a broad definition of misleading actions[412] covering 'a wide range of circumstances'.[413] These include the provision of false or misleading information about a product or trader, including the provision of factually correct information 'in a misleading way'.[414] The DMCCA also relies on a broad definition of misleading omissions which includes the omission of 'material information' needed by 'an average consumer' to take 'an informed transactional decision'.[415] As observed in the Explanatory Notes to the DMCCA, these provisions seek to ensure that 'consumers get from traders all the information they need to make informed decision in an upfront, clear, and timely manner'.[416]

Further examples of broad definitions under the DMCCA include the definition of unfair commercial practices in the form of omission of material information from an invitation to purchase,[417] relevant for capturing 'drip pricing'. 'Drip pricing' arises when traders initially show a base price (i.e. an initial price for a product) and then 'drip' (i.e. reveal) further fees to consumers, as they progresses through the checkout.[418] The DMCCA seeks to respond to these concerns by specifying that an unfair commercial practice in the form of omission of material information from invitation to purchase includes the omission of information regarding 'the *total* price of the product',[419] or the method of calculating the price, if this cannot be reasonably calculated in advance due to

407 Explanatory Notes to the DMCCA 2024, [1353]. 408 Ibid. 409 Ibid. [1431], [1432].
410 Section 225(4)(a) of the DMCCA 2024.
411 Explanatory Notes to the DMCCA 2024, [1429].
412 Sections 225(4)(a)(i) and 226 of the DMCCA 2024.
413 Explanatory Notes to the DMCCA 2024, [1353].
414 Sections 226(1)(a) and (2) of the DMCCA 2024.
415 Ibid. sections 225(4)(a)(i) and 227(1)(a) and (2).
416 Explanatory Notes to the DMCCA 2024, [1358].
417 Sections 225(4)(b) and 230 of the DMCCA 2024.
418 Department for Business and Trade, 'Estimating the Prevalence and Impact of Online Drip Pricing', September 2023, p. 6.
419 Sections 230(1) and 230(2)(b) of the DMCCA 2024 (emphasis added). Cf. CPUTRs 2008, Regulation 6(4), which referred to 'the price' of the product.

'the nature of the product'.[420] An 'invitation to purchase' is also defined broadly to refer to a commercial practice 'involving the provision of information to a consumer' which indicates a product's characteristics and price, and 'enables, or purports to enable' a consumer's decision 'whether to purchase the product or take another transactional decision in relation to the product'.[421] Moreover, unlike the previous position under the CPUTRs,[422] the assessment whether an omission of material information from an invitation to purchase amounts to an unfair commercial practice is no longer subject to a 'transactional decision test'. Yet, while the definition of an 'invitation to purchase'[423] is broad and can include the provision of 'minimal' information regarding a product's characteristics and price,[424] there is a risk that the inclusion of a reference to 'price' in this definition[425] could leave some consumers unprotected. As highlighted in the Parliamentary debates before the adoption of the DMCCA, 'many rogue traders who target vulnerable consumers do not give a price when offering to do work', and their practices may fall outside the definition of an 'invitation to purchase'.[426]

A second reason why the DMCCA should be commended is due to some of the changes in language adopted in the Act, compared with the CPUTRs. For example, with reference to aggressive commercial practices, section 228(2)(d) states that 'in determining whether a commercial practice uses harassment, coercion or undue influence, account must be taken of...whether the practice exploits any vulnerability of a consumer'. The references to consumer vulnerability include 'any vulnerability' due to age, physical or mental health, credulity or circumstances.[427] This is preferable when compared to the language in Regulation 7(2)(c) of the CPUTRs, which referred to a trader's exploitation 'of any specific misfortune or circumstance' which is 'of such gravity as to impair the consumer's judgment', and 'of which the trader is aware, to influence the consumer's decision' regarding that product.[428]

The DMCCA also reflects a preferable choice of language when defining 'vulnerable persons' when compared with the CPUTRs. The DMCCA makes a number of references to the 'average consumer',[429] described as being 'reasonably well informed, observant, and circumspect'[430] (the average consumer attributes). Where a commercial practice is targeted at a particular group, the 'average consumer' is an average member of that group (the average targeted consumer), and the average consumer attributes are 'are to be

420 Section 230(2)(c) of the DMCCA 2024. 421 Ibid. section 230(10).
422 Regulation 6 of the CPUTRs 2008. 423 Section 230(10) of the DMCCA 2024.
424 Explanatory Notes to the DMCCA 2024, [1374].
425 Section 230(10)(a) of the DMCCA 2024.
426 DMCC Bill Briefing Paper (Sept 07, 2023), pp. 31–32, with reference to the intervention from Seema Malhotra (Labour), Public Bill Committee 4 July 2023 cc 323-4.
427 Section 247(4) of the DMCCA 2024. 428 Regulation 7(2)(c) of the CPUTRs 2008.
429 See, for example, Sections 225(4)(a), 226(1)(b) and 227(2) of the DMCCA 2024.
430 Ibid. section 246(2).

read accordingly'.[431] Moreover, where a group of consumers is 'particularly vulnerable' to a commercial practice in a way that traders 'could reasonably be expected to foresee', and due to this vulnerability, the commercial practice is causing consumers 'to take a transactional decision that they would not have taken otherwise',[432] references to the 'average consumer' are to be read as referring to the average 'vulnerable' consumer, and the average consumer attributes are 'are to be read accordingly'.[433] A group of consumers may be vulnerable due to factors such as 'age', 'physical or mental health', 'credulity' or the 'circumstances' in which they find themselves.[434] The approach to defining vulnerable consumers under the DMCCA is preferable to the text previously adopted under the CPUTRs. While Regulation 2(5)(a) of the CPUTRs referred to vulnerability factors as 'mental or physical infirmity, age or credulity',[435] the DMCCA adopts a broader approach, listing the vulnerability factors as an open list (with reference to these as 'among other things').[436] The DMCCA also moves away from the reference to 'mental or physical *infirmity*' adopted in the CPUTRs,[437] to refer to 'physical or mental *health*'.[438] Furthermore, while the CPUTRs did not mention circumstantial vulnerability, the DMCCA includes reference to 'the circumstances [consumers] are in' as a factor for assessing vulnerability.[439] The DMCCA also removes the reference included previously in the CPUTRs, which stated that the provisions concerning vulnerable consumers were 'without prejudice to the common and legitimate advertising practice of making exaggerated statements which are not meant to be taken literally',[440] and which overlooked the preference of some neurodiverse consumers for a literal interpretation of words.[441]

A third reason for commending the DMCCA is due to the flexibility embodied in section 242, which enables the Secretary of State to adopt regulations to amend (i.e. modify, add to, or remove from) the list of unfair commercial practices under Schedule 20, to extend the private right of redress under section 232(7), or to amend the description of material information regarding an invitation to purchase under section 230(2).[442] The DMCCA also imposes the requirement for consultation with 'such persons as the Secretary of State considers appropriate', before adopting such regulations.[443] Yet, this provision

431 Ibid. section 246(4). 432 Ibid. sections 247(1) and (3). 433 Ibid. section 247(2).
434 Ibid. section 247(4). 435 Regulation 2(5)(a) of the CPUTRs 2008.
436 Section 247(4) of the DMCCA 2024.
437 Regulation 2(5)(a) of the CPUTRs 2008 (emphasis added).
438 Section 247(4)(b) of the DMCCA 2024 (emphasis added).
439 Ibid. section 247(4)(d). See Peter Cartwright, 'The Vulnerable Consumer and the Digital Markets, Competition and Consumers Bill in the UK' (2023) 12(5) *Journal of European Consumer and Market Law* 173–76.
440 Regulation 2(6) of the CPUTRs 2008.
441 Agustín Vicente and Ingrid Lossius Falkum, 'Accounting for the Preference for Literal Meanings in Autism Spectrum Conditions' (2023) 38(1) *Mind and Language* 119–40 at 119.
442 Sections 242(1)–(4) of the DMCCA 2024.
443 Ibid. section 242(5).

could have gone further in specifying explicitly that before adopting these regulations, the Secretary of State needs to consult, among other key stakeholders, consumer organisations and DDPOs.

A fourth positive aspect of the DMCCA refers to the increased enforcement power of the Competition and Markets Authority (CMA)[444] regarding the prohibitions on unfair commercial practices under section 225 of the Act.[445] Part 3 (enforcement of consumer protection law), under Chapter 4 (direct enforcement powers of CMA), grants the CMA the power to investigate suspected infringements of consumer protection law[446] which, as clarified in the Explanatory Notes to the DMCCA, can act as 'a trigger for the use of CMA's direct enforcement powers under this Chapter'.[447] These include the power to issue infringement notices and penalties, and online interface notices.[448] Traders can appeal CMA decisions to the High Court.[449]

Despite these positive developments, the DMCCA presents a range of challenges. Some of these have been referred to above (e.g. inclusion of reference to 'price' in the definition of 'invitation to purchase';[450] insufficient emphasis on the need to consult with consumer organisations and DDPOs when considering amendments to the DMCCA).[451] The remainder of this section focuses on two challenges: the continued reliance on the distinction between average and vulnerable consumers which rests on an unrealistic vision of average consumers, and the insufficient emphasis on neurodiversity when considering the scope of unfair commercial practices under the DMCCA framework.

Firstly, the DMCCA continues to rely on a distinction between average consumers,[452] average targeted consumers,[453] and average vulnerable consumers,[454] and on an unrealistic image of the average consumer as someone who is 'reasonably well informed, observant, and circumspect'.[455] Yet, as Sax and Helberger point out, the 'classic distinction' between vulnerable and non-vulnerable consumers 'is collapsed', as 'every consumer is potentially vulnerable', depending on circumstances.[456] Circumstantial vulnerability can be due to the architecture of the online environment, if this is designed by traders to manipulate consumer behaviour. Consequently, 'vulnerability becomes the rule, rather than the exception'.[457] Regulatory measures must reflect this universal vulnerability. They should also seek to protect consumers not only as economic actors but also as citizens, considering the 'collateral harm' to social values (such as autonomy, dignity and inclusion) which can be caused by unfair commercial practices.[458]

444 Ibid. section 231(3). 445 Ibid. section 231. 446 Ibid. section 180.
447 Explanatory Notes to the DMCCA 2024, [1066]. 448 Sections 181–84 of the DMCCA 2024.
449 Ibid. section 202. 450 Ibid. section 230(10)(a). 451 Ibid. section 242.
452 See, for example, sections 225(4)(a), 226(1)(b) and 227(2) of the DMCCA 2024.
453 Ibid. section 246(4). 454 Ibid. section 247. 455 Ibid. section 246(2).
456 Marijn Sax and Natali Helberger, 'Digital Vulnerability and Manipulation in the Emerging Digital Framework' in Natali Helberger and others, 'Digital Fairness for Consumers', Report for BEUC (European Consumer Organisation), Brussels, March 2024, 11–24, at 11.
457 Ibid. 458 Ibid. 13.

The definition of vulnerable consumers under the DMCCA includes reference to the circumstances of the transaction, alongside factors such as 'age', 'physical or mental health' or 'credulity'.[459] The Explanatory Notes to the DMCCA provide as examples of consumer vulnerability to unfair commercial practices, the potential vulnerability of elderly consumers to pressure selling, of consumers with physical injuries to 'misleading advertising' promising cures, as well as contextual vulnerability due to circumstances such as 'being in mourning, going through a divorce, or losing a job'.[460] These examples refer to personal circumstances affecting consumers. Reference to circumstantial vulnerability presented in the DMCCA should be interpreted broadly to include environmental barriers (e.g. due to the architecture of the online environment) and attitudinal barriers (e.g. negative attitudes from traders).

Secondly, the regulatory framework on the protection of consumers from unfair trading could have gone further in considering neurodiversity (e.g. when assessing whether a commercial practice falls within the list of prohibited practices under Schedule 20 of the DMCCA). Neurodiversity, which refers to 'acknowledging differences in brain function and behavioural traits as normal variation of the human population', includes neurodivergence (e.g. autism, ADHD, dyslexia, dyspraxia, dyscalculia, dysgraphia, Tourette's syndrome) and neurotypicality.[461] It promotes an understanding of 'the strengths of each neurodiverse individual',[462] and a perception of neurodivergence as a 'variation in functioning, rather than a disorder to be cured'.[463] In a regulatory framework where the focus on assessing vulnerability is based on the context of the transaction, rather than on the medical condition of individuals, more emphasis must be placed on developing an online market architecture which acknowledges the variety of ways in which people process information, and should take these aspects of human diversity into account when assessing the scope of unfair commercial practices. To explore this point in more detail, we must consider (i) what is meant by harmful 'online choice architecture' (or 'dark patterns') and the potential negative impact of such practices on consumers, (ii) why such practices pose a particular risk for neurodivergent consumers, (iii) why the DMCCA regulatory framework, as it stands, does not go far enough in addressing neurodiversity and (iv) call on legislative developments, including by relying on the power conferred to the Secretary of State under section 242 to adopt regulations[464] to expand the list of unfair commercial practices under Schedule 20, following consultations with consumer organisations and DDPOs.

'Online choice architecture' (OCA), which refers to the way in which traders present 'information and choices' about their products to consumers in the digital marketplace, can play a key role 'in influencing consumer and market

[459] Section 247(4) of the DMCCA 2024. [460] Explanatory Notes to the DMCCA 2024, [1440].
[461] Fung and others 'Neurodiversity', 3201. [462] Ibid. [463] Ibid. (quoting Jim Sinclair).
[464] Section 242 of the DMCCA 2024.

outcomes'.[465] In seeking to promote their products, traders may choose to rely on design features that use 'persuasion, emotion and trust'.[466] When these design techniques are used 'systematically' to 'manipulate consumers into actions' that they would not have taken otherwise, resulting in negative experiences for consumers but benefiting traders,[467] we are looking at harmful OCA,[468] or 'dark patterns'.[469] Dark patterns can influence consumers without their knowledge,[470] as they 'work on a subconscious level' to 'exploit consumers' cognitive vulnerabilities' such as their 'limited attention' or 'biases'.[471] These biases include the *status quo* bias (e.g. accepting a default option),[472] fear-based biases linked to loss aversion (e.g. making a purchase after being notified about the scarcity of a particular item),[473] or the anchoring bias (e.g. continuing with a purchase despite the addition of 'drip pricing', due to being 'anchored' to the 'initial headline price').[474] While these techniques can lead to positive outcomes for traders such as increases in sales, they can have a negative impact on consumers,[475] including financial and emotional harm.[476]

Due to the extensive range of dark patterns employed by traders and the need to provide a structure around which to group these manipulative practices, this discussion suggests a classification of these patterns into four categories. The first category focuses on dark patterns designed to lure consumers to choose a particular product by employing methods such as creating a false sense of urgency (we could call these 'inducing' patterns). The second category is concerned with dark patterns which target consumers who are in the process of buying a product (e.g. they have added the product to the basket), with the aim of manipulating them into purchasing an additional pre-selected product, or inadvertently signing up to a service or subscription (we could call these 'burdening' patterns). The third category of dark patterns is, like the previous category, focused on the stage where consumers are in the process of buying a product, but in this case, the aim is to manipulate consumers into giving away personal data which can be used by traders for the purpose of targeted advertising (we could call these 'encroaching' patterns). The fourth category focuses on dark patterns designed to make it difficult for consumers to leave a contract such as a subscription agreement (we could call these 'constraining' patterns).

Under the classification suggested earlier, the first set of deceptive designs to be considered come under the category of 'inducing' patterns. Traders employing these types of dark patterns seek to lure consumers into choosing their products by employing a range of manipulative methods. These include

[465] ICO and CMA, 'Harmful Design'. [466] Petterson, 'Dark Patterns and Disability'. [467] Ibid.
[468] ICO and CMA, 'Harmful Design'. [469] Firth, 'Practical Web Inclusion'.
[470] Petterson, 'Dark Patterns and Disability'. [471] Which? 'Dark Patterns'.
[472] ICO and CMA, 'Harmful Design'. [473] Petterson, 'Dark Patterns and Disability'.
[474] Martin Brenncke, 'A Theory of Exploitation for Consumer Law: Online Choice Architectures, Dark Patterns, and Autonomy Violations' (2024) 47(1) *Journal of Consumer Policy* 127–64, at 132.
[475] Petterson, 'Dark Patterns and Disability'. [476] Which? 'Dark Patterns'.

'bait advertising', where traders entice consumers 'by advertising a product at a very low price' despite not having available a reasonable stock,[477] as well as 'bait and switch', where deceptive practices include 'deliberately' using another company's 'trade mark' to 'attract the consumer's attention', and then exploiting 'the opportunity thus created to switch the consumer's purchasing intention to his own product or service'.[478] They also include the commercial practice described as 'advertorial', which refers to the promotion of a product 'in the form of an article' written in a way that resembles 'informative journalistic content' and which 'fits with its surrounding context' without making it clear to the consumer that this is, in fact, 'a paid advertisement'.[479] A further source of concern is the deceptive practice involving a forced sense of urgency (known as 'urgency claims'[480] or 'forced urgency'),[481] which seeks to pressure consumers into making a quick decision to purchase a product. These can take the form of time limitations (e.g. countdown timers indicating when a deal will expire),[482] 'act fast' claims, 'scarcity claims'[483] (e.g. notifications about the low stock levels of a product),[484] and 'popularity claims'[485] (e.g. notifications that a product is in high demand,[486] or is being viewed by other users).[487] In an open letter directed to online traders before the adoption of the DMCCA, the CMA reminded the business community to ensure that any urgency claims made online can be substantiated by 'adequate records to show that these claims genuinely reflect selling conditions'.[488] While this proactive approach from the CMA is to be welcomed, the message to the business community could have done more to highlight the impact of such patterns on consumers, including consumers with disabilities, and to stress vulnerability concerns posed by the context of the online design architecture.

The second category of harmful OCA to be considered, which could be grouped under the name of 'burdening' patterns, refers to deceptive designs which target consumers in the process of buying a product, with the aim of manipulating them into inadvertently signing up to services or subscriptions, or buying additional products. Examples of such patterns include 'basket sneaking' (also known as 'sneak into basket'), where traders add into

[477] 'Directive on Unfair Commercial Practices Comes into Force' (2008) 51(Jan) *European Newsletter* 11–12, at 12.

[478] *OCH-Ziff Europe* v. *OCH Capital* [2010] EWHC 2599 (Ch); [2011] Bus. L.R. 632, [82] (Mr Justice Arnold). See Alice Blythe, 'Confusion Online: Does the Test for Trade Mark Confusion on the Internet Differ from that Applied to Infringement in Other Spheres?' (2014) 36(9) *European Intellectual Property Review* 563–68, at 566.

[479] Alexandros Antoniou, 'Advertising Regulation and Transparency in Influencers' Endorsements on Social Media' (2021) 26(4) *Communications Law* 190–207, at 195.

[480] Competition and Markets Authority, 'Open Letter: Urgency Claims and Price Reduction Claims: Compliance Advice for Online Traders', 29 March 2023, 5.

[481] Firth, 'Practical Web Inclusion', p. 248. [482] Which? 'Dark Patterns'.

[483] CMA, 'Open Letter: Urgency Claims', 5. [484] Which? 'Dark Patterns'.

[485] CMA, 'Open Letter: Urgency Claims', 5. [486] Firth, 'Practical Web Inclusion', p. 248.

[487] Which? 'Dark Patterns'. [488] CMA, 'Open Letter: Urgency Claims', 5.

consumers' online shopping baskets additional products that consumers did not intend to buy, or pre-select an option for consumers where the additional product is added as the default option.[489] Further examples include the use of 'trick questions', where traders' choice of language is deliberately phrased to make it difficult for consumers to understand whether they are opting in or out of a service or subscription.[490] They also include 'hidden costs', where consumers are tricked into paying more for a product 'via pre-selected add-ons' that are 'embedded close to the final stage of payment'.[491]

The third category of dark patterns considered, which could come under the suggested term of 'encroaching' patterns, seek to manipulate consumers into giving away personal data, which is then used by traders for advertising purposes. Examples of such patterns include 'bundled consent', where a 'single consent option' manipulates consumers into agreeing 'to the use of their personal information for multiple separate purposes' such as 'consenting to the terms of use' and 'receiving marketing emails'.[492] They also include 'default privacy settings' where traders 'apply a predefined choice' which can be changed by consumers only through taking 'active steps', which are often cumbersome (e.g. having to 'dig deep into a service's settings').[493] Further examples include the dark pattern known as 'confirm shaming' (or 'confirmshaming'), where consumers are manoeuvred into choosing an option favourable to traders (e.g. consumers agree to give away their personal information in exchange for a discount), by phrasing the alternative choice in a manner that 'shames' consumers 'into compliance' (e.g. 'no thanks, I don't want to save money',[494] or 'nahh, I hate savings').[495] 'False hierarchy' is another example of dark patterns where consumers are presented with two options, and the option more favourable to traders stands out more due to its position on the page, colour or size.[496] Other instances of deceptive patterns include 'harmful nudges' (also known as 'dark nudges) and 'sludge' (also known as 'friction'), where consumers find it easy to make choices which benefit traders (e.g. allowing personalised adverts with one click), but find it difficult to choose the option which benefits them (e.g. having to take several steps to reject personalised adverts).[497] One further example of a dark pattern refers to 'nagging', where consumers who try to complete an order are interrupted by pop-ups inviting them to sign up to an email subscription list and redirect them to the sign up page.[498]

The fourth group of harmful OCA, which falls under the suggested category of 'constraining' patterns, is concerned with deceptive designs that seek to make it difficult for consumers to leave a contract such as a subscription contract. Examples include 'forced continuity' (also known as 'hotel California' or

[489] Firth, 'Practical Web Inclusion', p. 253. [490] Which? 'Dark Patterns'.
[491] Consumer Policy Research Centre (CPRC) (Australia), 'Duped by Design: Manipulative Online Design: Dark Patterns in Australia', June 2022.
[492] ICO and CMA, 'Harmful Design'. [493] Ibid. [494] Which? 'Dark Patterns'.
[495] ICO and CMA, 'Harmful Design'. [496] Which? 'Dark Patterns'.
[497] ICO and CMA, 'Harmful Design'. [498] Which? 'Dark Patterns'.

'roach motel') patterns, where consumers encounter difficulties when seeking to cancel a subscription (e.g. following a free trial) and, as a result, risk remaining trapped into an unwanted subscription.[499] Further instances include the 'automatic renewal' of subscriptions as part of the 'default settings' employed by traders, and where consumers must take 'active steps' to change these settings.[500] This category of dark patterns is discussed in more detail in relation to subscription contracts in the section on information and cancellation rights.

The use of dark patterns by traders can cause harms to consumers. People may suffer economic harms due to spending more money than originally intended[501] after being manoeuvred into purchasing products that they did not want or need.[502] As Citizens Advice point out, this is particularly problematic 'at a time when cost of living pressures mean budgets are stretched to breaking point'.[503] People may also suffer social harms, including emotional harms (e.g. feeling manipulated by traders),[504] a negative impact on mental health,[505] privacy harms (e.g. personalised adverts which may seek to exploit a position of vulnerability such bereavement),[506] and harm to people's individual autonomy and human dignity (e.g. lack of confidence in participating in the digital marketplace).[507]

Dark patterns can be particularly problematic for neurodivergent consumers, who may be 'more vulnerable to the psychological tricks' used by deceptive OCA, and for whom the threshold for when a trader's design becomes a deceptive pattern 'may be lower' when compared with neurotypical consumers.[508] Regulatory measures designed to address the harms posed by dark patterns must consider neurodiversity. Within the category of 'inducing' patterns discussed earlier, deceptive designs, such as 'bait advertising', 'bait and switch' and 'advertorial', could cause neurodivergent consumers to feel powerless.[509] Furthermore, the 'forced urgency' pattern can trigger or aggravate in neurodivergent people feelings of anxiety and panic.[510] Neurodivergent people with anxiety may require a longer amount of time to complete an online purchase (for example, due to the need to exercise extra caution when inputting credit card information),[511] and may experience an enhanced level of pressure when faced with urgency claims such as 'act fast', 'low stock' or 'in high demand',[512]

[499] CPRC, 'Duped by Design'. [500] ICO and CMA, 'Harmful Design'.
[501] Which? 'Dark Patterns'.
[502] Citizens Advice, 'Response to Consultation on Improving Price Transparency and Product Information for Consumers', October 2023.
[503] Citizens Advice, 'Pushed to Purchase! Counting the Cost of Deceptive Digital Design in E-commerce', July 2023.
[504] Which? 'Dark Patterns'. [505] Citizens Advice, 'Pushed to Purchase'.
[506] CMA, 'Online Choice Architecture', 4.4. [507] Citizens Advice, 'Pushed to Purchase'.
[508] Petterson, 'Dark Patterns and Disability'. [509] Firth, 'Practical Web Inclusion', p. 258.
[510] Ibid.
[511] Home Office, 'Designing Accessible Services', https://ukhomeoffice.github.io/accessibility-posters/ (last accessed 12 July 2024).
[512] Which? 'Dark Patterns'.

which may manipulate them into making very quick decisions.[513] They may also be 'more susceptible to fear-based cognitive biases such as artificial scarcity or loss aversion'.[514] Moreover, the presence of a countdown timer in an online shopping environment may trigger a 'fear response', impede decision-making, and may cause panic attacks.[515] 'Forced urgency' patterns can also push consumers, including people with ADHD, into making impulsive decisions which are not in their best interest,[516] such as 'volatile overspending' on products that they cannot afford or do not need,[517] or an impulsive purchase of a larger quantity of a product than what they need.[518]

As part of the category of 'burdening' patterns considered earlier, harmful OCA such as 'basket sneaking' can have a negative impact on neurodivergent people, including some people with ADHD, as it can manoeuvre people into making impulsive purchases.[519] In addition, dark patterns in the form of 'trick questions' could have a negative impact on people with language processing conditions such as dyslexia, who may face difficulties in understanding the decisions that they are making, due to the way in which the choice was framed by traders.[520]

The category of 'encroaching' patterns discussed earlier also includes deceptive patterns which can have a negative impact on neurodivergent consumers. For example, 'default privacy settings' can affect neurodivergent people, including dyslexic people and people with ADHD, who may experience difficulties when reading long instructions and may be tempted to agree to options that they do not want.[521] Other dark patterns such as 'confirm shaming' can impact negatively on people who experience social anxiety, including some autistic people.[522] This is because 'confirm shaming' relies on manoeuvring consumers into selecting the option favourable to traders, which is framed as the 'good' choice, while the alternative option which may be more favourable to consumers, tends to be phrased as a 'bad' choice.[523] People may associate choosing the latter option with feeling of guilt or embarrassment, or with doing something 'morally wrong or socially unacceptable'.[524] Further challenges can also be caused by deceptive patters such as 'false hierarchy', where information is presented in a complex layout, and where the choices favourable to traders are given greater prominence. The use of complex layouts to present information can make it more difficult for neurodivergent people to process information, including autistic people and people with language processing conditions such as dyslexia.[525]

513 Firth, 'Practical Web Inclusion', p. 248. 514 Petterson, 'Dark Patterns and Disability'.
515 Ibid. 516 Firth, 'Practical Web Inclusion', p. 248.
517 Competition and Markets Authority, 'Consumer Vulnerability: Challenges and Potential Solutions', February 2019, 34.
518 Petterson, 'Dark Patterns and Disability'. 519 Firth, 'Practical Web Inclusion', p. 253.
520 Petterson, 'Dark Patterns and Disability'. 521 Ibid.
522 Firth, 'Practical Web Inclusion', p. 255. 523 ICO and CMA, 'Harmful Design'. 524 Ibid.
525 Home Office, 'Designing Accessible Services'.

Within the category of 'constraining' patterns referred to earlier, harmful OCA such as 'forced continuity' can affect neurodivergent people with communication anxiety, who may choose to continue with an unwanted subscription, when that subscription can only be cancelled by phoning the trader.[526] Challenges are also posed by the dark pattern of 'automatic renewal' of subscriptions, where consumers, including dyslexic people and people with ADHD, may inadvertently agree to that option due to difficulties reading long instructions.[527]

The regulatory framework under the DMCCA responds to a number of the dark patterns examined earlier. For example, the 'constraining' patterns of 'forced continuity' and 'automatic renewal' are covered by the regime for subscription contracts under Chapter 2 of part 2 of the DMCCA,[528] which is discussed in more detail in the section on information and cancellation. Further dark patterns which fall within the DMCCA regulatory regime include the 'inducing' patterns discussed earlier, which include 'bait advertising', 'bait and switch', 'advertorial' and 'forced urgency', and which are prohibited by Schedule 20 as part of the list of commercial practices considered as unfair in all circumstances.[529] However, unlike the CPUTRs, which used the labels of 'bait advertising', 'bait and switch' and 'advertorial' for the first three of these patterns,[530] the DMCCA does not use these labels to describe the corresponding patterns. This is regrettable, as these labels could have assisted with consumer education on recognising these patterns. Moreover, these provisions could have gone further in protecting neurodivergent consumers. For instance, Schedule 20(7), which prohibits the dark pattern of 'forced urgency', focuses on the commercial practice of 'falsely stating that a product will only be available for a limited time, or that it will only be available on particular terms for a limited time', with the purpose of provoking 'an immediate decision' and denying consumers 'sufficient opportunity or time to make an informed choice'.[531] Thus, while false urgency is prohibited by the DMCCA, the Act could have gone further in addressing the negative impact that urgency-related claims can have on consumers, even when these claims are accurate. This is particularly pertinent for neurodivergent consumers, who may have a lower threshold than neurotypical consumers for when a trader's design becomes a deceptive pattern,[532] and for whom, design features such as countdown timers or scarcity claims could trigger or aggravate feelings of panic and anxiety.[533]

526 Firth, 'Practical Web Inclusion', p. 261.
527 Petterson, 'Dark Patterns and Disability'.
528 Chapter 2 (Subscription Contracts) in part 4 (Consumer Rights and Disputes) of the DMCCA 2024.
529 DMCCA 2024, Schedule 20(5): 'bait advertising', Schedule 20(6): 'bait and switch', Schedule 20(12): 'advertorial', and Schedule 20(7): 'forced urgency'.
530 CPUTRs 2008, Schedule 1(5): 'bait advertising', Schedule 1(6): 'bait and switch', Schedule 1(11): 'advertorial'.
531 Schedule 20(7) of the DMCCA 2024.
532 Petterson, 'Dark Patterns and Disability'.
533 Firth, 'Practical Web Inclusion', p. 232.

An enhanced protection for consumers, including neurodivergent consumers, from the harmful effect of dark patterns, could also rely on a broad interpretation of unfair commercial practices.[534] When assessing whether 'commercial practices' amount to 'unfair commercial practices', the assessment threshold must consider neurodiversity. An example could be provided regarding the measures condemning contraventions of 'the requirements of professional diligence', which refer to practices falling short of 'the standard of skill and care' reasonably expected from traders to be exercised towards consumers, assessed with reference to traders' 'field of activity', and corresponding with 'honest market practice', or 'the general principle of good faith'.[535] The concepts of 'good faith' and 'honest market practice' are not defined in the DMCCA, and this led Citizens Advice to express concern that this could result in inconsistent interpretations, leaving 'the door open to poor practices' which fall outside the scope of existing regulatory measures.[536] Some guidance is provided in the Explanatory Notes to the DMCCA, which note that 'good faith' refers to 'fair and open dealing', ensuring that traders do not 'take advantage of consumer's lack of experience or unfamiliarity with a product', and which assess 'honest market practices' and 'good faith' with reference to whether traders have considered 'the legitimate interests or expectations of the average consumer in the particular sector'.[537] The threshold for such considerations should take into account the variety of ways in which people process information or respond to pressure. A broad interpretation of the concepts of 'honest market practices' and 'good faith', where traders consider the interests and expectations of all consumers, including neurodivergent consumers, could contribute towards addressing harmful OCA. As Citizens Advice emphasise, interpretations of concepts such as 'good faith' must 'evolve to respond to the unique challenges that the digital world presents', given that the choices employed by traders when designing the online architecture 'can result in widespread detriment for consumers' if such choices 'are not made with due care'[538] for all consumers.

The regulatory framework on unfair commercial practices must go further in challenging and preventing the harmful effect of 'dark patterns' on consumers, including neurodivergent consumers.[539] This call for further legislative developments could rely, *inter alia*, on the power conferred to the Secretary of State under section 242 to adopt regulations to amend the list of unfair commercial practices under Schedule 20, including by modifying or adding to that list.[540] These measures should be based on principles of universal design, and

[534] Sections 225(4)(a) and 226–29 of the DMCCA 2024.
[535] Ibid. sections 225(4)(a)(i) and 229(1).
[536] Citizens Advice, 'Response to Consultation on Price Transparency'.
[537] Explanatory Notes to the DMCCA 2024, [1371], [1372].
[538] Citizens Advice, 'Response to Consultation on Price Transparency'.
[539] Firth, 'Practical Web Inclusion', p. 232.
[540] Section 242(1) of the DMCCA 2024.

should be developed in consultation with key stakeholders,[541] including organisations of neurodivergent people.

4.2.4 Regulating Information, Cancellation and Additional Charges

The key provisions regulating information, cancellation and additional charges in B2C contracts are comprised in the CCRs 2013. For subscription contracts, the regulation of these issues is comprised in the DMCCA 2024. This discussion starts with the latter framework to provide continuity with the discussion in the previous section, before moving on to discuss the CCRs in more detail.

The DMCCA introduces a new regulatory regime for the provision of information and cancellation rights regarding subscription contracts in Chapter 2 of part 4 (consumer rights and disputes).[542] Many of these provisions are expected to come into force[543] in the spring of 2026, to allow businesses sufficient time to adapt to the new rules.[544] A 'subscription contract'[545] is defined as a trader-consumer contract where the trader supplies goods, services or digital content to the consumer[546] in exchange for payment, is either a contract that falls within section 254(2) or 254(3), and is not an excluded contract.[547] A contract falls within section 254(2) if it is a fixed-term or indefinite contract which automatically renews, making the consumer automatically liable for payment, and the consumer has a right to bring that contract to an end.[548] For a contract to fall within section 254(3), it must be a contract where goods, services or digital content are provided to the consumer initially free of charge or at a reduced rate, this is done for a specified period of time, but once this period of time comes to an end, the consumer is automatically liable for payment (or for payment at the full rate), and the consumer has a right to bring that contract to an end before incurring such liability.[549] Schedule 22 provides a list of contracts excluded from this definition, including contracts for utilities and financial services.[550] The Explanatory Notes to the DMCCA clarify that the CCRs 'continue to apply' to contracts falling outside the definition of 'subscription contracts' under the DMCCA, 'unless otherwise excluded' by the CCRs.[551]

The DMCCA rules on subscription contracts focus on traders' duties to provide consumers with relevant information before entering into a subscription contract, send reminder notices before consumers become liable for renewal payments, and enable consumers to exercise their right to end a subscription

[541] Ibid. section 242(5).

[542] Chapter 2 (Subscription Contracts) of part 4 (Consumer Rights and Disputes) of the DMCCA 2024.

[543] Section 339 of the DMCCA 2024.

[544] Hansard, HL, vol. 49, col. 2085, 13 March 2024 (Lord Offord of Garvel).

[545] Section 254 of the DMCCA 2024. [546] Ibid. section 280(1). [547] Ibid. sections 254(1).

[548] Ibid. section 254(2). [549] Ibid. section 254(3). [550] Ibid. Schedule 22.

[551] Explanatory Notes to the DMCCA 2024, [1454].

contract.[552] They also cover consumer rights if traders breach these duties, and their rights to cancel subscription contracts during cooling-off periods.[553] Provision also cover circumstances where traders fail to provide consumers with information about cooling-off rights, and any potential defences available to traders.[554] They also confer on the Secretary of State powers to make further provisions regarding the cancellation of subscription contracts by adopting regulations.[555] Some of these provisions are explored in more detail in the next paragraphs, and this discussion is followed by a reflection on why the adoption of these rules was necessary, and whether these provisions go sufficiently far in protecting consumers, including consumers with disabilities.

Traders have a duty to provide consumers with two sets of relevant information before entering into subscription contracts.[556] Firstly, the 'key pre-contract information' listed in part 1 of Schedule 23[557] must be provided for all subscription contracts, even if apparent from the context of the transaction.[558] For contracts falling within section 254(2), traders must inform consumers, *inter alia*, about their on-going obligation to pay, unless consumers take steps to bring that contract to an end.[559] If a contract falls within section 254(3), traders must inform consumers, among others, that they will start being charged (or will be charged at a higher rate), unless consumers take steps to bring that contract to an end before incurring such liabilities.[560] Consumers must also be informed of the frequency with which payments will be taken and the amount to be paid,[561] and any contract terms which allow for a price to be varied during the course of a contract must comply with the fairness requirement in part 2 of the CRA.[562] Secondly, the 'full pre-contract information' listed in part 2 of Schedule 23[563] must be provided to consumers 'only to the extent that' is 'applicable to the contract' and is 'not already apparent from the context'.[564] This includes information about the main characteristics of products, traders' identity and address, payments, delivery charges and traders' 'complaint handling policy',[565] as well as information about consumers' right to cancel subscription contracts during 'the initial cooling-off period', any cancellation rights during the 'renewal cooling-off period' and statutory rights under part 1 of the CRA.[566] Traders must provide consumers with this information 'as close in time to entering into the contract as practicable'.[567] Information is 'made available' to consumers only if they 'can reasonably be expected to' 'know how to access it and be able to access it.[568] Traders must also provide this information 'in clear and plain language', written information must be 'in a legible form', and oral

[552] Sections 256–61 of the DMCCA 2024. [553] Ibid. sections 262–66.
[554] Ibid. sections 268–71. [555] Ibid. section 267. [556] Ibid. sections 256–57.
[557] Ibid. section 256(1) and part 1 of Schedule 23. [558] Ibid. section 256(1)(a).
[559] Ibid. Schedule 23(2). [560] Ibid. Schedule 23(3). [561] Ibid. Schedule 23(4).
[562] Explanatory Notes to the DMCCA 2024, [1486].
[563] Section 256(1)(b) and part 2 of Schedule 23 of the DMCCA 2024. [564] Ibid. section 256(5).
[565] Ibid. Schedules 23(14)–(20). [566] Ibid. Schedules 23(21)–(23). [567] Ibid. section 256(2).
[568] Ibid. section 256(6).

information must be 'audible and comprehensible'.[569] While these provisions are to be welcomed, a stronger degree of protection for consumers, including consumers with disabilities, would have been delivered if the DMCCA stated explicitly[570] that the information must be provided in accessible formats, and be based on principles of universal design.

Traders are also under a duty to send consumers reminder notices before they become liable for renewal payments, and these notices must include the information required under Schedule 23 part 3.[571] Traders must inform consumers, *inter alia*, that they 'will become liable for the renewal payment', unless they take steps to end the contract, the date when the renewal payment is due, the amount of the payment, and the steps that must be taken by consumers if they want to end the subscription contract.[572] Reminder notices must be given to consumers 'in such a way' that required information 'is more prominent than any other information given to the consumer at the same time.[573] Regrettably, these provisions fail to mention explicitly the need for reminder notices to be provided in accessible formats, reflective of principles of universal design.

Furthermore, traders are under a duty to enable consumers to exercise their right to end subscription contracts in a 'straightforward' way, and 'without having to take any steps which are not reasonably necessary'.[574] Practices 'likely to breach' these provisions include contracts where it was easy for consumers to sign up online, 'at the click of a button', but where they encountered 'more onerous' processes (e.g. having to phone traders) when seeking to exit these contracts.[575] Further examples include requiring consumers 'to go through an excessive number of steps' to 'turn off auto-renewal online', or not being presented with a 'clear and prominent option to turn off auto-renewal'.[576] While references to 'accessible means to end a subscription contract' are included in the Explanatory Notes to the DMCCA, such references are not explicit in the Act itself. Moreover, neither the DMCCA, nor the Explanatory Notes provide further details on what is meant by 'accessible means' in this context. A stronger degree of protection could have been provided for consumers, including consumers with disabilities, if the call for addressing accessibility barriers was explicit in the DMCCA.

Consumers may seek to exercise their right to end a subscription contract by 'notifying the traders' in the form of 'a clear statement setting out their decision to bring the contract to an end'.[577] In the case of subscription contracts entered into online, traders must allow consumers 'to bring the contract

[569] Ibid. section 272(8).

[570] The Explanatory Notes to the DMCCA 2024 [1473] indicate that 'the full pre-contract information must be accessible', but without going into details on what is meant by 'accessibility' in this context.

[571] Sections 258–59 and part 3 of Schedule 23 of the DMCCA 2024.

[572] Ibid. Schedules 23(30), (31), (34), (37) and (39).

[573] Ibid. section 259(2).

[574] Ibid. sections 260(1) and 261.

[575] Explanatory Notes to the DMCCA 2024, [1544].

[576] Ibid.

[577] Sections 260(2) and (6) of the DMCCA 2024.

to an end online', and to make sure that 'instructions for doing so are displayed online' in a place where consumers are 'likely to find them'.[578] Traders may be in breach of these provisions if the online cancellation mechanisms are 'not clearly and prominently labelled', or can only be accessed by 'activating hover text or a drop-down menu'.[579] Traders may also make available other additional means for cancelling the contract.[580] Where consumers exercise their right to cancel or bringing to an end a subscription contract, traders must provide an 'end of contract notice' to acknowledge this,[581] which must be 'in writing on a durable medium'.[582] A stronger degree of protection could have been provided by an explicit call to provide 'end of contract' notices in accessible formats.

The DMCCA also covers consumer rights in the event of breach of these duties by traders,[583] and their rights to cancel subscription contracts during cooling-off periods.[584] There is an implied term in every subscription contract that traders have complied with the duties to provide consumers with, *inter alia*, key pre-contract information and reminder notices.[585] If traders are in breach of this implied term, consumers have a right to cancel the subscription contract.[586] This is interpreted broadly to cover 'a failure to comply with any part' of these requirements, such as the partial provision of information.[587] Subscription contracts also imply a term that traders have complied with the duties to provide consumers with the full pre-contract information.[588] Consumers also have the right to cancel subscription contracts during 'initial' and 'renewal' cooling-off periods.[589] As simplified in the Explanatory Notes to the DMCCA, a 'cooling-off period' refers to a 'a 14-day period where a consumer may cancel their contract for any reason'.[590] Traders must provide consumers with a 'cooling-off notice' for each renewal cooling-off period, notifying consumers, *inter alia*, that their subscription contract is continuing, and that they have a renewal cooling-off cancellation right.[591] The DMCCA could have gone further in calling explicitly for the accessibility of 'cooling-off notices', and of the cancellation procedure during the 'cooling-off' periods.

Subscription-based business models can be beneficial for consumers, who can 'receive goods, services, and digital content on an ongoing basis', in exchange for a recurring payment.[592] They include subscriptions for streaming services (e.g. video), publications (e.g. newspapers), beauty products (e.g.

[578] Ibid. section 260(4). [579] Explanatory Notes to the DMCCA 2024, [1548].
[580] Ibid. [1547]. [581] Section 261 of the DMCCA 2024.
[582] Explanatory Notes to the DMCCA 2024, [1550]. [583] Sections 262–63 of the DMCCA 2024.
[584] Ibid. sections 264–66. [585] Ibid. sections 256(1)(a) and 258.
[586] Ibid. sections 263(1) and (2). [587] Explanatory Notes to the DMCCA 2024, [1557].
[588] Sections 256(1)(b) of the DMCCA 2024. [589] Ibid. sections 264–66.
[590] Explanatory Notes to the DMCCA 2024, [1573].
[591] Sections 266(1) and (2) of the DMCCA 2024.
[592] Department for Business, Energy, and Industrial Strategy (BEIS), 'Consumer and Competition Reform: Subscriptions Regs Impact Assessment', July 2021.

skincare) or groceries (e.g. food boxes).[593] However, as Citizens Advice warns, this business model 'can be abused' by traders, 'leading to subscription traps'.[594] Consumers may find themselves bound by subscription contracts they do not want due to signing up by accident, signing up to a free trial and then overlooking to cancel the subscription, or wanting to cancel a subscription but encountering difficulties in doing so.[595] Some of these challenges can be associated with 'dark patterns', including the 'constraining patterns' referred to in the previous section, which include the deceptive practices of 'forced continuity' and 'automatic renewal'.[596] 'Forced continuity' refers to a harmful OCA where consumers find it easy to sign up to a subscription contract, but find it difficult to cancel the agreement.[597] 'Automatic renewal' refers to a deceptive pattern where subscription contracts are renewed automatically as part of the 'default settings' presented by traders, which consumers can change only by taking 'active steps'.[598] This takes advantage of the *status quo* bias, where consumers are more likely to accept a default option.[599]

'Subscription traps' cause economic harm for consumers, such as financial losses caused by having to pay subscription fees for services or products that they do not want or cannot afford.[600] Citizens Advice have raised concerns that these harmful practices tend to have the hardest impact on 'marginalised groups and people on low incomes'.[601] Moreover, the negative impact of these dark patterns goes beyond economic harms to include social harms, including emotional harms, harm to consumers' mental health[602] and harms to their individual autonomy and human dignity, due to being manipulated by traders.[603] For example, consumers may experience stress when trying to cancel subscription contracts and being faced with complex cancellation processes.[604]

'Subscription traps' can pose a particular set of challenges for neurodivergent consumers and it is, therefore, important that regulatory responses to these challenges consider neurodiversity. For example, the 'automatic renewal' dark pattern can pose problems for neurodivergent people, including dyslexic people and people with ADHD, who may experience difficulties when reading long instructions and, as a result, may agree to options that they do not want.[605] The 'forced continuity' dark pattern can be problematic for people who experience communication anxiety, including some autistic people, who may choose to carry on with a subscription contract they do not want, when the only way to cancel that contract is to have a phone conversation with the trader.[606] In empirical research with autistic people which focused on

[593] Citizens Advice, 'Half a Billion Pounds Spent on Subscriptions That Rolled over without People Realising during the Cost-of-Living Crisis', 1 December 2022.
[594] Citizens Advice, 'Subscription Traps', November 2022. [595] Ibid.
[596] See the discussion in the section on 'unfair commercial practices'.
[597] Firth, 'Practical Web Inclusion', p. 261. [598] ICO and CMA, 'Harmful Design'. [599] Ibid.
[600] Citizens Advice, 'Subscription Traps'. [601] Ibid. [602] Which? 'Dark Patterns'.
[603] Citizens Advice, 'Pushed to Purchase'. [604] Citizens Advice, 'Subscription Traps'.
[605] Petterson, 'Dark Patterns and Disability'. [606] Firth, 'Practical Web Inclusion', p. 261.

preferred modes of communication, Howard and Sedgewick found that email was the preferred choice when contracting service providers, while phone calls were the lest preferred option.[607] The research concluded that 'autistic people are highly averse to making or receiving phone calls' due to challenges in auditory processing, communication anxiety, or a preference for 'planning and predictability'.[608] As Howard and Sedgewick note, 'mode of communication can be either enabling or disabling for autistic people' and 'a reliance on phone calls', rather than written forms of communications, 'can create barriers to access'.[609]

The DMCCA provisions regulating subscription contracts could address some of these challenges. As a result of the measures requiring traders to provide consumers with key and full pre-contract information about subscription contracts,[610] consumers are better informed about their rights and obligations. As stated in the Explanatory Notes to the DMCCA, 'all the pre-contract information should be easily understood by the average consumer'.[611] Yet, the DMCCA could have gone further in protecting all consumers, including consumers with disabilities, as these measures could have called explicitly for the provision of information in accessible formats, rooted in principles of universal design.

The DMCCA provisions requiring traders to send consumers reminder notices before consumers become liable for renewal payments,[612] could assist people who sign up for subscription contracts, often as part of free trials, and then overlook to cancel their subscription.[613] The DMCCA also requires traders to enable consumers to exercise their right to end a subscription contract, by ensuring that this right can be exercised in a 'straightforward' way, and without the need for steps which are 'not reasonably necessary'.[614] Moreover, in the case of subscription contracts entered into online, traders must ensure that consumers can 'bring the contract to an end online'.[615] This could address some of the concerns faced by consumers, including people with hearing and/or speech-related disabilities, or who are reluctant to use the phone due to communication anxiety, for whom the use of the phone as the sole mechanism to cancel subscription contracts could pose access barriers.

While these measures are to be welcomed, the DMCCA could have done more in challenging the 'dark patterns' employed by traders to 'trap' consumers in subscription contracts in the first place, including the use of 'auto-renewals' for 'opt out' free trials, which seek to 'capitalise on consumer inertia'.[616] Citizens Advice caution that reminder notices may not be enough to

[607] Philippa Howard and Felicity Sedgewick, 'Anything but the Phone!': Communication Mode Preferences in the Autism Community' (2021) 25(8) *Autism* 2265–78.

[608] Ibid. [609] Ibid. [610] Sections 256 and 257 of the DMCCA 2024.

[611] Explanatory Notes to the DMCCA 2024, [1476].

[612] Sections 258 and 259 of the DMCCA 2024. [613] Citizens Advice, 'Subscription Traps'.

[614] Sections 260(1) and 261 of the DMCCA 2024. [615] Ibid. section 260(4)(a).

[616] Citizens Advice, 'Subscription Traps'.

protection consumers, as these notices are unlikely to resolve all the challenges 'caused by inertia and product design'.[617] In addition to measures designed to educate consumers to recognise and avoid subscription traps,[618] regulatory provisions must go further and, with a few exceptions (e.g. insurance contracts, repeat prescriptions), ban the use of opt-out auto-renewals of subscription contracts.[619] As advocated by Citizens Advice, subscriptions after free trials should generally be based on an opt-in, rather than an opt-out mechanism.[620] This would be beneficial not only in responding to the economic harm caused by subscription traps but also to the social harm, including harm to people's mental health,[621] or to autonomy and human dignity, caused by being manipulated by traders.[622] Further measures would also need to focus on a safer design of the online choice architecture, to reduce the risk of people accidentally entering into subscription contracts.[623] Moreover, people with disabilities and DDPOs must be included in this search for solutions.

The remainder of this section discusses the provisions regulating information, cancellation, and additional charges in B2C contracts under the CCRs 2013. The CCRs, which implemented most of the provisions of Directive 2011/83/EU,[624] contain the key provisions regulating traders' information duties to consumers, consumers' cancellation rights and the issue of additional charges.[625] The CCRs consolidate the measures included previously in SI 2000 No. 2334[626] and SI 2008 No. 1816,[627] and make provisions, *inter alia*, for the information to be supplied by traders regarding the purchase of goods, digital content, or services in distance, off premises, and on premises contracts,[628] and for consumer cancellation rights regarding distance and off-premises contracts.[629]

'Distance contracts' are B2C transactions concluded 'under an organised distance sales or service-provision scheme', without the parties' 'simultaneous physical presence', and 'with the exclusive use of one or more means of distance communication up to and including the time' of the conclusion of the contract.[630] Examples include contracts via websites, telephone, email or letter.[631] 'Off-premises contracts' as B2C transactions involving the parties' 'simultaneous physical presence' in a place which is not the trader's 'business premises' and either the contract was concluded there, or the consumer made the offer there, or the trader 'personally and individually addressed' the consumer there and a contract was concluded immediately after on the trader's

[617] Ibid. [618] Citizens Advice, 'Pushed to Purchase'.
[619] Citizens Advice, 'Subscription Traps'. [620] Ibid. [621] Which? 'Dark Patterns'.
[622] Citizens Advice, 'Pushed to Purchase'. [623] Citizens Advice, 'Subscription Traps'.
[624] Directive 2011/83/EU, amended by Directive 2019/2161. [625] Parts 2–4 of the CCRs 2013.
[626] Consumer Protection (Distance Selling) Regulations 2000 (SI 2000 No. 2334), superseded by the CCRs 2013. See Regulation 2(a) of the CCRs 2013.
[627] Cancellation of Contracts Made in a Consumer's Home or Place of Work etc. Regulations 2008 (SI 2008 No. 1816), superseded by the CCRs 2013. See Regulation 2(b) of the CCRs 2013.
[628] Part 2 of the CCRs 2013. [629] Ibid. part 3. [630] Ibid. Regulation 5.
[631] Burrows, 'Principles of the English Law of Obligations', 1.12.

business premises or 'through any means of distance communication'.[632] This definition also includes contracts concluded during an excursion organised by traders 'with the aim or effect of promoting and selling goods or services' to consumers.[633] Examples of off-premises contracts include contracts concluded at the consumer's home,[634] and may include contracts where the negotiations extended beyond a single visit.[635] These provisions recognise the fact that in such circumstances, consumers may be 'under potential psychological pressure' to conclude the contract, or may be 'confronted with an element of surprise, irrespective whether or not' they 'solicited' the trader's visit.[636] Transactions that are neither distance contracts, nor off-premises contracts, fall within a residual category defined in Regulation 5 as 'on-premises contracts'.[637]

The CCRs do not apply, *inter alia*, to contracts for gambling, financial services and immovable property.[638] Moreover, while Directive 2011/83/EU excluded from its application, among others, contracts for social services and for healthcare,[639] these are not excluded (in the case of social services contracts), or not excluded entirely (in the case of healthcare contracts) from the CCRs.[640] The CCRs do not apply to contracts for 'the supply of a medicinal product by administration by a prescriber, or under a prescription or directions given by a prescriber' or 'the supply of a product by a health care professional' in certain circumstances identified in the Regulation.[641] While the partial inclusion of contracts for healthcare in the CCRs is to be welcomed, the absence of a full inclusion is problematic. As noted by the OFT before the adoption of the CCRs, the provision of effective information and cancellation rights in contracts for healthcare is important, given the vulnerability of consumers targeted by traders in this sector.[642]

The requirements placed by part 2 of the CCRs on traders to provide information to consumers, apply to distance, off-premises and on-premises contracts which fall within the scope of these Regulations.[643] In addition to the exclusion of certain contracts for healthcare mentioned earlier,[644] part 2 also excludes off-premises contracts where the payment made by consumers is 'no more than £42'.[645] Contracts falling within the scope of part 2 of these Regulations are 'treated as including a term' that traders have complied with the pre-contract information requirements under Regulations 9 (on-premises contracts), 10–12 (off-premises contracts) and 13, 14 and 16 (distance contracts).[646] Where traders have provided the pre-contract information required

[632] Regulation 5(a), (b) and (c) of the CCRs 2013. [633] Ibid. Regulation 5(d).
[634] Recital 21 of Directive 2011/83/EU. [635] Whittaker, 'Consumer Contracts', 40-085.
[636] Recital 21 of Directive 2011/83/EU. [637] Regulation 5 of the CCRs 2013.
[638] Ibid. Regulation 6(1)(a), (b) and (c). [639] Articles 3(3)(a) and (b) of Directive 2011/83/EU.
[640] Regulations 7(2), 27(2) and (4) of the CCRs 2013.
[641] Ibid. Regulations 7(2)(a) and (b). See Whittaker, 'Consumer Contracts', 40-085.
[642] Office of Fair Trading, 'Response to the Consultation on the Implementation of the Consumer Rights Directive 2011/83/EU' OFT1461, November 2012, 2.21.
[643] Regulation 7(1) of the CCRs 2013. [644] Ibid. Regulation 7(2). [645] Ibid. Regulation 7(4).
[646] Ibid. Regulation 18.

under these Regulations, the information is treated as included as a contract term.[647] For on-premises contracts, pre-contract information requirements include information relating to the main characteristics and total price of the products.[648] This information must be provided if 'not already apparent from the context', in a 'clear and comprehensible manner'.[649] This requirement should be read broadly to address accessibility concerns in the provision of information. Traders are not expected to provide consumers with pre-contract information if the transaction involves a 'day-to-day transaction' performed 'immediately' at the time of concluding the contract.[650] The pre-contract information requirements for off-premises and distance contracts call on traders to give consumers information relating to, *inter alia*, the main characteristics and total price of the products.[651] This information must be provided in 'a clear and comprehensible manner'.[652]

Regrettably, the CCRs place insufficient emphasis on accessibility requirements in the provision of information. While measures such as Regulations 9(1), 10(1) and 13(1) call on traders to provide consumers, with 'clear and comprehensible' pre-contract information,[653] there is no explicit reference in these provisions to the accessibility of information. The CCRs reflect the language of Directive 2011/83/EU.[654] This Directive also specifies that when providing the required information, traders should 'take into account the needs of the consumers who are particularly vulnerable' due to their 'mental, physical or psychological infirmity, age or credulity', that this should be done 'in a way which the trader could reasonably be expected to foresee', but that 'taking into account such specific needs should not lead to different levels of consumer protection'.[655] This approach is problematic, because it reflects a medicalised, paternalistic understanding of vulnerability which overlooks the context of the transaction and any environmental barriers to access. The Directive also fails to specify what is meant by the reasonable expectation on traders to foresee any specific needs of consumers, and does not refer explicitly to an interpretation of this expectation to include constructive knowledge based on the circumstances of transactions (such as grossly imbalanced transactions to the detriment of consumers). Moreover, the requirements for the provision of information in a 'clear and comprehensible' under this Directive are less generous in ensuring the appropriateness of information to consumers, when compared to previously adopted provisions. For example, Directive 97/7/EC stated that the information required from traders to be given to consumers should be provided not only in a 'clear and comprehensible manner', but also 'in a way appropriate' to the means of communication used, and 'with due regard' to, *inter*

[647] Sections 11(4)(5), 12(2)(3), 36(3)(4), 37(2)(3) and 50(3)(4) of the CRA 2015.
[648] Schedule 1(a)–(f) of the CCRs 2013. [649] Ibid. Regulation 9(1). [650] Ibid. Regulation 9(2).
[651] Ibid. Regulations 10(1) and 13(1) and Schedules 2(a)–(c), (f), (j) and (s).
[652] Ibid. Regulations 10(1)(a) and 13(1)(a).
[653] Ibid. Regulations 9(1), 10(1) and 13(1) and Schedules 1 and 2.
[654] Articles 5(1), 6(1) and 8(1) of Directive 2011/83/EU. [655] Ibid. recital 34.

alia, 'the principles of good faith in commercial transactions'.[656] It is important that these values are not lost following the repeal of this directive by Directive 2011/83/EU.[657] To provide effective protection for consumers, the information requirements comprised in the CCRs should be read broadly to include reference to accessible information based on principles of universal design.

Part 3 of the CCRs includes provisions on the circumstances in which consumers can cancel distance contracts and off-premises contracts. These provisions do not apply, *inter alia*, to 'off-premises contracts' where 'the payment made by the consumer is no more than £42'.[658] In the case of distance and off-premises contracts that fall within the scope of part 3, consumers may cancel 'at any time' within the cancellation period and 'without giving any reasons', and 'without incurring any liability', except in situations where, among others, the consumer chose enhanced delivery, or handled the goods and diminished their value, or requested the early supply of a service.[659] The CCRs have increased the 'normal cancellation period' (or 'cooling-off' period) from the seven days included in the previous legislation, to 14 days.[660] The cancellation period can be extended to 12 months if traders fail to provide consumers in distance and off-premises contracts with the required pre-contract information on their cancellation rights.[661] The CCRs also make provisions regarding the supply of services and digital content in the cancellation period, stating that traders must not begin the supply of services or digital content during the 14 days cooling-off period unless they have consumers' 'express request' (regarding services) or 'express consent' (regarding digital content) to do so.[662]

Part 4 of the CCRs is concerned with protection from additional charges and clarifies that consumers are not expected to pay any sums 'in addition to the remuneration agreed for the trader's main obligation' unless traders have obtained consumers' 'express consent' to such payment before concluding the contract.[663] Such consent cannot be inferred from 'the consumer not changing a default option' such as 'pre-ticked box on a website'.[664] Moreover, where traders operate a telephone helpline for consumers after the conclusion of a contract, consumers are 'not bound to pay more than the basic rate' for the phone call.[665]

As we have seen, the CCRs have introduced many positive developments for protecting consumers regarding the regulation of information, cancellation, and additional charges in B2C transactions falling within the scope of these measures. At the same time, these Regulations pose many challenges, as they

[656] Article 4(2) of Directive 97/7/EC of the European Parliament and of the Council of 20 May 1997 on the protection of consumers in respect of distance contracts, OJ 1997 No. L114, 4 July 1997, pp. 19–27, repealed by Directive 2011/83/EU. See Whittaker, 'Consumer Contracts', 40-003.

[657] Article 31 of Directive 2011/83/EU. [658] Regulation 27(3) of the CCRs 2013.

[659] Ibid. Regulation 29(1). [660] Ibid. Regulation 30(2). See Regulation 11 of SI 2000 No. 2334.

[661] Regulation 31 of the CCRs 2013. [662] Ibid. Regulations 36(1)(a) and 37(1)(a).

[663] Ibid. Regulation 40(1). [664] Ibid. Regulation 40(2). [665] Ibid. Regulation 41(1).

reflect an approach rooted in economic values, without sufficient emphasis on the social context of transactions. We have already discussed the challenges posed by an insufficient emphasis on the accessibility needs of consumers regarding information requirements. A second challenge is posed by gaps in the protection provided to consumers, manifested across a range of provisions within the CCRs. For example, Regulation 7(4) on the provision of information, and Regulation 27(3) on cancellation rights, state that the relevant provisions are not applicable to off-premise contracts where the consumer's payment 'is no more than £42'.[666] These measures seek to 'avoid placing an administrative burden' on traders in low value transactions.[667] Furthermore, in relation to cancellation rights, this reinforces an understanding of these rights as 'an exceptional instrument of consumer protection'.[668] Rather than recognising the more vulnerable position of consumers in B2C transactions, this approach seems to balance the parties' interests, protecting traders' interests in lower value transactions. Yet, as Watson argues, an exclusion of transactions such as doorstep selling contracts on the basis of costs, provides an 'example of sacrificing protection in favour of simplification', in a context where consumers are in the most need of protection.[669] Moreover, as noted by the OFT before the adoption of the CCRs, information and cancellation provisions should apply to all off-premises contracts.[670] Far from compromising any objectives for the simplification of the law in this area, this would provide greater clarity for parties in off-premises contracts.[671]

A further example in the CCRs of a gap in protecting consumers is provided by Regulation 11, which excludes from the information requirements for off-premises contracts under Regulation 10(1), service contracts where consumers have 'explicitly requested' traders to carry out repair or maintenance work, the parties' obligations are 'to be performed immediately' and the consumer is to pay £170 or less for the transaction.[672] As emphasised by the OFT before the adoption of the CCRs, 'immediate home repairs" should not be subject to a more relaxed information regime, given that the absence of 'essential information' in a durable medium regarding the service to be provided and any cancellation rights, could 'lead to disputes' about what the parties have agreed, and to 'lower consumer protection measures in an area in which vulnerable consumers are at risk'.[673] Potential gaps in protection are also illustrated by Regulation 9(2) regarding on-premises contracts, which excludes from the information requirements under Regulation 9(1), day-to-day transactions performed

[666] Ibid. Regulations 7(4) and 27(3).

[667] Jonathon Watson, 'Withdrawal Rights' in Christian Twigg-Flesner (ed.), *Research Handbook on EU Consumer and Contract Law* (Cheltenham: Edward Elgar Publishing, 2016), pp. 241–65, at p. 255.

[668] Ibid. p. 241. [669] Ibid. p. 255.

[670] OFT, 'Response to the Consultation on the Implementation of Directive 2011/83/EU', 1.10.

[671] Ibid. [672] Regulations 11(1)(a)–(d) of the CCRs 2013.

[673] OFT, 'Response to the Consultation on the Implementation of Directive 2011/83/EU', 1.11.

immediately at the time of the contract.[674] While information obligations for such transactions could impose 'unnecessary and unduly onerous' burdens on traders in 'some circumstances', the OFT emphasised the need for more clarity on what amounts to a 'day-to-day transaction performed immediately'.[675] Such ambiguities provide a source of concern for consumers, particularly when the attempts to redress these ambiguities seek to balance the parties' interests. Yet, given that the starting point in B2C transactions is one in which consumers are at a disadvantage (e.g. access to resources or information), the regulatory focus should be not on balancing the parties' interests, but on prioritising the interests of consumers.

A third challenge is posed by the fact that the CCRs place insufficient weight on addressing certain aspects of the imbalance of power between parties in B2C transactions. For example, Regulation 9(3) on the provision of information to consumers in on-premises contracts states that in the case of contracts 'for the supply of digital content other than for a price paid by the consumer', the information provided by traders under the Regulations 'is to be treated as included' as a contract term, and that pre or post-contractual changes to that information are 'not effective unless expressly agreed' between the parties.[676] Similar provisions are presented under Regulations 10(5) (off-premises contracts) and 13(6) (distance contracts).[677] A stronger degree of consumer protection would be provided if these measures specified that the express agreement between these parties to such changes needed to be based on an informed view. Regarding cancellation provisions for distance and off-premises contracts, Regulation 34(2) notes that traders must reimburse consumers for payments made for the delivery of goods, unless consumers 'expressly choose' an enhanced, more expensive delivery method.[678] Moreover, Regulation 36(1) specifies regarding the supply of services in the cancellation period, that traders must not supply services during the cooling-off period, unless consumers have made 'an express request' on a durable medium.[679] Regulation 37(1) makes broadly similar provisions regarding the supply of digital content, referring to consumers' 'express consent' and acknowledgement that their cancellation rights would be lost following such consent.[680] Once again, the reference to consumers' express request or consent does not state explicitly that this needs to be informed. As Watson notes, the reference to an 'express request' (compared to an 'express consent') provides a stronger degree of consumer protection, as 'a request implies that a consumer has seized the initiative' regarding the start of the performance.[681] One further example of this challenge is provided by Regulation 40(1), which states that consumers should not be expected to make payments additional to what was agreed between the parties regarding

[674] Regulations 9(1) and (2) of the CCRs 2013.
[675] OFT, 'Response to the Consultation on the Implementation of Directive 2011/83/EU', 1.7.
[676] Regulation 9(3) of the CCRs 2013. [677] Ibid. Regulations 10(5) and 13(6).
[678] Ibid. Regulation 34(2). [679] Ibid. Regulation 36(1). [680] Ibid. Regulations 37(1)(a) and (b).
[681] Watson, 'Withdrawal Rights', pp. 257–58.

traders' main obligations, 'unless, before the consumer becomes bound by the contract, the trader obtained the consumer's express consent'.[682] As above, references to express consent are not accompanied by explicit references to informed consent. A stronger degree of consumer protection would be provided if courts adopted an interpretation of these provisions to require the consumers' consent to be free and informed.[683] Moreover, consent should be made based on information that considers consumers' accessibility needs.

The emphasis on economic values and the insufficient focus on social values manifested in the CCRs can be traced largely to Directive 2011/83/EU. This Directive is rooted in economic values, overlooking social values such as the protection of human dignity. These measures reflect an approach in which the provision of information by traders could protect consumers' economic interests (who can make better choices about goods and services contracts), and information and cancellation rights can redress imbalances of power between the parties (as consumers have more information and time to consider the implications of transactions).[684] Yet, this approach overlooks assessments whether the information provided is accessible and appropriate to the consumers' circumstances, whether the cooling-off period is sufficiently long, and whether consumers have effective access to advice when considering the information presented by traders. It also relies on an unrealistic assumption that consumers, once provided with information, will act rationally in the use of the information and the choices they make.[685] The next section explores in more detail the challenges posed by an unrealistic vision of the market and of the consumers' use of the information provided. This discussion calls for an approach to the provision of information focused on consumers as both economic and social actors, which considers accessibility concerns and the context of the transaction.

4.3 Challenging an Approach That Places Insufficient Focus on the Contextual Vulnerability of Consumers

The current regulatory framework on consumer protection places insufficient focus on the vulnerability of consumers, relying instead on a vision of consumers as confident, self-sufficient economic actors in pursuit of self-interest. Such a vision overlooks the diversity of experiences (including with regards to barriers to access) encountered by consumers in the market, and the vulnerability created by the context of the transactions. For measures that seek to differentiate between 'average consumers' and 'vulnerable consumers', the average consumers tend to be perceived through an unrealistic lens as self-sufficient actors who

682 Regulation 40(1) of the CCRs 2013. 683 Whittaker, 'Consumer Contracts', 40-070.

684 Ibid. 40-062. See recitals 3–5 of Directive 2011/83/EU.

685 Peter Cartwright, 'Publicity, Punishment and Protection: The Role(s) of Adverse Publicity in Consumer Policy' (2012) 32(2) *Legal Studies* 179–201 at 180.

can look after their own interests if they have sufficient access to information about the product or service contracted for,[686] while vulnerable consumers are perceived through a stigmatising lens as people dependent on the 'benevolent protection' of others.[687] The distinction between average and vulnerable consumers is rooted in the EU legal framework,[688] which has been challenged for 'sacrificing' the interests of vulnerable consumers in favour of the interests of self-reliant average consumers who are 'reasonably well informed, reasonably observant and circumspect',[689] and who are seen as playing an important role in pursuing the economic objectives of 'deregulation' and 'market integration'.[690] While some of the EU measures that influenced UK consumer contract law rely on the average/vulnerable consumer dichotomy,[691] other EU instruments refer to vulnerable consumers mainly in the non-binding preamble of Directives,[692] reflecting the absence of 'a clear vision' to protect vulnerable consumers.[693]

The characterisation of consumers as 'average' or 'vulnerable' represents an unrealistic portrayal of people. The reference to 'the average consumer' overlooks the fact that all people can be vulnerable, depending on the circumstances of the transaction.[694] For example, consumers can be vulnerable not only when faced with unfair commercial practices but also when entering into contracts for the supply of goods, digital products or services, due to the complexity of certain transactions. Moreover, any stigmatising reference to vulnerable consumers as a separate group in need of special protection fails to perceive people as 'holders of rights' entitled to 'full social and economic inclusion'.[695] Furthermore, the generic reference to 'vulnerable consumers' overlooks the 'diversity of consumers and their needs', the different causes of vulnerability and the need for targeted measures to respond to challenges faced by individuals in the contractual sphere.[696] Such responses should reflect a proactive, rather than reactive approach to tackling social barriers and promoting equality, and should be informed by consultation with, *inter alia*, people with disabilities and DDPOs. The responses also need to have their basis on the social sphere of the contractual realm, informed by citizenship values such as equality, autonomy, and human dignity. Vulnerability should be understood as a 'social construction' dependent on the situation in which consumers may find themselves in relation to traders,[697] and regulatory responses should recognise

686 Lisa Waddington, 'Vulnerable and Confused: The Protection of "Vulnerable" Consumers under EU Law' (2013) 38(6) *European Law Review* 757–83, at 765.

687 Maker, 'From Safety Nets', 831.

688 See, for example, Articles 5(2)(b) and (3) of Directive 2005/29/EC.

689 Case C-210/96, *Gut Springenheide and Tusky* v. *Oberkreisdirektor des Kreises Steinfurt* [1998] ECR I-3599, [38].

690 Waddington, 'Vulnerable and Confused', 765.

691 For example, Directive 2005/29/EC.

692 For example, Directive 2011/83/EU.

693 Waddington, 'Vulnerable and Confused', 771.

694 Ibid. 768.

695 Maker, 'From Safety Nets', 830.

696 Waddington, 'Vulnerable and Confused', 765.

697 Maker, 'From Safety Nets', 833.

differences between consumers,[698] and address the 'varied and complex disadvantages' that may be faced by consumers.[699]

Contextual sources of consumer vulnerability include inaccessible information ('informational vulnerability'), inaccessible products ('supply vulnerability'), difficult to access redress mechanisms ('redress vulnerability'), susceptibility to pressure ('pressure vulnerability') and an amplified impact of loss due to circumstances ('impact vulnerability).[700] This discussion is based on the 'taxonomy of vulnerability' presented by Cartwright.[701] After reflecting on these aspects of consumer vulnerability regarding some of the key provisions explored in this chapter, this discussion seeks to add one further source of vulnerability, which is explored in more detail in the next chapter, and which could be referred to as 'influence vulnerability'. This aspect of consumer vulnerability refers to the limited opportunities of consumers (including consumers with disabilities) to influence the regulatory framework, when compared to the much louder voices of industry players.

'Informational vulnerability'[702] can take various forms and can be traced, *inter alia*, to inaccessible information about products, ranging from the absence of appropriate information in accessible formats (e.g. Braille, Easy Read), to the overprovision of complex information about products.[703] This results in 'information asymmetries' between the parties, placing consumers at a disadvantage.[704] In the absence of appropriate information for their needs, consumers face difficulties in choosing goods and services that 'reflect their true preferences'.[705] In contrast, well-informed consumers on matters such as price, quality and terms of trade are in a better position to compare the goods and services available in the market and make choices suitable to their needs, at the same time providing traders with the competitive incentives to improve their products.[706]

Issues concerning the absence of information could be remedied by regulatory measures requiring traders to disclose information about their products.[707] Such measures seek to correct 'information asymmetries' between the parties,[708] and are seen to be both 'market friendly' (as a lighter form of regulation) and respectful of consumer autonomy (as they enable consumers to take responsibility for their choices).[709] These measures are also 'likely to be favoured by those who see the correction of market failure' to be 'the primary rationale of regulation'.[710] These justifications rest on economic rationales

698 Cartwright, 'Consumer Protection', p. 29.

699 Devenney, 'The Consumer Rights Act 2015', p. 246.

700 Cartwright, 'Vulnerable Financial Consumers', 119. 701 Ibid. 702 Ibid.

703 Cartwright, 'Consumer Protection', p. 31. 704 Ibid. p. 20.

705 Geraint Howells, 'The Potential and Limits of Consumer Empowerment by Information' (2005) 23(3) *Journal of Law and Society* 349–70 at 355.

706 Howard Beales, Richard Craswell and Steven Salop, 'The Efficient Regulation of Consumer Information' (1981) 24(3) *Journal of Law and Economics* 491–539 at 492.

707 Cartwright, 'Consumer Protection', p. 31. 708 Ibid. p. 48.

709 Cartwright, 'Vulnerable Financial Consumers', 125.

710 Cartwright, 'Consumer Protection', p. 48.

for intervention. However, it is important that social considerations are also addressed, to ensure the equal access of consumers to information. For example, while the CCRs require traders to provide information to consumers regarding contracts that fall within the scope of the Regulations,[711] these measures place insufficient emphasis on accessibility needs. Although the CCRs call on traders to provide 'clear and comprehensible information' to consumers before the conclusion of the contract on matters including the main characteristics of the products,[712] these provisions fail to state explicitly that this information must also be accessible and appropriate to consumers.

Measures requiring traders to disclose information to consumers must consider the needs of vulnerable consumers, including those who encounter accessibility barriers.[713] Following the example of accessibility requirements for the packaging of medical products, which assist persons with visual disabilities, by requiring the inclusion of labels in Braille,[714] such accessibility requirements should be extended to other products and other accessibility solutions, including the provision of information in Easy Read formats. Regulatory responses should consider not only the economic costs of inclusion, but also the social costs of exclusion,[715] and should reflect a perception of consumers not just as economic actors, but also as citizens and social actors, with an interest in participation in society on an equal basis with others.

Informational vulnerability can also stem from the provision of information which is too complex for consumers to understand or use effectively. This may be due factors such as the use of complex technical language, or to the quantity of information provided. Rather than helping consumers to make informed choices, the excessive provision of information can be counterproductive, leaving consumers in a state of confusion.[716] Faced with such 'information overload', consumers often choose to ignore the information.[717] This position contrasts with the idealised and unrealistic visions of a 'perfect market' where consumers are presented with 'perfect information' about the products on offer, and exercise rational choices based on the information provided.[718] In reality, however, consumers often do not behave in a rational manner.[719]

Challenges to the 'traditional model of rational consumer decision-making' are posed, among others, by studies in neuroscience, which highlight the important role played by emotions in decision-making.[720] Moreover, studies

711 Regulations 6 and 7(1) of the CCRs 2013.

712 Ibid. Regulations 9(1), 10(1) and 13(1) and Schedules 1(a) and 2(a).

713 Cartwright, 'Consumer Protection', p. 31.

714 Regulation 259 of the Human Medicines Regulations (SI 2012 No. 1916).

715 Interview with Guido Gybels, RNID, 17 August 2009 in Varney, 'Disability and Information Technology'.

716 Cartwright, 'Vulnerable Financial Consumers', 125–26.

717 Ibid.

718 Cartwright, 'Consumer Protection', p. 20.

719 Cartwright, 'Publicity, Punishment and Protection', 180.

720 Christoph Busch, 'The Future of Pre-contractual Information Duties: From Behavioural Insights to Big Data' in Twigg-Flesner (ed.), *Research Handbook*, pp. 221–40 at p. 227.

in cognitive psychology and behavioural economics have stressed that 'people do not always make rational and deliberate decisions on how to allocate their attention to information'.[721] Generally, the complexity of information available to consumers contributes to issues of 'bounded rationality', which refers to situations where consumers are unable to make the best use of the information available in the market, including due to limitations in people's capacity to process that information.[722] Contrary to assumptions about the average, self-sufficient and rational consumers, people do not act in a 'perfectly rational' manner, including due to information constraints.[723] Consumers are often 'over-confident' in their assessment of how much they know about a product, as they rely on their 'subjective knowledge' (perceived knowledge), rather than on their 'objective knowledge' (actual knowledge) about the product.[724] Measures to enhance consumers' objective knowledge, such as campaigns to educate consumers, can contribute towards better decision-making.[725] Consumer education campaigns must be constructed with accessibility in mind, with information provided in accessible formats, including Easy Read. We must also move away from unrealistic visions of the rational consumer and recognise, as Howells suggests, that 'we are all to some extent vulnerable because of the limitations of the human mind', including in the understanding and processing of information.[726] Calls for the accessibility of information should not be confined to equality provisions (e.g. under EqA), but should also be reflected, to a greater extent than it is currently the case, in consumer law and policy. Consumers would also benefit from the provision of a reduced, but more relevant amount of information,[727] provided in a 'simple and consistent manner'.[728] Examples could include, where appropriate, an 'increased use of product scores' similar to the hygiene rating system used for restaurants.[729]

An aspect of informational vulnerability which is closely connected with the issue of 'redress vulnerability' is the fact that consumers have a limited understanding of their rights under consumer contract law, leading to the reflection that 'the average consumer' may, in fact, be 'more vulnerable than the legislator assumes'.[730] Consequently, regulatory measures must be supplemented

721 Ibid. 226.

722 Herbert Simon, *Models of Bounded Rationality* (Cambridge, MA: MIT Press, 1982).

723 Maker, 'From Safety Nets', 833.

724 Mike Varney, 'Services, Consumer Information and Remedies in the Electronic Communications Sector: A Yet Unanswered Challenge?' in Christian Twigg-Flesner and Gonzalo Villalta Puig (eds.), *Boundaries of Commercial and Trade Law* (Munich: Seller European Publishers, 2011), pp. 127–52, at p. 132, with reference to Mattila, Anna and Jochen Wirtz, 'The Impact of Knowledge Types on the Consumer Search Process: An Investigation in the Context of Credence Services' (2002) 13(3) *International Journal of Service Industry Management* 214–30 at 216.

725 Ibid. 726 Howells, 'Potential and Limits', p. 359.

727 Busch, 'The Future of Pre-contractual Information', p. 231.

728 Cartwright, 'Consumer Protection', p. 52.

729 Busch, 'The Future of Pre-contractual Information', p. 230.

730 Waddington, 'Vulnerable and Confused', 769.

by further guidance for consumers regarding their rights and remedies,[731] available in accessible formats. However, we must not overestimate the role that information can play in empowering consumers, nor overlook the need for targeted measures to address the various sources of vulnerability affecting consumers.[732] Under the current regulatory framework, including under the CCRs, the provision of information by traders is focused on counterbalancing information asymmetries between the parties. Yet, this model is based on an unrealistic understanding of consumers and their vulnerabilities. To use the vision of concentric spheres of contract law presented in this book, the model of the rational consumer discussed earlier has as its starting point the economic sphere of contract law, based on a vision of consumers as economic actors in pursuit of self-interest. A better degree of protection would be provided to consumers by a regulatory framework that has as its starting point the social sphere of contract law, which considers consumer vulnerability and the need to address social concerns for equality of citizenship, relational autonomy and the protection of human dignity.

A second form of consumer vulnerability is 'supply vulnerability', where consumers are faced with a limited choice of products,[733] including due to a limited availability of accessible products. Examples of accessibility barriers include products inaccessible to people with visual disabilities (e.g. payments reliant solely on using touchscreen technology), hearing disabilities (e.g. services without sign language interpretation), dexterity disabilities (e.g. inaccessible keypads) or cognitive disabilities (e.g. the absence of a quiet space to discuss complex products). Particular challenges are faced by consumers with non-visible disabilities such as neurodivergent consumers, whose differences (e.g. in processing information) are often overlooked by traders when developing their products.[734] Measures to address issues of 'supply vulnerability' include duties on providers of essential services (e.g. utilities) to ensure the access of vulnerable consumers to these services.[735] They also include the development of new products,[736] which should be based in principles of universal design. Moreover, proactive measures are needed to combat discrimination, including disability discrimination, and promote equality of access to goods and services, and social participation.[737] While instruments such as the CRA focus, *inter alia*, on the 'satisfactory quality' of goods or digital content, and the 'reasonable care and skill' employed in the provision of services,[738] these measures must be complemented by an effective regulatory framework which ensures that products are accessible in the first place. To some extent, and without overlooking the challenges associated with this framework, the CRA presents a credible regime for regulating products in B2C transactions. Nevertheless, the effectiveness of this framework can be undermined if the preceding steps (e.g. product

731 Devenney, 'The Consumer Rights Act 2015', p. 258. 732 Ibid. p. 264. 733 Ibid.
734 Guevara, 'Ableness as Property', 18. 735 Cartwright, 'Consumer Protection', p. 23.
736 Ibid. 737 Maker, 'From Safety Nets', 820. 738 Sections 9, 34 and 49 of the CRA 2015.

accessibility) and the succeeding steps (e.g. enforcement mechanisms) present additional challenges. The regulatory realm would benefit from a more explicit link between the equality framework under the EqA (including equal access to goods and services for persons with disabilities) and the consumer protection framework under the CRA. This could include a more explicit link between issues concerning the fitness of goods for a specific purpose under section 10 of the CRA, and consumers' accessibility requirements. This would reflect a perception of consumers as both social and economic actors and would create a stronger bridge between human rights and contract law.

A third form of vulnerability in B2C transactions concerns 'redress vulnerability' where consumers encounter 'difficulties in obtaining redress' due to 'costs, time, or process-related constraints'.[739] Examples of process-related constraints include measures that place insufficient focus on vulnerability. Section 9 of the CRA relies on a 'reasonable person' test to assess whether the goods are of satisfactory quality,[740] but misses out 'assessments of reasonableness from the perspective of individuals' who are 'particularly disadvantaged' due to the circumstances of the transaction, when compared with objectively reasonable consumers.[741] Furthermore, section 54(3) of the CRA regarding service contracts, presents a two-tiered approach in the provision of remedies.[742] Consumers can only rely on the remedy of price reduction if they have first provided traders with opportunities of repeat performance. This overlooks situations where, due to the circumstances of the transaction, consumers may feel vulnerable to allow traders the opportunity of repeat performance (e.g. consumers may feel vulnerable due to the presence of a particular trader on their premises) and may wish to go directly to the remedy of price reduction. Where consumers have 'lost confidence' in a trader, they may be able to rely on the remedies of breach of contract under general contract law which, in the case of repudiatory breaches of contract (such as a serious breach that goes to the root of the contract) may allow consumers, *inter alia*, to treat the contract as discharged.[743] Nevertheless, the CRA could have responded to a more satisfactory extent to the concerns expressed by the OFT in a consultation response, which stressed that it is 'unrealistic to expect consumers' to offer traders the opportunity of repeat performance 'in every case' and 'whatever the circumstances', including in circumstances where 'the original service was exceptionally poor'.[744] The CRA framework reveals an insufficient focus on contextual vulnerability.

Concerns regarding an insufficient focus on consumer vulnerability are also present in relation to the regulation of unfair terms under the CRA. For example, section 64 excludes from the application of the fairness test under

[739] Cartwright, 'Vulnerable Financial Consumers', 121. [740] Section 9(2) of the CRA 2015.
[741] Waddington, 'Vulnerable and Confused', 762. [742] Section 54(3) of the CRA 2015.
[743] Whittaker, 'Consumer Contracts', 40-586.
[744] OFT, 'Response to the Draft Consumer Rights Bill Proposals', 4.3.

section 62, terms concerning the subject matter of the contract, or the appropriateness of the price compared with the value of the goods supplied, if these terms are 'transparent' and 'prominent'.[745] Transparency is assessed by considering whether the term is expressed in plain and intelligible language, with the additional requirement of legibility in the case of written terms, while to evaluate prominence, reference is made to whether the term was brought to consumers' attention 'in such a way that an average consumer would be aware of the term'.[746] The average consumer is seen as someone who is 'reasonably well informed, observant and circumspect',[747] and these provisions make no reference to any accessibility requirements to enable consumers to become 'reasonably well informed'. As Howells notes, the definition of the average consumer expects, in fact, 'above average qualities', while considering vulnerable consumers as 'atypical' and overlooking people's universal vulnerability.[748] A stronger degree of protection would be provided by an explicit acknowledgement of vulnerable consumers within the fairness test and the core exemptions under sections 62 and 64 of the CRA.

Issues of 'redress vulnerability' are also manifested in provisions that overlook the challenges posed by inequalities of bargaining power between traders and consumers. For example, a term is considered to be unfair if 'contrary to the requirement of good faith, it causes *a significant imbalance* in the parties' rights and obligations under the contract', to the consumer's detriment.[749] A similar reference to such 'significant imbalance' is made when assessing the fairness of consumer notices.[750] This sets a high bar for consumers, who could have benefited from a stronger degree of protection had the 'significant imbalance' threshold and the 'incompatibility with good faith' had been set as alternative factors to assess unfairness.[751] Further examples of regulatory responses that could have gone further to address inequalities of bargaining power between consumers and traders, are also reflected in relation to the cancellation rights under the CCRs. These rights are not available in a range of circumstances, including in 'off-premises contracts' where 'the payment made by the consumer is no more than £42', or contracts 'where the consumers specifically requested a visit from the traders for the purpose of carrying out urgent repairs or maintenance'.[752] Such limitations illustrate attempts within the regulatory framework to balance the parties' rights,[753] rather than to prioritise consumer interests over the economic interests of traders. Consumers would enjoy a stronger degree of protection within a regulatory framework that uses as its starting point the social sphere of contract law, which places more emphasis on imbalances of power between the parties and the need to respond not only

[745] Sections 62, 64(1)(a), (b) and (2) of the CRA 2015. [746] Ibid. sections 64(3) and (4).
[747] Ibid. section 64(5). [748] Howells, 'Potential and Limits', p. 359.
[749] Section 62(4) of the CRA 2015 (emphasis added). [750] Ibid. section 62(6).
[751] Beale, 'Legislative Control of Fairness', p. 243.
[752] Regulations 27(3) and 28(1)(e) of the CCRs 2013. [753] Watson, 'Withdrawal Rights', p. 253.

to economic concerns, but also to the social concerns of consumers, including the protection of human dignity.

'Pressure vulnerability' constitutes a fourth type of vulnerability affecting consumers, and focuses on situations where, due to the circumstances of the transactions, consumers may be 'particularly susceptible to trickery or pressure'.[754] Rather than focusing solely on traders' unacceptable behaviour (e.g. aggressive commercial practices), or placing the spotlight on consumers' medical conditions, the regulatory framework needs to consider, in its assessment of vulnerability, the context of transactions. Consumer susceptibility to pressure may arise from a range of factors, including insufficient information about their options, individual circumstances (e.g. bereavement, financial difficulties), or sellers exercising 'psychological pressure', particularly when individuals are vulnerable to 'having their emotional weaknesses exploited'.[755] This latter form of pressure is particularly problematic, especially as it is often difficult to draw a line between 'exploitative' and 'persuasive' commercial practices.[756]

To some extent, the DMCCA provisions protect consumers affected by pressure vulnerability, including consumers who have been subject to, *inter alia*, aggressive practices 'likely to cause the average consumer to take a transactional decision that the consumer would not have taken otherwise.[757] Such practices cover situations involving 'harassment, coercion or undue influence', with the latter referring to the exploitation of a position of power by traders, to 'apply pressure' on consumers, in a way which significantly limits their ability to make an informed decision'.[758] Circumstances when traders may be placed in a position of power over consumers include situations where consumers are 'in a vulnerable position'.[759] Regrettably, this reference to circumstantial vulnerability was included in the Explanatory Notes to the DMCCA, rather than made explicit in the Act itself. Further unfair commercial practices covered by the DMCCA include the practices listed in Schedule 20, which are considered unfair 'in all circumstances', and include giving consumers the impression that they 'cannot leave the premises until a contract is formed', or 'explicitly telling a consumer' that the trader's 'job or livelihood' would be at risk unless the consumer buys a product.[760] Such tactics are likely to place consumers under pressure, including emotional pressure.

While acknowledging the merits of the DMCCA in seeking to protect consumers affected by pressure vulnerability due to unfair commercial practices, these provisions could have gone further in the level of protection provided, including for consumers with disabilities. Drawbacks include the continued reliance of the DMCCA on the distinction between average, targeted and vulnerable consumers, where average consumers are seen as 'reasonably

[754] Cartwright, 'Vulnerable Financial Consumers', 121. [755] Ibid. 122. [756] Ibid. 123.
[757] Sections 225(4)(a)(i) and 228 of the DMCCA 2024. [758] Ibid. sections 228(1) and (3)(b).
[759] Explanatory Notes to the DMCCA 2024, [1368].
[760] Schedules 20(26) and (32) of the DMCCA 2024.

well informed, observant, and circumspect'.[761] This reflects an unrealistic perception of consumers and overlooks the circumstantial vulnerability affecting all consumers faced with the use of dark patterns in the online market architecture.[762] Dark patterns can be particularly problematic for neurodivergent consumers, who may be 'more vulnerable to the psychological tricks' used by deceptive OCA, and for whom the threshold for when a trader's design becomes a deceptive pattern 'may be lower' when compared with neurotypical consumers.[763] For example, for some consumers, design features such as false scarcity claims could trigger or aggravate feelings of panic and anxiety.[764] Regulatory measures designed to address the harms posed by dark patterns must acknowledge the variety of ways in which people process information, or respond to pressure. Moreover, it is important that these measures consider both economic and social harms caused by these practices, including emotional harms, the negative impact on people's mental health and harms to people's individual autonomy and human dignity.[765] A vision of contract law which seeks to protect both economic and social values would be closer to addressing these concerns.

Measures to address pressure vulnerability also include the provision of more information to educate consumers above their options. This is a valuable 'long term strategy' that could respond to both pressure and redress vulnerability.[766] However, information must be provided in an accessible format and must be appropriate to the consumers' circumstances. Closely connected to the provision of information are the requirements under the CCRs to allow a cooling-off period for distance and off-premises contracts, where consumers can cancel their contract without the need to offer any reason for such cancellation.[767] The cooling-off period allows consumers 'to reach a more informed purchasing decision' while not being subjected to the traders' sales tactics.[768] The effectiveness of the cooling-off period as a mechanism of consumer protection may depend on the availability of information in accessible formats (e.g. Easy Read). It may also depend on the availability of an appropriate period of time during the cancellation period for the consumer to become fully informed.[769] While the normal cancellation period under Regulation 30 of the CCRs is 14 days, this may not be sufficient in certain circumstances. Directive 2019/2161, which became effective in EU law after the end of the Brexit transition period and does not affect the body of assimilated EU law, amended Directive 2011/83/EU to add to Article 9 on the consumer's right

[761] Ibid. sections 225(4)(a), 226(1)(b), 227(2), 246(2), (4) and 247.
[762] Sax and Helberger, 'Digital Vulnerability and Manipulation', 11.
[763] Petterson, 'Dark Patterns and Disability'. [764] Firth, 'Practical Web Inclusion', p. 248.
[765] Citizens Advice, 'Pushed to Purchase'.
[766] Cartwright, 'Vulnerable Financial Consumers', 128. [767] Regulation 29(1) of the CCRs 2013.
[768] William Whitford, 'The Functions of Disclosure Regulation in Consumer Transactions' (1973) 19(3) 2 *Wisconsin Law Review* 400–70 at 462.
[769] Cartwright, 'Vulnerable Financial Consumers', 129.

to withdrawal (equivalent to Regulation 30 of the CCRs) a subsection (1a) which extended the consumer's cancellation rights to 30 days if consumers concluded the contract 'in the context of the trader's unsolicited visit to the consumer's home' or during an excursion organised by traders 'with the aim or effect' of securing a contract with consumers.[770] This places greater focus on the circumstances of the transaction and the contextual vulnerability experienced by consumers.

The need to protect consumers placed in vulnerable situations due to the context of the transaction could be articulated more clearly in the regulatory framework. For the CCRs, this challenge can be traced back to Directive 2011/83/EU. In justifying the availability of cancelation rights in off-premises contracts, recital 37 of this Directive clarifies that consumers should enjoy such cancellation rights due to 'the potential surprise element' or 'psychological pressure' experienced when approached by traders in such contexts. Yet this explicit recognition of contextual vulnerability is confined to the non-binding preamble of the Directive. A stronger degree of consumer protection could have been provided if contextual vulnerability was recognised more explicitly in the body of Directive 2011/83/EU and in the CCRs, which implemented this Directive. A regulatory framework reliant on a short cancellation period is based on the assumption that consumers act rationally, and that during the cooling-off period, they can make an informed decision regarding the transaction.[771] Reflecting the vision of concentric spheres presented in this book, such an approach uses as its stating point the economic sphere where individuals are presumed to act as rational economic actors. Conversely, a framework that extends the cancellation period to be more 'consumer friendly',[772] taking into account contextual vulnerability, reflects a more realistic perception of consumers, including with regards to more complex contracts. Such an approach uses as its starting point the social sphere of contract law.

A fifth form of consumer vulnerability is 'impact vulnerability', which considers circumstances where the losses suffered by some consumers due to entering into disadvantageous transactions have a greater impact on them than on other consumers, due to their circumstances.[773] For example, according to a report of the UNCRPD Committee regarding the UK, persons with disabilities are 'more likely to live in poverty' and to have a disposable income which is 'approximately 44 per cent lower than that of other working-age adults'.[774] Some of the measures to address impact vulnerability include a requirement on traders to disclose information about their products, aiming to prevent consumers entering into contracts for products that they do not need or cannot

770 Article 9(1a) of Directive 2011/83/EU, as added by Directive 2019/2161.

771 Watson, 'Withdrawal Rights', pp. 244–45.

772 Ibid.

773 Cartwright, 'Vulnerable Financial Consumers', 121.

774 UN Committee on the Rights of Persons with Disabilities, 'Report on Follow-up to the Inquiry concerning the United Kingdom of Great Britain and Northern Ireland', 22 March 2024, UN Doc CRPD/C/GBR/FUIR/1, [16].

afford.[775] Such information must be provided in accessible formats, appropriate to the circumstances of consumers (e.g. responding to needs for supported decision-making).[776] The regulatory framework must also consider imbalances of power, to the detriment of consumers, caused by the combination of information deficits and circumstances of 'emotional or social instability' caused, *inter alia*, by 'family disruption, illness, financial hardship, or simply time pressure'.[777] Such enhanced reduction in bargaining power places consumers deeper into the social sphere of the contractual realm, calling for appropriate regulatory responses rooted in social values, including the protection of human dignity.

This book seeks to highlight one additional form of vulnerability affecting consumers, which could be termed 'influence vulnerability'. This form of vulnerability refers to the fact that the voices of consumers (including consumers with disabilities and DDPOs) do not have the same level of impact in influencing the regulatory framework, when compared with the voices of industry players. There is considerable discrepancy between the influence exercised over the regulatory realm by consumers on the one hand, and traders on the other, as the latter are better organised and better equipped, having access to more resources, including information and financial resources.[778] For example, during the consultation process that led to the adoption of the CRA, while the Government received several responses from industry players, there were no responses from DDPOs to any of the consultation papers which informed the adoption of this Act.[779] Furthermore, no DDPOs appear to be included in the list of organisations that responded to the Government consultation on 'Smarter Regulation', which informed the DMCCA.[780] DDPOs are organisations where the majority of board members are persons with disabilities.[781] Without effective mechanisms to enable citizenship voices (including the voices of persons with disabilities and DDPOs) to shape the regulatory framework, measures risk overlooking matters such as the accessibility barriers encountered by individuals in the market (including inaccessible products, or inaccessible information). The best persons to identify accessibility concerns and to educate policymakers and traders about the solutions to address such accessibility barriers are people with disabilities themselves, and their voices should

[775] Cartwright, 'Consumer Protection', p. 31. [776] Maker, 'From Safety Nets', 820.

[777] Ibid. 833.

[778] Interview with Guido Gybels, RNID, 17 August 2009 in Varney, 'Disability and Information Technology'.

[779] See, for example, BIS, 'Enhancing Consumer Confidence by Clarifying Consumer Law'.

[780] Government Department for Business and Trade, 'Consultation outcome: Government response to consultation on 'Smarter Regulation: Improving consumer price transparency and product information for consumers', Annex 1: List of organisations that responded to the consultation', 24 January 2024.

[781] Saskia van Veen, Barbara Regeer and Joske Bunders, 'Meeting the Challenge of the Rights-Based Approach to Disability: The Changing Role of Disability-Specific NGOs and DPOs' (2013) 31(3) *Nordic Journal of Human Rights* 360–81 at 360.

be heard 'at every level of decision-making'.[782] In Chapter 5, which focuses on the connection between human rights and contract law, part two of the discussion explores the extent to which the current framework on public consultations facilitates the participation of DDPOs in consultation processes, and what measures could be put in place to enhance such involvement. These voices can play an important role in shaping a vision of contract law that responds to both economic and social values, understands vulnerability as being contextual, and perceives individuals as both consumers and citizens.

4.4 Conclusion

In the model of balance scales within concentric economic and social spheres presented in this book, the role of the state within the contractual realm can be envisaged as being twofold. Starting with the outer (interventionist) social sphere, the state is a protector of vulnerable parties ('function one'), focused on upholding citizenship values (such as equality, autonomy and human dignity), and reflecting an understanding of vulnerability as based on the context of the transaction, rather than the medical condition of individuals. In exercising this function, in pursuit of fairness or public policy considerations, the state could also refuse to enforce grossly asymmetrical transactions. The state also has a role within the inner (non-interventionist) economic sphere ('function two'), as the facilitator of transactions, by creating an environment where parties can deal with confidence in pursuit of their freedom if contract. Within the inner economic sphere, the state also exercises the role of enforcer of transactions (e.g. if a party is in breach of contract), protecting values such as sanctity of contracts.

This model recognises that the starting point for regulating B2C agreements is within the social sphere, rather than the economic sphere of contract law, so that individuals can be seen not just as consumers (and economic actors), but also as citizens (and social actors), with all the rights that citizenship entails. For this purpose, the state's exercise of 'function one' (as the protector of vulnerable parties within the social sphere of contract law) can be seen as a conduit of fairness within the contractual realm, providing fertile ground to pursue a vision of contract law which is closer to UNCRPD values, including autonomy and human dignity. In addition to the starting point referred to above, if things go wrong in the consumer–trader contractual relations (such as a grossly asymmetrical transaction to the detriment of consumers, due to unfair commercial practices on the part of traders), the state's response must extend beyond the economic sphere into the social sphere of contract law. Moreover, when pursuing its role as protector of vulnerable parties (e.g. by refusing to enforce a transaction on fairness or public policy grounds), such considerations should prevail over protecting the security of transactions.

782 Gerard Goggin and Christopher Newell 'An End to Disabling Policies? Toward Enlightened Universal Service' (2000) 16(2) *The Information Society* 127–33 at 131.

The boundaries between these functions are fluid. In the context of regulating B2C transactions, when the state exercises 'function one' effectively, putting in place a multi-layered response to address imbalances of power, including in the pre-contractual framework (e.g. to ensure that no one is discriminated against on the basis of, *inter alia*, disability, and that goods are accessible), the entry into contract (including measures to challenge unfair commercial practices that pressure or mislead people to enter into an agreement), or the context of transactions (including measures to challenge unfair terms), the state can then direct its focus on 'function two'. Many of the situations where things go wrong in consumer-trader relations could be addressed by the state exercising 'function two'. However, in situations such as grossly asymmetrical transactions at the detriment of consumers, involving traders' unacceptable conduct such as the inclusion of unfair terms in standard form contracts, the transaction reverts into the 'danger zone' within the social sphere, where the state would exercise 'function one' as the protector of vulnerable parties. In the event of tensions between the state's exercise of functions one and two, 'function one' should prevail, as this is rooted in the social sphere of contract law. In areas where the regulatory measures adopted by the state are ineffective, consumers remain in the 'danger zone' within the social sphere, which warrants state intervention through the exercise of 'function one'.

The discussion so far has stressed the relevance of the social sphere of contract law, as part of the concentric sphere structure presented in this book (in Chapter 2), its role within the vision of balance scales that address concerns regarding vitiating factors (in Chapter3), and as part of regulatory responses in B2C transactions (in this chapter). This sphere provides fertile ground for an understanding of contract law which is close to the UNCRPD vision, where concerns for social values (such as autonomy and human dignity) prevail over concerns for economic values (such as freedom and sanctity of contract). Chapter 5 seeks to explore in more detail why and how to strengthen the social sphere of contract law and the bridges between private law and human rights.

5

The Third Bridge

Constitutional Values

I stepped from plank to plank
So slow and cautiously...

(Emily Dickinson, American poet, 1830–1886
CXXXVI, Complete Poems, 1924)

Bridges have always been powerful symbols of connectivity and imagination, whether we are evoking with our mind's eye the poignancy of Dickinson's '*I stepped from plank to plank*',[1] or Turner's unfinished canvas *The Thames above Waterloo Bridge*.[2] When seeking paths that link the economic and social spheres of contract law, a journey mapped within the frameworks of English contract law and the UNCRPD is bound to encounter incomplete bridges. In the realm of English contract law, the construction starts from strong foundations of principles such as freedom and sanctity of contract, rooted in economic values. Yet, as the journey progresses towards social values, the bridges narrow, the gaps between the boards become further apart, and the journey is shakier. Anyone starting from the realm of the UNCRPD, attempting a crossing from the solid foundation of social values into the economic sphere is likely to encounter similar difficulties. This vision of incomplete bridges would make any traveller think twice before attempting the crossing. This perspective may account for the hesitation observed in English contract law to recognise that substantive fairness does matter, or in the reluctance of the UNCRPD Committee to articulate more explicitly that human dignity considerations rank higher than negative interpretations of freedom of contract. To overcome such hesitancy and complete these bridges, we must have the destination in sight, to identify the obstacles currently standing in the way and, most of all, to be aware of why action is needed.

The third and final bridge examined in this book looks at the connection between constitutional values and contract law, promoting a perception of contracting parties as citizens, rather than mere economic actors. While the

[1] Emily Dickinson, 'CXXXVI', *Complete Poems* (Boston: Little, Brown and Co, 1924).
[2] Joseph Turner, *The Thames above Waterloo Bridge*, c. 1830–1835 painting, Tate, London.

reference to constitutional values could cover a broad spectrum, this discussion, structured in two sections, focuses on four values crucial to the UNCRPD, which can be seen as aspects of equality of citizenship, and which could strengthen and shape the social sphere of contract law. Section 5.1 concentrates on the values of autonomy and human dignity. Although central to the UNCRPD, the connection between these values and the contractual sphere requires a reading between the lines of the UNCRPD Committee's decision in *Nyusti and Takács* v. *Hungary* (*Nyusti*).[3] Yet, implicit in this decision is the recognition that citizenship values permeate not just the public domain, but also the private sphere, that contractual relations are not confined to the economic sphere but are located within a wider social sphere, and that in the event of a conflict between the protection of autonomy and human dignity on the one hand, and freedom of contract on the other, the former values prevail. The discussion considers that many of the challenges associated with pursuing citizenship values in English contract law (including a focus on economic interests and procedural fairness, and insufficient emphasis on social consideration and substantive fairness) may stem from possible concerns not to upset well-established principles such as freedom of contract. Consequently, this section calls for a positive interpretation of freedom of contract in English contract law, which is closer to the UNCRPD values of autonomy and human dignity, interpreted broadly to also consider the inter-relation between people, and the need to protect contracting parties placed in a position of vulnerability due to the context of the transaction.

Section 5.2 focuses on the values of participation and inclusion. The discussion examines how these values promoted by the UNCRPD can enhance the influence of persons with disabilities and DDPOs in shaping future legislative developments in English contract law, including consumer contract law. This analysis seeks to address challenges related to issues of influence vulnerability identified in Chapter 4. While there are many steps that must be taken to respond to concerns posed by influence vulnerability, this discussion centres specifically on measures to enhance the participation of DDPOs in public consultations. DDPOs are organisations where the majority of board members are persons with disabilities.[4] The reason for placing the spotlight on public consultations is because of the absence of any responses from DDPOs to the consultations that informed the adoption of the CRA.[5] Moreover, the list of organisations that responded to the Government consultation on 'Smarter Regulation', focused on 'improving price transparency and product

[3] *Nyusti and Takács* v. *Hungary*, CRPD/C/9/D/1/2010, 11 March 2010.

[4] van Veen, Regeer and Bunders, 'Meeting the Challenge', 360.

[5] Department for Business, Innovation and Skills (BIS), 'Enhancing Consumer Confidence through Effective Enforcement: Consultation on Consolidating and Modernising Consumer Law Enforcement Powers', March 2012; BIS, 'Enhancing Consumer Confidence by Clarifying Consumer Law'; BIS, 'Consultation on Extending the Range of Remedies Available to Public Enforcers of Consumer Law', November 2012; Law Commission and Scottish Law Commission, 'Unfair Terms in Consumer Contracts: A New Approach? Issue Paper, July 2012.

information for consumers', which informed the DMCCA, does not appear to include DDPOs.[6] The involvement of DDPOs in public consultations is particularly pertinent in the current context of shaping consumer contract law, given the consultation conducted, or due to be conducted by the Government and the CMA following the adoption of the DMCCA.[7]

5.1 Interpreting Current Principles, Doctrines and Statutory Provisions in English Contract Law in Light of UNCRPD Values

Within the realm of English contract law, strong economic foundations connect feebly with social considerations. Yet, we must ensure that contract law embraces not only economic values, but also social values. A complete vision of contract law should not be confined to a horizontal axis which epitomises the relation between parties connected through contracts.[8] It should also acknowledge a vertical axis which represents the relation between the state and the people, who are seen not just as economic actors, but also as citizens.[9] Consequently, citizenship values, including the protection of autonomy and human dignity, should permeate all areas of law, including contract law. These principles should be interpreted broadly to reflect both the economic and the social dimensions of contract law. A narrow interpretation of these principles focuses on their individualistic dimension, with autonomy being confined to pursuing self-interest by parties seen as economic actors (individual autonomy),[10] and with human dignity perceived as having a role in empowering individuals to exercise their individual autonomy and pursue their individual interests (human dignity as empowerment).[11] This vision is associated with a unidimensional role of contract law confined to the economic sphere, where the main function of the state is to act as the facilitator of transactions.[12] Conversely, a broad interpretation of these principles considers the wider, social dimension of the contractual sphere. It adopts a broad view of personhood, recognising that autonomy is relational and taking into account the interdependence between people (relational autonomy).[13] It also includes an understanding of human dignity which recognises that the context of transactions may call for state intervention to protect the interests of

[6] Department for Business and Trade (DBT), 'Consultation Outcome: Government Response to Consultation on 'Smarter Regulation: Improving Consumer Price Transparency and Product Information for Consumers', Annex 1: List of organisations that responded to the consultation, 24 January 2024.

[7] See, for example, Competition and Markets Authority, 'Digital Markets Competition Regime Guidance: Consultation Document', 24 May 2024.

[8] Teubner, 'Contracting Worlds', 400. Charles Fried, *Contract as Promise: A Theory of Contractual Obligation* (2nd ed., Oxford: Oxford University Press, 2015), pp. 72–73.

[9] Teubner, 'Contracting Worlds', 400. [10] Atiyah, 'An Introduction', p. 9.

[11] Brownsword, 'Modern Understanding of Human Dignity', p. 302.

[12] Teubner, 'Contracting Worlds', 400.

[13] Dhanda, 'Constructing a New Human Rights Lexicon', 50.

contracting parties who find themselves in a position of vulnerability due to gross imbalances of power between the parties (human dignity as constraint).[14] This view is associated with a multidimensional role of contract law,[15] which also includes the social sphere, which recognises that the state has a role in protecting vulnerable parties,[16] and which accommodates a concern for the protection of human rights within the private sphere.[17] This section starts with a reflection on the potential of the UNCRPD values of autonomy and human dignity to shape our understanding of the contractual legal framework and protect individuals not just as economic actors, but also as citizens. Section 5.2 reflects on the insufficient focus on these values in English contract law and calls for the interpretation of principles, doctrines and statutory provisions in light of these values, to strengthen the connection between the economic and social spheres of contract law.

5.1.1 The UNCRPD: A Benchmark for Protecting Autonomy and Human Dignity

When examining the UNCRPD with the contractual sphere in mind, the Convention appears, at first instance, to be relatively silent. There is no equivalent provision to Article 15(2) of the UN CEDAW, which makes explicit reference to the equal right to conclude contracts and the equal right and equal opportunities to exercise legal capacity.[18] While Article 12 of the UNCRPD reaffirms the equal right of persons with disabilities to recognition as persons before the law[19] and to enjoy legal capacity 'in all aspects of life',[20] there is no explicit call on States Parties to provide persons with disabilities with equal opportunities to exercise legal capacity. There is also no explicit reference to equality in the contractual sphere, although this is implicit, including in the call on States Parties to take all appropriate measures to ensure the equal right of persons with disabilities to 'control their own financial affairs' and 'have equal access to bank loans, mortgages and other forms of financial credit'.[21] The UNCRPD acknowledges that some persons with disabilities may require support in exercising legal capacity,[22] and that safeguards must be put in place to ensure that 'measures relating to the exercise of legal capacity' are, *inter alia*, free of undue influence.[23] Yet, the Convention is unclear on the extent to which the right to exercise legal capacity can be restricted (if at all), and on the link between the concepts of legal, mental and contractual capacity.[24]

The guidance offered by the UNCRPD Committee on how to interpret the Convention in the contractual sphere is also limited. In its General Comment 1,[25]

[14] Brownsword, 'Modern Understanding of Human Dignity', p. 302.
[15] Teubner, 'Contracting Worlds', 400. [16] Herring, 'Vulnerable Adults', p. 226.
[17] Deutch, 'Are Consumer Rights Human Rights?', 553. [18] Article 15(2) of the UN CEDAW.
[19] Article 12(1) of the UNCRPD. [20] Ibid. Article 12(2). [21] Ibid. Article 12(5).
[22] Ibid. Article 12(3). [23] Ibid. Article 12(4).
[24] Bartlett, 'The United Nations Convention', 768.
[25] UNCRPD Committee, 'General Comment No. 1'.

other than two references to Article 15 of the UN CEDAW,[26] the UNCRPD Committee refers only once to the equal right to exercise legal capacity by entering into contracts. This reference is part of its discussion on the provision of support to exercise legal capacity.[27] The Committee calls on public and private actors to provide information in accessible formats, to enable persons with disabilities to perform legal acts required to conclude contracts,[28] but provides no further guidance on how this should operate in practice. Regarding the concepts of legal and mental capacity, the Committee distinguishes the concept of universal legal capacity (the ability to hold and exercise rights, duties) from mental capacity (the decision-making skills which may be influenced by external factors and vary from person to person).[29] Yet, it insists that legal standing (to hold rights) and legal agency (to exercise rights) cannot be separated and adopts an absolute stance on mental capacity assessments based on functional tests focused on an individual's ability to process information, finding these to be incompatible with Article 12 of the UNCRPD.[30]

The Committee also fails to consider the issue of contractual capacity involving a party who may act outside a framework of support to enter into a grossly imbalanced transaction to their detriment, whilst lacking the mental capacity to understand the consequences of the transaction. While the starting point should always be a presumption of contractual capacity and a focus on support to exercise capacity[31] (e.g. accessible information, informal or formal support arrangements),[32] the exercise of universal legal capacity could be facilitated by a legal framework where parties can rely, when appropriate, on defences such as contractual incapacity, but where disability and incapacity are never conceptually equated.[33]

If an intervention may amount to indirect discrimination on the basis of disability, this may be objectively justified only if it pursues a legitimate aim.[34] Such legitimate aim may be to protect the human dignity[35] of a party (A) in a situation of financial risk,[36] due to entering into a grossly asymmetrical contract while being in a vulnerable position where the other party (B) decided to proceed with the transaction without ensuring that A received appropriate independent legal advice regarding the transaction, despite B having (actual or constructive) knowledge of A's condition.[37] A's vulnerability, which derives from the context of the transaction, may be due to the fact that their consent was affected by vitiating factors such as incapacity, unconscionability or undue influence. Intervention should also be permitted only on an objective basis that moves beyond A's medical condition to include environmental factors such as the circumstances of the transaction (e.g. whether A entered into a grossly

[26] Ibid. [6], [35]. [27] Ibid. [17] with reference to Article 12(3) UNCRPD. [28] Ibid.
[29] Ibid. [13]. [30] Ibid. [14], [15]. [31] Article 12(3) of the UNCRPD.
[32] UNCRPD Committee, 'General Comment No. 1', [17].
[33] Bach, 'The Right to Legal Capacity', 21. [34] Martin, 'Achieving CRPD Compliance', p. 30.
[35] Article 3(a) of the UNCRPD. [36] Ibid. Article 11.
[37] Martin, 'Achieving CRPD Compliance', p. 30.

imbalanced contract without accessible and appropriate independent advice) and only if it constitutes a reasonable means to achieve a legitimate aim.[38] Regrettably, the UNCRPD Committee provided no guidance on how vitiating factors in contract law (including incapacity, unconscionability or undue influence), could act as a safety net in such circumstances.

The jurisprudence of the UNCRPD Committee illustrates further missed opportunities to provide guidance on how concepts such as contractual capacity and freedom of contract should be interpreted in light of the Convention. For example, the decision in *Nyusti*[39] highlighted States Parties' obligations to take 'all appropriate measures' to eliminate discrimination on the basis of disability by private parties such as banks[40] and ensure that such private parties offering services to the public 'take into account all aspects of accessibility'.[41] Despite the merits of this decision, the UNCRPD Committee failed to engage explicitly with the issue of freedom of contract or to challenge the negative interpretation of this concept presented by the private bank and endorsed by the State to resist intervention in pursuing equality objectives. Because of the significance of this case in illustrating the tension between negative interpretations of freedom of contract focused on economic concerns and positive interpretations focused on social values (including autonomy and human dignity), the decision in *Nyusti* and its wider implications that should be read between its lines, is examined in more detail in this section.

In *Nyusti*, when seeking to justify its refusal to provide accessible ATMs and enable its customers with visual disabilities to use these facilities independently, the bank stressed that independent use of ATMs would increase banking security risks for these customers, 'due to their special situation',[42] reflecting a paternalistic perception of people with disabilities as objects of care, rather than as subjects of rights.[43] Overlooking the security risks faced by anyone who has to rely on others to access their bank account[44] and the infringement on human dignity associated with inaccessible services, the bank insisted that the availability of accessible ATMs would motivate people with visual disabilities to use these facilities 'without help', endangering their 'personal safety'.[45] The bank also approached the issue of equal access to financial services from a solely economic perspective focused on the cost of inclusion (rather than the wider social costs of exclusion),[46] insisting that the provision

[38] Ibid. [39] *Nyusti and Takács* v. *Hungary*, CRPD/C/9/D/1/2010, 11 March 2010.

[40] Ibid. [9.4] with reference to Article 4(1)(e) of the UNCRPD.

[41] Ibid. with reference to Article 9(2)(b) of the UNCRPD.

[42] *Nyusti and Takács* v. *Hungary*, CRPD/C/9/D/1/2010, 11 March 2010, [2.5].

[43] Bielefeldt, 'New Inspiration', 397.

[44] Anna Lawson, 'Accessibility Obligations in the UN Convention on the Rights of Persons with Disabilities: *Nyusti and Takacs* v. *Hungary*' (2014) 30 *South African Journal on Human Rights* 380–92.

[45] *Nyusti and Takács* v. *Hungary*, CRPD/C/9/D/1/2010, 11 March 2010, [2.12].

[46] Interview with Guido Gybels, RNID, 17 August 2009 in Varney, 'Disability and Information Technology'.

of accessible ATMs would impose on it 'an unexpected financial burden'.[47] The bank's approach was also problematic in their interpretation of freedom of contract based on a negative, non-interventionist approach (rather than a positive approach that justifies intervention to protect social values such as equality, autonomy and human dignity),[48] as it stressed that an obligation to provide accessible services would amount to interference into the parties' contractual relations and infringe their freedom of contract.[49] Perhaps even more concerning is the positive reception of these arguments in Hungary's highest courts, as both the Court of Appeal and the Supreme Court agreed with the cost-based vision of accessibility and negative interpretation of freedom of contract presented by the bank.[50] This position was ultimately challenged before UNCRPD Committee, which, in a judgement that engaged more with accessibility arguments than with the issue of freedom of contract, found Hungary to be in breach of its obligations under Article 9(2)(b) UNCRPD to ensure that private entities offering facilities and services open to the public consider all accessibility aspects for persons with disabilities.[51]

While the applicants in *Nyusti* were ultimately successful in their claim under Article 9(2)(b) UNCRPD,[52] they did not provide sufficient justifications to enable the UNCRPD Committee to consider their claim under Article 12(5) UNCRPD, concerning the equal right of persons with disabilities to control their financial affairs.[53] Nevertheless, their successful claim should have provided the Committee with more scope to engage with the wider issue of asymmetrical power in contracts involving individuals and private entities such as banks. The Committee should have challenged a narrow, market individualist[54] understanding of freedom of contract that assumes that parties are free to pursue their own interest in the contractual sphere, placing insufficient weight on the inequality of bargaining power illustrated in the asymmetrical relation between individuals and banks, and on the proliferation of standard form contracts based on a 'take it or leave it basis'.[55] The UNCRPD Committee should have also contested negative visions of freedom of contract based on non-intervention by the state, in favour of a positive understanding of this concept where intervention is permitted if required to pursue wider social values such as the protection of autonomy and human dignity.[56]

In the contractual sphere, the UNCRPD Committee's decision in *Nyusti* is more significant for what can be read between the lines, rather than for what was stated explicitly. Implicit in this decision is the recognition that Convention rights permeate not just the public domain, but also the private

[47] *Nyusti and Takács* v. *Hungary*, CRPD/C/9/D/1/2010, 11 March 2010, [2.5].
[48] Collins, 'The Impact of Human Rights Law', 5.
[49] *Nyusti and Takács* v. *Hungary*, CRPD/C/9/D/1/2010, 11 March 2010, [2.5] and [2.12].
[50] Ibid. [2.13]–[2.16]. [51] Ibid. [10] and [9.4] with reference to Article 9(2)(b) of the UNCRPD.
[52] Ibid. [9.4]. [53] Ibid. [8.3].
[54] Adams and Brownsword, 'Understanding Contract Law', p. 194.
[55] Kessler, 'Contracts of Adhesion', 632. [56] Collins, 'The Impact of Human Rights Law', 5.

sphere, affecting the contractual relationships between parties. The Committee endorsed, albeit implicitly, the perception that the contractual relation of the applicants (who were consumers with disabilities) with the bank, was not confined to the economic sphere and, therefore, should not be rooted in a non-interventionist stance. Instead, the contractual relationship was located within a wider, social sphere, where intervention may be justified in pursuing equality objectives. A further significant aspect of the UNCRPD Committee's decision in *Nyusti* is the implicit recognition that in a process of balancing human dignity and freedom of contract, the protection of human dignity is ranked as a higher value that justifies interference with freedom of contract.

The issues explored in *Nyusti* are not confined to one isolated incident or to one jurisdiction. Barriers encountered by persons with disabilities in the contractual sphere continue to remain prevalent and are likely to increase, given the rise in the number of people with disabilities, including people developing mental health conditions such as dementia.[57] Such barriers have a negative impact on the extent to which people with disabilities can exercise their right to full and equal enjoyment of all human rights and fundamental freedom, including the right to independent living, and to the protection of their human dignity.[58] Moreover, service providers continue to resist calls for equality on the basis of paternalistic perceptions of disability, cost-related considerations and negative interpretations of freedom of contract,[59] while state actors appear to be more inclined to listen to industry voices than the views presented by people with disabilities.[60] In seeking to challenge negative interpretations of freedom of contract and to promote a positive understanding of this concept based on the values promoted by the UNCRPD, we must pick up what the UNCRPD Committee should have explored more explicitly and in more depth in *Nyusti* and subsequent decisions,[61] in highlighting the relevance and importance of values such as human dignity in the contractual realm.

The framework of values advanced by the UNCRPD rests on a human rights-based understanding of disability, moving away from a focus on the medical condition of individuals[62] and building on the social model of disability, concerned with addressing the social barriers faced by persons with disabilities when accessing a particular context.[63] In the contractual realm, barriers such as the unavailability of accessible information may lead to asymmetry in the parties' bargaining positions, enhancing consumer vulnerability.[64] Furthermore, barriers such as inaccessible services and facilities may produce

[57] Prince and others, 'Dementia UK', p. 5. [58] Articles 1 and 19 of the UNCRPD.

[59] *Nyusti and Takács* v. *Hungary*, CRPD/C/9/D/1/2010, 11 March 2010, [2.13]–[2.16].

[60] Anthony Ogus, *Regulation, Legal Form and Economic Theory* (Oxford: Hart Publishing, 2004), p. 22.

[61] *Bacher* v. *Austria*, CRPD/C/19/D/26/2014, 6 April 2018.

[62] Paragraph (e), Preamble and Article 1 of the UNCRPD.

[63] Fraser Butlin, 'The UN Convention on the Rights of Persons with Disabilities'.

[64] Trebilcock and Elliott, 'Scope and Limits of Legal Paternalism', p. 62.

isolation, dependence on others,[65] or lack of confidence to approach service providers, or to decline unwanted offers of goods or services.[66] The UNCRPD recognises the need to adapt society to accommodate the full spectrum of abilities,[67] including in its general principles a call for accessibility,[68] 'full and effective participation and inclusion in society'[69] and 'respect for difference and acceptance of persons with disabilities as part of human diversity and humanity'.[70] In addition, the States Parties' general obligations include a call to 'take all appropriate measures to eliminate discrimination on the basis of disability' by private enterprises,[71] while the provisions on accessibility call on States Parties to ensure that such requirements are considered by private entities offering services to the public.[72] These obligations contribute towards meeting the Convention's overall purpose to promote 'the full and equal enjoyment of all human rights and fundamental freedoms by all persons with disabilities' and 'respect for their inherent dignity',[73] reflecting a perception of persons with disabilities as citizens with full entitlements in society.

In meeting these objectives, an important role can be played by a vision of contract law that perceives people not only as economic actors in pursuit of self-interest but also as participants in the wider social sphere,[74] and which aims to protect citizenship values such as equality, autonomy, human dignity, participation and inclusion.[75] Furthermore, the concept of autonomy should be interpreted broadly to include relational autonomy, recognising our inter-dependence.[76] Based on this perspective, contract law is not confined to a unidimensional role to enable transactions in the economic realm, but reflects a multidimensional role that permeates the economic and social spheres, as it facilitates transactions and connects people into mutual relations.[77] In this vision, concepts such as freedom of contract should not be restricted to a narrow, negative interpretation concerned with resisting state intervention, and should, instead, be interpreted broadly to consider social values alongside economic concerns. A clear message would, therefore, be welcomed from the UNCRPD Committee to articulate expressly the link between Convention values and the contractual sphere, especially as the UNCRPD constitutes a benchmark in assessing the effectiveness of domestic frameworks in pursuing equality objectives.

The UNCRPD has been recognised by the European Court of Human Rights (ECtHR) as providing a 'universal consensus' on the protection of persons with disabilities from discrimination.[78] The 'embedding' of the UNCRPD in

[65] World Health Organisation and the World Bank, *Summary World Report on Disability*, WHO/NMH/VIP/11.01, 2011, p. 11.
[66] Maker, 'Ensuring Equality', 192. [67] Lawson, 'The United Nations Convention', 573.
[68] Article 3(f) of the UNCRPD. [69] Ibid. Article 3(c). [70] Ibid. Article 3(d).
[71] Ibid. Article 4(1)(e). [72] Ibid. Article 9(2)(b). [73] Ibid. Article 1.
[74] Cass Sunstein, *After the Rights Revolution: Reconceiving the Regulatory State* (Harvard: Harvard University Press, 1990), p. 58.
[75] Article 3 of the UNCRPD. [76] Dhanda, 'Constructing a New Human Rights Lexicon', 49.
[77] Teubner, 'Contracting Worlds', 400.
[78] *Glor* v. *Switzerland* (Application No. 13444/04), 30 April 2009, [53].

the ECtHR jurisprudence[79] provides an important step in the complex, interconnected bridge linking (i) the UNCRPD and the ECHR, (ii) the ECHR and the HRA and (iii) the HRA and English contract law. While the UK has incorporated the ECHR into domestic law via the HRA, the UNCRPD, ratified by the UK in 2009, has not been incorporated and is of limited direct assistance in domestic courts.[80] Nevertheless, the relevance of the UNCRPD values as a benchmark to be pursued, cannot be overlooked,[81] particularly if we consider the influence of the UNCRPD on the ECtHR and, in turn, the influence of the Strasbourg jurisprudence in interpreting the HRA at domestic level.[82]

The transformative potential of the UNCRPD is one element within a wider process of shaping private law in general, and contract law in particular, under the influence of human rights.[83] Rather than having a direct influence on domestic law, the UNCRPD is more likely to be relied on to support a particular interpretation of rights under the ECHR,[84] including Article 14 ECHR (prohibition of discrimination), relied on in combination with provisions such as Article 8 ECHR (right to respect for private and family life) or Article 1 (protection of property) of the First Protocol to the ECHR.[85] Whilst more progress could have been achieved in bridging provisions such as Article 1 of the First Protocol to the ECHR with the interpretation of domestic statutes[86] and common law doctrines[87] in disputes between private parties, this continues to be a realistic endeavour, especially given that courts (as public authorities) must act in a manner compatible with ECHR rights,[88] including with regards to dispute between private parties.[89] However, this bridge is more likely to be built on the basis of an indirect influence of the ECHR (interpreted in light of the UNCRPD) and the HRA on private law.[90] As Brownsword notes, the HRA

[79] Ibid.; *Kiss* v. *Hungary* (Application No. 38832/06), 20 May 2010, [42], [44]. See Fraser Butlin, 'The UN Convention on the Rights of Persons with Disabilities', 430–31.

[80] *R. (on the application of NM)* v. *Islington LBC* [2012] EWHC 414 (Admin) [98] (Sales J). See Canruh, 'Use of the UNCRPD in Social Security Cases', 115.

[81] *AH* v. *West London Mental Health Trust* [2011] UKUT 74 (AAC) [16] (Carnwath LJ).

[82] Sections 3(1) and 4 of the HRA 1998.

[83] See, for example, sections 28–31 of the EqA 2010.

[84] *AH* v. *West London Mental Health Trust* [2011] UKUT 74 (AAC) [16] (Carnwath LJ). See Canruh, 'Use of the UNCRPD in Social Security Cases', 119.

[85] Article 1 of the Protocol to the Convention for the Protection of Human Rights and Fundamental Freedoms, Paris, 20 March 1952. See Dan Friedmann and Daphne Barak-Erez 'Introduction' in Friedmann and Barak-Erez (eds.), 'Human Rights in Private Law', pp. 1–9.

[86] *Wilson* v. *First County Trust Ltd* [2003] UKHL 40 (with reference to the Consumer Credit Act 1974 (c. 39)). See Roger Brownsword, 'General Considerations' in Michael Furmston (ed.) *The Law of Contract: Butterworths Common Law Series* (6th ed., London: LexisNexis, 2017), 1.215.

[87] *Versloot Dredging BV* v. *HDI Gerling Industrie Versicherung AG (The DC Merwestone)* [2016] UKSC 45 (with reference to the common law doctrine of forfeiture). See François Du Bois, 'The Impact of Human Rights on English Contract Law' in Luca Siliquini-Cinelli and Andrew Hutchison (eds.), *The Constitutional Dimension of Contract Law* (New York: Springer Publishing, 2017), pp. 1–37 at pp. 23–25.

[88] Section 6(1) of the HRA 1998.

[89] *Campbell* v. *Mirror Group Newspapers Ltd* [2004] UKHL 22, [132] (Baroness Hale).

[90] du Bois, 'Private Law in the Age of Rights', p. 25.

has 'some degree of indirect horizontal application' and, while the Act does not provide private parties with 'freestanding private law pegs on which new causes can be hung', once a claim is brought on an established cause of action in private law, courts must handle that claim 'in a way that is compatible with the values represented by the Convention rights'.[91] The influence of the HRA on private law could be seen as a 'hidden catalyst for change',[92] providing 'an explicit tilt towards acceptance of human rights'.[93] A conduit for the influence of human rights on private law (even if indirect), can be provided by reliance on 'public policy',[94] which may limit freedom of contract in the event of grossly imbalanced agreements,[95] and which may include transactions incompatible with Convention rights.[96]

The influence of the UNCRPD (even via the indirect route provided by the ECHR and the HRA), could challenge negative interpretations of freedom of contract (based on non-intervention) in favour of positive interpretations promoting the protection of human dignity.[97] Although there is no express reference to human dignity in the HRA or the ECHR, this concept is part of 'the infrastructure on which the entire superstructure of human rights is constructed',[98] including the UNCRPD,[99] and has been recognised by the ECtHR to be 'the very essence of the Convention'.[100] Human dignity is considered to be 'the resource needed to intensify and broaden the impact' of human rights in the contractual sphere, although caution must be adopted when interpreting this concept (whether as empowering parties to exercise individual autonomy, or constraining such exercise on the basis of wider social values).[101] Yet, both of these interpretations of human dignity can be accommodated within a vision of contract law based on two concentric spheres, as the empowerment dimension of this concept is manifested in the inner, economic sphere, while its

91 Brownsword, 'Freedom of Contract', p. 181.

92 Hugh Beale and Nicola Pittam, 'The Impact of the Human Rights Act 1998 on English Tort and Contract Law' in Friedmann and Barak-Erez (eds.), *Human Rights in Private Law*, pp. 131–159 at p. 159.

93 Brownsword, 'Freedom of Contract', p. 159.

94 Aharon Barak, 'Constitutional Human Rights and Private Law' in Friedmann and Barak-Erez (eds.), *Human Rights in Private Law*, pp. 13–42 at p. 22.

95 Waddams, 'Sanctity of Contracts', p. 6. 96 Brownsword, 'General Considerations', 1.232.

97 Collins, 'The Impact of Human Rights Law'.

98 Brownsword, 'Freedom of Contract', p. 188. See the Preamble and Articles 1, 22 and 23 of the Universal Declaration of Human Rights, GA Res 217A (III), 10 December 1948, A/810; Preamble and Article 10 of the International Covenant on Civil and Political Rights, GA Res 2200A (XXI), 16 December 1966; preamble and Article 13 of the International Covenant on Economic, Social and Cultural Rights, GA Res 2200A (XXI), 16 December 1966.

99 Paragraphs (a), (h) and (y), Preamble of the UNCRPD. See also Articles 1, 3(a), 8(1)(a), 16(4), 24(1)(a), 25(d) of the UNCRPD.

100 *Pretty* v. *The United Kingdom* (Application No. 2346/02), 29 April 2002, [65]. See Sarah Arduin, 'Article 3: General Principles' in Ilias Bantekas, Michael Stein and Dimitris Anastasiou (eds.), *The UN Convention on the Rights of Persons with Disabilities: A Commentary* (Oxford: Oxford University Press, 2018), pp. 84–105.

101 Brownsword, 'Freedom of Contract', pp. 183–84 and 188.

constraint role is relevant in the outer, social sphere. The UNCRPD provides us with a benchmark to understand autonomy not only as individual, but also as relational, challenging narrow conceptions focused on pursuing self-interest in favour of broad interpretations focused on inter-dependence between human beings and the provision of support.[102]

5.1.2 Challenging an Insufficient Emphasis on Autonomy and Human Dignity in English Contract Law

The UNCRPD sparked the need to re-examine statutory provisions, doctrines and principles in English contract law, including the principle of freedom of contract, in light of the values pursued by the Convention. The UK ratified the UNCRPD in 2009 and, although this instrument has not been incorporated into national law and is of limited direct assistance in domestic courts,[103] its relevance cannot be ignored. Through its ratification, the UK undertook that 'wherever possible, its laws will conform to the norms and values' enshrined in the Convention.[104] This section emphasises that UNCRPD values, including the protection if autonomy and human dignity, could (and should) inform our interpretation of English contract law.

Freedom of contract is a foundational concept of English contract law, emphasising that parties are free to choose whether to enter into a contract, who to contract with, and under which terms.[105] However, this freedom is not absolute, and courts may decline to enforce contracts affected, *inter alia*, by vitiating factors.[106] They may also decline to enforce, among others, unfair contract terms in B2C transactions.[107] A narrow interpretation of freedom of contract focused on negative liberty (defined as freedom from state control)[108] would seek to resist interference, limiting it to procedural factors (e.g. vitiation of consent), unconcerned with substantive considerations of fairness (e.g. whether the parties entered into a grossly asymmetrical contract). This vision is not concerned with who the contracting parties are (e.g. whether there is a gross imbalance in their bargaining power)[109] and reflects a narrow conception of autonomy, perceiving the parties as economic actors in pursuit of their individual interests (individual autonomy).[110] It also reflects a narrow understanding of human dignity confined to emboldening people to pursue their individual interests (human dignity as empowerment).[111] Moreover, this view associates English contract law with a unidimensional role confined to

102 Dhanda, 'Constructing a New Human Rights Lexicon', 49.
103 *R. (on the application of NM)* v. *Islington LBC* [2012] EWHC 414 (Admin) [98] (Sales J).
104 *AH* v. *West London Mental Health Trust* [2011] UKUT 74 (AAC) [16] (Carnwath LJ).
105 Adams and Brownsword, 'Understanding Contract Law', p. 194.
106 Spark, 'Vitiation of Contracts'. 107 Section 62(1) of the CRA 2015.
108 Collins, 'The Impact of Human Rights Law', 5.
109 Adams and Brownsword, 'Understanding Contract Law', p. 194.
110 Collins, 'The Impact of Human Rights Law', 5.
111 Brownsword, 'Modern Understanding of Human Dignity', p. 302.

the economic sphere,[112] where the role of the state is seen as the facilitator of transactions.[113]

An alternative vision of freedom of contract is to focus on positive values such as promoting respect for autonomy and human dignity (interpreted broadly), where the state would refuse to enforce terms or transactions that harm such values.[114] This would reflect a broad, relational conception of autonomy, focused on the inter-dependence between human beings,[115] where contract law facilitates transactions that connect people into mutual relations within a wider social sphere[116] (relational autonomy).[117] It would also reflect a broad understanding of human dignity which recognises that, in certain circumstances, the state may need to intervene to protect the interests of a contracting party where circumstances (e.g. gross asymmetry of bargaining power) placed them in a position of vulnerability, resulting in a grossly imbalanced transaction (human dignity as constraint).[118] Within this alternative vision, contract law has a multidimensional role[119] which recognises the state's function to protect vulnerable parties in the contractual realm.[120]

Many of the challenges discussed in Chapters 3 (on vitiating factors) and four (in the regulation of B2C transactions) can be associated with a vision of contract law based on a narrow understanding of freedom of contract. The first challenge is linked to a narrow interpretation of the scope for intervention. Many of the doctrines concerning vitiating factors are confined by a narrow interpretation of their relevant triggers. For example, if a party (A) seeks to rely on the incapacity defence for contracts governed by the common law (which are outside the control of the court[121] and do not involve the purchase of necessary goods and services),[122] A needs to show both his mental incapacity and the other party (B)'s knowledge of his condition.[123] This can be a very high threshold if courts interpret the knowledge requirement to be confined to actual knowledge, or if any acceptance of constructive knowledge in this definition[124] is limited to situations where A's incapacity is apparent,[125] rather than where B ought to have known about A's incapacity due to the circumstances of the transaction.

As a second challenge, the current framework appears focused on limited intervention with the parties' freedom of contract, confined to procedural grounds. For example, B could seek to resist challenges based on undue influence or unconscionability by stressing that A exercised his free will when

112 Teubner, 'Contracting Worlds', 400.
113 Brownsword, 'Themes for the Twenty-First Century', p. 38.
114 Collins, 'The Impact of Human Rights Law', 5. 115 Ibid. 6.
116 Teubner, 'Contracting Worlds', 400.
117 Dhanda, 'Constructing a New Human Rights Lexicon', 50.
118 Brownsword, 'Modern Understanding of Human Dignity', p. 302.
119 Teubner, 'Contracting Worlds', 400. 120 Waddams, 'Sanctity of Contracts', p. 6.
121 Section 15 of the MCA 2005. 122 Ibid. section 7.
123 *Imperial Loan* v. *Stone* [1892] 1 QB 599, [601]. 124 *Dunhill v. Burgin* [2014] UKSC 18, [25].
125 Whittaker, 'Personal Incapacity', para 11-081, para 9-081.

entering into the contract[126] after having received independent legal advice.[127] This approach is driven by concerns to uphold the security of transactions[128] (making it harder for A to be released from their contractual obligations on the basis of vitiating factors), facilitate commercial convenience[129] (enabling B to point to the independent legal advice received by A) and ensure certainty[130] (as procedural factors appear to be easier to assess than substantive considerations). Nevertheless, this approach risks leaving vulnerable parties with insufficient protection of their economic interests (e.g. entering into a grossly imbalanced transaction, to their detriment) and social interests (e.g. harm to their human dignity and the wider social implications of allowing such grossly imbalanced contracts with vulnerable parties to be enforceable). Furthermore, insufficient weight is placed on whether the independent legal advice was appropriate to A,[131] and whether it addressed both economic and social considerations.

Challenges associated with a focus on procedural grounds for intervention and an insufficient focus on the wider social context of the transaction are also present regarding the statutory framework for the protection of consumers in B2C agreements. For example, under part 2 of the CCRs, traders are required to provide consumers with information regarding distance, off-premises and on-premises contracts that fall within the scope of the Regulations,[132] but these provisions fail to place sufficient emphasis on the need for that information to be accessible to consumers. Measures such as Regulations 9(1), 10(1) and 13(1) require traders to provide consumers, before the conclusion of the contract, with 'clear and comprehensive information' on matters such as the main characteristics of the goods, digital content or services,[133] with the aim of addressing issues such as 'informational vulnerability' in which consumers lack access to appropriate information about products.[134] However, these measures do not call explicitly for this information to be appropriate to the consumers' circumstances and to be provided in an accessible format.

A third challenge is due to the fact that the current framework appears to be unconcerned with who the contracting parties are.[135] It seeks to provide a 'middle course' that protects the interests of both parties,[136] assuming that they approached the transaction from an unconstrained bargaining position.[137] Once again, this provides insufficient protection to vulnerable contracting

[126] *Inche Noriah* v. *Shaik Allie bin Omar* [1929] AC 127.
[127] *RBS* v. *Etridge* [2001] UKHL 44, [20].
[128] Adams and Brownsword, 'Understanding Contract Law', p. 192.
[129] Herring, 'Vulnerable Adults', p. 249.
[130] Adams and Brownsword, 'Understanding Contract Law', p. 189.
[131] Trebilcock and Elliott, 'Scope and Limits of Legal Paternalism', p. 79.
[132] Regulations 6 and 7(1) of the CCRs 2013.
[133] Ibid. Regulations 9(1), 10(1) and 13(1) and Schedules 1(a) and 2(a).
[134] Cartwright, 'Vulnerable Financial Consumers', 119.
[135] Adams and Brownsword, 'Understanding Contract Law', p. 194.
[136] Watts, 'Contracts Made by Agents', 145.
[137] Herring, 'Vulnerable Adults', pp. 228 and 257.

parties. In cases where A seeks to rely on the incapacity defence, the requirement to show B's knowledge of incapacity as a condition for rendering the contract voidable may protect B's interests but places insufficient weight on A's lack of consent,[138] resulting in an imbalanced approach.[139] Similarly, in cases where A seeks to render a contract voidable on grounds of undue influence, any assumption of a balanced bargaining position distorts subsequent assessments of whether access to independent legal advice redressed this alleged balance. Furthermore, attempts to 'balance' the interests of parties such as individuals and banks overlook the gross asymmetry in these parties' bargaining positions and access to resources.[140]

The regulatory framework for B2C transactions presents its own sets of challenges, as although measures are designed to address imbalances of power between the contracting parties, the provisions could go further in responding to these imbalances and to consumer vulnerability, including 'redress vulnerability'. As discussed in Chapter 4, redress vulnerability results from constrained related to time, resources or processes.[141] For example, the fairness test under section 62 of the CRA considers a contract term to be unfair if 'contrary to the requirement of good faith', the term 'causes a significant imbalance' in the parties' contractual rights and obligations to the consumer's detriment.[142] The requirement for such a balance to be 'significant' sets a high threshold to be met by consumers.[143] Concerns are also posed by the provisions under section 64 of the CRA, which exclude from the application of the fairness test under section 62, terms concerning the appropriateness of the contract price compared with the value of the goods supplied, or terms concerning the subject matter, if these terms are 'prominent' and 'transparent'.[144] A term is 'prominent' if it was brought to the consumer's attention in a way that would make 'an average consumer' (i.e. someone who is 'reasonably well informed, observant and circumspect') aware of the term.[145] Furthermore, a term is 'transparent' if expressed in plain and intelligible language, and in the case of written contract terms, it is also legible.[146] These measures fail to make explicit reference to accessibility requirements in the provision of these terms which would be relevant to enable consumers to become 'reasonably well informed'. Moreover, these provisions place insufficient emphasis on the issues of consumer vulnerability, such as accessibility barriers encountered in the market (including the online marketplace), relying instead on an unrealistic vision of confident, self-reliant consumers.

138 Goudy, 'Contracts by Lunatics', 150.
139 Hudson, 'Mental Incapacity Revisited', 181.
140 Auchmuty, 'Men Behaving Badly', 271.
141 Cartwright, 'Vulnerable Financial Consumers', 121.
142 Section 62(4) of the CRA 2015. See also section 62(6) for a similar approach regarding consumer notices.
143 Burrows, 'Principles of the English Law of Obligations', 1.222.
144 Sections 64(1) and (2) of the CRA 2015.
145 Ibid. sections 64(4) and (5).
146 Ibid. section 64(3).

As a fourth challenge, this framework reflects narrow conceptions of autonomy (focused on individual autonomy)[147] and human dignity (focused on empowering parties to pursue their individual interests).[148] This framework places insufficient emphasis on the need for intervention to protect parties in a position of vulnerability due to the context of the transaction (human dignity as constraint).[149] For example, the *non est factum* doctrine illustrates a narrow understanding of vulnerability reliant on factors such as 'defective education, illness or innate incapacity',[150] overlooking the context of the transaction and the challenges of being presented with a complex document for signature.[151]

At the root of these concerns is a narrow interpretation of freedom of contract, where the state can intervene only in narrowly defined circumstances shaped by procedural factors, and where contract law has a unidimensional role limited to enforcing agreements.[152] Intervention, when permitted as part of procedural mechanisms, is confined to the economic realm, and is not understood to be transcending economic and social spheres. Such a framework overlooks the role of the state as a central pivot in enforcing (or refusing to enforce, where appropriate) the contractual relations between the parties.[153]

There is, however, an alternative vision of freedom of contract and of the state's role in the contractual sphere. This vision understands the role of contract law as multidimensional, transcending economic and social spheres,[154] and actively enforcing positive values such as the protection of autonomy and human dignity, interpreted broadly.[155] For example, in the context of vitiating factors, rather than perceiving the protection of vulnerable contracting parties as 'interference' with freedom of contract due to procedural concerns, this could be understood as a circumstance where the state refuses to enforce grossly imbalanced contracts[156] which have stepped out of an inner, non-interventionist sphere of contract law concerned with economic values, into a wider sphere shaped by social values.

Firstly, this alternative vision of freedom of contract relies on a broader interpretation of the scope for intervention, including a broader interpretation of the relevant triggers for vitiating factors such as incapacity, unconscionability, undue influence or *non est factum*, to include B's constructive knowledge regarding A's vulnerability, based on the circumstances of the transaction and to also include B's passive unacceptable conduct of going ahead with a grossly imbalanced transaction despite having such constructive knowledge. By adopting a broader interpretation of the scope for intervention, this vision reflects the view that the state cannot stay neutral in situations where, for example, a stronger party seeks to take advantage of the vulnerable position of the other

147 Collins, 'The Impact of Human Rights Law', 5.
148 Brownsword, 'Modern Understanding of Human Dignity', p. 302. 149 Ibid.
150 *Saunders* v. *Anglia Building Society* [1971] AC 1004, [1016] (Lord Reid).
151 Herring, 'Vulnerable Adults', p. 237. 152 Ibid. 225. 153 Shiffrin, 'Paternalism', 227.
154 Teubner, 'Contracting Worlds', 400. 155 Collins, 'The Impact of Human Rights Law', 5.
156 Chen-Wishart, 'Undue Influence: Vindicating Relationships of Influence', 231.

party, resulting in a grossly asymmetrical transaction.[157] It also reflects the connection between private law principles and doctrines and concerns for the protection of human rights, even if such concern is translated into the realm of contract law by reference to pursuing public policy or fairness-based considerations.[158]

The task of connecting economic and social values in English contract law would not take us into unchartered territories, but would be part of a rebuilding process. As Waddams reminds us, courts can rely on a general power, inherited from the Court of Chancery, to modify grossly imbalanced contracts.[159] While this power has been marginalised and confined to a piecemeal approach for intervention[160] (despite the express provisions of the Judicature Act 1873 that conflicts between law and equity should prioritise the latter),[161] this residual power for intervention has been 'inherited by the modern court' and 'can be revived', when required.[162] Consequently, Waddams calls for a 'more fluid interrelation between the idea of enforceability of contracts and the limitations of enforceability', where contracts are 'enforceable, unless their enforcement' is 'highly unreasonable'.[163] The idea of the inner and outer spheres of contract law is compatible with this vision, although the path presented in this book is one of broadening the current doctrines (such as undue influence, unconscionability, duress, *non est factum*, misrepresentation, and incapacity) to take account of social factors such as the protection of autonomy and human dignity, narrowing the gaps between the planks on the bridge. Nevertheless, the perception of this endeavour as a rebuilding process and the knowledge that there is a safety net provided by the general reserve power of the court to intervene into grossly asymmetrical contracts,[164] can provide the impetus to move forward.

Secondly, a vision of contract law that responds to both economic and social concerns would place more emphasis on substantive grounds for intervention, within a clear framework which considers the need for legal certainty. For example, in the context of contractual incapacity, as a factor for assessing whether B ought to have known about A's mental incapacity or vulnerability, this framework could consider either procedural factors alone or a combination of substantive and procedural factors (e.g. a grossly imbalanced contract where A received no independent legal advice).[165] Yet, this framework should not go as far as advocating intervention on the basis of substantive factors alone,[166] as the scope of such an assessment would be too uncertain. Instead, concerns for the substantive fairness of the transaction could be seen as a trigger for raising procedural protections.

The exercise of universal legal capacity (protected by the UNCRPD) can operate more effectively in a legal framework where parties can rely, when appropriate,

157 Kimel, 'Neutrality', 478. 158 Friedmann and Barak-Erez, 'Introduction', p. 3.
159 Waddams, 'Sanctity of Contracts', p. 220. 160 Ibid. p. 4.
161 Sections 24 and 25 of the Supreme Court of Judicature Act 1873.
162 Waddams, 'Sanctity of Contracts', pp. 8, 170 and 220. 163 Ibid. 221. 164 Ibid. 4.
165 *York Glass Co Ltd* v. *Jubb* [1925] All ER 285, [292]. 166 *Archer* v. *Cutler* [1980] 1 NZLR 386.

on legal concepts such as an incapacity defence in contract law that reflects not only economic but also social values. As Collins states, 'principles such as respect for the liberty and dignity of the individual' should influence not only the public sphere but should also 'guide all legal regulation of civil society'.[167] Once private law is perceived as 'a form of social regulation', it becomes legitimate to question whether particular concepts protect adequately autonomy and human dignity.[168] Collins concedes that the interplay between human rights law and private law could either lead private law to become more receptive 'to arguments about fairness', or stimulate instead 'a restatement of a more liberal, *laissez-faire* approach in private law', but that 'both directions of development seem to be on the cards'.[169] A key factor that may skew the outcome in favour of the former approach is the ability to develop 'a balancing mechanism suitable for contract law' that protects rights without undermining freedom of contract.[170] The vision of concentric economic and social spheres presented in this book (including the idea of parties connected by a lever within balance scales, with the state in the middle as the fulcrum), sought to advance such a mechanism.

Referring more broadly to vitiating factors and the pursuit of wider social values, rather than perceiving the state's refusal to enforce a contract affected by vitiating factors, as 'intervention' with the parties' freedom of contract, a grossly imbalanced transaction is seen as stepping out of a non-interventionist sphere into a sphere where the state is prepared to intervene to protect social values such as autonomy and human dignity. Moreover, certainty-related concerns about pursuing substantive fairness can be alleviated by a framework that does not allow intervention based on substantive fairness alone, but where substantive fairness is a trigger for investigating the procedural fairness of the transaction. In this framework, a combination of A's vulnerability and B's unacceptable conduct could be seen to act as a weight pushing A into a danger zone located within a sphere rooted in social values, and A could be lifted out of this danger zone only by a counterweight that addresses not only economic but also social concerns about A's position. A gross contractual imbalance between the parties would trigger a concern to protect values associated with the vertical axis that symbolises the relationship between individuals and the state, including human dignity. Consequently, courts should not be too quick in concluding that A has been lifted out of this danger zone unless these social considerations are also addressed. For example, for cases where A seeks to rely on doctrines such as undue influence or unconscionability to escape a grossly imbalanced transaction, courts should look not only at whether A received legal advice but also at whether the advice was appropriate to A's circumstances. This would involve a changed perception of A as both an economic and a social actor, requiring an examination of whether the advice provided to A considered the need to protect not only his financial interests but also his autonomy and human dignity.

[167] Collins, 'The Impact of Human Rights Law', 1. [168] Ibid. 3. [169] Ibid. 4. [170] Ibid.

Thirdly, a vision of contract law focused on both economic and social values would show concern for who the contracting parties are (e.g. assessing whether any independent legal advice received was appropriate and accessible) and would not assume that parties started from a balanced position, as such assumptions tend to favour the stronger party.[171] One illustration of the challenges associated with attempts to balance the interests of contracting parties and the important of social values in assessing this balance can be provided regarding the issue of contractual capacity. The law regarding the validity of contracts entered into between A (who lacked the mental capacity to understand the nature of the transaction) and B (who was unaware of the incapacity and acted in good faith), has been described as 'a battleground' of conflicting policies.[172] The most appropriate response in such circumstances is a balanced approach that protects the interests of both parties to the transaction. Yet, the history of this area of law has witnessed a shift from extreme responses (which protected the interests of only one of the parties), to imbalanced approaches. The predominant approach, based on the nineteenth-century Court of Appeal decision in *Imperial Loan*,[173] illustrates such imbalance. In a desire to uphold the security of transactions, this decision has left A with a very high threshold to invalidate the contract for want of capacity. This approach, which fails to place sufficient weight on A's lack of consent,[174] seems to require him to show not only his incapacity to understand the transaction but also B's knowledge of it.[175] In an attempt to redress this imbalance, the New Zealand Court of Appeal decision in *Archer* permitted contracts to be invalidated for want of capacity, irrespective of B's knowledge, if the contract was unfair.[176] However, this decision failed to articulate the practical implications of an unfairness test and left B with insufficient means to protect his interests, resulting in yet another imbalanced approach. *Archer* ultimately failed due to its over-ambition.[177] By opening up the possibility for substantive unfairness alone to invalidate the transaction, *Archer* went too far, seeking to disrupt in too significant a manner the current parameters of contract law.

The Supreme Court decision in *Dunhill*[178] provides hopes that a middle ground can be found to protect the interests of both A and B. These hopes rest on Lady Hale's interpretation of the *Imperial Loan* rule, confirming that B's knowledge of incapacity is not limited to actual knowledge and can include constructive knowledge.[179] Unlike *Archer*, this reflects a more realistic attempt to balance the interests of both contracting parties, based on a small but potentially significant step and working within the current parameters of English

171 Herring, 'Vulnerable Adults', p. 228.
172 Brucken and others, 'Mental Illness and the Law of Contracts', 1025.
173 *Imperial Loan* v. *Stone* [1892] 1 QB 599.
174 Goudy, 'Contracts by Lunatics', 150.
175 *Imperial Loan* v. *Stone* [1892] 1 QB 599, [601].
176 *Archer* v. *Cutler* [1980] 1 NZLR 386, [401].
177 See *Hart* v. *O'Connor* [1985] AC 1000.
178 *Dunhill* v. *Burgin* [2014] UKSC 18.
179 Ibid. [25].

contract law. Hopefully, subsequent cases will clarify the meaning of constructive knowledge in a way that would secure a balanced approach between the interests of both contracting parties. It is important to exercise cautious optimism, as Lady Hale's formulation of the *Imperial Loan* rule is open to two potential interpretations. A narrow understanding of constructive knowledge (limited to situations where incapacity is apparent)[180] would bring no significant changes and would merely retell the tale of imbalance associated with *Imperial Loan*. Conversely, a broad interpretation of constructive knowledge (to include situations where B ought to have known about the incapacity, due to the circumstances of the transaction) would signal the beginning of a new story. This would be a story rooted in an existing, but insufficiently explored legal basis,[181] setting the basis for a more balanced approach to protect the interests of both contracting parties. A narrow interpretation of constructive knowledge would be a step in the wrong direction. It would be a retrograde step for twenty-first century contract law, at a time when measures to protect the autonomy and human dignity of persons who lacked mental capacity are moving forward.

Fourthly, by focusing on the relation between the parties and the rules that should govern these relations within a wider social context,[182] this alternative framework demonstrates concern with issues of relational autonomy, including values such as interdependence and mutuality.[183] Moreover, a vision of contract law focused on both economic and social values considers the need for intervention to protect parties in a position of vulnerability due to the context of the transaction.[184] By adopting a broad, positive interpretation of freedom of contract that includes social values, this vision recognises the interconnected economic and social spheres of contract law[185] and the contribution that private law can play in securing social objectives such as the protection of human dignity.[186]

The relevance of a vision of contract law based on concentric economic and social spheres is not confined solely to vitiating factors affecting contractual relations, or to the need to address imbalances of power in B2C transactions. Vulnerability can arise at various stages of the contracting process. Consequently, addressing gross imbalances of power between the parties, which could harm human dignity, requires a multi-layered approach combining public and private law measures.[187] In addition to an effective framework regarding vitiating factors, which can act as a safety net enabling individuals to invalidate grossly imbalanced transactions,[188] and provisions regulating,

[180] Whittaker, 'Personal Incapacity', 11-088.
[181] *York Glass Co Ltd* v. *Jubb* [1925] All ER 285, [292] (Warrington LJ).
[182] Chen-Wishart, 'Undue Influence: Vindicating Relationships of Influence', 231.
[183] Herring, 'Vulnerable Adults', p. 228.
[184] Brownsword, 'Modern Understanding of Human Dignity', p. 302.
[185] Teubner, 'Contracting Worlds', 400. [186] Collins, 'The Impact of Human Rights Law', 1–2.
[187] Collins, 'Regulating Contracts', p. 361. [188] Maker, 'From Safety Nets', 831.

among other concerns, unfair contract terms and unfair commercial practices in B2C transactions, the protection of social values in the contractual sphere also requires provisions for combating discrimination and promoting equality of access to goods and services.

Whenever a trader refuses to enter into a contract with an individual (or offers less favourable terms) on discriminatory grounds such as disability, or whenever it imposes, for example, unfair terms on a 'take it or leave it basis', leaving the individual with a choice between accepting these terms or having no access to the goods or services,[189] such circumstances transcend the non-interventionist economic sphere of contracting, stepping into a wider social sphere. In this social dimension, parties cannot hide behind narrow interpretations of freedom of contract that seek to resist state interference. In fact, rather than 'interfering' with contractual relations between the parties, the state is exercising its function within the social sphere as the protector of vulnerable parties, guided by public policy and fairness-based considerations. While the state also has a role within the economic sphere of contract law as the enforcer of transactions, this role is secondary to its function within the social sphere. Within this social sphere, we can locate the measures adopted for regulating consumer-trader relations, and we should also locate the measures for controlling vitiating factors affecting the contractual relations between the parties. At the same time, this sphere also accommodates provisions to combat discrimination and promote equality in the contractual sphere, including regarding access to goods and services, illustrating the interplay between public law and private law.[190]

When we talk about parties who are in a vulnerable position in the contractual sphere due to the context of the transaction, and the measures to safeguard the interests of these parties, we should not see these measures as the state 'interfering' with freedom of contract. Freedom of contract should never be used to condone the behaviour of a contracting party (such as a trader), or to attempt to bring transactions behind the closed doors of a private realm not open to scrutiny.[191] Instead, this foundational concept of private law should be shaped by positive values that reflect both the economic and social dimensions of contract law, and the interplay between private law and human rights.[192] This positive interpretation of freedom of contract is closer to UNCRPD values, such as equality, autonomy and the protection of human dignity. Although the UNCRPD has no binding force in the UK (as this instrument was signed and ratified, but not incorporated into domestic law),[193] the Convention has persuasive authority[194] and, therefore, its values should not be overlooked.

[189] Kessler, 'Contracts of Adhesion', 632. [190] Collins, 'Regulating Contracts', p. 361.
[191] Collins, 'The Vanishing Freedom', 72.
[192] Deutch, 'Are Consumer Rights Human Rights?', 554.
[193] *R. (on the application of NM)* v. *Islington LBC* [2012] EWHC 414 (Admin) [98] (Sales J).
[194] *AH* v. *West London Mental Health Trust* [2011] UKUT 74 (AAC) [16] (Carnwath LJ).

5.2 Influencing Future Legislative Developments in English Contract Law to Reflect UNCRPD Values

One of the sources of consumer vulnerability discussed in Chapter 4 was that of influence vulnerability, where the voices of consumers (including consumers with disabilities and DDPOs) do not have the same level of impact in influencing the regulatory framework, when compared with industry voices. This can lead to the adoption of provisions favourable to traders, at the expense of consumer interests (e.g. the reluctance, due to business lobbying, to extend the strict liability standard applicable to goods and digital content in part 1 of the CRA, to also cover services such as the maintenance or storage of consumer goods or digital content).[195] It can also lead to measures that fail to place sufficient emphasis on matters such as accessibility concerns and, therefore, fail to engage sufficiently with issues such as the protection of autonomy and human dignity (e.g. the price/subject matter core exemptions in part 2 of the CRA, which refer to transparency and prominence, but which do not refer explicitly to accessibility requirements).[196] This can be problematic for people, including people with disabilities, faced with accessibility barriers due to the context of the transaction (e.g. inaccessible information or products). Without disability voices to educate policymakers about these barriers and the solutions to address them, adopted measures risk overlooking these matters of concern, or risk reflecting a lack of clear understanding of these challenges and of what is needed to facilitate equal access to information, products or services.

One approach towards increasing the influence of people with disabilities and DDPOs in shaping future legislative developments in English contract law (including consumer contract law) is by adopting measures to enhance the participation of DDPOs in public consultations. The reason for focusing this discussion on public consultations, rather than on other steps that should also be taken to address issues of influence vulnerability, is due to the absence of any responses from DDPOs to the consultations that led to the adoption of the CRA.[197] Furthermore, the list of organisations that responded to the consultation on 'Smarter Regulation' which informed the DMCCA, does not appear to include DDPOs.[198] After a brief background on the important contribution that DDPOs can bring to consultations, providing expertise based on the lived experiences of persons with disabilities, the discussion reflects on the potential of the UNCRPD to act as a benchmark for the values of participation and inclusion. The analysis then moves on to the English legal and policy

[195] Sections 9 and 34 (strict liability standard) and 49 (negligence-based standard) of the CRA 2015. See Willett, 'Re-theorising Consumer Law', 199.

[196] Section 64(2) of the CRA 2015.

[197] BIS, 'Enhancing Consumer Confidence through Effective Enforcement'; BIS, 'Enhancing Consumer Confidence by Clarifying Consumer Law'; BIS, 'Consultation on Extending the Range of Remedies'; Law Commission and Scottish Law Commission, 'Unfair Terms in Consumer Contracts'.

[198] DBT, 'Consultation Outcome'.

framework on public consultations, questioning its effectiveness in promoting engagement from DDPOs.

As a State Party to UNCRPD, the UK is subject to the general obligation under Article 4(3) to 'closely consult with and actively involve' persons with disabilities 'through their representative organizations' in relevant decision-making processes.[199] The discussion calls for a wider interpretation of consultation standards developed by the courts, informed by UNCRPD values, including participation and inclusion. These values are a crucial aspect of the wider objective for pursuing equality of citizenship which has relevance in all areas of law, including contract law. By enhancing the participation and inclusion of persons with disabilities and DDPOs in public consultations, adopted measures, including in the field of consumer contract law, would be more responsive to addressing issues of contextual vulnerability, and would strengthen and shape the social sphere of contract law.

5.2.1 Background: DDPOs and Contributions to Public Consultations

This chapter relies on a definition of DDPOs as registered charities, led and controlled by people with disabilities (minimum 75 per cent of board members).[200] Distinguished from organisations *for* people with disabilities (which tend to focus on the provision of services and may reflect a medical understanding of disability focused on the medical condition of individuals),[201] DDPOs are organisations *of* people with disabilities. These organisations are focused on empowerment, build on the social model of disability (which 'shifts the perspective from the individual to the environment's role in defining [and] amplifying the effects of impairments')[202] and reflect a human rights model of disability (which calls for the full and equal enjoyment of all human rights and fundamental freedoms by people with disabilities).[203] Developed as 'a direct action against the assumptions' of medical and social care professionals that they 'owned disability',[204] DDPOs are 'vehicles of self-representation'.[205] They have a crucial role to play in identifying social barriers and the solutions to remove these barriers in promoting the rights of persons with disabilities to full and equal enjoyment of all human rights and fundamental freedoms.[206] Participation in public consultations is one facet for fulfilling that role.

199 Article 4(3) of the UNCRPD.

200 Department of Health, 'User-Led Organisations Project Policy' (September 2007), para. 24.

201 Joshua Malinga and Trynos Gumbo, 'Advocacy and Lobbying: The Road Map from Charity to Human Rights' in Edurne García Iriarte, Roy McConkey and Robbie Gilligan (eds.), *Disability and Human Rights: Global Perspectives* (London: Palgrave, 2016), pp. 49–67 at p. 58.

202 van Veen, Regeer and Bunders, 'Meeting the Challenge', 360.

203 Article 1 of the UNCRPD.

204 Hurst, 'Disabled People's Organisations', p. 25.

205 Malinga and Gumbo, 'Advocacy and Lobbying', p. 52.

206 Articles 1, 4(3) and 33(3) of the UNCRPD.

DDPOs are important actors in enhancing the participation of persons with disabilities in policymaking[207] to influence decisions[208] and promote social inclusion.[209] They give people with disabilities a voice in policymaking and provide expertise, given their unique insight into the impact of policies on the lives of people with disabilities.[210] Organisations working at grassroot level 'will often have the best data for policymaking', as being user-led provides an insight into the impact of policy changes in the community.[211] DDPOs can also develop solutions based on the lived experiences of their users.[212] People with disabilities are 'experts by experience',[213] with practical understanding of overcoming barriers to participation,[214] and the user-led status puts DDPOs in a unique position to recognise what people with disabilities are going through, as often, these are shared experiences.[215] This practical knowledge provides DDPOs with an unparalleled understanding of the social changes needed for ensuring the 'equalisation of opportunities' and the 'enhancement of rights' for persons with disabilities.[216] Furthermore, by sharing the practical experiences of people with disabilities with other stakeholders, DDPOs facilitate the mainstreaming of disability issues in policymaking.[217]

The reference to public consultations employed in this chapter refers to formal written public consultation exercises conducted by public authorities. Such consultations are an important stage in policymaking, as they facilitate the public scrutiny of preliminary findings, and enable citizens to have a voice in the development of new or revised policies.[218] They also provide voluntary organisations with 'useful arenas' to influence policymaking.[219] Consultations

[207] Priscille Geiser, Stefanie Ziegler and Ute Zurmühl, 'Support to Organisations Representative of Persons with Disabilities', Policy Paper, July 2011.

[208] García Iriarte, McConkey and Gilligan (eds.), 'Disability and Human Rights', p. 6.

[209] Sian Williams, 'Confident Commissioning: Building Relationships between Local Authorities and Disabled People's User-Led Organisations', South-East Network of Disabled People's Organisations, June 2014, 280.

[210] Ibid. 51.

[211] Interview with Lorna Carter (Chair), Disability Nottinghamshire (Mansfield, 27 January 2016), research funded by the Society of Legal Scholars (SLS) Research Activities Fund (joint bid with Mike Varney).

[212] Williams, 'Confident Commissioning', 51.

[213] Interview with Hannah Tutt (Chairperson), Centre for Independent Living Kent (CiLK) (now Disability Assist) (Ashford, 4 March 2016), research funded by the SLS Research Activities Fund (joint bid with Mike Varney).

[214] Interview with Dave Thompson (Development Manager), Access Dorset (Bournemouth, 23 February 2016), research funded by the SLS Research Activities Fund (joint bid with Mike Varney).

[215] Interview with Jonathan Toye (Coordinator), West Norfolk Disability Information Service (WNDIS) (King's Lynn, 25 February 2016), research funded by the SLS Research Activities Fund (joint bid with Mike Varney).

[216] Hurst, 'Disabled People's Organisations', p. 25.

[217] van Veen, Regeer and Bunders, 'Meeting the Challenge', 378–79.

[218] Government Consultation Principles 2018, [B], [I]. See previously Government Code of Practice on Consultation 2008, [1.1], [5].

[219] Erik Lundberg, 'Does the Government Selection Process Promote or Hinder Pluralism? Exploring the Characteristics of Voluntary Organizations Invited to Public Consultations' (2013) 9(1) *Journal of Civil Society* 58–77.

enable public authorities to access external expertise and adopt informed decisions which consider public experiences.[220] An effective consultation exercise can 'identify hidden issues or groups'.[221] Public authorities that facilitate the participation of DDPOs in public consultation are in a better position to understand the barriers encountered by persons with disabilities in society and the solutions needed to address these barriers.

In addition to the potential practical impact of this discussion in highlighting incentives and barriers encountered by DDPOs to participating in public consultations and the potential solutions to address these barriers, this section explores an area that has not yet received sufficient attention in academic literature. Research on public consultations tends to stress the value of public participation in policymaking but does not focus specifically on the participation of people with disabilities in public consultation.[222] Conversely, research on disability equality often refers to the importance of ensuring that people with disabilities have a voice in policymaking, but do not focus specifically on the involvement of DDPOs in public consultations.[223] This discussion focuses specifically on the participation of DDPOs in public consultations, to explore the key factors affecting such involvement, the effectiveness of the current legal and policy framework on public consultations to facilitate such participation, and the measures needed to enhance participation.

5.2.2 The UNCRPD: A Benchmark for Protecting Participation and Inclusion

The UNCRPD has been credited with transforming the disability movement's mantra 'nothing about us without us'[224] from 'a campaign anthem' to 'a non-negotiable principle of disability rights'.[225] In addition to being the first binding international human rights instrument focused specifically on the rights of persons with disabilities, the Convention has been commended for relying on the most inclusive negotiation process.[226] This process involved the highest level of participation from persons with disabilities and their representative organisations, covering a wide range of disabilities.[227]

[220] Erik Lundberg and Erik Hysing, 'The Value of Participation: Exploring the Role of Public Consultations from the Vantage Point of Interest Groups' (2015) 39(1) *Scandinavian Political Studies* 1–21 at 9.

[221] Andrew Power, Janet Lord and Allison DeFranco, *Active Citizenship and Disability* (Cambridge: Cambridge University Press, 2013), p. 455.

[222] See, for example, James Fishkin, 'Making Deliberative Democracy Practical: Public Consultation and Dispute Resolution' (2011) 26(4) *Ohio State Journal on Dispute Resolution* 611–26.

[223] See, for example, Arie Rimmerman, *Social Inclusion of People with Disabilities* (Cambridge: Cambridge University Press, 2014).

[224] James Charlton, *Nothing about Us without Us: Disability Oppression and Empowerment* (Berkeley: University of California Press, 1998).

[225] Dhanda, 'Constructing a New Human Rights Lexicon', 50.

[226] Kanter, 'The Promise and Challenge', 308.

[227] Geiser, Ziegler and Zurmühl, 'Support to Organisations', 14.

Participation and inclusion are 'essential ingredients' of the Convention,[228] which stresses in its preamble that persons with disabilities 'should have the opportunity to be actively involved in decision-making processes about policies and programmes, including those directly concerning them'.[229] The UNCRPD lists 'full and effective participation and inclusion in society' as part of its general principles,[230] while its general obligations include a requirement on States Parties to 'closely consult with, and actively involve' persons with disabilities, 'through their representative organisations', when developing policies and legislation to implement the UNCRPD, and in 'other decision-making practices concerning issues relating to' persons with disabilities.[231] The Convention also stresses that 'persons with disabilities and their representative organisations shall be involved and participate fully' in the process of monitoring the implementation of the UNCRPD at national level.[232] These requirements should be interpreted widely, particularly when read in light of the Convention's ethos to ensure the 'full and equal enjoyment of all human rights and fundamental freedoms by all persons with disabilities and to promote respect for their inherent dignity'.[233] As Article 4(3) UNCRPD clarifies, the requirement to consult and involve persons with disabilities, through their representative organisations, is not limited to measures for implementing the Convention, but also covers any other 'decision-making practices concerning issues relating to persons with disabilities'.[234] This should include provisions adopted in the field of contract law, including consumer contract law. The UNCRPD, which calls for 'respect for difference' and for the 'acceptance of persons with disabilities as part of human diversity and humanity',[235] implies that all human issues are disability issues and that all decision-making practices that have an impact on people can be seen as decision-making 'concerning issues relating to persons with disabilities'.[236] In its General Comment 7 on Articles 4(3) and 33(3) UNCRPD, the UNCRPD Committee explains that the phrase 'concerning issues relating to persons with disabilities' must be interpreted broadly to include 'the full range of legislative, administrative and other measures' that may have a direct or indirect impact on the rights of people with disabilities, to facilitate mainstreaming and the adoption of inclusive measures.[237]

The consultation requirements advanced by the Convention promote a perception of persons with disabilities as active citizens rather than as 'passive recipients of care'.[238] Unlike the medical approach to disability (which perceives persons with disabilities as 'different from the wider society'),[239] the

[228] Ibid. [229] Paragraph (o), Preamble of the UNCRPD. [230] Ibid. Article 3(c).
[231] Ibid. Article 4(3). [232] Ibid. Article 33(3). [233] Ibid. Article 1. [234] Ibid. Article 4(3).
[235] Ibid. Article 3(d). [236] Ibid. Article 4(3).
[237] UN Committee on the Rights of Persons with Disabilities, 'General Comment No. 7: Article 4.3 and 33.3 (Participation with persons with disabilities in the implementation and monitoring of the Convention)', 21 September 2018, UN Doc. CRPD/C/GC/7, [18].
[238] Geiser, Ziegler and Zurmühl, 'Support to Organisations', 12.
[239] Paul Harpur, 'Time to Be Heard: How Advocates Can Use the Convention on the Rights of Persons with Disabilities to Drive Change' (2010) 45(3) *Valparaiso University Law Review* 1271–96 at 1273.

UNCRPD builds on the social model of disability (focused on tackling socially constructed participation barriers),[240] to advance a human-rights–based approach.[241] The human rights paradigm acknowledges people with disabilities as subjects of rights[242] with full and equal entitlements to exercise these rights and participate as active members of society.[243] DDPOs have a key role in promoting the citizenship values of autonomy, human dignity, inclusion and participation.[244] They are a vehicle for social change to ensure the full and equal enjoyment of all human rights by persons with disabilities.[245]

The human rights paradigm promoted by the UNCRPD recognises the responsibility of the state and of other key stakeholders to respect and facilitate the exercise of human rights by persons with disabilities.[246] It acknowledges that reactive measures designed to ensure that people are not treated less favourably because of a specified characteristic must be complemented by proactive measures focused on tackling systemic forms of discrimination.[247] As participation is a key aspect of citizenship, proactive measures must be put in place to ensure that all citizens can contribute to political discussions.[248] The language adopted in the Convention, requiring States Parties to 'closely consult' and to 'actively involve' people with disabilities, though their representative organisations, in decision-making,[249] sends a clear message that the consultation cannot be a token effort. Effective compliance with this requirement involves the development of a partnership between public authorities and organisations representing persons with disabilities. The development of such partnership is also suggested with regards to the process of implementing the UNCRPD at national level and the monitoring of this process, as the Convention calls on States Parties to ensure that the civil society, particularly people with disabilities and their representative organisations are 'involved and participate fully in the monitoring process'.[250] The requirement for the 'full' involvement and participation of these key stakeholders, presented in Article 33(3) UNCRPD, echoes the call for 'close consultation' and 'active involvement' of these stakeholders advanced under Article 4(3) UNCRPD. The Convention does not refer explicitly to DDPOs, and the reference to 'representative organisations' does not appear to make a distinction between organisations *of* and organisations *for* persons with disabilities. Nevertheless, in

240 Michael Oliver, *Understanding Disability: From Theory to Practice* (2nd ed., Basingstoke: Palgrave Macmillan, 2009).
241 Harpur, 'Time to Be Heard', 1275.
242 Office of the United Nations High Commissioner for Human Rights (OHCHR), 'The Convention on the Rights of Persons with Disabilities: Training Guide', Professional Training Series No. 19, 2014, 10.
243 van Veen, Regeer and Bunders, 'Meeting the Challenge', 361.
244 Williams, 'Confident Commissioning', 12.
245 Hurst, 'Disabled People's Organisations', p. 25.
246 OHCHR, 'Training Guide', 10.
247 Fredman, 'Equality: A New Generation?', p. 163.
248 Robert Drake, *Understanding Disability Policies* (Basingstoke: Palgrave 1999), p. 41.
249 Article 4(3) of the UNCRPD.
250 Ibid. Article 33(3).

General Comment 7, the UNCRPD Committee clarifies that 'representative organisations' in these provisions refers to organizations *of* persons with disabilities.[251] The Committee also calls for mandatory consultations with people with disabilities and their representative organisations, prior to the adoption of both mainstream and disability-specific measures, insisting that these consultations must be accessible.[252]

The UNCRPD sets an important benchmark regarding the participation of persons with disabilities and DDPOs in policymaking, focusing on promoting the full and equal enjoyment of all human rights and fundamental freedoms and reflecting a perception of persons with disabilities as active citizens.[253] It calls for genuine consultation with people with disabilities and DDPOs, promoting a partnership between these stakeholders and policymakers.[254] It also suggests that the requirement to consult with these stakeholders on 'issues relating to persons with disabilities' can apply to all issues affecting people, given that disability is an aspect of human diversity.[255] These can include issues related to contractual relations, including consumer-trader transactions. The next section explores the extent to which the English framework on public consultations reflects these values. The UNCRPD is a landmark instrument in promoting the rights of persons with disabilities, but its impact is conditioned by the extent to which States Parties reflect these values in their domestic laws and policies.[256]

5.2.3 Public Consultations in England: An Effective Framework for the Participation and Inclusion of DDPOs?

The English legal and policy framework on public consultations has already been analysed at length in the literature.[257] This discussion focuses specifically on how the limitations of the current framework affect DDPOs (including the framework on judicial review and the potential for Cabinet Office guidelines, when followed, to address some of the challenges identified), examining what is problematic about this framework, how does it need to change, and why is it important that such changes are implemented.

Under English law, there is no general legal requirement to consult with anyone, unless the legislation which gives the power to make Statutory Instruments or other regulatory policies requires it.[258] Public consultation standards have been developed by courts in England, most notably the principles presented by Mr. Sedley QC (as he then was) and adopted by Mr. Justice Hodgson in

[251] UNCRPD Committee, 'General Comment No. 7', [10]. [252] Ibid. [15], [22].
[253] Articles 1, 3, 4(3) and 33(3) of the UNCRPD. [254] Ibid. Articles 4(3) and 33(3).
[255] Ibid. Articles 3(d) and 4(3).
[256] Geiser, Ziegler and Zurmühl, 'Support to Organisations', 16.
[257] See, for example, Clive Sheldon, 'Consultation: Revisiting the Basic Principles' (2012) 17(2) *Judicial Review* 152–60.
[258] *Bates* v. *Lord Hailsham of St Marylebone* [1972] 1 WLR 1373, [1378] (Megarry J).

R. v. Brent LBC Ex p. Gunning (*Gunning*), which seek to ensure that (i) consultations are conducted when the proposals are 'still at a formative stage', (ii) 'sufficient reasons' are provided for the consultation, to enable 'intelligent consideration and response', (iii) 'adequate time' is provided for consideration and response and (iv) the product of the consultation is considered 'conscientiously' when statutory proposals are being finalised.[259] However, there is no general principle regarding who should be consulted[260] and how the process should be tailored to the needs of those being consulted.

The first and fourth *Gunning* principles seek to ensure that the consultation exercise is genuine,[261] as consultations on decisions that have already been made are futile, due to their 'predetermined outcome'.[262] It also aims to ensure that decision-makers consider the submissions presented by individuals and groups to reach an 'informed decision' that 'meets the interests and needs of the community'.[263] Most importantly, by enabling the public voice to shape decision-making, this process seeks to ensure that 'democratic values extend to administrative actions'.[264] Yet, while the *Gunning* principles require decision-makers to consider 'conscientiously' the product of the consultation,[265] they include no express requirement to provide feedback on how the submissions have informed the final policy and why specific suggestions have not been adopted. Furthermore, decision-makers enjoy discretion on what they are consulting on,[266] and cases where the courts have intervened to find the scope of a consultation as too restricted have been 'exceptional',[267] although, following *R. (on the application of Moseley)* v. *Haringey LBC*,[268] an argument could be made that the requirements over the provision of information might mean that the scope of the consultation has to be extended in at least some cases. To support this latter point, reference may be made to the 'Judge Over Your Shoulder' (JOYS) Government guidance to civil servants on, *inter alia*, consultations, which notes that 'consultation helps to ensure that the decision maker is in possession of all relevant information, allows people to have their voices heard, and often results in better and fairer decision making'.[269]

259 *R.* v. *Brent LBC Ex p. Gunning* (1985) 84 LGR 168, [189], (Hodgson J).

260 Sheldon, 'Consultation', 152.

261 *Agricultural, Horticultural and Forestry Industry Training Board* v. *Aylesbury Mushrooms* [1972] 1 WLR 190, [194], (Donaldson J), referring to 'a genuine invitation, extended with a receptive mind, to give advice'.

262 Sheldon, 'Consultation', 152.

263 Andrew Edgar, 'Procedural Fairness for Decisions Affecting the Public Generally: A Radical Step Towards Public Consultation' (2014) 33(1) *University of Tasmania Law Review* 56–82 at 59.

264 Ibid. 265 *R.* v. *Brent LBC Ex p. Gunning* (1985) 84 LGR 168, [189], (Hodgson J).

266 *Nichol* v. *Gateshead MBC* (1988) 87 LGR 435.

267 *Vale of Glamorgan Council* v. *Lord Chancellor* [2011] EWHC 1532 (Admin), [25].

268 *R. (on the application of Moseley)* v. *Haringey LBC* [2014] UKSC 56.

269 Government Legal Department, 'JOYS: The Judge Over Your Shoulder', 6th ed., May 2022, [2.67].

The second and third *Gunning* principles are focused on ensuring that the consultation exercise provides sufficient information that can be considered in adequate time,[270] and this may include information on the proposed action, the potential implications and impact of the proposal and the evidential basis for the proposal.[271] It may also include the proposed criteria for reaching the final decision.[272] What amounts to 'adequate time' to consider this information is generally at the discretion of the decision-maker (subject to any prescribed statutory requirements).[273] Unfortunately, the *Gunning* principles fail to consider the consultation process in light of those being consulted. There is no explicit reference to matters such as the need for accessible information or the need to consider those being consulted when exercising discretion regarding the time allocated for consultations. Subsequent cases considered the complexity of the information provided as part of the consultation exercised and called for information to be published in a form that can be understood by those consulted (with reference to the inclusion of 'complicated and indigestible' financial information in a consultation document).[274] However, more is needed to make explicit the requirement that the information provided as part of the consultation document must be in a format that is accessible to people with disabilities. The *Gunning* principles are focused on traditional forms of consultation which are predominantly written and reliant largely on consultation documents, but which may not provide the best format for engaging grassroot organisations such as DDPOs. Furthermore, while these principles refer to the need to allocate appropriate time for consultation, they make no explicit reference to the allocation of other resources to facilitate effective consultation.

Some optimism may have been gleaned from the call in subsequent cases that if consultation is embarked upon, 'it must be carried out properly',[275] although the narrow interpretation of what is meant by 'proper consultation' largely replicates the *Gunning* principles. For conducting a 'proper' consultation, public authorities must let interested parties 'know in clear terms what the proposal is' and 'why it is under positive consideration', telling consultees 'enough (which may be a good deal) to enable them to make an intelligent response'.[276] This obligation 'may be quite onerous' but 'goes no further than this'.[277] This replicates the focus of the *Gunning* principles on the consultation process itself, without giving sufficient attention to those being consulted.

A public body which engages in a consultation process 'must do so fairly' and what amounts to a 'fair consultation' depends on the circumstances of

[270] *R.* v. *Brent LBC Ex p. Gunning* (1985) 84 LGR 168, [189], (Hodgson J).

[271] Edgar, 'Procedural Fairness', 58.

[272] *R. (on the application of Capenhurst)* v. *Leicester City Council* [2004] EWHC 2124 (Admin).

[273] Sheldon, 'Consultation', 156.

[274] *R. (on the application of Breckland DC)* v. *Electoral Commission Boundary Committee for England* [2009] EWCA Civ 239, [69].

[275] *R.* v. *North and East Devon HA Ex p. Coughlan* [2001] QB 213, [108], (Lord Woolf).

[276] Ibid. [112] (Lord Woolf). [277] Ibid.

the case and on the nature of the proposals under consideration.[278] The reference to the 'rather open-ended doctrine of fairness' may provoke some concerns regarding potential uncertainty and the risk that 'different judges could reach different views on the lawfulness of the consultation process on the same facts'.[279] On this regard, Sheldon warns that 'possibly, the underlying merits of the decision in question could influence the outcome of any challenge' and, consequently, decision-makers should 'approach the consultation with more care and seriousness when the subject-matter is likely to prove particularly controversial'.[280] The reference to fairness should not be a cause for concern. It could provide an opportunity to move away from a narrow interpretation of the *Gunning* principles. The call for 'fair consultation' could be interpreted broadly, informed by the UNCRPD, to require consultations to be accessible to people with disabilities and DDPOs. While decision-makers enjoy a broad level of discretion regarding the consultation process, the topic of consultation and who should be consulted (subject to any statutory requirements),[281] they must also comply with the requirement to consult 'fairly'.[282] This includes fairness in deciding the subject matter, the timing of the consultation and who should be consulted.[283] A broad reading of this fairness requirement, informed by the UNCRPD, may increase the set of circumstances where public authorities are expected to consult with people with disabilities and DDPOs.

An important mechanism for the involvement of people with disabilities and DDPOs in public consultations is provided by section 149 of the EqA, which places on public authorities a PSED.[284] In the exercise of their functions, public authorities must have 'due regard' to, *inter alia*, the need to 'eliminate discrimination' and 'advance equality of opportunities' between people with and without disabilities, including by encouraging people with disabilities 'to participate in public life' and to 'foster good relations' between people with and without disabilities.[285] The PSED has been commended for reflecting a substantive vision of equality focused on proactive measures[286] and for aspiring towards engagement with the civil society, promoting a 'real connection' between decision-makers and the people affected by the decisions.[287] However, the transformative potential[288] of the PSED is curtailed by the language

278 *R. (on the application of Edwards)* v. *Environment Agency* [2006] EWCA Civ 877, [90], (Auld LJ).
279 Sheldon, 'Consultation', 152. 280 Ibid.
281 *R. (on the application of Greenpeace)* v. *Secretary of State for Trade and Industry* [2007] EWHC 311 (Admin), [62], (Sullivan J).
282 *R. (on the application of Edwards)* v. *Environment Agency* [2006] EWCA Civ 877.
283 *R. (on the application of Milton Keynes Council)* v. *Secretary of State for Communities and Local Government* [2011] EWCA Civ 1575, [32], (Pill LJ).
284 Section 149 of the EqA 2010. 285 Ibid. sections 149(1)(a)–(c) and (3).
286 Bob Hepple, *Equality: The Legal Framework* (Oxford: Hart Publishing, 2011), p. 163.
287 Nick O'Brien, 'Positive about Equality: The Public-Sector Duty under Threat' (2013) 84(4) *The Political Quarterly* 486–96 at 487.
288 Hepple, 'Equality', p. 1.

adopted in section 149 of the EqA, as a requirement to have 'due regard' to achieve equality is rather weak and could have been formulated as a stronger commitment to take steps to achieve this objective.[289] This duty should be reinterpreted in light of the UNCRPD as a call for proactive steps to ensure equality of citizenship and to involve people with disabilities and DDPOs in 'decision-making structures and processes',[290] including targeted involvement in public consultations. Another hinderance to the transformative potential of the PSED is posed by the focus of the EqA on the medical model of disability.[291] The model that should guide the PSED should be the human rights model advanced by the UNCRPD.[292]

A reinterpretation of the PSED in light of the UNCRPD could reverse the backward trajectory taken by the EqA, when it failed to build on the DED introduced in 2005 through an amendment to the DDA 1995.[293] The DED required public authorities to have 'due regard' to 'encouraging participation' by persons with disabilities in public life[294] and this requirement was strengthened by placing specific duties on public authorities to produce disability equality schemes and involve people with disabilities in the search for solutions.[295] Unfortunately, these specific duties have been 'drastically pruned back' under the EqA framework.[296] Moreover, a subsequent review of the PSED stopped short of abolishing the equality duty, concluding (with insufficient regard to DDPOs submissions) that this duty lacked an effective positive impact and amounted to burdensome red tape.[297] A reinterpretation of the PSED in light of the UNCRPD would repair the damage caused by the 'dilution of rights' under the EqA.[298]

The discussion so far has called for a reinterpretation of the public consultation standards developed by courts in England and of the PSED under section 149 of the EqA, in light of the human rights vision of disability pursued by the UNCRPD. In the absence of a general legal requirement to consult with DDPOs, a broad reading of the legal requirement to 'fair' public consultations,[299] informed by the UNCRPD, may increase the set of circumstances where public authorities would be expected to consult with people with disabilities and DDPOs. Furthermore, a broad reading of the PSED, building on the requirements previously advanced by the DED and informed by the

[289] Sandra Fredman, 'The Public Sector Equality Duty' (2011) 40(4) *Industrial Law Journal* 405–27.
[290] Ibid. 412. [291] Section 6(1) of the EqA 2010. [292] Article 4(3) of the UNCRPD.
[293] Section 49A of the DDA 1995, as amended by section 3 of the DDA 2005.
[294] Ibid. section 49A1(f). [295] Ibid. section 49B.
[296] Lawson, 'Disability and Employment', 386.
[297] Government Equalities Office, 'Review of the Public Sector Equality Duty: Report of the Independent Steering Group', September 2013, 31.
[298] Eilionóir Flynn, *From Rhetoric to Action: Implementing the UN Convention on the Rights of Persons with Disabilities* (Cambridge: Cambridge University Press, 2011), p. 236.
[299] *R. (on the application of Edwards)* v. *Environment Agency* [2006] EWCA Civ 877, [90], (Auld LJ).

UNCRPD, would expect public authorities to involve people with disabilities and DDPOs in the search for solutions in removing barriers to equality. This could enhance the chances of applicants who would seek to challenge through judicial review the decisions of a public authority where the public consultation was inadequate, and where the public body failed to comply with the PSED.[300] Furthermore, a reinterpretation of the public consultation standards and of the PSED in light of the UNCRPD would move away from the current reliance on 'retrospective and individualised' measures to pursue equality objectives, such as applications for judicial review, and would place the emphasis on 'proactive and collective' measures for pursuing these goals.[301] However, the success of these objectives is dependent on an 'internal cultural change' where public authorities perceive equality as a common goal to be pursued by working in partnership with key stakeholders,[302] including people with disabilities and DDPOs.

One step towards achieving such cultural change would be through the development of an effective structure framing public consultations. Where Regulatory Impact Assessments are required, public authorities must comply with the Better Regulation Framework, and in these cases, there is a clearer structure for public consultations.[303] Some inspiration for an effective protocol for public consultations could also be provided by the Cabinet Office consultation principles.[304] Similar to the *Gunning* principles, the Cabinet Office consultation principles of 2018 stress that 'consultations should have a purpose' and that responses should be taken into account when policy is taken forward.[305] However, these principles state further that consultations 'should facilitate scrutiny' and that policymakers should 'explain the responses that have been received' and make clear how these responses have informed the policy.[306] This embeds a call on decision-makers to provide feedback on the responses received. Furthermore, unlike the *Gunning* principles, which focus on the consultation procedure without considering those being consulted, the Cabinet Office consultation principles make provisions for targeted consultations that would consider 'the full range of people' affected by the proposed measure and 'whether representative groups exist'.[307] Consultations should also be tailored to 'the needs and preferences of particular groups', including people with disabilities, who 'may not respond to traditional consultation methods', and should employ methods that suit these groups, which may include informal

[300] See, for example, *R. (on the application of Bracking)* v. *Secretary of State for Work and Pensions* [2013] EWCA Civ 1345, where the applicant was unsuccessful in proving that the public consultation was inadequate, but successful in arguing that the PSED was not met. See Helen Carr, 'The Public-Sector Equality Duty: A Mainstay of Justice in an Age of Austerity' (2014) 36(2) *Journal of Social Welfare and Family Law* 208–10 at 210.

[301] Fredman, 'Public Sector Equality Duty', 408. [302] Ibid. 423.

[303] Department for Business and Trade, 'Better Regulation Framework: Guidance', September 2023, [3.5].

[304] Government Consultation Principles 2018. [305] Ibid. [B]. [306] Ibid. [I]. [307] Ibid. [F].

consultations using 'digital tools' and 'open and collaborative approaches'.[308] The Cabinet Office consultation principles recognise that drafting responses may prove burdensome to consultees and seek to reduce this burden by calling for clear and concise consultation documents, with questions that are easy to understand and answer.[309] Those consulting should 'avoid lengthy documents' and merge consultations on related topics.[310] Furthermore, the consultation principles acknowledge that organisations such as charities 'may need more time' to respond to consultations.[311]

Despite the merits of the Cabinet Office consultation principles in calling for targeted and tailored consultations,[312] these guidelines are applicable only to Central Government consultations, have no legal force and should be read in the context of reduced, rather than increased resources. Furthermore, the 2018 guidelines appear to have been watered down when compared with the 2013 Consultation Principles[313] and the 2008 Government Code of Practice on Consultations, which were more explicit in calling for 'accessible' consultations processes.[314] As explained in the 2008 document, to reach a wider audience, consultation documents should be provided in alternative formats, including Easy Read, Braille and audio versions, and methods should include alternative arrangements such as focus groups, public meetings or online tools.[315] The 2008 document went further in its insistence that 'the burden of consultation' should be 'kept to a minimum', stressing in its explanatory notes that all consultation documents should include 'a standard table of basic information' to assist consultees in making a quick decision whether a consultation is relevant to them.[316] Furthermore, the 2008 document was more explicit when calling for the allocation of an appropriate time for consultation, stressing that 'consultation should normally last for at least 12 weeks, with consideration given to longer timescales where feasible'.[317] This recognised that many organisations may want to consult with the people they represent before drafting their response, and that this process requires time.[318] As a further drawback, the 2018 Cabinet Office consultation principles, while recognising public consultation as an 'on-going process' of engagement,[319] did not include the call previously comprised in the 2013 consultation principles, that policymakers should seek to achieve 'real engagement' rather than merely follow 'bureaucratic process'.[320]

Interest groups tend to be sceptical of the power of responses to public consultations as instruments to shape policymaking, because public consultations are 'one of the last stages in the policymaking process'.[321] Rather than relying on written responses to consultations, they seek to influence

[308] Ibid. [D], [F], [G]. [309] Ibid. [A]. [310] Ibid. [311] Ibid. [G]. [312] Ibid. [F].
[313] Government Consultation Principles 2013.
[314] Government Code of Practice on Consultation 2008, criterion 4. [315] Ibid. [4.4], [4.5].
[316] Ibid. [4.5], criterion 5. [317] Ibid. criterion 2. [318] Ibid. [2.1].
[319] Government Consultation Principles 2018, [D].
[320] Government Consultation Principles 2013, 1.
[321] Lundberg and Hysing, 'The Value of Participation', 9–11.

policies through other strategies that tend to be more effective, including meetings with policymakers and media campaigns.[322] Public consultations tend to be perceive as 'merely symbolic', confined to 'information sharing' and not a genuine route to shape policymaking.[323] Consultation is classified as 'tokenism' in Arnstein's 'ladder of citizen participation', alongside 'information' and 'placation' (where participants can advise but cannot decide), as these methods lack a mechanism to ensure that the views of participants are considered by policymakers to inform change.[324] Lower on this ladder are non-participation mechanisms such as 'manipulation' and 'therapy', where decision-makers aim to 'educate' or 'cure' people.[325] The higher end of Arnstein's 'ladder of citizen participation' includes mechanisms such as 'partnerships' (where citizens 'negotiate and engage in trade-offs' with policymakers), 'delegated power' and 'citizen control' (where citizens become the decision-makers).[326] Arnstein's scepticism about the impact of consultation as an instrument of citizen participation is based on the fact that if this mechanism is 'not combined with other methods of participation' and 'offers no assurances that citizen concerns and ideas' will be considered', then participation 'remains just a window-dressing ritual'.[327] In such a setting, citizens are seen as 'statistical abstractions' who have 'participated in participation' and policymakers can point towards 'evidence that the have gone through the motions of involving "those people"'.[328]

Such scepticism towards public consultations has been echoed in interviews with DDPO representatives, who commented that 'you cannot always see the purpose' of a consultation and that, often it is as if policymakers are 'trying to dot the Is and cross the Ts, to make sure that they have been doing their job', leaving people with the feeling that 'whoever runs the consultation does it to tick a box'.[329] DDPO representatives expressed doubt that if they invested time to respond to public consultations, their responses would make any difference in shaping policymaking.[330] This doubt is augmented by the insufficient level of feedback that DDPOs receive on their submissions to public consultations, leaving organisations to question that 'if we respond, what will they do with the information?'.[331] If public consultations are to be a channel that enables policymakers to reach informed decisions that meet community needs,[332] they must enable the submission of views that are 'representative of the population at large',[333] including the views of people with disabilities and DDPOs. However, to achieve 'real engagement'[334] with DDPOs, policymakers must provide an

322 Ibid. 323 Ibid. 1.
324 Sherry Arnstein, 'A Ladder of Citizen Participation' (1969) 35(4) *Journal of the American Institute of Planners* 216–24 at 216.
325 Ibid. 326 Ibid. 327 Ibid. 328 Ibid. 329 Interview with Jonathan Toye (WNDIS).
330 Ibid. 331 Interview with Lorna Carter (Disability Nottinghamshire).
332 Edgar, 'Procedural Fairness', 59.
333 Keith Culver and Paul Howe 'Calling All Citizens: The Challenges of Public Consultation' (2004) 47(1) *Canadian Public Administration* 52–75 at 53.
334 Government Consultation Principles 2013.

'on-going' rather than an 'occasional' process of involvement in shaping policymaking,[335] based on a partnership between these stakeholders.

DDPO representatives spoke about the need for 'effective consultation'[336] and 'real commitment' from policymakers.[337] This would require from public authorities engagement with DDPOs not just as part of the public consultation itself, but through upfront engagement and follow up responses, in the form of 'a whole engagement with all the questions on the table'.[338] DDPO representatives should be involved earlier on in policymaking and before the launch of the consultation process,[339] as public authorities are likely to receive more responses if the consultation documents are drafted with the involvement of people who understand the subject 'from a disability-perspective'.[340] People with disabilities and DDPOs are also likely to respond to more consultations if the consultation process is followed up by effective feedback on how the submissions received have informed the adopted measures. DDPO representatives have commented that 'if we invest time and resources to respond to public consultations, we expect public authorities to come back to tell us what they have done and what kind of conclusions they have drawn', insisting that 'this loop is quite important, as you know that you are being listened to'.[341] Effective consultation requires 'an element of accountability' where public authorities consider the views presented by people with disabilities and DDPOs and either adopt the course of action suggested by these stakeholders, or provide clear explanations why these suggestions cannot be put in place.[342]

Effective consultation also requires from public authorities willingness to listen and to change based on the views presented in the consultation responses.[343] Public authorities must recognise the mutual benefits of direct engagement with people with disabilities and DDPOs.[344] In fact, public authorities could 'avoid several pitfalls by consulting early' with DDPOs and by taking on board the lived experiences of people with disabilities.[345] There is 'no substitute for direct involvement if you want to do good policymaking'.[346] If measures are adopted with input from people with disabilities, it is more likely that accessibility is considered at the outset,[347] rather than as an afterthought.

335 Williams, 'Confident Commissioning', 70.
336 Interview with Emily Morton (Operations Manager), Disability Sheffield (Sheffield, 11 February 2016), research funded by the SLS Research Activities Fund (joint bid with Mike Varney).
337 Interview with Dave Thompson (Access Dorset).
338 Interview with Guido Gybels (policy expert) (London, 10 March 2016), research funded by the SLS Research Activities Fund (joint bid with Mike Varney).
339 Lundberg and Hysing, 'The Value of Participation', 17.
340 Interview with Dave Thompson (Access Dorset).
341 Ibid.
342 OHCHR, 'Training Guide', 37.
343 Flynn, 'From Rhetoric to Action', p. 209.
344 Williams, 'Confident Commissioning', 109.
345 Interview with Dave Thompson (Access Dorset).
346 Interview with Guido Gybels (policy expert).
347 Disability Rights UK, 'Inclusive Communities: Guidance for Disabled People's Organisations (DPOs)', 2014, 16.

This input should be sought in the development of all laws and policies.[348] Public authorities often display a narrow understanding of 'disability issues' confined to areas such as healthcare or social security and do not always realise the benefits of participation from people with disabilities in consultations beyond these issues.[349] Yet, given that disability is an aspect of human diversity,[350] all human issues are disability issues. Public authorities must 'get away from the assumption' that a proposed measure has no relevance to people with disabilities unless some relevance can be expressly identified and must start instead from the assumption that 'whatever they do, it has relevance' to people with disabilities.[351] Therefore, unless public authorities 'can demonstrate that this is not the case', they need to show that they have taken into account the interests of all stakeholders, including people with disabilities.[352]

DDPOs have commented that public consultations are often not tailored to encourage responses from people with disabilities. Documents are not always provided in accessible formats,[353] and even when organisations have asked for the provision of accessible documents, such formats can be 'very difficult to get hold of'.[354] Additional barriers may be posed by inaccessible consultation documents or websites that host the consultation documents, which include graphics unreadable by screen readers, or information accessible only by using a mouse rather than the keyboard.[355] These websites are often based on 'a maze' of 'partly interconnected sites', with unclear names and structures.[356] The 'information inequity' associated with the segregation of the public into 'information rich' and 'information poor' has worrying implications for the lives of persons with disabilities,[357] including participation in the political sphere.

To ensure that public consultations are tailored to the needs of persons with disabilities, the consultation documents and the websites hosting these documents must be accessible. A tailored approach in conducting public consultations would also require a move beyond the traditional form of written public consultations.[358] On-line public consultation, if based on accessible documents and hosted on accessible websites, could contribute towards enhancing citizenship participation in the political sphere.[359] Whilst most

[348] OHCHR, 'Training Guide', 11. [349] Disability Rights UK, 'Guidance for DPOs', 30.

[350] Article 3(d) of the UNCRPD. [351] Interview with Guido Gybels (policy expert). [352] Ibid.

[353] Interview with Sophie Fournel (CEO), Centre for Independent Living Kent (CiLK) (now Disability Assist) (Ashford, 4 March 2016), research funded by the SLS Research Activities Fund (joint bid with Mike Varney).

[354] Interview with Emily Morton (Disability Sheffield).

[355] Richard Moberly, 'The Americans with Disabilities Act in Cyberspace: Applying the 'Nexus' Approach to Private Internet Websites' (2004) 55(3) *Mercer Law Review* 963–99.

[356] Jim Macnamara, 'The Quadrivium of Online Public Consultation: Policy, Culture, Resources, Technology' (2010) 45(2) *Australian Journal of Political Science* 227–44 at 236.

[357] Vandana Chaudhry and Tom Shipp, 'Rethinking the Digital Divide in Relation to Visual Disability in India and the United States: Towards a Paradigm of "Information Inequity"' (2005) 25(2) *Disability Studies Quarterly*.

[358] Government Code of Practice on Consultation 2008, 5.

[359] Macnamara, 'Quadrivium of Online Public Consultation', 227.

consultations are constructed in a prescribed format based on written submissions, the on-line environment opens the way for consultations based on interactive discussions in on-line consultation forums.[360] Technology can provide a way to consult more effectively, but care is needed to ensure that such forums for discussion are accessible.[361] An increased openness by public authorities on the measures adopted to enhance the accessibility of their websites and the adoption of effective measures to enforce accessibility standards, could contribute towards addressing the barriers encountered by people with disabilities when accessing public consultations.[362] Such measures would reflect a human rights vision of disability focused on full and equal participation in society as citizens.[363] However, it is important that the call for alternative formats of public consultations is not confined to the on-line environment. In fact, there is a risk that 'over-reliance in digital channels' would 'reinforce the influence of organisations that already have considerable influence' and would do little to enhance the 'voices of hard to reach or seldom-heard groups'.[364] Such groups include people with disabilities, who are 'significantly less likely to have access to the internet' or to use information and communication technologies.[365] Public authorities would receive more responses from DDPOs if the public consultations were conducted in the form of face to face discussions. DDPO representatives commented that public authorities conducting consultations 'would get a lot more responses if they made time to come to talk to us (e.g., at our meetings)', as 'it is much easier to have a conversation than to type a written response'.[366] DDPOs have called on public authorities to develop 'more creative ways' of eliciting responses to public consultations from people with disabilities and their representative organisations, such as 'recording discussions',[367] or conducting 'large consultation groups',[368] or asking a DDPO to facilitate deliberations with people with disabilities and other DDPOs.[369]

In their call for tailored public consultations, DDPOs pointed not only to the barriers posed by inaccessible consultation formats, but also to the burden posed by consultations with limited timeframes, with documents drafted in complex language and with insufficient resources allocated to facilitate the

[360] Ibid. 236.

[361] House of Lords, Secondary Legislation Scrutiny Committee, 'The Government's New Approach to Consultation: Work in Progress', 22nd Report of Session 2012–13, 10 January 2013 (submission from the Institute of Chartered Accountants, Scotland), 44.

[362] Jonathan Lazar and Paul Jaeger, 'Reducing Barriers to Online Access for People with Disabilities' (2011) 27(2) *Issues in Science and Technology* 68–82.

[363] Article 1 of the UNCRPD.

[364] House of Lords, 'New Approach to Consultation' (submission from the Consultation Institute), 48.

[365] Ibid. (submission from Disability Rights UK), 49.

[366] Interview with Sophie Fournel (CiLK, now Disability Assist).

[367] Interview with Emily Morton (Disability Sheffield).

[368] Interview with Lorna Carter (Disability Nottinghamshire).

[369] Interview with Dave Thompson (Access Dorset).

participation of organisations such as DDPOs. With reference to the time barrier for responding to public consultations, DDPO representatives commented on the time pressures they faced in balancing their advocacy roles with the day to day work of providing support in the community. Whilst recognising the importance of responding to public consultations to enable people with disabilities to have a voice in policymaking, this activity is much lower in the DDPO's list of priorities than the more immediate pressure to respond to people in need of support.[370] DDPO representatives commented that responses to public consultations 'should be much higher a priority, but we are firefighting all the time', as 'we are dealing with people with real issues now instead of maybe'.[371] In addition to the 'balancing act' between their advocacy and service provision roles, DDPOs are also faced with the pressure of 'keeping the organisation afloat',[372] commenting that 'we find ourselves juggling balls in the air all the time' and that one of the key priorities that takes precedence over responses to public consultations is having to secure funding to enable their survival as organisations.[373]

The timeframes allocated by public authorities for the submission of responses to public consultations are generally short,[374] and there is often no coordination between Government departments in the launch of consultations, resulting in 'multiple consultations' with 'overlapping deadlines'.[375] Public authorities must recognise the challenges encountered by DDPOs in responding to consultations. While some organisations may consider that it is their 'civic duty' to respond to consultations, Lundberg and Hysing note that 'this would be a precarious foundation' for any public consultation framework, especially given the time and resource pressures encountered by DDPOs.[376] Consequently, when dealing with consultations, public authorities should consider the preferences of organisations such as DDPOs regarding the time and formats of consultations.[377] They should also allocate longer time frames for the submission of responses to consultations, and a 'pre-warning that a public consultation is going to come out', to allow DDPOs to plan and integrate their responses to 'existing meetings'.[378]

In addition to time pressures, DDPOs are also confronted with the barrier posed by the complexity of consultation documents. DDPOs have commented negatively on the length of consultation documents where 'even the summary

[370] Issue raised in the interviews with Lorna Carter (Disability Nottinghamshire), Sophie Fournel and Hannah Tutt (CiLK, now Disability Assist), Emily Morton (Disability Sheffield), Dave Thompson (Access Dorset) and Jonathan Toye (WNDIS).

[371] Interview with Sophie Fournel (CiLK, now Disability Assist).

[372] Interview with Emily Morton (Disability Sheffield).

[373] Interview with Dave Thompson (Access Dorset).

[374] Issue raised in the interviews with Sophie Fournel and Hannah Tutt (CiLK, now Disability Assist), and Emily Morton (Disability Sheffield).

[375] House of Lords, 'New Approach to Consultation', 33.

[376] Lundberg and Hysing, 'The Value of Participation', 18. [377] Ibid.

[378] Interview with Emily Morton (Disability Sheffield).

is not very accessible',[379] and which are 'time consuming to take up',[380] and have called on public authorities to provide more focused documents that 'get to the point',[381] and to provide an indication of how long it is likely to take consultees to respond.[382] Additional barriers are posed by limited human and financial resources. DDPOs commented that whilst they wished to have someone assigned to draft responses to public consultations, this was not possible due to resource limitations.[383] DDPOs have called on public authorities to allocate funds as part of consultation budgets.[384] On a similar note, Gybels comments that 'in all public consultation exercises, there must be resources allocated' for the translation of technical information for users, for the provision of support to engage with user groups and for ensuring engagement with a representative set of users from across the board.[385] In allocating resources to facilitate engagement with user groups, including DDPOs, public authorities should consider not only the cost of inclusion but also the wider social costs of exclusion.[386]

Persons with disabilities and DDPOs are often reluctant to engage in public consultations due to the lack of an effective structure framing such consultations.[387] Public authorities should rely on an effective protocol for public consultations. Rather than merely 'ticking the box' to show that they have consulted, public authorities should have to show the steps taken and the outcome of the consultation.[388] As part of a 'structured engagement', public authorities should have to 'identify the issues, tackle them before, during and after the consultation, capture what they have done, check that they had the right level of engagement, analyse the responses and provide feedback'.[389] Such a framework, embedded in a formal consultation protocol, could be used to 'drive engagement at both sides of the debate'.[390] It should be reinforced by a 'broader infrastructure' that supports this engagement, such as 'local contact points and national contact points for key topics'.[391] As part of this formal consultation protocol, public authorities should be under an obligation to follow 'a formal process of identifying' relevant stakeholders,[392] which should include people with disabilities and DDPOs.

Public authorities need to formalise their relationships with DDPOs, involve DDPO representatives as members of scrutiny committees, examine 'equality impact assessments associated with specific proposals' and consider the impact of these proposals on persons with disabilities.[393] This would contribute

[379] Ibid. [380] Interview with Lorna Carter (Disability Nottinghamshire).
[381] Interview with Sophie Fournel (CiLK, now Disability Assist).
[382] Interview with Jonathan Toye (WNDIS).
[383] Issue raised in the interviews with Lorna Carter (Disability Nottinghamshire), Sophie Fournel and Hannah Tutt (CiLK, now Disability Assist), Emily Morton (Disability Sheffield), Dave Thompson (Access Dorset) and Jonathan Toye (WNDIS).
[384] Ibid. [385] Interview with Guido Gybels (policy expert). [386] Ibid. [387] Ibid. [388] Ibid.
[389] Ibid. [390] Ibid. [391] Ibid. [392] Ibid.
[393] Disability Rights UK, 'Inclusive Communities: Guidance for Local Authorities', 2014, 25.

towards establishing 'a firm structure' for ensuring the participation of persons with disabilities in policymaking.[394] A further step could be through legislative reform introducing a legal requirement to consult with DDPOs. However, some DDPOs have expressed scepticism that this alone would be a preferred way forward, expressing concern that without an enhanced perspective from public authorities regarding the benefits of consulting with DDPOs, a mandatory requirement to consult with these organisations would be another box ticking exercise. To be effective, the consultation with DDPOs must be driven by 'a will to do it', rather than by an obligation to conduct such consultation exercises.[395] Formal consultation protocols must be accompanied by attitudinal changes on the part of policymakers to recognise the benefits of direct engagement with persons with disabilities and DDPOs. There are 'cultural issues that need to be addressed', including the fact that policymakers tend to place greater weight on the views of industry representatives, when compared with the views of representatives of user groups, and tend to consider the interests of persons with disabilities by reliance on 'second hand opinions from other stakeholders', rather than by direct engagement with DDPOs.[396] Therefore, any requirements on public authorities to comply with formal consultation protocols must be part of a 'holistic view' of 'sincere and connective engagement' based on trust, shared values[397] and an understanding of the benefits of direct engagement with relevant stakeholders.

To be effective in shaping policymaking, consultation mechanisms must be complemented by other models of citizenship participation, such as partnerships between citizens and decision-makers (e.g. joint policy boards).[398] Their success is reliant on a large range of factors, including the presence of 'an organised power base in the community' and resources to pay the leaders of citizen groups 'reasonable honoraria for their time-consuming efforts', and to hire 'technicians, lawyers and community organisers'.[399] DDPOs can play an important role in providing an organised community powerbase. The success of these partnerships is measured by the extent to which citizen groups such as DDPOs have 'genuine bargaining in influence' over policy outcomes.[400]

DDPOs should be enabled to educate policymakers 'on an ongoing basis' about the interest of persons with disabilities[401] and should have an input 'at every level of decision-making', to ensure that the interests of persons with disabilities are protected effectively. Equality for persons with disabilities can be achieved only with the appropriate political will to support this.[402] One way in

[394] Ibid. [395] Interview with Lorna Carter (Disability Nottinghamshire).

[396] Interview with Guido Gybels (policy expert).

[397] Ken Haddow, 'Consultation, the Way Forward' (2013) 31(1) *Journal of Energy and Natural Resources Law* 81–90 at 90.

[398] Arnstein, 'Ladder of Citizen Participation', 216. [399] Ibid. [400] Ibid.

[401] Jenifer Simpson, 'Inclusive Information and Communication Technologies for People with Disabilities' (2009) 29(1) *Disability Studies Quarterly*.

[402] Flynn, 'From Rhetoric to Action', p. 215.

which such will can be manifested into practice is by looking at the channels available to persons with disabilities and DDPOs to influence policymaking, to shape proposals before they are presented for consultation, to participate in consultations and have an impact on the measures ultimately adopted by policymakers. The effectiveness of laws and policies in removing the barriers to equality encountered by persons with disabilities and ensuring their full and equal enjoyment of all human rights and fundamental freedoms[403] depends on the extent to which these measures have listened to the voices of persons with disabilities. To fully understand the barriers to disability equality and the measures needed to remove these barriers, there is no substitute for direct engagement with persons with disabilities and DDPOs.[404]

5.2.4 Way Forward?

The UNCRPD has called on all States Parties, including the UK, to adopt all appropriate measures for implementing the Convention and in any decision-making processes on issues relating to persons with disabilities, to 'closely consult with and actively involve' persons with disabilities, 'through their representative organisations'.[405] In fulfilling their obligations, States Parties are to be guided by the Convention's general principles (e.g. full and effective participation and inclusion of persons with disabilities in society) and objectives (e.g. 'full and equal enjoyment of all human rights and fundamental freedoms' by persons with disabilities), to interpret these requirements widely, understanding that all human issues are disability issues and that all decision-making processes that impact of people are processes on issues relating to persons with disabilities.[406] These processes must reflect a rights-based understanding of disability where the state and other key stakeholders have a responsibility to facilitate the exercise of these rights.[407] Moreover, the participation of persons with disabilities and DDPOs in decision-making should involve a genuine engagement by public authorities with these stakeholders, developing a partnership between them.[408] While meeting these objectives is reliant on a range of actions, one of these measures is to enhance the participation of DDPOs in public consultations.

In the UK, in the absence of mandatory domestic legal requirements to consult with DDPOs, a reinterpretation of the public consultation principles developed by courts, and of the PSED under the EqA, in light of UNCRPD values, could lead to an increased set of circumstances where public authorities would be expected to consult with persons with disabilities and DDPOs. These measures should be supplemented by a consultation protocol to provide the structure for framing the consultation exercise, supported by an infrastructure

403 Article 1 of the UNCRPD. 404 Interview with Guido Gybels (policy expert).
405 Articles 4(1)(a) and (3) of the UNCRPD. 406 Ibid. Articles 1, 3(c) and 4(3).
407 OHCHR, 'Training Guide', 10.
408 UNCRPD Committee, 'General Comment No. 7', [48], [94(u)].

based on national and local contact points and required to identify relevant key stakeholders,[409] including persons with disabilities and DDPOs. Most importantly, these measures must be accompanied by attitudinal changes where public authorities recognise the benefits of direct engagement with persons with disabilities and DDPOs. Such recognition should go beyond procedural issues (which may assist public authorities to 'fend off' judicial review challenges regarding the decision-making process or their compliance with PSED),[410] and should consider substantive issues, including wider social benefits and the protection of citizenship values such as equality.

If measures are adopted without the voices of persons with disabilities, provisions are based on 'stereotypical and inaccurate beliefs' about disability.[411] DDPO representatives commented that without the involvement of persons with disabilities in policymaking, laws and policies would not be 'a true reflection of what society (including the disability community) requires'[412] and policymakers would risk making mistakes.[413] The involvement of persons with disabilities and DDPOs in policymaking would ensure that proposed measures are disability-proofed in light of UNCRPD values.[414] As emphasised by Disability Rights UK, given that disability is part of the human experience, all decisions should be inclusive decisions, and the best was to ensure this is to involve persons with disabilities in decision-making.[415]

The adoption of the UNCRPD, with a high level of involvement from persons with disabilities and DDPOs, provides a clear example of what can be achieved successfully when persons with disabilities speak with 'a strong voice'.[416] It also illustrates the importance of a 'healthy infrastructure' of DDPOs where these organisations join forces to prioritise key areas for action.[417] The UNCRPD could assist DDPOs in 'opening new doors' for cooperation with policymakers in pursuit of measures that reflect a rights-based understanding of disability.[418] The impetus for such increased cooperation is provided by calls from the UNCRPD Committee presented in 2017, requiring the UK to 'allocate financial resources to support organisations representing persons with disabilities' and develop mechanisms to ensure the involvement of organisations of persons with disabilities 'in the planning and implementation of all legislative measures that affect the lives of persons with disabilities'.[419] These calls

409 Interview with Guido Gybels (policy expert). 410 Sheldon, 'Consultation', 159.

411 Anthony Tusler, 'How to Make Technology Work: A Study of Best Practices in United States Electronic and Information Technology Companies' (2005) 25(2) *Disability Studies Quarterly*.

412 Interview with Lorna Carter (Disability Nottinghamshire).

413 Interview with Jonathan Toye (WNDIS). 414 Flynn, 'From Rhetoric to Action', p. 200.

415 Disability Rights UK, 'Guidance for DPOs', 16.

416 Power, Lord and DeFranco, 'Active Citizenship', p. 454.

417 Flynn, 'From Rhetoric to Action', p. 199.

418 van Veen, Regeer and Bunders, 'Meeting the Challenge', 379.

419 UN Committee on the Rights of Persons with Disabilities, 'Concluding Observations on the Initial Report of the United Kingdom of Great Britain and Northern Ireland', 3 October 2017, CRPD/C/GBR/CO/1, [11(a)].

follow the UNCRPD Committee's expressed concern about the absence of sufficient mechanisms to facilitate an effective participation of organisations of persons with disabilities in decision-making processes on issues affecting persons with disabilities, and the 'lack of comprehensive mechanisms and sufficient resources', which have a negative impact on the ability to coordinate the UNCRPD implementation in the UK.[420]

Similar calls were made by the UNCRPD Committee in a 2016 report[421] which condemned the grave and systematic violations of the rights of persons with disabilities to independent living, work and social protection,[422] due to the cumulative impact of measures adopted by the UK on social security schemes, work and employment from 2010.[423] The recommendations presented by the UNCRPD Committee in this report included a call on the UK Government to establish 'mechanisms and system of human rights-based indicators' to monitor 'in close consultation with persons with disabilities and their representative organisations', the impact of 'different policies and programmes' on the enjoyment by persons with disabilities of their human rights.[424] The UNCRPD Committee also stressed that the involvement of persons with disabilities and their representative organisations in policymaking and consultation processes 'should not be merely symbolic'.[425] These concerns continue to be an issue. In a follow-up report issued by the UNCRPD Committee in 2024, the Committee emphasised that concerns remained regarding 'the obligation to closely consult and actively involve disabled people through their representative organizations in decision-making affecting their lives'.[426]

Under the current economic climate with reduced financial resources, it is important that public authorities work in partnership with DDPOs in the search for solutions that respond to the needs of all people, including persons with disabilities.[427] It is also imperative that in this partnership, public consultations move beyond a primary focus on the economic implications of the proposed measures, to also consider the wider social implications of these measures,[428] and that persons with disabilities are perceived not as service users but as citizens with full and equal entitlements in society. A reinterpretation of the public consultation principles developed by courts in England[429] and of the PSED under the EqA,[430] in light of the human rights vision of

420 Ibid. [10(b)], [68].

421 UN Committee on the Rights of Persons with Disabilities, 'Inquiry Concerning the United Kingdom of Great Britain and Northern Ireland Carried Out by the Committee under Article 6 of the Optional Protocol to the Convention: Report of the Committee', 6 October 2016, CRPD/C/15/R.2/Rev.1.

422 Articles 19, 27 and 28 of the UNCRPD.

423 UNCRPD Committee, 'Inquiry', [113].

424 Ibid. [114].

425 Ibid. [38].

426 UNCRPD Committee, 'Follow-Up to the Inquiry', [73].

427 Williams, 'Confident Commissioning', 13.

428 Interview with Guido Gybels (policy expert).

429 *R.* v. *Brent LBC Ex p. Gunning* (1985) 84 LGR 168; *R. (on the application of Edwards)* v. *Environment Agency* [2006] EWCA Civ 877; *R.* v. *North and East Devon HA Ex p. Coughlan* [2001] QB 213; *R. (on the application of Moseley)* v. *Haringey LBC* [2014] UKSC 56.

430 Section 149 of the EqA 2010.

disability pursued by the UNCRPD, could lead to an increased set of circumstances where policymakers would be expected to consult with persons with disabilities and DDPOs, including in the area of contract law. Furthermore, the adoption of a consultation protocol reflecting the UNCRPD values (including the full and equal enjoyment of all human rights and fundamental freedoms by persons with disabilities[431] and the full and effective participation and inclusion of persons with disabilities in society)[432] would provide a structure for framing the consultation exercise[433] and ensure the involvement of DDPOs in the planning and implementation of all laws and policies affecting persons with disabilities.[434] Such involvement should go beyond a mere bureaucratic process, resulting in a genuine partnership between DDPOs and public authorities.

The urgency for reform is emphasised by the concerns expressed by the UNCRPD Committee that in the UK there are insufficient mechanisms to facilitate the effective participation of key stakeholders such as DDPOs in decision-making processes affecting persons with disabilities.[435] These limited opportunities to influence policymaking are even more concerning if we consider them alongside the limited avenues to challenge adopted measures through processes such as judicial review.[436] Any review of the English legal and policy framework on public consultations cannot overlook the concerns presented by the UNCRPD Committee, and should not seek to preserve the *status quo* or adopt a patchwork approach where consultation is merely symbolic.[437] Instead, such review should be guided by UNCRPD values, pursuing not only economic objectives but also social values such as equality of citizenship and the protection of autonomy and human dignity.

5.3 Conclusion

Whichever area of life we navigate, as people, we never stop being citizens. This term is to be understood not in a narrow sense, confined to nationality, but in a wider sense based on values such as equality, autonomy, human dignity, participation and inclusion. We are not just economic actors but also social actors. While this may seem more apparent on a vertical axis, in our affiliation with the state, the same is true on a horizontal axis, in our relationships with other private parties. Even in the contractual sphere, where we may

[431] Article 1 of the UNCRPD. [432] Ibid. Article 3(c).

[433] Interview with Guido Gybels (policy expert).

[434] UNCRPD Committee, 'Concluding Observations', [11(a)]. [435] Ibid. [10(b)].

[436] Nick O'Brien, 'Disability Discrimination Law in the United Kingdom and the New Civil Rights History: The Contribution of Caroline Gooding' (2016) 43(3) *Journal of Law and Society* 444–68 at 466. See, for example, *Rex (Eveleigh and others)* v. *Secretary of State for Work and Pensions* [2023] EWCA Civ 810, [84]–[86] (Elisabeth Laing LJ) and [95]–[96] (Bean LJ), where a Government 'survey' that informed the National Disability Strategy could not be assessed under the *Gunning* criteria, as it could not be classed as a 'consultation'.

[437] UNCRPD Committee, 'Inquiry', [38].

appear as economic actors in pursuit of our self-interests, we always remain social actors, with the equivalent values that this entails, including in pursuing public policy and fairness-based considerations. Consequently, we should not perceive our contracting world as a single, economic sphere, separated from human rights-based considerations, but as concentric spheres that link economic and social values.

The endeavour of connecting economic and social values in the contractual realm requires a network of bridges, rather than a single construction. As discussed throughout this book, there are at least three bridges that require completion. The first bridge, within private law, links the inner economic sphere of contract law with its outer social sphere. The second bridge, centred on regulation, makes further connections between economic and social values in the contractual sphere, regarding measures designed to protect parties in weaker bargaining positions, such as consumers. The third bridge, which was the focus of the discussion in this chapter, explores the link between constitutional values and private law, concentrating on an enhanced perception of contracting parties as citizens. This latter bridge is based on a more complex construction, including a reliance on stepping stones linking English contract law, the HRA, the ECHR and the UNCRPD. The architectural landscape of these interconnected bridges reveals a project that has already started, but which remains incomplete, being reliant on advancements at both domestic and supranational level.

This chapter focused on four key values of relevance to the public and private realms: autonomy and human dignity (discussed in Section 5.1) and participation and inclusion (discussed in Section 5.2). These values are aspects of a wider focus on promoting equality of citizenship, a pursuit relevant to all areas of law, including contract law. The recognition of the outer social sphere of contract law plays a key role in connecting these citizenship values within private law, and promoting a vision of contract law that perceives individuals as more than merely economic actors. The measures promoted in this chapter to enhance the participation and inclusion of persons with disabilities and DDPOs in public consultations could contribute towards a regulatory framework in contract law (including consumer contract law) that is more responsive to economic and social considerations. Moreover, the current framework in English contract law would benefit from a broader interpretation of principles, doctrines and statutory provisions focused on protecting values such as autonomy and human dignity, whether through stronger links with equality provisions, or when relying on measures to regulate unfair contract terms, or when refusing to enforce transactions affected by vitiating factors. Such steps should not be seen as ‘interference’ with freedom of contract. Instead, they should be perceived as instances where the transaction between the parties stepped out of an inner, non-interventionist sphere, into a wider sphere of contract law informed by social considerations. As freedom of contract is not absolute, it is important that the boundaries of this concept are shaped by positive values such as the protection of equality and human dignity, reflecting a broad, relational conception of autonomy which recognises the interdependence between people and where contract law has a multidimensional role that permeates social and economic spheres. Under this approach, contract law is brought closer to the vision of equality advanced by the UNCRPD, informing our understanding of the correlation between abstract concepts and real people.

6

Conclusion

Embracing Complementarity in Contract Law

> Two roads diverged in a wood, and I—
> I took the one less travelled by,
> And that has made all the difference
>
> (Robert Frost, American poet, 1874–1963
> 'The Road Not Taken' (1916))

An initial, passing glance at the intricate web of the English legal system may perceive human rights and private law as paths leading to different realms, akin to the divergent roads in Robert Frost's poem, 'The Road Not Taken'.[1] Such a perspective may see economic concerns as shaping the path of contract law, with social values showing the way to another sphere. In this vision, the role of contract law is confined to the unidimensional role of enforcing agreements between private parties, acting in pursuit of self-interest.[2] The dominant values of this realm are freedom and sanctity of contract, and as long as these agreements are unaffected by vitiating factors, they are generally enforceable, irrespective of outcomes.[3] Yet, given the increase in the ageing population and the consequential rise of contracts entered into by parties who develop cognitive disabilities such as dementia, or the rise in social isolation seen during pandemics such as COVID-19,[4] increasing people's vulnerability to pressure to enter into grossly asymmetrical transactions, we must re-assess the lens through which we perceive the role of contract law. This book calls for a re-examination of the role of contract law in light of the UNCRPD, insisting on the adoption of a multi-dimensional lens[5] that responds to both economic and social concerns in the contractual sphere. Rather than perceiving social values as 'the road not taken' by contract law, the discussion promotes a perception of the contractual realm as based on two concentric spheres: an inner sphere focused on economic values (such as freedom and sanctity of contract) and an outer sphere guided by social values (including dignity-related considerations

[1] Robert Frost, *Mountain Interval* (New York: Henry Holt, 1916).
[2] Teubner, 'Contracting Worlds', 400–02.
[3] Adams and Brownsword, 'Understanding Contract Law', p. 192.
[4] Banerjee and Rai, 'Social Isolation', 525.
[5] Teubner, 'Contracting Worlds', 400.

and substantive fairness concerns), where grossly imbalanced transactions step outside the inner, non-interventionist sphere, into an outer sphere warranting intervention.

The analysis of English contract law explored in this book, with a view of determining whether contracting parties are protected as both economic and social actors, whether the regulatory framework safeguards values such as autonomy and human dignity, and whether vulnerability is assessed based on the context of the transaction rather than the medical condition of individuals, has revealed a framework beset by challenges. Both the discussion on common law principles and doctrines examined in Chapter 3, and the analysis of the regulatory framework on consumer protection in Chapter 4, indicate a focus on procedural fairness, showing *how* parties may be protected by, among others, vitiating factors, unfair contract terms, or unfair commercial practices, but with insufficient clarity on *why* intervention may be necessary. This framework reflects an approach entrenched in economic values, with an insufficiently articulated focus on social considerations. Conversely, the UNCRPD framework assessed in Chapter 5 is culpable of the exact opposite. While it seeks to substantiate *why* the interests of vulnerable contracting parties should be protected,[6] it is less clear on *how* this should be achieved. Furthermore, while social values (including equality and the protection of autonomy and human dignity) are clearly articulated,[7] references to the economic sphere do not share the same degree of clarity and strength. Using the model of concentric economic and social spheres advanced in this book, we can see that in both cases, the challenges can be linked to weaknesses in delineating the social sphere of contract law which connects economic values in contract law with human rights values.

English contract law and the UNCRPD have much to learn from each other on how to address the barriers they encounter in completing the bridges that link economic and social values. English contract law has much to teach the UNCRPD Committee, including the importance of recognising the power of contract law in shaping how we treat each other.[8] Lessons that English contract law can learn from the UNCRPD include the fact that social values, such as relational autonomy and human dignity, rank higher than economic concerns rooted in individualistic perspectives of autonomy. The task to complete these bridges would not be overwhelming. It would not involve a new construction, but building on work already begun, such as 'the fall' in negative interpretations of freedom of contract documented by Atiyah decades ago,[9] or the more recent pursuit of fairness values in CRA.[10] It would require, for example, express recognition in English contract law that substantive fairness does matter, and an articulation from the UNCRPD Committee that dignity considerations rank higher than negative interpretations of freedom of contract.

[6] Preamble and Articles 1 and 12 of the UNCRPD. [7] Ibid. Article 3.

[8] Chen-Wishart, 'Undue Influence: Vindicating Relationships of Influence'.

[9] Atiyah, 'Rise and Fall of Freedom of Contract'. [10] Part 2 of the CRA 2015.

One path towards succeeding in this endeavour is by embracing the idea of complementarity in contract law. Starting from the premise that a scientific way of thinking can provide us with analogies to address challenges that exist outside the scientific domain, the concept of complementarity enables us to accept the coexistence of ideas that may appear, initially, to be mutually exclusive.[11] Just as an electron can behave both as a particle and as a wave,[12] accepting that 'neither of these descriptions are absolutely right or absolutely wrong',[13] we can transpose this concept of complementarity to ideas such as individual and collective rights, accepting that we cannot make one absolute and the other relative,[14] and that we need to acknowledge their coexistence to gain a richer understanding of society.[15] This approach would enable us to see economic and social values in contract law not as antagonistic, but as complementary parts of interconnected spheres of contract law. It would also allow us to see the role of contract law as being about both the enforcement of agreements and the protection of contracting parties, including via regulatory means,[16] with the former focusing on the inner, economic sphere of contract law, and the latter being concerned with the outer, social sphere. Embracing complementarity in contract law would also enable us to see that the concept of human dignity can pursue both empowerment and enforcement objectives,[17] depending on whether the focus is on the inner or outer spheres of contract law. Crucial in this endeavour is the recognition of the outer, social sphere of contract law, without which we are left facing 'choppy waters',[18] with no immediate bridge in sight.

Rather than a single construction to bring together economic and social values in contract law, this endeavour requires a network of bridges focused on private law principles and doctrines (the first bridge), regulation (the second bridge), and the connection between constitutional values and private law, linking the UNCRPD, the ECHR, the HRA and English contract law (the third bridge). Recognising the outer social sphere of contract law, rooted in the value of human dignity, can act as a keystone holding these constructions together. Contract law can be seen as being concerned with both economic and social values, with both enforcing transactions and protecting vulnerable parties,[19] and with both individual and relational autonomy.

While we may not be able to redesign the law of contract starting with a blank canvas, we can choose the lens through which we interpret common law

[11] Oppenheimer, 'Science and the Common Understanding'; Cox, 'Robert Oppenheimer'.

[12] Ibid. See Niels Bohr, *Atomic Theory and the Description of Nature* (Cambridge: Cambridge University Press, 1934).

[13] Cox, 'Robert Oppenheimer'.

[14] Oppenheimer, 'Science and the Common Understanding'.

[15] Cox, 'Robert Oppenheimer'.

[16] Brownsword, 'Themes for the Twenty-First Century', p. 41.

[17] Ibid. p. 183.

[18] Ibid. p. 199 (with reference to conflicting interpretation of human dignity in the context of debates about human rights, human dignity, and freedom of contract).

[19] Ibid. p. 41.

principles, doctrines and regulatory provisions, and we can choose the values that would guide future developments in this area of law. In the last stanza of his poem *The Road Not Taken*, Robert Frost tells us that '*Two roads diverged in a wood, and I—I took the one less travelled by, And that has made all the difference*'.[20] Whilst these verses could be 'read in a great variety of ways', one potential interpretation is an encouragement 'not to limit ourselves to only one choice'.[21] Returning to the realm of contract law, both paths, the economic and the social, are part of the same vision. By adopting a model of concentric spheres in contract law, connected by bridges, and by embracing the idea of complementarity in contract law, we accept a new perspective, enabling us to see merging roads, where once, they seemed to be diverging.

[20] Frost, 'Mountain Interval'.

[21] Jane Williams, 'Freedom', Something Understood, BBC Radio 4, 21 July 2019.

Bibliography

Adams, John and Roger Brownsword, 'The Ideologies of Contract' (1987) 7 *Legal Studies* 205–23.

Adams, John and Roger Brownsword, *Understanding Contract Law* (5th ed., London: Sweet & Maxwell, 2007).

Antoniou, Alexandros, 'Advertising Regulation and Transparency in Influencers' Endorsements on Social Media' (2021) 26(4) *Communications Law* 190–207.

Apostolopoulou, Zoe, 'Equal Treatment of People with Disabilities in the EC: What Does "Equal" Mean?' (2004) Jean Monnet Working Paper 09/04.

Arduin, Sarah, 'Article 3: General Principles' in Ilias Bantekas, Michael Stein and Dimitris Anastasiou (eds.), *The UN Convention on the Rights of Persons with Disabilities: A Commentary* (Oxford: Oxford University Press, 2018), pp. 84–105.

Arnstein, Sherry, 'A Ladder of Citizen Participation' (1969) 35(4) *Journal of the American Institute of Planners* 216–24.

Arstein-Kerslake, Anna, 'An Empowering Dependency: Exploring Support for the Exercise of Legal Capacity' (2016) 18 *Scandinavian Journal of Disability Research* 77–92.

Atiyah, Patrick, 'Contract and Fair Exchange' (1985) 35 *University of Toronto Law Journal* 1–24.

Atiyah, Patrick, *An Introduction to the Law of Contract* (5th ed., Oxford: Clarendon Press, 1995).

Atiyah, Patrick, *Essays on Contract* (Oxford: Clarendon Press, 1986).

Atiyah, Patrick, *The Rise and Fall of Freedom of Contract* (Oxford: Clarendon Press, 1979).

Auchmuty, Rosemary, 'Men Behaving Badly: An Analysis of English Undue Influence Cases' (2002) 11 *Social and Legal Studies* 257–82.

Bach, Michael, *The Right to Legal Capacity under the UN Convention on the Rights of Persons with Disabilities: Key Concepts and Directions for Law Reform* (Toronto: IRIS, 2009).

Banerjee, Debanjan and Mayank Rai, 'Social Isolation in Covid-19: The Impact of Loneliness' (2020) 66 *International Journal of Social Psychiatry* 525–27.

Bantekas, Ilias, Michael Stein and Dimitris Anastasiou (eds.), *The UN Convention on the Rights of Persons with Disabilities: A Commentary* (Oxford: Oxford University Press, 2018).

Barak, Aharon, 'Constitutional Human Rights and Private Law' in Dan Friedmann and Daphne Barak-Erez (eds.), *Human Rights in Private Law* (Oxford: Hart Publishing, 2001), pp. 13–42.

Bartlett, Peter, 'Re-thinking the Mental Capacity Act 2005: Towards the Next Generation of Law' (2023) 86(3) *Modern Law Review* 659–700.

Bartlett, Peter, 'The United Nations Convention on the Rights of Persons with Disabilities and Mental Health Law' (2012) 75 *Modern Law Review* 752–78.

Bartlett, Peter, and Marianne Schulze, 'Urgently Awaiting Implementation: The Right to be Free from Exploitation, Violence and Abuse in Article 16 of the Convention on the Rights of Persons with Disabilities (CRPD)' (2017) 53 *International Journal of Law and Psychiatry* 2–14.

Beale, Hugh and Nicola Pittam, 'The Impact of the Human Rights Act 1998 on English Tort and Contract Law' in Dan Friedmann and Daphne Barak-Erez (eds.), *Human Rights in Private Law* (Oxford. Hart Publishing, 2001), pp. 131–159.

Beale, Hugh, 'Legislative Control of Fairness: The Directive on Unfair Terms in Consumer Contracts' in Jack Beatson and Daniel Friedman (eds.), *Good Faith and Fault in Contract Law* (Oxford: Oxford University Press, 1995), pp. 231–61.

Beale, Hugh, 'Misrepresentation' in Hugh Beale and others (eds.), *Chitty on Contracts*, 2 vols. (34th ed., London: Sweet & Maxwell, 2021), vol. I, Chapter 10, paragraph 10-001 et seq.

Beale, Hugh, 'Mistakes as to the Terms or as to Identity' in Hugh Beale and others (eds.), *Chitty on Contracts*, 2 vols. (35th ed., London: Sweet & Maxwell, 2023), vol. I, Chapter 5, paragraph 5-001 et seq.

Beale, Hugh, 'Undue Influence and Unconscionability' in Andrew Dyson, James Goudkamp and Frederick Wilmot-Smith (eds.), *Defences in Contract* (Oxford: Hart Publishing, 2019), pp. 87–110.

Beale, Hugh, and others (eds.), *Chitty on Contracts*, 2 vols. (34th ed., London: Sweet & Maxwell, 2021).

Beale, Hugh, and others (eds.), *Chitty on Contracts*, 2 vols. (35th ed., London: Sweet & Maxwell, 2023).

Beales, Howard, Richard Craswell, and Steven Salop, 'The Efficient Regulation of Consumer Information' (1981) 24(3) *Journal of Law and Economics* 491–539.

Beatson, Jack, and Daniel Friedman (eds.), *Good Faith and Fault in Contract Law* (Oxford: Oxford University Press, 1995).

Bennett, Howard, 'Statements of Fact and Statements of Belief in Insurance Contract Law and General Contract Law' (1998) 61(6) *Modern Law Review* 886–98.

Benöhr, Iris, *EU Consumer Law and Human Rights* (Oxford: Oxford University Press, 2013).

Benson, Peter (ed.) *The Theory of Contract Law: New Essays* (Cambridge: Cambridge University Press, 2001).

Benson, Peter, 'The Unity of Contract Law' in Peter Benson (ed.), *The Theory of Contract Law: New Essays* (Cambridge: Cambridge University Press, 2001), pp. 118–205.

Bielefeld, Shelley, 'Compulsory Income Management and Indigenous Peoples: Exploring Counter Narratives amidst Colonial Constructions of "Vulnerability"' (2014) 36 *Sydney Law Review* 695–726.

Bielefeldt, Heiner, 'New Inspiration for the Human Rights Debate: The Convention on the Rights of Persons with Disabilities' (2007) 52 *Netherlands Quarterly of Human Rights* 397–99.

Bigwood, Rick, 'Contracts by Unfair Advantage: From Exploitation to Transactional Neglect' (2005) 25 *Oxford Journal of Legal Studies* 65–96.

Bigwood, Rick, 'Undue Influence: 'Impaired Consent' or 'Wicked Exploitation'?' (1996) 16 *Oxford Journal of Legal Studies* 503–15.

Bigwood, Rick, *Exploitative Contracts* (Oxford: Oxford University Press, 2003).

Birks, Peter and Chin Nyuk Yin, 'On the Nature of Undue Influence' in Jack Beatson and Daniel Friedman (eds.), *Good Faith and Fault in Contract Law* (Oxford: Clarendon Press, 1997), pp. 57–97.

Blythe, Alice, 'Confusion Online: Does the Test for Trade Mark Confusion on the Internet Differ from that Applied to Infringement in Other Spheres?' (2014) 36(9) *European Intellectual Property Review* 563–68.

Brenncke, Martin, 'A Theory of Exploitation for Consumer Law: Online Choice Architectures, Dark Patterns, and Autonomy Violations' (2024) 47(1) *Journal of Consumer Policy* 127–64.

Brownsword, Roger, 'Developing a Modern Understanding of Human Dignity' in Dieter Grimm, Alexandra Kemmerer and Christoph Mollers (eds.), *Human Dignity in Context* (Baden-Baden: Nomos, 2018), pp. 299–324.

Brownsword, Roger, 'Freedom of Contract, Human Rights and Human Dignity' in Dan Friedmann and Daphne Barak-Erez (eds.), *Human Rights in Private Law* (Oxford: Hart Publishing, 2001), pp. 181–200.

Brownsword, Roger, 'General Considerations' in Michael Furmston (ed.), *The Law of Contract: Butterworths Common Law Series* (6th ed., London: LexisNexis, 2017).

Brownsword, Roger, *Contract Law: Themes for the Twenty-First Century* (Oxford: Oxford University Press, 2006).

Brucken, Robert and others, 'Mental Illness and the Law of Contracts' (1959) 57 *Michigan Law Review* 1020–1118.

Burgess, Andrew, 'Consumer Adhesion Contracts and Unfair Terms: A Critique of Current Theory and a Suggestion' (1986) 15 *Anglo-American Law Review* 255–80.

Burns, Fiona, 'The Elderly and Undue Influence Inter Vivos' (2003) 23 *Legal Studies* 251–83.

Burrows, Andrew (ed.), *Principles of the English Law of Obligations* (Oxford: Oxford University Press, 2015).

Burrows, Andrew, *A Casebook on Contract* (6th ed., Oxford: Hart Publishing, 2018).

Burrows, Andrew, *A Restatement of the English Law of Contract* (Oxford: Oxford University Press, 2016).

Burrows, Andrew, *A Restatement of the English Law of Unjust Enrichment* (Oxford: Oxford University Press, 2012).

Burrows, Andrew, *The Law of Restitution* (3rd ed., Oxford: Oxford University Press, 2011).

Busch, Christoph, 'The Future of Pre-contractual Information Duties: From Behavioural Insights to Big Data' in Christian Twigg-Flesner (ed.), *Research Handbook on EU Consumer and Contract Law* (Cheltenham: Edward Elgar Publishing, 2016), pp. 221–40.

Callaghan, Sascha and Christopher Ryan, 'An Evolving Revolution: Evaluating Australia's Compliance with the Convention on the Rights of Persons with Disabilities in Mental Health Law' (2016) 39 *University of New South Wales Law Journal* 596–624.

Campbell, David, *Contractual Relations: A Contribution to the Critique of the Classical Law of Contract* (Oxford: Oxford University Press, 2022).

Canruh, Deniz, 'Use of the UNCRPD in Social Security Cases before UK Courts and Tribunals' (2019) 26 *Journal of Social Security Law* 112–25.

Carr, Helen, 'The Public-Sector Equality Duty: A Mainstay of Justice in an Age of Austerity' (2014) 36(2) *Journal of Social Welfare and Family Law* 208–10.

Cartwright, John, *Contract Law: An Introduction to the English Law of Contract for the Civil Lawyer* (3rd ed., Oxford: Hart Publishing, 2016).

Cartwright, Peter, 'Publicity, Punishment and Protection: The Role(s) of Adverse Publicity in Consumer Policy' (2012) 32(2) *Legal Studies* 179–201.

Cartwright, Peter, 'The Vulnerable Consumer and The Digital Markets, Competition and Consumers Bill in the UK' (2023) 12(5) *Journal of European Consumer and Market Law* 173–6.

Cartwright, Peter, 'Understanding and Protecting Vulnerable Financial Consumers' (2015) 38 *Journal of Consumer Policy* 119–38.

Cartwright, Peter, *Consumer Protection and the Criminal Law* (Cambridge: Cambridge University Press, 2001).

Charlton, James, *Nothing about Us without Us: Disability Oppression and Empowerment* (Berkeley: University of California Press, 1998).

Chaudhry, Vandana and Tom Shipp, 'Rethinking the Digital Divide in relation to Visual Disability in India and the United States: Towards a Paradigm of "Information Inequity"' (2005) 25(2) *Disability Studies Quarterly*. https://doi.org/10.18061/dsq.v25i2.553

Chen-Wishart, Mindy, 'Duress, Undue Influence and Unconscionable Dealing' in Hugh Beale and others (eds.), *Chitty on Contracts*, 2 vols. (34th ed., London: Sweet & Maxwell, 2021), vol. I, Chapter 11, paragraph 11-001 et seq.

Chen-Wishart, Mindy, 'Practical Benefit and the Emperor's New Clothes' in Jack Beatson and Daniel Friedman (eds.), *Good Faith and Fault in Contract Law* (Oxford: Oxford University Press, 1995), pp. 123–50.

Chen-Wishart, Mindy, 'The Nature of Vitiating Factors in Contract Law' in Gregory Klass, George Letsas and Prince Saprai (eds.), *Philosophical Foundations of Contract Law* (Oxford: Oxford University Press, 2014), pp. 294–318.

Chen-Wishart, Mindy, 'The *O'Brien* Principle and Substantive Unfairness' (1997) 56 *The Cambridge Law Journal* 60–70.

Chen-Wishart, Mindy, 'Undue Influence: Beyond Impaired Consent and Wrongdoing towards a Relational Analysis' in Andrew Burrows and Alan Rodger (eds.), *Mapping the Law: Essays in Memory of Peter Birks* (Oxford: Oxford University Press, 2006), pp. 201–22.

Chen-Wishart, Mindy, 'Undue Influence: Vindicating Relationships of Influence' (2006) 59 *Current Legal Problems* 231–66.

Chinn, Deborah and Homeyard, Claire, 'Easy Read and Accessible Information for People with Intellectual Disabilities: Is It worth it? A Meta-Narrative Literature Review' (2017) 20(6) *Health Expectations* 1189–200.

Citizens Advice, 'Pushed to Purchase! Counting the Cost of Deceptive Digital Design in E-commerce', July 2023.

Citizens Advice, 'Response to Consultation on Improving Price Transparency and Product Information for Consumers', October 2023.

Citizens Advice, 'Subscription Traps', November 2022.

Collins, Hugh, 'Private Law, Fundamental Rights, and the Rule of Law' (2018) 121 *West Virginia Law Review* 1–25.

Collins, Hugh, 'The Impact of Human Rights Law on Contract Law in Europe' *Cambridge Legal Studies Research Paper* 13/2011.

Collins, Hugh, 'Regulating Contract Law' in Christine Parker and others (ed.), *Regulating Law* (Oxford: Oxford University Press, 2004), pp. 13–32.

Collins, Hugh, *Regulating Contracts* (Oxford: Oxford University Press, 1999).

Collins, Hugh, *The Law of Contract* (4th ed., London: Lexis Nexis, 2003).

Collins, Hugh, 'The Vanishing Freedom to Choose a Contractual Partner' (2012) 76 *Law and Contemporary Problems* 71–88.

Competition and Markets Authority, 'Consumer Vulnerability: Challenges and Potential Solutions', February 2019.

Competition and Markets Authority, 'Open Letter: Urgency Claims and Price Reduction Claims: Compliance Advice for Online Traders', 29 March 2023.

Competition and Markets Authority, 'Unfair Contract Terms Explained', CMA37(a), 31 July 2015.

Conklin, Kathy, Richard Hyde, and Fabio Parente, 'Assessing Plain and Intelligible Language in the Consumer Rights Act: A Role for Reading Scores?' (2019) 39(3) *Legal Studies* 378–97.

Cook, W.G.H., 'Mental Deficiency and the English Law of Contract' (1921) 21 *Columbia Law Review* 424–41.

Cox, Brian, 'Robert Oppenheimer', Reith Revisited, BBC Radio 4, 27 September 2017.

Culver, Keith and Paul Howe, 'Calling all Citizens: The Challenges of Public Consultation' (2004) 47(1) *Canadian Public Administration* 52–75.

Dawson, John, 'A Realistic Approach to Assessing Mental Health Laws' Compliance with the UNCRPD' (2015) 40 *International Journal of Law and Psychiatry* 70–9.

Dawson, John, 'Economic Duress: An Essay in Perspective' (1947) 45 *Michigan Law Review* 253–90.

De Bhailís, Clíona, 'Introduction to Contractual Capacity' in Eilionóir Flynn and others (eds.), *Global Perspectives on Legal Capacity Reform: Our Voices, Our Stories* (London: Routledge, 2019), pp. 47–9.

Department for Business and Trade (DBT), 'Consultation Outcome: Government Response to Consultation on 'Smarter Regulation: Improving Consumer Price Transparency and Product Information for Consumers', 24 January 2024.

Department for Business, Innovation and Skills (BIS), 'Consultation on Extending the Range of Remedies available to Public Enforcers of Consumer Law', November 2012.

Department for Business, Innovation and Skills (BIS), 'Enhancing Consumer Confidence through Effective Enforcement: Consultation on Consolidating and Modernising Consumer Law Enforcement Powers', March 2012.

Department for Business, Innovation and Skills (BIS), 'Enhancing Consumer Confidence by Clarifying Consumer Law: Consultation on the Supply of Goods, Services and Digital Content', July 2012.

Deutch, Sinai, 'Are Consumer Rights Human Rights?' (1994) 32 *Osgoode Hall Law Journal* 537–78.

Devenney, James and Adrian Chandler, 'Unconscionability and the Taxonomy of Undue Influence' (2007) 8 *Journal of Business Law* (August) 541–68.

Devenney, James, 'The Consumer Rights Act 2015 and Related Reforms: An Epic Disappointment?' in Roger Halson and David Campbell (eds.), *Research Handbook on Remedies in Private Law* (Cheltenham: Edward Elgar Publishing, 2019), pp. 257–93.

Devenney, James, 'The Legacy of the Cameron-Clegg Coalition Programme of Reform of the Law on the Supply of Goods, Digital Content and Services to Consumers' (2018) 6 *Journal of Business Law* 485–511.

Dhanda, Amita, 'Constructing a New Human Rights Lexicon: Convention on the Rights of Persons with Disabilities' (2008) 5 *Sur: International Journal of Human Rights* 43–59.

Dick, Robert, 'Administration of Estates and the Mentally and Physically Infirm' (1975) 2 *Estates and Trusts Quarterly* 256–302.

Diduck, Alison, '*Royal Bank of Scotland Plc v Etridge* (No 2): Commentary' in Rosemary Hunter, Clare McGlynn and Erika Rackley (eds.), *Feminist Judgments, from Theory to Practice* (Oxford: Hart Publishing, 2010).

Dinerstein, Robert, 'Implementing Legal Capacity under Article 12 of the UN *Convention on the Rights of Persons with Disabilities*: The Difficult Road from Guardianship to Supported Decision-Making' (2012) 19 *Human Rights Brief* 8–74.

Disability Rights UK, 'Inclusive Communities: Guidance for Disabled People's Organisations (DPOs)', 2014.

Dixon, Jeremy, Judy Laing and Christine Valentine, 'A Human Rights Approach to Advocacy for People with Dementia: A Review of Current Provision in England and Wales' (2018) *Dementia* 1–16.

Dobransky, Kerry and Eszter Hargittai, 'The Disability Divide in Internet Access and Use' (2006) 9 *Information, Communication and Society* 314–334.

Drake, Robert, *Understanding Disability Policies* (Basingstoke: Palgrave, 1999).

Du Bois, François, 'Private Law in the Age of Rights' in Daniel Visser and Elspeth Reid (eds.), *Private Law and Human Rights in Scotland and South Africa* (Edinburgh: Edinburgh University Press, 2013), pp. 12–36.

Du Bois, François, 'The Impact of Human Rights on English Contract Law' in Luca Siliquini-Cinelli and Andrew Hutchison (eds.), *The Constitutional Dimension of Contract Law* (New York: Springer Publishing, 2017), pp. 1–37.

Edgar, Andrew, 'Procedural Fairness for Decisions Affecting the Public Generally: A Radical Step towards Public Consultation' (2014) 33(1) *University of Tasmania Law Review* 56–82.

Eisenberg, Melvin, 'The Theory of Contracts' in Peter Benson (ed.), *The Theory of Contract Law: New Essays* (Cambridge: Cambridge University Press, 2001), pp. 206–64.

Enonchong, Nelson, *Duress, Undue Influence and Unconscionable Dealing* (4th ed., London: Sweet & Maxwell, 2023).

Erevelles, Nirmala, *Disability and Difference in Global Contexts: Enabling a Transformative Body Politic* (New York: Palgrave Macmillan, 2011).

Feintuck, Mike, *'The Public Interest' in Regulation* (Oxford: Oxford University Press, 2004).

Fejős, Andrea, 'Social Justice in EU Financial Consumer Law' (2019) 24 *Tilburg Law Review* 68–88.

Fineman, Martha Albertson, 'Beyond Identities: The Limits of an Antidiscrimination Approach to Equality' (2012) 92 *Boston University Law Review* 1713–70.

Fineman, Martha Albertson, 'The Vulnerable Subject and the Responsive State' (2010) 60 *Emory Law Journal* 251–76.

Fineman, Martha Albertson, 'Vulnerability and Inevitable Inequality' (2017) 4 *Oslo Law Review* 133–49.

Fineman, Martha Albertson, 'Vulnerability and Social Justice' (2019) 53 *Valparaiso University Law Review* 341–69.

Firth, Ashley, *Practical Web Inclusion and Accessibility: A Comprehensive Guide to Access Needs* (1st ed., New York: Apress, 2019).

Fishkin, James, 'Making Deliberative Democracy Practical: Public Consultation and Dispute Resolution' (2011) 26(4) *Ohio State Journal on Dispute Resolution* 611–26.

Flynn, Eilionóir and others (eds.), *Global Perspectives on Legal Capacity Reform: Our Voices, Our Stories* (London: Routledge, 2019).

Flynn, Eilionóir, 'Mental (in)Capacity or Legal Capacity: A Human Rights Analysis of the Proposed Fusion of Mental Health and Mental Capacity Law in Northern Ireland' (2013) 64 *Northern Ireland Legal Quarterly* 485–505.

Flynn, Eilionóir, *From Rhetoric to Action: Implementing the UN Convention on the Rights of Persons with Disabilities* (Cambridge: Cambridge University Press, 2011).

Fraser Butlin, Sarah, 'The UN Convention on the Rights of Persons with Disabilities: Does the Equality Act 2010 Measure up to UK International Commitments?' (2011) 40 *Industrial Law Journal* 428–38.

Fredman, Sandra, 'Equality: A New Generation?' (2001) 30 *Industrial Law Journal* 145–68.

Fredman, Sandra, 'The Public Sector Equality Duty' (2011) 40(4) *Industrial Law Journal* 405–27.

Fridman, Gerald, 'Lawyers as Agents' (1987) 36 *University of New Brunswick Law Journal* 9–40.

Fried, Charles, *Contract as Promise: A Theory of Contractual Obligation* (2nd ed., Oxford: Oxford University Press, 2015).

Friedmann, Dan and Daphne Barak-Erez, 'Introduction' in Dan Friedmann and Daphne Barak-Erez (eds.), *Human Rights in Private Law* (Oxford: Hart Publishing, 2001), pp. 1–9.

Friedmann, Dan, and Daphne Barak-Erez (eds.), *Human Rights in Private Law* (Oxford: Hart Publishing, 2001).

Frost, Robert, *Mountain Interval* (New York: Henry Holt, 1916).

Fung, Lawrence and others 'Neurodiversity: An Invisible Strength?' (2022) 74(9) *Jom* 3200–2.

García Iriarte, Edurne, Roy McConkey and Robbie Gilligan (eds.), *Disability and Human Rights: Global Perspectives* (London: Palgrave, 2016).

Gauke, David, Christopher Charlton, and Jonathan Pratt, 'Retained EU Law Act receives Royal Assent', Macfarlanes, 13 July 2023.

Geiser, Priscille, Stefanie Ziegler and Ute Zurmühl, 'Support to Organisations Representative of Persons with Disabilities', *Policy Paper*, July 2011.

Gilmore, Grant, *The Death of Contract* (Columbus: Ohio State University Press, 1974).

Goggin, Gerard and Christopher Newell 'An End to Disabling Policies? Toward Enlightened Universal Service' (2000) 16(2) *The Information Society* 127–33.

Gooding, Piers, Anna Arstein-Kerslake and Eilionóir Flynn 'Assistive Technology as support for the Exercise of Legal Capacity' (2015) 29 *International Review of Law, Computers and Technology* 245–65.

Goudy, Henry, 'Contracts by Lunatics' (1901) 17 *Law Quarterly Review* 147–54.

Graham, Cosmo, *Regulating Public Utilities: A Legal and Constitutional Approach* (Oxford: Hart Publishing, 2000).

Guevara, Angelica, 'Ableness as Property' (2020) *Denver Law Review Forum*, University of Wisconsin Legal Studies Research Paper No. 1593, 1–39.

Haddow, Ken, 'Consultation, the Way Forward' (2013) 31(1) *Journal of Energy and Natural Resources Law* 81–90.

Hamdy, Ronald and others, 'Patients with Dementia Are Easy Victims to Predators' (2017) 3 *Gerontology and Geriatric Medicine* 1–8.

Hanisch, Halvor, 'Recognising Disability' in Jerome Bickenbach, Franziska Felder and Barbara Schmitz (eds.), *Disability and the Good Human Life* (Cambridge: Cambridge University Press, 2014), pp. 113–38.

Harpur, Paul, 'Time to Be Heard: How Advocates Can Use the Convention on the Rights of Persons with Disabilities to Drive Change' (2010) 45(3) *Valparaiso University Law Review* 1271–96.

Hepple, Bob, *Equality: The Legal Framework* (Oxford: Hart Publishing, 2011).

Herr, Stanley, Lawrence Gostin and Harold Hongju Koh (eds.), *The Human Rights of Persons with Intellectual Disabilities: Different but Equal* (Oxford: Oxford University Press, 2003).

Herring, Jonathan, *Vulnerable Adults and the Law* (Oxford: Oxford University Press, 2016).

Higgins, P, 'The Effect of Insanity on Agency Transactions' (1961) 1 *University of Tasmania Law Review* 569–79.

Hogg, Martin, *Promises and Contract Law: Comparative Perspectives* (Cambridge: Cambridge University Press, 2011).

Howard, Philippa and Felicity Sedgewick, '"Anything but the Phone!": Communication Mode Preferences in the Autism Community' (2021) 25(8) *Autism* 2265–78.

Howells, Geraint and Christian Twigg-Flesner (eds), 'Consolidation and Simplification of UK Consumer Law', Report for the Department for Business, Innovation and Skills (BIS), November 2010.

Howells, Geraint, 'The Potential and Limits of Consumer Empowerment by Information' (2005) 23(3) *Journal of Law and Society* 349–70.

Hudson, Anthony, 'Agency and Insanity' (1959) 37 *Canadian Bar Review* 497–503.

Hudson, Anthony, 'Mental Incapacity Revisited' (1986) *The Conveyancer and Property Lawyer* 178–86.

Hunter, Rosemary, Clare McGlynn and Erika Rackley (eds.), *Feminist Judgments, from Theory to Practice* (Oxford: Hart Publishing, 2010).

Hurst, Rachel, 'Disabled People's Organisations and Development: Strategies for Change' in Emma Stone (ed.) *Disability and Development: Learning from Action and Research on Disability in the Majority World* (Leeds: Disability Press, 1999), pp. 25–35.

Ibbetson, David, *A Historical Introduction to the Law of Obligations* (Oxford: Oxford University Press, 1999).

Information Commissioner's Office and the Competition and Markets Authority, 'Harmful Design in Digital Markets: How Online Choice Architecture Practices can undermine Consumer Choice and Control over Personal Information, Joint Position Paper', August 2023.

Kanter, Arlene, 'The Promise and Challenge of the United Nations Convention on the Rights of Persons with Disabilities' (2007) 34 *Syracuse Journal of International Law and Commerce* 287–322.

Kaufman-Scarborough, Carol, 'Social Exclusion: A Perspective on Consumers with Disabilities' in Susan Dunnett, Kathy Hamilton and Maria Piacentini (eds.), *Vulnerable Consumers: Conditions, Contexts and Characteristics* (London: Routledge, 2015), pp. 157–69.

Kayess, Rosemary and Phillip French, 'Out of Darkness into Light? Introducing the Convention on the Rights of Persons with Disabilities' (2008) 8 *Human Rights Law Review* 1–34.

Kessler, Friedrich, 'Contracts of Adhesion: Some Thoughts about Freedom of Contract' (1943) 43 *Columbia Law Review* 629–42.

Kimel, Dori, 'Neutrality, Autonomy, and Freedom of Contract' (2001) 21 *Oxford Journal of Legal Studies* 473–94.

Kimel, Dori, *From Promise to Contract: Towards a Liberal Theory of Contract* (Oxford: Hart Publishing, 2005).

Kronman, Anthony T, 'Contract Law and Distributive Justice' (1980) 89 *Yale Law Journal* 472–511.

Law Commission & Scottish Law Commission, 'Unfair Terms in Consumer Contracts: A New Approach?' *Issue Paper*, July 2012.

Law Commission and the Scottish Law Commission, 'Unfair Terms in Contracts', *LAW COM* No. 292, Cm 6464, February 2005.

Law Commission, 'Consumer Prepayments on Retailer Insolvency', *Law Com* No. 368, July 2016.

Law Commission, 'Twelfth Report on the Transfer of Title to Chattels', Cmnd 2958, 1966.

Lawson, Anna, 'Accessibility Obligations in the UN Convention on the Rights of Persons with Disabilities: *Nyusti and Takacs v Hungary*' (2014) 30 *South African Journal on Human Rights* 380–92.

Lawson, Anna, 'Disability and Employment in the Equality Act 2010: Opportunities Seized, Lost and Generated' (2011) 40(4) *Industrial Law Journal* 359–83.

Lawson, Anna, 'The United Nations Convention on the Rights of Persons with Disabilities: New Era or False Dawn?' (2007) 34 *Syracuse Journal of International Law and Commerce* 563–618.

Lazar, Jonathan and Paul Jaeger, 'Reducing Barriers to Online Access for People with Disabilities' (2011) 27(2) *Issues in Science and Technology* 68–82.

Lewis, Oliver, 'Advancing Legal Capacity Jurisprudence' (2011) 6 *European Human Rights Law Review* 700–14.

Lucy, William, *Philosophy of Private Law* (Oxford: Oxford University Press, 2007).

Lundberg, Erik and Erik Hysing, 'The Value of Participation: Exploring the Role of Public Consultations from the Vantage Point of Interest Groups' (2015) 39(1) *Scandinavian Political Studies* 1–21.

Lundberg, Erik, 'Does the Government Selection Process Promote or Hinder Pluralism? Exploring the Characteristics of Voluntary Organizations Invited to Public Consultations' (2013) 9(1) *Journal of Civil Society* 58–77.

MacDonald Eggers, Peter, *Vitiation of Contractual Consent* (London: Routledge, 2016).

MacKay, Don, 'The United Nations Convention on the Rights of Persons with Disabilities' (2007) 34 *Syracuse Journal of International Law and Commerce* 323–32.

MacMillan, Catharine, 'Rogues, Swindlers and Cheats: The Development of Mistake of Identity in English Contract Law' (2005) 64 *Cambridge Law Journal* 711–44.

Macnamara, Jim, 'The Quadrivium of Online Public Consultation: Policy, Culture, Resources, Technology' (2010) 45(2) *Australian Journal of Political Science* 227–44.

Maker, Yvette and others, 'Ensuring Equality for Persons with Cognitive Disabilities in Consumer Contracting: An International Human Rights Law Perspective' (2018) 19 *Melbourne Journal of International Law* 178–99.

Maker, Yvette and others, 'From Safety Nets to Support Networks: Beyond 'Vulnerability' in Protection for Consumers with Cognitive Disabilities' (2018) 41 *University of New South Wales Law Journal* 818–45.

Malinga, Joshua and Trynos Gumbo, 'Advocacy and Lobbying: The Road Map from Charity to Human Rights' in Edurne García Iriarte, Roy McConkey and Robbie Gilligan (eds.), *Disability and Human Rights: Global Perspectives* (London: Palgrave, 2016), pp. 49–67.

Marshall, Thomas Humphrey, *Citizenship and Social Class, and Other Essays* (Cambridge: Cambridge University Press, 1950).

Martin, Wayne and others, 'Achieving CRPD Compliance. Is the Mental Capacity Act of England and Wales Compatible with the UN Convention on the Rights of Persons with Disabilities? If Not, What Next? An Essex Autonomy Project Position Paper', Report submitted to the UK Ministry of Justice, 22 September 2014.

McKendrick, Ewan, 'Contract: In General' in Andrew Burrows (ed.), *Principles of the English Law of Obligations* (Oxford: Oxford University Press, 2015).

McMeel, Gerard, 'Philosophical Foundations of the Law of Agency' (2000) 116 *Law Quarterly Review* 387–411.

Melish, Tara, 'The UN Disability Convention: Historic Process, Strong Prospects and Why the U.S. Should Ratify' (2007) 14 *Human Rights Brief* 37–47.

Millett, Peter, 'Equity's Place in the Law of Commerce' (1998) 114 *Law Quarterly Review* 214–22.

Moberly, Richard, 'The Americans with Disabilities Act in Cyberspace: Applying the 'Nexus' Approach to Private Internet Websites' (2004) 55(3) *Mercer Law Review* 963–99.

Morgan, Jonathan, *Great Debates in Contract Law* (3rd ed., Basingstoke: Palgrave Macmillan, 2020).

Nilsson, Anna, 'Who Gets to Decide? Right to Legal Capacity for Persons with Intellectual and Psychosocial Disabilities', Council of Europe, CommDH/IssuePaper(2012)2, Strasbourg, 20 February.

O'Brien, Eimear, 'Are You treating your Vulnerable Customers Fairly?' (2017) 6 *Compliance and Risk Journal* 10.

O'Brien, Nick, 'Disability Discrimination Law in the United Kingdom and the New Civil Rights History: The Contribution of Caroline Gooding' (2016) 43(3) *Journal of Law and Society* 444–68.

O'Brien, Nick, 'Positive about Equality: The Public-Sector Duty under Threat' (2013) 84(4) *The Political Quarterly* 486–96.

Office of Fair Trading, 'Guidance on the Consumer Protection from Unfair Trading Regulations 2008', May 2008.

Office of Fair Trading, 'Office of Fair Trading, 'Response to the Law Commission Issues Paper: Unfair Terms in Consumer Contracts', OFT1465, November 2012.

Office of Fair Trading, 'Response to the Consultation on the Implementation of the Consumer Rights Directive 2011/83/EU' OFT1461, November 2012.

Office of Fair Trading, 'Response to the Draft Consumer Rights Bill Proposals' OFT1502, September 2013.

Office of the United Nations High Commissioner for Human Rights, 'The Convention on the Rights of Persons with Disabilities: Training Guide', Professional Training Series No. 19, 2014.

Ogus, Anthony, *Regulation, Legal Form and Economic Theory* (Oxford: Hart Publishing, 2004).

Oliver, Michael, *The Politics of Disablement* (Basingstoke: Palgrave Macmillan, 1990).

Oliver, Michael, *Understanding Disability: From Theory to Practice* (2nd ed., Basingstoke: Palgrave Macmillan, 2009).

Onions, Charles Talbut (ed.), *The Oxford Dictionary of English Etymology* (1st ed., Oxford: Oxford University Press, 1996).

Oppenheimer, Robert, 'Science and the Common Understanding', The Reith Lectures, BBC Radio 4, 1953.

Peel, Edwin, *Treitel on the Law of Contract* (15th ed., London: Sweet and Maxwell, 2020).

Petterson, Adrian, 'Dark Patterns and Disability: Ethical Failings of Designing for Normal', TEDxUofT, University of Toronto, 29 January 2022.

Phang, Andrew, 'Economic Duress: Recent Difficulties and Possible Alternatives' (1997) 5 *Restitution Law Review* 53–65.

Phang, Andrew, 'Economic Duress: Uncertainty Confirmed' (1992) 5 *Journal of Contract Law* 147–56.

Pollock, Frederick, *Principles of Contract* (13th ed., London: Stevens & Sons, 1950).

Power, Andrew, Janet Lord, and Allison DeFranco, *Active Citizenship and Disability* (Cambridge: Cambridge University Press, 2013).

Prince, Martin and others, *Dementia UK: Second Edition – Overview* (London: Alzheimer's Society, 2014).

Procacci, Giovanna, 'Poor Citizens: Social Citizenship versus Individualisation of Welfare' in Colin Crouch, Klaus Eder and Damian Tambini (eds.), *Citizenship, Markets and the State* (Oxford: Oxford University Press, 2001), pp. 49–68.

Quinn, Gerard, 'Personhood and Legal Capacity: Perspectives on the Paradigm Shift of Article 12 CRPD', HPOD Conference, Harvard, 2010.

Réaume, Denise, 'Discrimination and Dignity' (2003) 63 *Louisiana Law Review* 1–51.

Rehema, Joy and Emer O'Shea, 'I have the Strength to speak up for Myself: Nikona nguvu ya kujiongelelea' in Eilionóir Flynn and others (eds.), *Global Perspectives on Legal Capacity Reform: Our Voices, Our Stories* (London: Routledge, 2019), pp. 50–60.

Reynolds, Francis, 'Agency' in Hugh Beale and others (eds.), *Chitty on Contracts*, 2 vols. (34th ed., London: Sweet & Maxwell, 2021), vol. I, Chapter 22, paragraph 22-001 et seq.

Rimmerman, Arie, *Social Inclusion of People with Disabilities* (Cambridge: Cambridge University Press, 2014).

Russell, Marta and Ravi Malhotra, 'Capitalism and the Disability Rights Movement' in Marta Russell (ed.), *Capitalism and Disability: Selected Writings* (edited by Keith Rosenthal) (Chicago: Haymarket Books, 2019), pp. 1–10.

Russell, Marta, 'Backlash, the Political Economy, and Structural Exclusion' (2000) 21 *Berkeley Journal of Employment and Labor Law* 335–66.

Russell, Marta, 'What Disability Civil Rights Cannot Do' in Marta Russell, *Capitalism and Disability: Selected Writings* (edited by Keith Rosenthal) (Chicago: Haymarket Books, 2019), pp. 62–73.

Sax, Marijn and Natali Helberger, 'Digital Vulnerability and Manipulation in the Emerging Digital Framework' in Natali Helberger and others, 'Digital Fairness for Consumers', Report for BEUC (European Consumer Organisation), Brussels, March 2024, 11–24.

Scanlon, Thomas M., 'Promises and Contracts' in Peter Benson (ed.), *The Theory of Contract Law: New Essays* (Cambridge: Cambridge University Press, 2001), pp. 86–117.

Selznick, Philip, 'Focusing Organisational Research on Regulation' in Roger Noll (ed.), *Regulatory Policy and Social Sciences* (Barkley: University of California Press, 1985), pp. 363–7.

Series, Lucy, 'Relationships, Autonomy and Legal Capacity: Mental Capacity and Support Paradigms' (2015) 40 *International Journal of Law and Psychiatry* 80 91.

Sheldon, Clive, 'Consultation: Revisiting the Basic Principles' (2012) 17(2) *Judicial Review* 152–60.

Shiffrin, Seana, 'Paternalism, Unconscionability Doctrine and Accommodation' (2000) 29 *Philosophy and Public Affairs* 205–50.

Shuchman, Philip, 'Consumer Credit by Adhesion Contracts' (1962) 35 *Temple Law Quarterly* 125–40.

Simon, Herbert, *Models of Bounded Rationality* (Cambridge, MA: MIT Press, 1982).

Simpson, Alfred, *A History of the Common Law of Contract: The Rise of the Action of Assumpsit* (Oxford: Oxford University Press, 1996).

Simpson, Jenifer, 'Inclusive Information and Communication Technologies for People with Disabilities' (2009) 29(1) *Disability Studies Quarterly*. https://doi.org/10.18061/dsq.v29i1.167

Smith, Adam, *An Inquiry Into the Nature and Causes of the Wealth of Nations* (2nd ed., London: Strahan and Cadell eds. 1778), Volumes I and II.

Smith, Deirdre, 'Who Says You're Disabled? The Role of Medical Evidence in the ADA Definition of Disability' (2007) 82 *Tulane Law Review* 1–76.

Smith, Stephen, 'In Defence of Substantive Fairness' (1996) 112 *Law Quarterly Review* 138–58.

Smith, Stephen, *Atiyah's Introduction to the Law of Contract* (6th ed., Oxford: Clarendon Press, 2005).

Smith, Stephen, *Contract Theory* (Oxford: Oxford University Press, 2004).

Smits, Jan, *Contract Law: A Comparative Introduction* (2nd ed., Cheltenham: Edward Elgar Publishing, 2017).

Spark, Gareth, *Vitiation of Contracts: International Contractual Principles and English Law* (Cambridge: Cambridge University Press, 2013).

Sunstein, Cass, *After the Rights Revolution: Reconceiving the Regulatory State* (Harvard: Harvard University Press, 1990).

Teubner, Gunther, 'Contracting Worlds: The Many Autonomies of Private Law' (2000) 9 *Social and Legal Studies* 399–417.

Thal, Spencer, 'The Inequality of Bargaining Power Doctrine: The Problem of Defining Contractual Unfairness' (1988) 8 *Oxford Journal of Legal Studies* 17–33.

Tiplady, David, 'The Judicial Control of Contractual Unfairness' (1983) 46 *Modern Law Review* 601–18.

Trebilcock, Michael, and Steven Elliott, 'The Scope and Limits of Legal Paternalism: Altruism and Coercion in Family Financial Arrangements' in Peter Benson (ed.), *The Theory of Contract Law: New Essays* (Cambridge: Cambridge University Press, 2001), pp. 45–85.

Treitel, Guenter, *An Outline of the Law of Contract* (6th ed., Oxford: Oxford University Press, 2004).

Tusler, Anthony, 'How to Make Technology Work: A Study of Best Practices in United States Electronic and Information Technology Companies' (2005) 25(2) *Disability Studies Quarterly*. https://doi.org/10.18061/dsq.v25i2.551

Twigg-Flesner, Christian (ed.) *Research Handbook on EU Consumer and Contract Law* (Cheltenham: Edward Elgar Publishing, 2016).

UN Committee on the Rights of Persons with Disabilities, 'Concluding Observations on the Initial Report of the United Kingdom of Great Britain and Northern Ireland', 3 October 2017, CRPD/C/GBR/CO/1.

UN Committee on the Rights of Persons with Disabilities, 'General Comment No. 1: Article 12 (Equal Recognition before the Law)', 19 May 2014, UN Doc CRPD/C/GC/1.

UN Committee on the Rights of Persons with Disabilities, 'General Comment No. 7: Article 4.3 and 33.3 (Participation with persons with disabilities in the implementation and monitoring of the Convention)', 21 September 2018, UN Doc. CRPD/C/GC/7.

UN Committee on the Rights of Persons with Disabilities, 'Inquiry Concerning the United Kingdom of Great Britain and Northern Ireland carried out by the Committee under Article 6 of the Optional Protocol to the Convention: Report of the Committee', 6 October 2016, CRPD/C/15/R.2/Rev.1.

UN Committee on the Rights of Persons with Disabilities, 'Report on Follow-up to the Inquiry concerning the United Kingdom of Great Britain and Northern Ireland', 22 March 2024, UN Doc CRPD/C/GBR/FUIR/1.

van Veen, Saskia, Barbara Regeer and Joske Bunders, 'Meeting the Challenge of the Rights-Based Approach to Disability: The Changing Role of Disability-Specific NGOs and DPOs' (2013) 31(3) *Nordic Journal of Human Rights* 360–81.

Vanhala, Lisa, *Making Rights a Reality? Disability Rights Activists and Legal Mobilization* (Cambridge: Cambridge University Press, 2011).

Varney, Eliza, *Disability and Information Technology* (Cambridge: Cambridge University Press, 2013).

Varney, Mike, 'Services, Consumer Information and Remedies in the Electronic Communications Sector: A Yet Unanswered Challenge?' in Christian Twigg-Flesner and Gonzalo Villalta Puig (eds.), *Boundaries of Commercial and Trade Law* (Munich: Seller European Publishers, 2011), pp. 127–52.

Vicente, Agustín and Ingrid Lossius Falkum, 'Accounting for the Preference for Literal Meanings in Autism Spectrum Conditions' (2023) 38(1) *Mind and Language* 119–40.

Waddams, Stephen, 'Unconscionability in Contracts' (1976) 39 *Modern Law Review* 369–93.

Waddams, Stephen, *Principle and Policy in Contract Law* (Cambridge: Cambridge University Press, 2011).

Waddams, Stephen, *Sanctity of Contracts in a Secular Age: Equity, Fairness and Enrichment* (Cambridge: Cambridge University Press, 2019).

Waddington, Lisa, 'Vulnerable and Confused: The Protection of "Vulnerable" Consumers under EU Law' (2013) 38(6) *European Law Review* 757–83.

Watson, Jonathon, 'Withdrawal Rights' in Christian Twigg-Flesner (ed.), *Research Handbook on EU Consumer and Contract Law* (Cheltenham: Edward Elgar Publishing, 2016), pp. 241–65.

Watts, Peter, 'Contracts Made by Agents on Behalf of Principals with Latent Mental Incapacity: The Common Law Position' (2015) 74 *Cambridge Law Journal* 140–54.

Watts, Peter, *Bowstead and Reynolds on Agency* (23rd ed., London: Sweet & Maxwell, 2023).

Which? '*Dark Patterns: How Consumer Choices are manipulated Online*', 23 March 2023.

Whittaker, Simon, 'Consumer Contracts' in Hugh Beale and others (eds.), *Chitty on Contracts*, 2 vols. (34th ed., London: Sweet & Maxwell, 2021), vol. II.

Whittaker, Simon, 'Distinctive Features of the New Consumer Contract Law' (2017) 133 *Law Quarterly Review* 47–72.

Whittaker, Simon, 'Personal Incapacity' in Hugh Beale and others (eds.), *Chitty on Contracts*, 2 vols. (24th ed., London: Sweet & Maxwell, 2021), vol. I, Chapter 12, paragraph 12-001 et seq.

Willett, Chris, 'Re-theorising Consumer Law' (2018) 77(1) *Cambridge Law Journal* 179–210.

Williams, Sian, 'Confident Commissioning: Building Relationships between Local Authorities and Disabled People's User-Led Organisations', *South-East Network of Disabled People's Organisations*, June 2014.

Wilson, Nicholas, 'Freedom of Contract and Adhesion Contracts' (1965) 14 *International and Comparative Law Quarterly* 172–93.

Index

For EU product safety concerns, contact us at Calle de José Abascal, 56–1°,
28003 Madrid, Spain or eugpsr@cambridge.org.

www.ingramcontent.com/pod-product-compliance
Ingram Content Group UK Ltd.
Pitfield, Milton Keynes, MK11 3LW, UK
UKHW051510240426
470322UK00008B/115
* 9 7 8 1 3 1 6 5 1 6 6 3 8 *